ON THE DEITIES OF SAMOTHRACE

Facing, A first sighting of Samothrace.

Studies in Continental Thought
John Sallis, editor

Consulting Editors
Robert Bernasconi
John D. Caputo
David Carr
Edward S. Casey
David Farrell Krell
Lenore Langsdorf

James Risser
Dennis J. Schmidt
Calvin O. Schrag
Charles E. Scott
Daniela Vallega-Neu
David Wood

F. W. J. SCHELLING

ON THE DEITIES OF SAMOTHRACE

Edited and translated by
**Alexander Bilda,
Jason M. Wirth, and
David Farrell Krell**

INDIANA UNIVERSITY PRESS

This book is a publication of

Indiana University Press
Herman B Wells Library 350
1320 East 10th Street
Bloomington, Indiana 47405 USA

iupress.org

© 2025 by Indiana University Press

All rights reserved
No part of this book may be reproduced or utilized in any form or by any means, electronic or mechanical, including photocopying and recording, or by any information storage and retrieval system, without permission in writing from the publisher. The paper used in this publication meets the minimum requirements of the American National Standard for Information Sciences—Permanence of Paper for Printed Library Materials, ANSI Z39.48-1992.

Manufactured in the United States of America

First printing 2025

Cataloging information is available from the Library of Congress.
ISBN 978-0-253-07110-1 (hardback)
ISBN 978-0-253-07111-8 (paperback)
ISBN 978-0-253-07112-5 (ebook)

CONTENTS

Translators' Preface   ix

General Introduction   1

PART ONE | F. W. J. Schelling, *On the Deities of Samothrace*

1. Schelling's Lecture, Endnotes, and Afterword   13
2. Explanatory Notes on Schelling's Lecture   91
3. Explanatory Notes on Schelling's Endnotes   121

PART TWO | Three Essays on Schelling's *Deities of Samothrace*

4. Schelling *archaeologicus*, by David Farrell Krell   145
5. The Importance of Schelling's *Deities of Samothrace* for His Own Work and for His Contemporaries, by Alexander Bilda   219
6. The Advent of the Return of the Cabiri, by Jason M. Wirth   281

Index   307

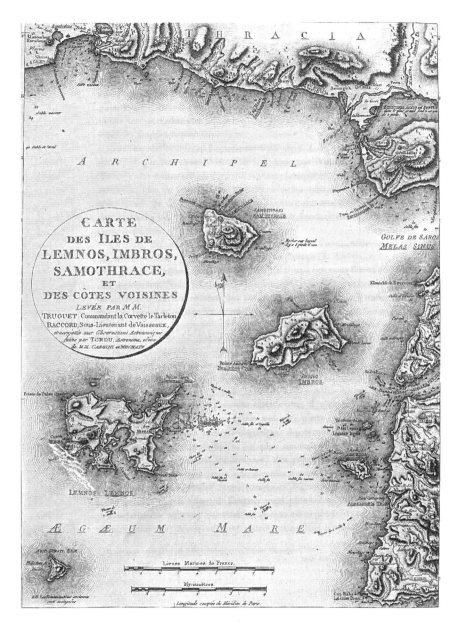

Samothrace is the northernmost of the three islands shown here, due west of the Gulf of Saros and the Turkish coast and due south of ancient Thrace. This map, from Schelling's own time, appears in M. G. F. A. de Choiseul-Gouffier (1752–1817), *Voyages pittoresques de la Grèce, Missions du Levant*.

TRANSLATORS' PREFACE

This is the first complete English translation in a critical edition of F. W. J. Schelling's remarkable 1815 lecture and subsequent book publication with extensive notes and an afterword. Despite the lecture's relatively modest length, this translation took several years and a combined effort to complete. Earlier editions (Robert F. Brown's 1977 edition with Scholars Press and Frank Scalambrino's 2019 version with Magister Ludi Press) largely avoid the challenging work of translating Schelling's copious, daunting, and linguistically complex endnotes. Those notes contain not only Schelling's sources but also his philosophical reflections and philological hypotheses, ranging across the German, French, Greek, Latin, Phoenician, Hebrew, Persian, Arabic, Syriac, and other languages. Our translation is complemented by our explanatory annotations on Schelling's lecture and endnotes and a critical essay by each of us.

We recommend that readers approach Schelling's text in two stages. Because the endnotes are so numerous and demanding, we suggest readers ignore them on their first reading of the lecture. They may instead imagine themselves present at the Bavarian Academy of Sciences in Munich on that October day in 1815, when Schelling addressed the academy and its patron, the king of Bavaria Maximilian I. Joseph. Understandably, the endnotes were not presented during the address. After reading the lecture—surely one of the most astonishing in the history of academe—readers may then want to delve more deeply into the matter, this time by poring over the many endnotes. Never mind if your Chaldean and Phoenician are not up to the challenge. Not many are up to it today, including the present translators, who have often had to seek the help of specialists in this or that language. At all events, the endnotes are richly suggestive and thought-provoking in any and every language.

Our citations of Schelling's major works follow the standard pagination of the original edition, established after Schelling's death by his son Karl and published as *Schellings Sämmtliche Werke* (Stuttgart-Augsburg: J. G. Cotta, 1856–1861), which contains two divisions and fourteen volumes. We cite the division, followed by the volume and page numbers. Hence (SW I/1, 1) refers to division one, volume one, page one. These designations are preserved in Manfred Schröter's reorganization of the material in *Schellings Werke: Nach der Originalausgabe in neuer Anordnung* (Munich: C. H. Beck, 1927) and also in Manfred Frank's selection of Schelling's writings in six paperback volumes (Frankfurt am Main: Suhrkamp, 1985). Readers should therefore have no problem finding the passages cited here. Schelling's Samothrace lecture and notes appear in division one, volume eight of SW. For readers who wish to find a particular part of Schelling's original in that edition, we have inserted between two straight lines the page number of each new page, for example, |347| for the opening page of the lecture.

The phrases in Schelling's lecture that are enclosed in fancy brackets {} are emendations that Schelling himself made in his personal copy of the published lecture. His son Karl added these suggested changes to his edition of his father's *Sämmtliche Werke*. On occasion, Schelling's published endnotes refer back to his lecture by paragraph number; to facilitate the reader's locating these references, we have numbered the paragraphs of the lecture, 1 through 20. We are fortunate to have been able to check the German text prepared by Schelling's son with the newest critical edition of the text; we are grateful to the editors of the historical-critical edition of Schelling's *Ueber die Gottheiten von Samothrace*, Christopher Arnold and Christian Danz, who kindly sent us a page proof of their recently published volume.[1]

---

1. See Hans Michael Baumgartner et al., eds., *Historisch-kritische Ausgabe im Auftrag der Schelling-Kommission der Bayerischen Akademie der Wissenschaften* (Stuttgart-Bad Cannstatt: Frommann-Holzboog, 1976). *Ueber die Gottheiten von Samothrace* appears as volume nineteen of division one (AA I/19). This edition too reproduces the page numbers of SW so that readers can find, in this new edition too, all references made in the present volume.

The present book is organized in two parts. After a general introduction that tries to situate *On the Deities of Samothrace* in Schelling's long career of thought, the first part contains Schelling's text (the lecture, endnotes, and afterword) along with our explanatory notes; the second part offers three essays that try to elucidate various aspects of Schelling's text. In our presentation of Schelling's address, we have introduced paragraph breaks where Schelling merely indicated them by numbers in the outside margin, again, 1 through 20. Otherwise the translation hopes to be a faithful rendering of the German text as it appears in Karl Schelling's edition. The address is followed by Schelling's own detailed endnotes and his concluding afterword or postface (*Nachschrift*) to the book.

After presenting Schelling's lecture and the complete set of his endnotes and afterword (chap. 1), we offer a series of explanatory notes to the lecture in which we hope to aid readers with Schelling's more abstruse references and allusions (chap. 2). We did not enter footnote numbers into Schelling's address to indicate our explanatory notes, since the address already contains well over a hundred of Schelling's own endnotes, and we did not wish to clutter his text any further. We trust that our readers' own puzzlement will take them to the appropriate explanatory notes, indicated by the *book page* number on which the word or phrase appears. We then (chap. 3) offer a second set of explanatory notes, this time on Schelling's endnotes, our explanatory notes now being indicated by the *endnote*, not page, number. These explanatory notes may seem to some to be editorial overkill, yet they are perhaps fewer than other readers might have wished: the content of Schelling's endnotes, to say nothing of his references to sources, is extraordinarily intricate, sometimes obscure, and invariably challenging. Clearly, these *Anmerkungen* are Schelling's work in progress; we have tried to offer some help but did not dare try to unravel all the mysteries here. Whenever Schelling (or, more likely, his son Karl) misquoted a source or cited it incorrectly, we have made the correction, usually without drawing attention to it. We have tried to translate Schelling's more familiar sources into English, but when the materials were quite rare, we offered a translation of the titles but also presented them in the original language so that researchers could locate them.

Finally, the three essays in part 2 of the book offer the translators' efforts to interpret particular aspects of *On the Deities of Samothrace*. David Farrell Krell, who also took the cover photo and all the photographs for the volume, focuses on the *archaeology* of the sanctuary of the "Great Gods" on the island of Samothrace, noting how recent finds and current scholarship sometimes confirm but also often challenge Schelling's reflections (chap. 4). Alexander Bilda's essay has a double purpose, namely, first, to interpret *The Deities* in the light of Schelling's thinking both before and after 1815, and second, to investigate how Schelling's contemporaries all over Europe received his efforts (chap. 5). Jason M. Wirth focuses on the position of *The Deities* in the context of Schelling's "positive" philosophy, that is, the culmination of his thinking toward the end of his life; he also asks whether, after two centuries have elapsed since Schelling reflected so profoundly on the Cabiri and the "Great Gods," it is time for them and for us to return to Samothrace (chap. 6).

We would like to thank Jason Giannetti for his generous and skillful assistance with the Hebrew passages. We would also like to thank Human Demesvar, Zahra Donyai, and Lena Rudolph of the University of Freiburg, who offered insight and invaluable help with other languages. Lena Rudolph also provided the index for the volume. Our thanks to John Sallis and Anna Francis, our editor at Indiana University Press, and the entire IUP staff; thanks also to freelancer Larry Baker, who worked diligently on the proofs of the book. We are also grateful to Professor Bonna D. Wescoat of Emory University, the director of excavations at Samothrace, for her hospitality, encouragement, and support of our project.

ON THE DEITIES OF SAMOTHRACE

The two sides of a medallion presented to Schelling by his Berlin students in 1841–42. An enthroned Philosophia reads the New Testament while supporting the Ten Commandments of the Old Testament. Behind her stands the Ephesian Artemis, an Ionian-Greek version of the Great Mother of Anatolia. Revelation and Mythology are thus united in this emblem of Schelling's final philosophy.

General Introduction

What in all the world could have induced a serious young philosopher, born into the Pietist Protestant southwestern corner of Germany in 1775 and educated to be a pious pastor and theologian, to deliver a lecture about goddesses who are sorceresses that play with fire and consort with dwarfs and kobolds? And to claim that these goddesses and dwarflike gods, themselves hungry, destitute, and longing to give birth, are the first to teach human beings something about the essence of deity, something that would make human life and death easier to bear?

F. W. J. Schelling presented that lecture, "On the Deities of Samothrace," on October 12, 1815, before the king of Bavaria, who paid the speaker an honorarium but must have been puzzled about what the lecture meant. No doubt at the king's right side sat the higher clergy, who must have been horrified rather than puzzled. The question as to what led Schelling to that strange place—a Greek isle settled by Phoenician sailors who founded what Schelling took to be the oldest and most august religious and philosophical system in history—is not easily answered. But we have to try, merely by way of introduction.

From his father, a Pietist pastor, theologian, and linguist, Schelling learned early in his childhood ancient Latin, Greek, Hebrew, and a number of Near Eastern languages, so he had the tools to examine some of the oldest historical documents we possess. He went to the Protestant seminary connected with the university at Tübingen (the so-called Tübinger Stift) at age fifteen and began publishing influential books of philosophy when he was twenty. The master's dissertation of this teenager at Tübingen had the title "A Critical-Philosophical Attempt to Explain the Oldest Philosophical Formulations on the Origins of Human Evil," and this interest in the most bedeviling question of ethics and religion—the origins of evil and the vaunted *freedom* of human beings to *do* evil—would resurface eighteen years later in one of his most important books, *On the Essence of Human Freedom*, concerning which, more in a moment. However, in 1793 young Schelling penned a second large essay, *On Myths, Historical Legends, and Philosophical Formulations of the Most Ancient World*, and this fascination with myths and the oldest narratives of human history in every culture to which he had access became a mainstay of his philosophy.

A year later he wrote a commentary on Plato's *Timaeus*, the influential Platonic dialogue—one of the few dialogues to survive the collapse of Greece and Rome and thus influence Western religion, philosophy, and science over the centuries—that offers a detailed account of the origins of the universe. That account featured the demiurge, the powerful god who "makes" and "fathers" the universe, and it was not difficult for the young and pious Schelling to want to ascend in thought to the supernal father. Yet the father and maker of the universe, whom Plato called the Logos, the Word, was not alone. In fact, according to Timaeus of Locri, Plato's spokesperson, the Logos had to persuade a second aboriginal deity to participate in shaping or bearing the cosmos, and this figure was Ananke, a female figure whom some translated as "Brute Necessity." Schelling never stopped thinking about the "necessity" that seems to set limits on "free" activity and demand an inquiry into good and evil in that universe, both of these qualities uncannily related to the necessitous female, whether as Demeter the Earthmother or as Eve.

By the time Schelling concluded the theological portion of his university education, he and his roommates in the Tübinger Stift had abandoned all thoughts of becoming pastors. Those roommates were G. W. F. Hegel, who became the most famous of the German Idealist philosophers, and Friedrich Hölderlin, who became one of the most renowned German poets. The three roommates, inspired by the French Revolution, conspired throughout the 1790s to revolutionize philosophy as a whole: in 1796–97 they announced their plans to develop a philosophy of freedom ("the representation *of me myself* as an absolutely free creature") that confronts the worlds of nature (by way of a "physics with wings") and politics ("we must proceed beyond the state!"), worlds where brute necessity holds sway. That bold program, "The Oldest Program toward a System in German Idealism," might in fact cause philosophy itself to dissolve into, or at least be entirely reshaped by, art and poetry:

And at the very end, the idea that unifies all, the idea of *beauty*.... The philosopher must possess as much aesthetic force as the poet.... Poesy will thereby attain a higher dignity; in the end she will again become what she was in the beginning—the instructress of humanity.... At the same time, we so often hear that the great mass of human beings must have a *sensuous religion*. Not only the masses but also the philosopher needs it. Monotheism of reason and of the heart, polytheism of the imagination and art, that is what we need! ... Thus the enlightened and unenlightened must at long last clasp hands; mythology must become philosophical, and the people rational, while philosophy must become mythological, to make the philosophers sensuous. Then eternal unity will prevail among us.[1]

Great expectations, no doubt. How well the careers of the three—Schelling, Hegel, and Hölderlin—realized those dreams will surely remain a matter of debate. Yet it is safe to say that all three devoted themselves to the task, with Schelling not the least energetic of the three.

During the 1790s, Schelling studied mathematics, the natural sciences, and medicine, deepening his understanding of nature and the organism. The ideas of Johann Gottlob Fichte at Jena University also influenced him strongly. Fichte's dynamic personality and personal brilliance were dedicating themselves to a unification of the Kantian critical philosophy in both its theoretical and practical aspects. Schelling very soon became convinced, however, that the ego-centered basis of Fichte's philosophy, a philosophy inherited from Descartes's famous *cogito sum*, "I think, I am," was unable to confront *nature* in a serious way. Still in his early twenties, Schelling published two influential books on nature philosophy, culminating in a third, *First Projection of a System of Nature Philosophy* (1799), where he developed an account of the universe as fundamentally organic. It was as though Timaeus's Ananke had taken him under her wing and tutored him. By 1809, in the essay on human freedom mentioned earlier, Schelling's critique of Cartesian subjectivism from the point of view of organic nature became quite pointed:

Modern European philosophy as a whole, from its beginning (in Descartes), has this common flaw: nature does not exist for it; it lacks a living ground.

---

1. See the presentation of "The Oldest System" in chapter 1 of David Farrell Krell, *The Tragic Absolute: German Idealism and the Languishing of God* (Bloomington: Indiana University Press, 2005), esp. 22–26.

Spinoza's realism is in this regard as abstract as Leibniz's idealism. Idealism is the soul of philosophy, realism its body; only the two together constitute a living whole. Never can the latter [i.e., realism, as "the body," *der Leib*, of philosophy] provide the principle, but it must be the ground and the medium in which the former actualizes itself, assuming flesh and blood. If a philosophy lacks this living fundamental—which is usually a sign that the ideal principle too was only feebly at work in it from the outset—it loses itself in the kind of system whose attenuated concepts of self-origination, modifications, etc. stand in sharpest contrast to the vital force and fullness of actuality. Yet wherever the ideal principle actually works its effects to a high degree, while failing to find the reconciling and mediating basis, it generates a turbid, wild enthusiasm that irrupts in self-mutilation or—as with the priests of the Phrygian goddess [i.e., the Great Mother of Asia, or Kybele]—self-emasculation. This in fact transpires in philosophy when reason and science are surrendered. (SW I/7, 356–57)

Yet if the *vocabularies* of realism and idealism are preserved when we talk of the "body" and the "soul," as though these were two items that needed to be conjoined, what becomes of a philosophy of organism? Is not the talk of the self-emasculation of idealism a kind of catachresis? What *is* this "living ground" of philosophy? And what role do physical and moral evil, evil and *illness*, play in such a ground?

These are the questions the 1809 essay pursues. Schelling has not lost his faith in a demiurge, a maker and father of the universe. But how does imperfection slip into the productions of a perfect maker and beneficent father? Schelling is impatient with the traditional responses, such as the influential reply that evil is merely "the absence of good." That is like saying that tuberculosis is the absence of healthy lung tissue. Should one not insist on a more precise diagnosis? The traditional responses to questions concerning physical and moral evil, says Schelling, merely displace the difficulty "one point farther down the line without resolving it" (SW I/7, 355). If nature and human freedom both derive from a divine source, then all the possibilities of nature—including nature's most dire and most destructive forces—and all the possibilities of humanity—including the worst that human beings can do—must in some mysterious way be contained in that divine source. Schelling does not shy from saying that "because nothing can be outside God" or "besides God" (*außer Gott*), the contradiction can be resolved only in this way: the things of nature "have their ground in whatever in God Himself is not *He Himself*, that is, in that which is the ground of His existence" (SW I/7, 359–60). What is this "ground" of God's existence, which presumably lies beyond or outside his perfect freedom to create? It is beginning to look as though Ananke is reclaiming her rights. Schelling continues: "If we wish to make this essence more accessible in human terms, we can say that it is the yearning felt by the eternal One to give birth to itself. Such yearning [*Sehnsucht*, "languor," "languishing"] is not the One itself, yet it is nonetheless co-eternal with it. It wants to give birth to God, that is, to the ungroundable unity; but to that extent, unity is not yet in the yearning itself" (ibid.).

It is safe to say that insight into the languor, languishing, and yearning that constitute the ground of God's existence will continue to haunt Schelling for the rest of his life. In the three drafts of what he hoped would be his major philosophical work, *The Ages of the World* (1811–1815), Schelling struggles to understand that ground. It is no longer a "fundament," no longer Descartes's *fundamentum inconcussum veritatis*, "the unshakable foundation of truth," which would be provided by a *cogito*, the Idealist's confident "I think." It is closer to what Kant in the second edition of his *Critique of Pure Reason* called, if only by a slip of the pen, "the unground," in any case a veritable "abyss of reason."

The first book of the projected three-volume *Ages of the World* was to tell the story of the "elevated past." That past would have to reveal the mystery of a deity that longs to give birth to itself and so creates a universe and a particular form of life that mirrors the deity. Whatever is known about the past comes down to us in the oldest myths and legends we have inherited, and Schelling knows he will have to *recount* those old stories. A dialectic of concepts will not be enough. Schelling again introduces the word *Sehnsucht*, the longing to give birth, and adds to it the word *Schmachten*, which more explicitly makes of that longing a *languishing* in destitution. If traditional accounts of creation hold that the creator was moved by an unaccountable yet perfect beneficence, a kind of overflowing generosity that fashioned a universe and a humankind that would reflect back to him his own glorious image, Schelling's account is far more dire: the deity is initially *alone*—there is nothing out there for it, so that its early life is one of loneliness, anxiety, and nightmare. The deity is initially a clenched fist, a force of sheer contraction and resistance to all otherness, a furious jealousy. The farthest reaches of the past are characterized by strife, supreme enmity, and revulsion. "Suffering is universal, not only with a view to human beings but also with a view to the Creator—suffering is the path to glory."[2] That path, as Schelling understands it, takes us from the moment of sheer contraction in the life of deity to the moment when the first stirrings of desire or yearning to give birth appear. Perhaps the development will culminate in a force of *love*; yet whatever such love might be, it will never supplant the force of a primeval *Sehnsucht*. If in 1809 Schelling was quick to introduce "the will of love" into his story of deity, by 1815 he is more likely to write of a longing that is well-nigh obsessive and addictive—a longing and languishing strongly related to *mourning*. No wonder Schelling found it impossible to formulate an account of the elevated past that he and his contemporaries could accept. He never published his musings on "The Past."

And so we arrive at the lecture hall in Munich on October 12, 1815, as Schelling is about to address the king and a number of colleagues who represent a wide range of the arts and sciences. After four frustrating years, years in which he failed to get into publishable shape his manuscript of the very first volume of *The Ages of the World*, the volume on "The Past," Schelling is heartened by a recent discovery. One of the most ancient mystery cults, namely, the cult that established itself on the island of Samothrace in the North Aegean Sea, not far from the Turkish coast, seems to him to answer the recalcitrant questions that have been plaguing him for some time. The cult of the Cabiri or "Great Gods" on Samothrace offers him the narrative he has been searching for. The cult involves an early form of Demeter or "Mother Earth," *Axieros* by name, who knows something about the desire to give birth to deity, and her daughter Persephone, known on Samothrace as *Axiokersa*, who inhabits both the land of the living and the land of the dead. A third deity, *Axiokersos*, is Hades, or perhaps also the mysterious god Dionysos. Finally, a fourth figure is mentioned, *Kasmilos* or *Kadmilos*, obviously related to the Phoenician Cadmus, who was said to have founded Greek Thebes but who otherwise is even more mysterious than Dionysos. In Schelling's view, the narrative that gathers up these Cabirian deities or "Great Gods," which is the story of their relative "potencies," will leave behind the acrimonious

---

2. We cite Schelling's two earlier versions of *Die Weltalter* from the edition by Manfred Schröter: F. W. J. Schelling, *Die Weltalter Fragmente: In den Urfassungen von 1811 und 1813*. Nachlaßband to the Münchner Jubiläumsdruck (Munich: Biederstein and Leibniz, 1946), here at 40.

debate between monotheists and polytheists. Schelling will argue that deity as such is a matter of *dynamic* and *developing* gods and goddesses who are companions, or *socii*, born together, working their effects together, yearning, languishing, and dying together.

The mystery religion at Samothrace, renowned throughout antiquity from the most ancient times until the fall of Rome, is cloaked in secrecy. Initiates are forbidden to talk about it. But this much we know: in addition to the familiar worship of chthonic deities who promise a rich harvest and the fertility of flocks, this religion also pledges aid to endangered seafarers. Many of the initiation practices are intriguing, and Schelling's audience will doubtless be astonished by a number of surprising aspects of the Cabiri themselves—their dwarflike appearance but magical powers, their relation to fire and the forge of Hephaistos but also to water and moisture, their enticing combination of masculine and feminine traits, and above all the *languor* and the *hunger* that characterize their lives—and that audience will be even more astonished by the importance Schelling takes these rites to have for the entire history of religion and philosophy.

Schelling will never forget Samothrace, certainly not six years later when he lectures at the University of Erlangen on his *dynamic* system of philosophy as a whole, and not even thirty years later when he is lecturing in Berlin on *The Philosophy of Mythology* and *Revelation*. Indeed, it will seem to him that the story of the Cabiri on Samothrace is every bit as revelatory as the Revelation he had been studying since his university years and as far back as his early childhood.

Schelling may not have solved all the philosophical problems he set out to solve, but over the many decades of his teaching and research he had amassed a wealth of material from the philosophies, mythologies, and mystery religions of Europe, the Middle East, India, and China, and he analyzed that material with extraordinary depth and seriousness of purpose. He also found in that same material good grounds for revising our inherited views of male and female aspects of both humankind and deity. His account of hunger, destitution, and desire, of languor and languishing in the life of the divine, would alter fundamentally most of the received views of deity. He also opened the door to a depth psychology that would delve into the shadow side of that "consciousness" of which modern and contemporary philosophers are still so inordinately proud. Finally, he brought philosophy closer to both our natural environment and to philosophy's textual history, so that this history might be pursued not as mere manipulation of abstract concepts but as the critical communication of the decisive narratives about both nature and culture—the stories that matter most to all the gods and goddesses there may be, to mortal women and men everywhere, and to everything that lives and dies on the earth.

PART ONE

F. W. J. Schelling, *On the Deities of Samothrace*

Facing, High above the Sanctuary of the Great Gods, on Mount Georgos, Samothrace.

1

Schelling's Lecture, Endnotes, and Afterword[*]

The isle of Samothrace looms out of the North Aegean Sea. In the beginning it seems to have been called Samos, but then, to distinguish it from Ionian Samos and because of its proximity to Thrace, it was later called Thracian Samos.[1] The geographers of antiquity surmised that during the earliest ages of humankind massive natural cataclysms struck these regions. It may have been that the waters of the Euxine Sea, swollen by flooding, first penetrated what is today the strait that separates the island from Thrace and then breached the Hellespont.[2] Or it may be that the {more profound} force of subterranean volcanic activity altered the level of the waters.[3] The oldest narratives from Samothrace, spun about natural monuments that one could point to, thus became memories that testified to these events. All the way back to those remote times, such memories evoked the honor that was shown to the gods of their native land and the protection that these gods afforded.[4] The terror of such cataclysmic memories was intensified by the ubiquitous tremors of an overwhelmingly powerful nature; the well-nigh inaccessible island,[5] thickly forested, emerged as one uninterrupted mountain chain.[6] During the siege of Troy, Poseidon was able to observe from the island's highest peak all that transpired on the slopes of Mount Ida, in Priam's city, as well as on and about the Danaean ships.[7]

---

[*] The title page of Schelling's book bears the full title, *On the Deities of Samothrace. A Lecture to the Public Assembly of the Bavarian Academy of Sciences on the Nameday of the King, October 12, 1815*. To a second printing of the book, Schelling added a subtitle, *Supplement to the Ages of the World*, referring to the book he had been working on since 1811 but was never able to complete and publish.—Tr.

There on Samothrace, in days now shrouded in the mists of time, a mysterious cult of the gods took root. And if the abundantly blessed Ionian Samos could boast of a man whom all held to be divine—namely, the man who first formed a brotherhood that had as its goal a higher form of humanity—the unprepossessing isle of Thracian Samos possessed something still more splendid in the history of humanity, to wit, the cult of the Cabiri. It is the oldest cult in all Greece, and it bestowed on the region the dawn of a more elevated and finer form of knowledge. The sun did not set on that cult until the ancient |348| faith itself foundered. From the forests of Samothrace, with their more mystery-laden history of gods, ancient Greece first received the belief in a future life. According to universal ancient testimony, those who were initiated into the rites were better prepared to live and to die, and happier in both their living and their dying.[8] Offering sanctuary to victims of misfortune and indeed to criminals—insofar as reconciliation could be achieved through confession and remission of sins[9]—the rites of Samothrace preserved a feeling of humanity in both archaic and more recent times of savagery. No wonder the name of this holy island came to be interwoven with all things of honor and renown.[10] The ancient stories told of Iasion and Dardanos, Orpheus and the Argonauts, but also Hercules and Ulysses are said either to have helped shape the cult mysteries there or to have been themselves initiated.[11] A neither improbable nor insignificant account lists Pythagoras among those who sought wisdom on the isle and found it.[12] The Macedonian king Philip, and his queen Olympia, who was still a child but soon to be the mother of Alexander the Great, first espied one another at the Cabirian orgies, and this was perhaps not without influence on the destiny of their future son.[13] Even during Roman rule, the freedom of Samothrace and its presumably theocratic constitution were respected.[14] There the last Macedonian king, who had been deprived of his kingdom, sought sanctuary; he was driven out not by the Romans, who were vigorous enough in exercising their rule, but by the holiness of the place, inasmuch as the king had polluted himself by murdering one of his own generals.[15] Noble Germanicus would have been initiated into the mysteries there shortly before his death had not the north wind repulsed his ship.[16] Authors from the late period of the Roman Empire mention the sacred precincts of Samothrace, which they clearly continue to revere.[17] And even if researchers of antiquity failed to recognize that the ongoing sacred rites bore traits of the archaic cult on Samothrace,[18] they were nonetheless able, following other traces, to ascertain the continuing influence of the cult up to the end of the second—and indeed on into the third—century of the Christian era.[19] Because public attention has today turned to ancient Greece with an energy more intense than ever before, it may well happen that one day this all but forgotten island will be explored the way others have been; perhaps |349| one will not discover art treasures here to match that unforgettable find from Aegina but what might be uncovered are monuments of the most ancient of faiths, fruits of research that would be more important to the entire history of our race than those treasures.[20]

Although there have been many earlier inquiries into this mystery cult, renewed investigation appears to be worthwhile from every point of view, but especially in light of the following considerations. The meaning of the various individual deities involved there is still swathed in darkness, even though, to be sure, more than one writer cites their Greek names. We know that Demeter, Dionysos, Hermes, and Zeus too were revered as Cabiri. Yet these are mere names to us, leaving open a doubt as to whether the Samothracian gods were actually one with them in terms of the fundamental concepts of these deities, or whether they were merely similar, merely comparable to them. Equally uncertain are the ways in which these gods may have differed as objects of a mystery doctrine, as opposed to objects of public worship and general belief. And yet only such unified knowledge can afford us fundamental insight into the meaning of the Samothracian doctrine, that is, into the genuine system that underlies it. A single report, which by great good fortune has survived, seems to have preserved the birth certificates and the sequence of the deities of Samothrace, along with their true names, inscribed at the time of their earliest origins.[21] It therefore seems justified to employ *this* report as the basis for all further investigation.

The passage preserved by the Greek interpreter who rescued all this for us offers the following account. One receives the rites of the Cabiri on Samothrace. Mnaseas says that the Cabirian deities are three in number: Axieros, Axiokersa, Axiokersos. Axieros is said to be Demeter; Axiokersa, Persephone; and Axiokersos, Hades. Some say that a fourth joins them, Kasmilos by name; he, according to Dionysodorus, is Hermes.[22] Mnaseas attaches considerable importance to the sequence of these personalities and their precise number, and even though he supplies their original names, he also gives us cause to seek out comparisons and search for the concept that underlies each deity. For it seems hazardous, indeed almost blasphemous, to adopt the names offered by this ancient historian while desiring to research their |350|

significance quite independently on the basis of other sources. We have every reason to believe that the one who knew their concealed names was also not uninformed concerning the general significance of those names. That they are not of Hellenic origin but—to put it as the Greeks themselves did—of barbarian provenance is acknowledged.[23] To which tongue and which nation they originally pertain is a question independent of every historiographical supposition. Here linguistics has to decide. That industrious scholar Zoëga, who spent his entire lifetime entombed in his Egyptological studies, found it quite natural to trace the roots of these names back to some dubious remnants of the ancient Egyptian language. Yet when his investigations brought to light only the most general and indeterminate sorts of meanings, instead of identifying particular and precise personalities, when, for instance, he calls Axieros the almighty and Kasmilos the supremely wise,[24] such explanations alone are enough to render his derivations suspect. Whether the treasures we have inherited from the languages of India prove to be more revealing in this regard must remain an open question. We think it better to strike out once again on a path opened by earlier researchers.

Whatever people it was that originally gave us these names and the gods designated by them, it seems certain that they were a seafaring nation. For because the most universal belief surrounding these gods is that they brought exceptional aid and rescue to mariners.[25] The origin and persistence of this belief allows us in effect no other explanation than that these gods were first known to a people who pursued their enterprise on the seas, a people who seem to have been particularly skilled in this respect. It also appears quite natural that when entering upon those waters that still today are quite treacherous, where gales and storms often forced them to remain on the islands in that vicinity much longer than their trade would have required of them, these strangers who had sailed from afar would want to bring their domestic gods with them. Thus the same ships that brought incense, indigo, or ivory also transplanted their gods and sanctuaries onto these Greek coasts and islands.[26] We recognize such a people who flourished in ancient times in the Phoenicians alone, whose perduring impact and long-lasting rule, and indeed whose very |351| settlements in these regions, history cannot gainsay.[27] To this add Herodotus's assurance that the protective deities of the Phoenicians, whose likenesses were affixed to the prows of their ships, resembled in outline those of the Egyptian Cabiri.[28] If, then, Samothrace received its gods from Phoenician sailors, whether directly or indirectly, and if in all probability the names and the gods themselves derived from that nation, there are strong grounds for trying to trace the meaning of those names in the roots of the Phoenician language—roots that are indisputably identical with those of ancient Hebrew. For we scarcely need reminding, and we can dispense with all proof of the fact, that in the Near East the names of the gods, as well as the proper names of human beings, have quite specific meanings.

We shall therefore strike out along the hazardous path of linguistic research, the path that invites us to investigate the provenance and derivation of names or words. We are not unapprised of the difficulty and thanklessness of such a task; cautious experts have taken pains to remind us of these hazards. We are not uninformed with regard to the anathemas pronounced almost universally by less reflective minds upon every such undertaking. Yet all research in and of itself is praiseworthy—all that matters is the manner of its conduct, its procedure. In an era when everyone quite readily feels equal to any and every challenge, it could well be that a new etymological craze jumbles everything with everything else; such a craze, in hectic, harebrained fashion, might scramble all the ancient fables of the gods. And yet investigation of the provenance and derivation of words, when pursued not blindly but artfully and in accord with the rules pertinent to that art, will always constitute the noblest portion of linguistic research.[29]

In view of this, we cannot leave without comment the word that the first three deities share as their prefix, as though it said nothing about the particular nature of each.[30] According to its literal sense, however, the first name, Axieros can {initially} mean nothing else in the Phoenician dialect than "hunger," "poverty," and as a consequence, "languishing" and "obsession."[31] Such an explanation may astonish at first, but a more penetrating observation will confirm it, {indeed immediately, |352| the instant we note that according to the ancient historian, Axieros had to be conceived of as the primal essence, the essence upon which all else succeeded}. We will not allow ourselves to be satisfied with the general claim that an essence that is *primal* without qualification, even if it is in itself an overflowing plenitude, must appear to itself as extreme poverty and supreme destitution, inasmuch as it possesses *nothing* to which it can communicate itself. Nor will we be satisfied with the claim that in the concept of *every* commencement there lies a concept of lack.[32] We hasten instead to recall something quite specific, to wit, Plato's figure of Penia, who, having mated with Poros, becomes the mother of Eros.

To be sure, the Greeks were wont to demand the rebirth of their most hoary deities during the {later} reign of Zeus. And so it is that the goddess Penia arrives at a feast that is being celebrated by all the other gods. Yet we cannot doubt that Plato here, as elsewhere, is offering us a freewheeling treatment of a fable long available to him, and that the initial material for his narrative is a fragment of ancient lore. According to that lore, Eros is the first of the gods to emerge from the cosmic egg, so that prior to Eros all we have is night, the night that bears the egg. For *night* is primordial in the entire nature of things: such lore belongs to all those nations that count time by nights,[33] although it is a distortion to think of this primal essence as uppermost. Yet what is the essence of night if not lack, destitution, and languor? And yet night as such is not gloom, not something inimical to light; it is rather the essence that waits upon light; it is languorous, desiring as night does to conceive. Another image of that primal nature whose entire essence is craving and obsession emerges as all-consuming fire. Fire itself is nothing, as it were, nothing but hunger for an essence, hunger that draws all things into itself. Hence the venerable proverb that says fire is the innermost and thus the oldest; everything that was introduced into the world passed through reductions of fire. For this reason it was also said that Hestia is esteemed as the most archaic {primal} of essences, with the concepts of Ceres and Proserpina serving as the most ancient of deities, blending as they do with the concept of Hestia.[34] As the femininity of this polynomial essence already suggests, all the names of primal nature—some obscurely, some more clearly—point in the direction of the concepts of languor and a languishing longing; this is especially so in the case of Ceres, the first deity of Samothrace who according to the ancient historian is altogether consumed by her {languorous} obsession.

—I am Deo, she replies to the daughters of Celeus when first announcing herself.[35]

That is to say, she is sick with languor, she is languishing, and the meaning of her pronouncement would be clear from the context even if etymological research failed to justify the sense we have of the word *deo*.[36] Like Isis, who goes in search of the vanished god, Ceres is entirely she who wanders in search of her missing daughter. She is altogether the seeker. Yet the primal ground of her concept lies still deeper. {The first is at the same time the nethermost}. With all that is deepest {however}, beneath which nothing else can be, there can only be obsession, that is, an essence that has less to do with being than with the struggle to be. For that reason the Egyptians held that Ceres is the queen of the dead.[37] The dead are generally thought to be in a state of helplessness, a state of impotent striving for actuality. The underworld itself is said to be the covetous and avaricious Dis or Amenthes. For in the most ancient days, the Athenians called their departed ones *Demetrians*,[38] precisely because those who were separated from the body and the visible world were thought to have been transported to a realm of unalleviated obsession; for the same reason, the Manes were called in Hebrew the languishing ones, the longing ones.[39] Someone might object by citing the words of the Latin poet, words less profound than admittedly quite witty, to the effect that hunger and Ceres never go together.[40] Yet it suffices to remember that we encounter not only a Ceres who is cornucopia but also a Ceres who is Erinyes, and because the Erinyes universally belong among the older deities,[41] the terrifying Ceres is in fact the more archaic one. For unquenchable enticement precedes the craving that has been stilled; the urgent need to conceive—which is a hunger that consumes all else—precedes abundance and fertile plenitude. The full meaning of the name Ceres is felt in the punishment meted out to Erysichthon, on whom the enraged goddess inflicts a voracity that can never be sated.[42] For no serious researcher will be unaware of the fact that the gods punish those who offend them precisely by returning them to the condition from which the gods' succor was intended to save them. For that reason, those in the underworld who have not been initiated into the mysteries suffer the particular punishment of struggling endlessly to fill a container that never can be filled.[43] |354| These indications seem to suffice for what we are here trying to explain. Yet we believe that we can bring the matter to a point of even greater certitude. A number of fragments from Phoenician cosmologies have survived, one of them placing time over all the gods, inasmuch as time encompasses all numbers—being pregnant with them, as it were—without itself being a number. Yet that which is closest to number, appearing therefore as the very first number, they call a languishing longing.[44] Another fragment of Phoenician cosmology, bearing upon its brow the mark of great antiquity, expresses itself in the following way: First there was a breath of gloomy air and turbid Chaos, all without boundary. Yet when the spirit of love was kindled in its own primordial beginnings and a contraction occurred, the resulting cincture was called *languor*, and thus commenced the creation of all things.[45] Here the commencement is posited as an ignition aimed toward and seeking itself. The resulting ligature is once again called languor, but now embodied, as it were, and in that way providing the occasion for the creation of all things. Indigenous therefore to Phoenician cosmogonies is the notion of languor as commencement, as the primal ground of the creation. Yet was this true also for Samothrace? A passage from Pliny answers this question for us when it lists among the works of Skopas a Venus, a Pothos—which is to say, a Languor—and a Phaethon; he adds that in cult practices on Samothrace, these deities were revered most highly.[46] It is also certain that among the Samothracian deities, there was one closely affiliated with the concept of languor. We may be fairly confident that we are acquainted with all the deities of Samothrace and that none of them better merits the designation granted by the ancient historian, to wit, languishing longing, than Demeter. This is the designation that is most appropriate to the goddess who was called Axieros.[47] We believe the explanation proffered here offers the highest degree of certainty that is possible in such investigations.

As far as the |355| designations of the second and third personalities are concerned, namely, Axiokersa and Axiokersos, the first thing we have to record is our astonishment over the fact that past researchers have overlooked the trace of the ancient root of the name Ceres in them; yet in the present context, everything points to a cult and a doctrine at the center of which stands Ceres. *Kersa* is actually the same name transmuted into a different dialect—for Ceres was once pronounced *Keres*.[48] And once we have deciphered the name Axieros, we will have discovered beyond all doubt that Axiokersa is Persephone. The name Axiokersa is yet one more proof of the well-known fact that Proserpina is but another name for Ceres, the daughter a further configuration of the mother. This is why their names, and often their images, were confounded.[49] Both Demeter and Persephone can be called *magicians* or *sorceresses* since that is the meaning of these words.[50] For as {a languishing for actuality, as} a hunger for essence, an appetite we recognize as the most intrinsic trait of all nature {which is replete with languor}, Ceres is the moving force through whose relentless assiduity everything is conjured as though by magic, conjured out of undecidability into figure and actuality. The originally figureless goddess, worshipped in the Roman temple as the imageless Vesta, the pure flame, now assumes shape in Persephone.[51] She becomes the primordial, proper, living figure of magic, the medium and the image, so to speak, that are bound up with an ineradicable sorcery. Our treatment of this aspect of the goddess's meaning may be brief, however, if only because Creuzer has already published his learned findings, which scarcely admit of any other synthesizing category than that of the magician-goddess, a category that is also immediately to be conceived of as the artist-goddess. Persephone is a sorceress {according to the expression of the ancients} insofar as the embodied existence that is to come commences with her; Persephone weaves the raiment of mortality and spins the bedazzlements of the senses. She is, moreover, the first link in the chain that connects the deepest to the highest, the beginning to the end.[52] Persephone is also called Maja, a name that is perhaps more than merely reminiscent of *Magia*.[53] As far back as Aeschylus, it was claimed that Artemis herself had something of Persephone about her;[54] the very name Artemis |356| in its natural derivation also refers to a sorceress.[55] And in general the concept of magic underlies *every* female divinity. In the same way that in ancient German lore concerning the gods, more intrinsically related to the Samothracian system than one might surmise, Freya allied herself with Odin, the two of them reputedly possessing formidable magical powers,[56] precisely so Axiokersa and Axiokersos are united by the concept of magic they share.

For this third figure, Axiokersos, is actually none other than the Egyptian Osiris, the Greek Dionysos, and the German Odin.[57] True, the Greek historian explains Axiokersos as Hades, and every interpreter understands this as properly referring to Pluto or Stygian Jupiter. As already Heraclitus taught, however, Hades and Dionysos are the same.[58] Osiris-Dionysos is king of the departed,[59] just as our German Odin, a benevolent god and the first to communicate to us the good news, is at the same time lord of the realm of the dead. *This* doctrine, according to which the *amiable* god Dionysos is Hades, is indisputably the felicitous conviction that was communicated by the mystery religions. Souls are conducted not down to the stern Zeus of the underworld but upward to the mild god Osiris: this is the arcane sense of the doctrine that Dionysos is Hades. A passage from Plutarch makes this abundantly clear[60] as does the inscription we find so often on Roman gravestones, "Live in blessedness with Osiris."[61] In this context, Persephone, as Kore and Libera, is the wife not of Hades but of Dionysos.[62] Nevertheless, in the generally received tradition, the name Hades perdured; thus Dionysos himself came to be known as Hades. Hence Dionysos or Osiris is Axiokersos, in the same way that Axiokersa-Persephone is Isis.[63] Yet what the name {Axiokersos} expresses most explicitly is difficult to say, inasmuch as we do not know him in his original configuration. Is this personage called Axiokersos simply because he is the consort of Axiokersa? Or is he a magician in some more elevated sense, as the one who surpasses the magic of Persephone, moderating its vigor, both conjuring and quelling by turns that primordial fire (for she too is fire)?[64] At all events, the answers to such questions could be elaborated only in investigations that |357| exceed the scope of the present lecture. Yet regardless of the more determinate meaning of the name, in contrast to its more general sense, Dionysos is himself a magical god, whether one thinks of him in terms of the terrifying images in which he punishes the Tyrrhenian sailors or in terms of his office as the inaugurator of nature, the god who alleviates all things,[65] or as the principle of moisture, which fends off desiccating fire.[66]

10   Thus, in any case, the first three Samothracian gods constitute the same sequence and the identical linkage in which we otherwise always and everywhere find Demeter, Persephone, and Dionysos. And now comes the fourth figure, Kasmilos by name, more usually called Kadmilos and Camillus. Concerning all these names, scholars are unanimous, insofar as they refer to a god who serves. So much would be clear to us by virtue of the Etruscan-Roman Camillus. But the servant of what god or of which gods? The equally unanimous view holds that he serves the company of those gods whose names precede his own; his very concept makes it clear that he is subordinated to them.[67] Would Kadmilos or Hermes therefore be subservient to Ceres, Proserpina, and Bacchus? For there is also no doubt about Kadmilos being Hermes. Mercury, the servant of these gods, otherwise and preeminently the messenger of the supreme god Zeus? True, Hermes calls Proserpina back from the underworld, albeit not at the behest of Ceres, but rather upon the command of Jupiter.[68] In Varro we find the expression "Camillus, a god, servant of the great gods."[69] Yet this does not tell us to which gods he was ministrant, even if we presuppose that the Cabirian deities are not to be distinguished from the Great Gods. For the number of the Great Gods is fixed at seven, to which an eighth may be added. Therefore, as a minion of the Great Gods, Camillus is not necessarily in service to those first three. However, if we grant that he attended the lesser and the superior gods simultaneously, then he was in service to the lesser gods only to the extent that he was the *mediator* between them and the higher deities and thus was himself superior; indeed, the *most appropriate* concept of Hermes is that he is the preeminent contact between the higher and the lower gods.[70] Hence he would serve the higher and the lower realms in quite distinct senses: he would be a true acolyte to the superior gods, serving as their obedient instrument, whereas to the

inferior gods he would be |358| a benevolent yet more sublime essence. We have to be extremely cautious about the all-too-readily affirmed supposition that Kadmilos accompanies the three deities as their servant, for this may cast a false light on the entire Samothracian system. Such doubts are in fact bolstered by the names themselves. For Kadmilos, with its Greek ending, derives from the original Kadmiel, which literally means "he who goes before the god."[71] This, in turn, in accord with Near Eastern usage, means nothing other than that he is the harbinger of the coming god, the god's herald. To that extent, he stands in the same relation to the unknown god that the so-called Angel of the Visage stands toward the Jehovah of the Old Testament.[72] For *visage* is the very meaning of *kadmi*, namely, "the one who goes before." Thus the Angel of the Visage is the messenger, the one at the forefront, as it were, the one who walks before divinity. Kadmilos is therefore not one of the prior gods; rather, he is a ministrant {only} to a future god, a god yet to come. His other name, no less informative, refers not to a god who precedes him but a god who follows him: Kasmilos does not at all mean a mere interpreter of deity, as the usual accounts say; surely it means the one prophesied by divinity as such, ahead of it, proclaiming the deity to come.[73] Thus these names most assuredly indicate a future god, a god to whom Kadmilos or Hermes—but also necessarily all the gods who precede him—stand in a relation of subservience; each of them is a mere ministrant, a herald, or one who announces the coming. We can therefore take it that the nature of the individual personalities themselves proves that the first, Axieros, is by no means given precedence as the unity and source of the gods and the world; nor does the doctrine of the Cabiri contain any sort of system of emanation in the Egyptian sense.[74] Far be it from the gods to follow one another in descending order; rather, they succeed upon one another in ascending order. True, Axieros is the first essence, but she is not uppermost. Among the four, Kadmilos is the last but also the highest.

Naturally, the reflective researcher tends to grasp everything that is human in as human a way as possible. Naturally, too, when researching the ancient teachings concerning the gods, he looks for some means that would allow him to unite the multiplicity of divine natures with the thought of the unity of god, a thought that seems necessary |359| and indelible in humankind. Yet the representation of the sundry gods as mere effluences of one self-reproducing primordial force in them all, as though in various radiations, is neither in itself clear nor is it comprehensible to the people.[75] Furthermore, the indeterminacy and nebulousness of this account do not accord with either the determinateness and sharpness of outline in each individual figure or the circumscribed number of these figures. And yet all of this cannot readily be brought into harmony with the way human beings think. For whoever, even once, has risen to the thought of one supreme essence from which all other natures are but outflowing tributaries will find it difficult to be confirmed in his esteem for these effluences, to say nothing of his finding them to be suitable objects of that profoundly felt piety we perceive in many of the wisest and best who were initiates in either the mysteries or the doctrines of the philosophers—in a Xenophon, for example. Matters are altogether different, however, if the sundry gods are not effluences of a supreme and uppermost divinity, flowing downward, each one weaker than the last, but far rather enhancements of a force that underlies them all as their very basis, enhancements that are finally all transfigured in one supreme personality; from that point of view, they are all links in a chain that ascends from the deepest to the highest, or they are like rungs on a ladder whose deeper-lying rungs cannot be skipped over if one wants to climb higher. But then, because they are mediators for human beings, operating in the space between them and supreme divinity, because they are but messengers, prophets, heralds of the coming god, our estimation of them assumes contours that accord also with the judgments of more estimable human beings. Such contours alone explain how the esteem shown to the many gods could take root so deeply—for such esteem was almost inexpugnable, and it persevered for quite a long time. The notion of emanation therefore does not seem appropriate to any kind of explanation of ancient teachings concerning the gods, nor does it seem helpful in explaining Samothracian teachings in particular. Such a notion shatters against the concept of Kadmilos rightly understood.

The four Samothracian deities concerning whom we have ancient testimony and who are therefore known to us thus form an ascending sequence, like a series of numbers, starting from the lower ones. Kadmilos, not subservient to the three others, rather prevails over them. This insight suddenly transforms the entire sequence into a living, continuous |360| procession; it opens for us the prospect of a further unfolding of the series that is familiar to us up to the number four. The next question, to be sure, is this: What is the nature of that El, that god whose herald and servant proves to be—all those prior gods, certainly, but especially and most immediately—Kadmilos? Indisputably, a new series of revelations begins with this god, a series by dint of which the sequence of personalities continues to the numbers seven and eight. Yet the complete unfolding of this series, which requires more resources than those contained in the transmissions we possess from Samothrace, is not to our purpose. For us it will suffice to open some sort of view—to the extent that this is possible—on the nature of the deity that follows {immediately} upon Kadmilos.

At the outset it is clear that those initial deities are the forces through whose preeminent efficacy and governance the totality of the world exists— clear, therefore, that they are worldly, cosmic deities. For all of them, taken together, are called Hephaistoi,[76] precisely in the sense meant by Alexander the Great when he said that Parmenio too was Alexander. Hephaistos himself is not a member of the Cabirian series in any sense, nor does his name turn up among those of the seven planets or in the cycle of the days of the week—the two phenomena that constitute the key, as I hope to show some day, to all systems of the gods. All of these, taken together as erstwhile deities or, we might also say, as ministrant deities, are Hephaistos.[77] The creation that pertains to Hephaistos is the world of necessity. He is the one who relentlessly compels the universe, holding it in thrall.[78] Yet he is {also the artful sculptor of the whole. He is also the one} also the one who shapes the intramundane seat of those gods who are indisputably superior to him.[79] Exactly this is what such ministrant deities do, in this way once again exhibiting what they are, namely, those who merely prepare the epiphany, paving the way for the revelation of the higher gods. One could say of them that they are not so much godlike as they are god-producing natures, theurgical natures, and that the entire linkage shows itself to be increasingly theurgical. If therefore those personalities who go before are {inner-} worldly deities, then the god for whom they are guides and leaders, the god whom Kadmilos directly *serves*, is the *trans*mundane god, the god who rules over them and is thereby lord of the world, the demiurge, or, in the supreme sense, Zeus.[80] Thus in Eleusis the god who was represented as Hermes or Kadmilos was called the sacred herald. Yet the highest of the high priests, the one who represented the highest of the gods, was the image and likeness of the maker of the world, and he was adorned as such.[81] The Etruscan-Roman Camillus was by no means an acolyte who ministered to any and every priest without distinction; although this has not generally been noted in the past, he was, according to the explicit accounts of the ancient authors, the boy who served the priest of Jupiter.[82] Therefore, in our view, since the priest represented

Zeus himself, Camillus stood in the same relation to Zeus as the Cabirian Kadmilos stood to the highest god. Thus the ascending series functions as follows: the deepest figure is Ceres, whose essence is hunger and obsession and who is the first and most distant commencement of all actual revealed being; Proserpina comes next, the essence or primordial commencement of all visible {extended} nature; then comes Dionysos, lord of the spirit world; and finally, Kadmilos or Hermes, prevailing over nature and the spirit world, having both realms beneath him inasmuch as he communicates with the transmundane.[83] Above all of these stands the demiurge, the god who is free with respect to the world.[84]

14 Hence the Cabirian doctrine embraced an ascensional system, starting from subservient personalities or nature deities and advancing to a supreme personality presiding over them all, a transmundane god.[85] Yet the depiction only now offered is far removed from that other avowal, first elaborated by Warburton but then found to be attractive to German scholars as well, according to which the proper secret of all the mystery religions of antiquity was the doctrine of the unity of God, indeed "unity" in a sense that excludes all multiplicity, which is precisely the sense that our current age attributes to the very concept of unity. Such a contradiction between the public worship of the gods and the mystery doctrines would be inconceivable in and of itself. Any such contradiction, as Sainte-Croix observes, could not have survived even for a brief time, much less endured for two millennia, without desecrating all the altars, indeed without shattering the tranquility of the citizenry. With one hand to create and with the other to annihilate, publicly to deceive and then to enlighten covertly, to institutionalize through laws the worship of the gods, rigorously prosecuting all sacrilege and then clandestinely |362| nurturing and encouraging disbelief—what a rule of law that would be![86] An age that in so many respects is accustomed to fraud {and even takes pride in it} might affirm such a thought, whereas antiquity—still forceful, forthright, and healthy—would unanimously condemn it.[87] In all probability, what was depicted in the mysteries was identical to what transpired in public worship, except that the former would draw out the latter's concealed concatenations; the mysteries probably differed from public worship no more than the esoteric or acroamatic presentations of the philosophers differed from their exoteric teachings. Running entirely against the grain of the whole of antiquity, however, is the concept of a monotheism that almost always is made to undergird the assertions we were only now discussing, a concept that one

can say is appropriate to neither the Old nor the New Testament, although somewhat more attributable to Mohammedanism; nor is such a concept appropriate to that quite splendid humanity that is perfectly mirrored in a saying of Heraclitus, a saying that Plato too applauded: The one wise essence does not want to be called that which is alone; it wants the name Zeus![88]

One might be tempted to draw a different series of conclusions from that admittedly hasty comparison between Samothracian and Old Testament notions—especially when, pursued further, such a comparison would lead to more profound areas of agreement. One might then see in such agreement renewed corroboration of older views held by Gerhard Vossius, Samuel Bochart, and other worthy researchers. According to them, the amassed doctrines concerning the pagan gods are merely a botched recounting of Old Testament history and the revelation disclosed to God's people.[89] Revelation is thereby taken to be the uttermost and ultimate standard, beyond which no historical explanation can go. Yet what if this supposition were merely arbitrary? What if in Greek lore concerning the gods (to say nothing of Indian and other Near Eastern teachings) the ruins of an insight jut forth, indeed, the debris of a scientific system that far exceeds the scope of the most ancient revelation we have in our written documents?[90] What if, in general, revelation did not so much open up a new stream of insights as constrain what earlier flowed freely into a more narrowly circumscribed but precisely for that reason more secure and sustaining riverbed? What if revelation, |363| after the ancient lore had been corrupted and had degenerated irremediably into idolatry, wisely restricted itself to one part of that primal system, but in so doing preserved precisely those traits that might lead us once again to the magnificently encompassing whole of the system?

Be all this as it may, such comparisons at least demonstrate that Greek beliefs concerning the gods can be traced back to more elevated sources than we find in Egyptian and Indian representations. Indeed, if the question arose as to which of the various systems of divine lore remained closer to the primal source, whether the Egyptian and Indian or the Greek, the unbiased researcher would hardly hesitate to decide in favor of the Greek. In the Greek fable, in that history of the gods poetized so marvelously by Homer for the Greeks, what prevails is an innocent, almost childlike fantasy that dissolves the tie that makes the many gods but one god; this is done experimentally, as it were, playfully, and with the reservation that the tie may have to be restored; in the Egyptian and Indian systems, by contrast, what dominates is a serious misunderstanding—indeed, one cannot overlook something demonic there, a spirit of error that seems to be intentionally at work, one that projects misunderstanding to the point of monstrosity and utter horror. Had that nation, which was so bound up with nature, namely, the Pelasgians, from which the entirety of Greek energy and splendor appears to have arisen,[91] themselves muddied the fundamental concepts, had they failed to preserve them in natural innocence and vigor, these notions could never have developed in the direction of such unadulterated beauty; no matter how highly we esteem the vital sensibility of the Greeks, they would never have been able to preserve those deeper connections so faithfully, so candidly, so openly in the very course of their play; it is the covert magic of those deeper connections that also strikes us when we allow the figures of their gods to assume dominion over us in their full poetic and artistic independence. The tie that is dissolved in the play of poetry is restored in the gravity of the mystery doctrines. Viewed historically, it cannot be doubted that these doctrines too come to the Greeks from foreign shores, from the barbarians. Yet why precisely from Egypt? Merely because Herodotus had heard from the priestesses of Dodona that the Pelasgians first learned the names of the deities from the Egyptians?[92] This same Herodotus, however, immediately before the reference to Egypt, concedes that the derivation of the names of the Greek gods from the Egyptian is merely an opinion;[93] it is an opinion that can be even less |364| decisive for us, insofar as Herodotus did not have access to the essential materials for a suitable judgment, documents that are now available to us.[94] A whole other world would have opened up for the father of history had he known of these ancient Hebrew documents; for he too had not failed to notice that the first Bacchic orgies in Greece were inherited from those Phoenicians who had settled in Boeotia with Tyrian Kadmos.[95] Concerning the mysteries of Samothrace, Herodotus asserts quite decisively that the island received them from the Pelasgians, who first dwelled there before they moved on to live among the Athenians.[96]

17   The single reason—itself merely a semblance—that might have urged some researchers to seek the primal source of the Cabirian cult in *Egypt* involves a particular tale that is recounted by our Ionian historian.[97] Kambyses is said to have traveled to Memphis, where he entered the temple of Hephaistos. There he jeered at the image of the god. For, as with the dwarflike figures on the prows of the Phoenician ships, it was the portrait of a pygmy. The blasphemer is also said to have forced his way into the temple

of the Cabiri, entry to which was forbidden to all but the priest who served there; laughing scornfully, he burned the temple's images, for they too were similar to images of Hephaistos.[98] The comparison of the Hephaistos and Cabiri images with the Phoenician patron gods, however, might well lead to the reverse derivation, that is, the derivation of Egypt's Cabiri from the Phoenician dwarf gods. Such a conclusion would be equally sustainable, inasmuch as Phoenicia, according to equally reliable testimony, belongs among the most ancient seats of the Cabiri.[99] Thus the tale in question offers us no conclusions concerning the earliest provenance of the Cabirian cult. That narrative is actually made only more quaint by the suggestion that the Cabiri were seen in their pygmy-like form in Memphis. We will not wish to speculate on how this form jibes with the notion that Hephaistos was the supreme god for both the Cabirian and Egyptian systems, such that all the remaining gods are but effluences from him. How does such a portrayal rhyme with the very designation "the Great Gods," which is universally attributed to the Cabiri? One of our older researchers wanted to eliminate the difficulty through mere interpretation.[100] Yet to no avail, because we have found indubitable traces of the fact that these same gods, even outside of Egypt, were |365| portrayed as dwarflike.[101] This occurred in poetic images and artistic representations alike, as in the poet who tells us that old Anchises carried the Penates of his fatherland out of Ilium in his hands,[102] which demonstrates at least how small these images depicting the gods must have been, gods that were closely related to the Cabirian. One might be tempted to say that at least the initial Cabiri were all ministering deities and were thus, as in the case of the Etruscan Camillus, portrayed as boys. However, boys are not dwarfs. The following account is therefore more suitable, especially since it rests on a representation that was demonstrably available.[103] Because they were gods, and because they were the most ancient essences, these figures were necessarily thought to be worthy, hence to be quite old; {and yet as ministrant essences or} as Camilluses, however, they were thought to be youthful, to be mere boys. The somewhat naive yet well-meaning makers of idols knew no other way to unite these conflicting concepts than through the figure of the dwarf. To be sure, we have to suppose, and meanwhile we have the wherewithal to justify this, that only the early Cabiri were sculpted in this form. For only as sons of Hephaistos, only insofar as they themselves were Hephaistoi, were the Cabiri to be seen in Memphis in the figure of pygmies. In addition, we believe, one among the traits of the human imagination, and a very common trait, to be found especially in old German and Nordic cultures, is that vast powers—more magical than natural—may be found united in the figure of the dwarf. According to an ancient etymology, not in the least to be rejected as absurd, our German word *Zwerg* {in Old German *Tuwerg*} has as its root the Greek word *theurgos*, and thus from its origin has the meaning of an essence possessing magical powers. {Who can fail to think of the artful—and thus in this respect Hephaistian—dwarfs of the Nordic sagas?} We may also recall our trolls, about whom our trusty countryman Georg Agricola still had so many robust tales to tell. For they too are, if we may say so, sons of Hephaistos, trafficking in metals as they do and even forging weapons out of them.[104] Because the very concept of supernatural strength is bound up with the figure of the pygmy, we do not find it at all strange when those who are otherwise viewed as dwarfs at a sudden turn may be |366| thought to be giants.[105] It should not seem so remarkable that among those who are apparently thought to be smaller still, namely, the Idaean Daktyloi,[106] none other than Hercules was named; nor the fact that the rather grotesque image of the oldest Cabiri was {later} transfigured into the splendid figures of the Dioskouroi.[107]

Thus the accounts we have of their form may also be traced back to the concept of magical, theurgical powers. The significance expressed by the name they share deserves to be treated now in the final part of our investigation. Yet here practically all researchers are of one persuasion. The concept of mighty, powerful gods is expressed in the name Cabiri, in accord with a like-sounding Hebrew word. The remaining doubts about this explanation[108] are all but routed by the single argument that these very gods, taken both singly and together, always and everywhere are called "the Great," "the Mighty."[109] However, what guarantees that precisely this concept was expressed by the word *Cabiri*? Not without basis does the doubt persist that properly speaking only the higher gods in the Cabirian system were called "the Great."[110] Yet the designation has an all too general ring to it and is not sufficiently indicative of the specific concept that we should allow ourselves to be carried away by the initial similarity. Our investigation itself compels us once again to offer a single comprehensive depiction of the peculiarities of the Cabiri. The earliest Cabiri, then, were magical or, to speak more specifically, theurgical forces or natures that brought the higher gods to efficacy.[111] Yet the Cabiri exercised their magic not singly but only in their indissoluble sequence and linkage; by dint of such magic, they drew the transmundane into actuality. Now the gods, brought to revelation by this magic, are also caught up in a magical connection with those forces. The entire Cabirian sequence thus constitutes a chain of enchantment that binds the deepest with the highest. Not a single link in this chain can go missing or can fail to be efficacious, lest the magic vanish. Just as mariners find no promise of rescue in the appearance of only one of the Dioskouroi but only under the sign of the two flames in unison, so the Cabiri are the Great Gods who bring rescue only by working in concert; they are worshipped not singly but only as a community.[112] |367| Thus the name, if it was to capture completely their common nature, must have expressed the concept of those who are indissolubly united (like the Dioskouroi) and indeed united by magic. If one had to invent a name for the designated concept, one could not conjure up a more illustrative name than *Cabiri*, as soon as one derives that name {not as is usually done, from the Hebrew *Kābbir*, which means merely *strength*, and this not even assuredly, but rather} from another word of that same language, a word that embraces both the concept of an indissoluble unity and the concept of magic.[113]

If this explanation seems the more probable one, due to the precise conjunction of word and state of affairs, an unexpected yet therefore all the more corroborating similarity raises this explanation to the level of certainty. There is a council of the gods, thus a cohesive totality of gods, that we find among the ancient Etruscans, gods whose individual names are unknown to us.[114] Taken together, however, they were called *Consentes* and *Complices*.[115] These words do no more than explain, or indeed provide a literal translation of, the name Cabiri, granted that the meaning we have accepted is ascribed to it. There were six male and six female essences in this council, but besides these we find Jupiter, to whom they were collectively subordinated. When one thinks of the double gender of all the ancient deities, albeit not in the sense that the two sexes were united unnaturally in one essence, but rather that each personality or, so to speak, each stage in the sequence of the gods was designated simultaneously by a masculine and a feminine deity,[116] one discovers here again the number seven, the Cabirian number, as it becomes absorbed into Jupiter, who expresses its unity.[117] These sundry gods were nonetheless together as one.[118] Thither, to the land of the Tuscians, as we know from our historical sources, the Pelasgians transplanted their gods; to the coast of Lavinium sailed Aeneas, with the Trojan Penates on board {which are but one with the Cabirian essences}. And concerning precisely these Tuscian gods, Varro assures us that they were called *Complices* because they can live only in company with one another, and only in company with one another can they die. It would be impossible to adduce anything further to this expression or to characterize more tellingly the true thought of those united gods. And so, |368| as a consequence, the significance of the name that has been the object of our research certifies the inner sense of the Cabirian system and testifies to the explanation that unfolds first of all from the procession of these gods. Its most profound sense, according to the lore surrounding the Cabiri, revered as holy, was that it depicted inalienable life itself as it advances in a series of enhancements from the deepest to the highest levels, and that it portrayed the universal magic and the theurgy that endure forever in the cosmos, whereby the invisible—which in effect is the transcendently actual—is ceaselessly brought to revelation and actuality. To be sure, there on Samothrace it was unlikely to have been proclaimed in expressions such as these; at all events, initiation into the mysteries was intended to commit the life and death of the individual to the higher gods, not to attain information about the universe. The lower gods were regarded as theurgic means toward the end of such commitment, and they were honored as such. Their magic stretched not downward into the visible world but upward. As a result of these rites, the initiate himself became a link in that enchanted chain, he himself a Cabir, taken up into that indestructible nexus and, as an ancient inscription puts it, welcomed into the company of the higher gods.[119] In *this* sense we may call the Cabiri or their acolytes the inventors of those magical incantations that, as Socrates says, the child in us must always conjure up in order to be healed by them, annealed to the point where the child in us is liberated from the fear of death.[120] Viewed from this one side, the doctrine proper was directed toward life and toward a reflection on how life should be lived; viewed from another side, however, the doctrine may have been thoroughly converted into sensuous imagery. In all probability that imagery depicted the chorus of gods as the ring dance of the stars.[121] And what more splendid image of the fundamental thought could be invented than the ineluctably prescribed movement of these celestial lights in whose choral dance no member can go missing without the whole collapsing, these lights concerning which the most appropriate thing to say is that they can only have been born together and that they can die only together—and at one stroke! Much (although in truth we know nothing about this) may have been concealed over the course of eons, numerous aspects (and this is the fate of many more of our elevated and better doctrines) may have been blurred and robbed of their meaning. Yet whatever |369| obfuscations they may have suffered and whatever particular directions these doctrines may have taken, the fundamental thought remained indestructible and the whole of the original doctrine remained unmistakable: a belief rescued from a remote and pristine age, the purest of all the beliefs of pagan antiquity, the closest approximation to the truth.

Today's celebration seemed a not altogether unsuitable occasion to try to riddle on the riddle of a belief that comes to us from the elevated past. For research into what is bygone constitutes the largest part of all scientific work. Whether we are investigating the oldest traits of peoples, their deeds of war and their constitutions; whether the likeness of extinct creatures can be restored thanks to the all but illegible imprints that an abundant nature has preserved; whether traces of the path that our Eearth has pursued in its development can be uncovered—such investigations always devolve upon times past. Yet of all the objects worthy of research, the worthiest is what once united human beings intrinsically, something in which myriad human beings—and sometimes the very finest representatives of their time—recognized that which required of them the supreme dedication of their lives. In the later periods of Roman Imperial rule, the erstwhile sacred name of the Cabiri was desecrated and used as a form of flattery: on coins bearing reproductions not only of busts of emperors such as the pious Antoninus or Marcus Aurelius but also showing the heads of emperors like Domitian, all of them sporting epithets of the Cabirian deities.[122] For us, in this moment, the most fitting application of the name may be permitted, inasmuch as it reminds us at the same time of that Cabirian confederation by which the ancient tyranny was first broken and the last spasms of a truly Typhonian empire, which threatened merely to end in a universal collapse of ethical life, was finally quelled. Yet the pristine feeling we are now experiencing refuses every alien expression and every artificial use. Such is the feeling we possess toward our beloved sovereign, the feeling by virtue of which we rejoin the ardent plea of his entire nation, that his well-being endure long and long.

The Sanctuary of the Great Gods, with Phengári, the "Mountain of the Moon," in the background.

Schelling's Endnotes

|370| Everyone who is not a stranger to investigations of this sort would, unless I were to reassure them, automatically believe that it would have been easier and more pleasant for the reader had the author worked the material contained in the following endnotes into his text rather than separating out the endnotes in this way. Yet etymological investigations, and especially those that have to compare words and passages from the writers of antiquity, do not lend themselves to a public lecture, particularly when delivered to a mixed audience. The author therefore had to submit to all the disadvantages that arise from such a segregation. First of all, the disadvantage that many of the assertions in the lecture itself are stated quite baldly; one might have found them more readily accessible had the material assembled here in the endnotes been introduced and developed step-by-step along with them. Another disadvantage is that the endnotes exceed the text in length; indeed, it sometimes seems that the endnotes lead an independent life of their own. With regard to the places where this happens, I therefore observe that many points that serve to explain the entire system, and not merely one of its parts, had to be explicated first of all in the endnotes. Several of these points thus seem to go beyond the text in scope, even though they are genuinely necessary for its grounding. Hence, whoever wishes to pass judgment on the intended whole will scarcely be able to avoid granting the endnotes their own careful study. If in what follows it almost seems as though excessive nervous energy has been expended on matters of linguistics, the author confesses that he prefers to be reprimanded for this excess than to be lauded for the opposite. For such investigations, if they are not conducted rigorously and with often painful scrupulousness, are absolutely worthless.

|371| 1. Samothrace—*attollitur*, "forced upward from the seabed." Pliny the Elder, *Natural History*, 4:23, 214 in the edition by Hard. Today called *Samothraki*, it faces the deltas of the Hebrus and Lyssus Rivers, not far from the entrance to the Gulf of Saros. An older name, Leukosia, according to the scholiast to Apollonius of Rhodes, *Argonautica*, line 917, is said to have been cited by Aristotle in his "Constitution of Samothrace." Other ancient authors, among them Pausanias, *Description of Greece*, "Achaia," 7:4, in the Kuhn edition at 530, also cite the name as Dardania. Diverse explanations are offered concerning the source of the allegedly later name Samos; some

of these are refuted simply by the fact that Homer already refers to the island as Samos. Strabo, *Geography*, 10:457 in the Paris edition, understood what was in all probability the case, namely, that the *height* of its mountains gave the name to these mountains and both of the islands we call Samos: ἐπειδὴ Σάμους ἐκάλουν τὰ ὕψη. "They called them Samos because of their heights." He may have been thinking of the word σῆμα, the Doric σᾶμα ("stone heap"): Samuel Bochart, *Sacred Geography*, 1:8, derives the same meaning with greater probability from Near Eastern roots. Compare the opinion of several commentators on Genesis 11:4 and Friedrich Münter's explanation of an inscription that refers to the Samothracian mysteries ([*Erklärung einer griechischen Inschrift, welche auf die Samothracischen Mysterien Beziehung hat,*] Copenhagen, 1810, 29). Accordingly, the name *Samos* would have belonged to the island already during those times when the Phoenicians sailed these waters. Only the supplemental designation "Thracian" would have come later, forming then by contraction the most recent name *Samothrace*, which Homer does not yet know. (See the note in Hesychios, *Lexicon*, 2:1148 in the Alberti edition and note also Virgil's expression, *Threiciamque Samon, quae nunc Samothracia fertur*, "Thracian Samos, which is now called Samothrace.") This is the meaning of the Strabo passage cited in the lecture text, in *Geography*, 7, fragments, ἐκαλεῖτο δὲ ἡ Σαμοθράκη Σάμος πρίν. "Samothrace, which was earlier called Samos." The basis of the name *Leukosia* we need not discuss here; it is doubtless similar to the more conspicuous case of *Melite* (Malta) to which Strabo refers (*Geography*, 10:472); it seems correct to judge that *Dardania* (namely, *insula*, "island") is just as little a proper name as *Electria* (*tellus*, "earth"); see in this respect the scholiast to Valerius Flaccus, *Argonautica*, 2:431 and Pliny, *Natural History*: *Callimachus eam antiquo nomine Dardaniam vocat*, "Callimachus calls it by its ancient name, Dardania."

2. This was the opinion of Strato, cited by Strabo, *Geography*, 1:49. The swelling of the sea was said to have been caused gradually by the rivers flowing into it.

3. The epithet "Earthshaker," which Poseidon bears in the |372| Homeric epics, and the continuous effects of subterranean magma in those waters make such a connection credible. Far back in human memory (at least all the way back to 237 BCE) the same sort of activity caused Therasia to be separated off from Thera (Santorini); shortly thereafter, between the two islands emerged a new island called Hiera (the holy island, according to Choiseul-Gouffier,

now called Great Cammeni), which was raised up by devastating tremors felt as far away as Rhodes and in many cities of the Near East; later, in 46 BCE, a new island, Thia ("the divine"), joined these others; see Pliny, *Natural History*, 4:23, 213. In the beginning of the sixteenth century, the Small Cammeni was formed; at the beginning of the eighteenth century, a new island, five miles in circumference, was forced to the surface by earthquakes, subterranean thunderings, and magma. See Choiseul-Gouffier, *Voyages pittoresques de la Grèce*, volume 1; *Missions du Levant*, volume 2.

4. At that time vast stretches of the Near East were covered over, some only temporarily, some forever. Dwellers on Samothrace reported that the lower parts of the island were also flooded; they fled to the highest mountain peaks and swore endless oaths to the gods of their fatherland in search of succor. According to Diodorus of Sicily, *The Library of History*, 5:47, 357 in the Wessel-Zweibrücken edition, altars could still be seen across the island, showing where rescue had been possible and thus revealing how high the flood waters had risen.

5. *Vel importuosissima omnium*, says Pliny, *Natural History*, 214. Sainte-Croix, *Recherches sur les mystères du paganisme*, 32, takes this to mean that Samothrace was "absolutely without a port." (He says this probably in order to emphasize his appended remark, "Superstition alone would have caused them to disembark on the island.") Sainte-Croix's reading does not accord with Pliny's superlative, however, nor with Livy, *Histories*, 45:6: *Demetrium est portus in promontorio quodam Samothracae*. "Demetrius is the port located on a promontory of Samothrace" (on the northern coast of the island, according to Choiseul-Gouffier, 2:123, where he believed he had found traces of the temple to Ceres); see also Plutarch, *Lives*, "Aemilius Paulus," chapter 26.

6. This is shown by the Homeric expression, ἐπ᾽ἀκροτάτης κορυφῆς Σάμου ὑληέσσης (*Iliad*, 13:12), "on the uppermost peak of forested Samos," and by the already cited statement by Pliny, *Samothrace attollitur monte Saoce decem millia passuum altitudinis*. "Samothrace was thrust upward by its Mount Saokis to over a thousand meters of altitude." Pliny also takes the name of this mountain (Σαωκίς) to be the name of the entire island; see Hesychios, *Lexicon*, 2:1161. Otherwise we know all too little about the |373| natural history of Samothrace. Whether the *Zerynthium antrum*, "the Zerynthian cave," especially sacred to the Cabiri and to Hecate, was located on the island itself or on the coast of Thrace is uncertain, inasmuch as several cities on the

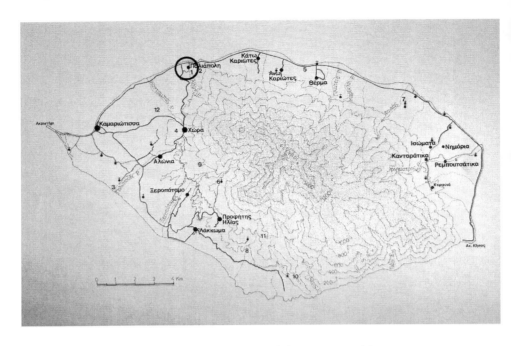

The ancient city of Samothrace, Paleopolis, and the Sanctuary of the Great Gods are in the northwest portion of the island, here circled.

mainland, along with the surrounding territories, belonged to Samothrace. Lucretius, *On the Nature of Things*, 6:1042–46: *Exsultare etiam Samothracia ferrea vidi … lapis hic Magnes cum subditus esset.* "I have even seen Samothracian iron dance … when this Magnet-stone was applied underneath." It cannot be entirely decided whether the iron mentioned here was extracted from the Samothracian mines alone (either on the island itself or on the mainland) or whether what is meant are idols, as Adrian Turnebus, *Adversaria* 20:2, suggests, or whether, as is more probable, iron rings, amulets, and talismans (no one would otherwise think of calling them "compasses" or "magnetic needles") that came from the region.

7. *The Iliad*, 13:10–14, in the translation by Voss:

> For he sat, astonished by the battle and the contest of weapons,
> High on the uppermost peak of the green-forested Samos of
> Thrace; there he saw, among all the mountain peaks, Ida,
> And he saw too the city of Priam and the Danaean ships.

8. Diodorus of Sicily, *The Library of History*, 1:49, 362–63.

9. We may conclude from the mention of this so-called rite of confession that no one could receive a communication from the gods without having confessed the most flagrant injustice he had committed during his life, just as this was demanded of Lysander: see Plutarch, *Apophthegmata Laconica*, in the Wyttenbach edition (Oxford, 1:639). Yet precisely this test shows that there were crimes that barred every approach to the gods. Hesychios (*Lexicon*, 2:293) says, not very specifically, Κοίης ἱερεὺς Καβείρων, ὁ καθαίρων φονέα, "A priest of the Cabiri may cleanse a murderer," but all the circumstances we know to exist, such as the rigorous standards applied in the Eleusinian mysteries, allow us to surmise that only involuntary manslaughter could have been granted such absolution.

10. *Sacram hanc insulam et augusti totam atque inviolati soli esse*, "This entire island is holy and is accessible only to the pure and the just," says the Roman L. Atilius in his address to the Samothracians, in Livy, *Histories*; Diodorus, *The Library of History*, 3:324, reports the view that the very name of the island means ἱερὰν νῆσον, "sacred island."

11. Diodorus, *The Library of History*, 5:49, *Extracts*; Apollonius of Rhodes, *Argonautica*, 1:915ff.; and *Argonautica Orphica*, 465. See the scholiast to Apollonius of Rhodes, *Argonautica*, as cited, with regard to Odysseus.

12. Iamblichus, *The Life of Pythagoras*, chapter 28.

|374| 13. Plutarch, *Lives*, "Alcibiades," chapter 2, expressly says that this woman her whole life long remained devoted to Orphic and Bacchic inspiration; indeed, he suggests that she belonged to the Klodonian and Mimallonian sects (see on these last Creuzer's *Symbolism and Mythology*, 3:208ff.). I do not know if the surmise has already been expressed that this Dionysian trait, passed on from mother to son, even if Alexander himself remained unconscious of it, induced the inebriate youth to cross the Indus.

14. *Samothrace, quae libera*, "Samothrace, which is free": Pliny, as cited in the *Natural History*. The supreme priest appears to have conducted himself as the lord of the land, *Obvius ... terris adytisque Sacerdos Excipit*, "Whether in the countryside or within the temple ... the priest stands out as the exceptional person," says Valerius Flaccus, *Argonautica*, 2:437–38. This is also suggested by Livy's words, *Theondam, qui summus magistratus apud eos erat (regem ipsi*

adpellant), "Theondas, who was the chief magistrate among them (they also called him king)."

15. Livy, *Histories,* 45:6; Plutarch, *Lives,* "Aemilius Paulus," at the end of chapter 26 says explicitly that Gnaeus Octavius granted him the protection of asylum (ἀσυλίαν) and that he was cut off only by the sea and by his sacrilege.

16. Tacitus, *Annals,* 2:53, *Extracts*: the pursuit of Mithridates prevented the Roman commander Voconius from being initiated on Samothrace. See Plutarch, *Lives,* "Lucullus," chapter 13. That exceptionally learned man, M. Terentius Varro, visited the site more for purposes of research than for initiation. See endnote 112, below.

17. Pliny, at the place cited in endnote 46, below.

18. To this belong the ministrations of the altar boys and also the initiation of children; see *Aelius Donatus's Commentary on Terence's "Phormio,"* act 1, scene 1, which tells us: *Terentius Apollodorum sequitur, apud quem legitur, in insula Samothrace a certo tempore pueros initiatos,* "According to Terence, following Apollodoros, in whom we read that on the island of Samothrace at certain times boys were initiated." See Johannes Meursius, *Eleusinia, sive, De Cereris Eleusinae sacro, Works,* 2:502.

19. Friedrich Münter, *A Samothracian Inscription,* 47, with good reason dates the inscription, which has to do with the Samothracian rites at the end of the second or the beginning of the third century of our era. The final cessation of the mysteries in general, as we know, occurred under Theodosius. See Sainte-Croix at 501.

20. Choiseul-Gouffier asserts the same thing; see 2:123.

21. Scholiast to Apollonius, *Argonautica,* line 917.

22. Whether by accident or for some other reason, Creuzer (2:294) names |375| Axiokersos before Axiokersa. We scarcely recognize any longer the passage as cited in Sainte-Croix at 27. In its main features, it is cited above according to the Parisian *scholia,* which shows that the interpretation of the names must also be ascribed to the ancient historian and not to the scholiast. Detailed information on the historian Mnaseas is to be found in Gerardus Vossius, *On the Greek Historians,* 4:96b, which also merits study in relation to the present investigation.

23. No one will take seriously the explanations propounded by the author of "Recherches sur les Cabires," in *Mémoires de l'Académie des Inscriptions*, 27, even though they refer to the Greek and even if Sainte-Croix (27) repeats them. That author goes so far as to contradict Herodotus, who assures us that the names of all the Greek gods, with only a few exceptions, are derived from the barbarians.

24. Georg Zoëga, *De origine et usu obeliscorum*, 220n.

25. According to both poets, the Argonauts seek to be initiated at Samothrace in order to secure better fortune in their sailing; it would be superfluous to heap up references to a matter so well attested. Persons who survived storms at sea caused votive tablets to be hung on the walls at Samothrace—as is shown here, and in other related matters, by the often-repeated words of Diagoras. Diagoras was also blamed for having published Cabirian secrets. See Cicero, *De natura deorum*, 3:37.

26. See Friedrich Münter, *A Samothracian Inscription*, 14. See Christian Friedrich Wilhelm Jacobs, "On the Graves of Memnon," *Denkschriften der Akademie*, 1809, 18.

27. On Thassos, the closest island neighbor of Samothrace, lying to the northwest, Herodotus saw a temple of Herakles, built by the Phoenicians who had sailed there in search of the kidnapped Europa "at least five generations earlier than Herakles, son of Amphitryon." See *Histories*, 2:44. Herodotus admired the goldmines that the Phoenicians were the first to dig on Thassos, mines by which the island received its name. See *Histories*, 6:47.

28. *Histories*, 3:37.

29. The lack of certitude with regard to etymological explanations, especially when it comes to the names of the gods, derives principally from the fact that each deity is capable of possessing sundry and quite varied qualities. It would be altogether remarkable if the etymology of the name failed to outline some sort of meaning, however, |376| a meaning that would accord with some characteristic of the deity. It is therefore important above all that a researcher have insight into the basic concept of a deity, as it were, the root of all its qualities: otherwise a whole series of derivations would overwhelm him, none of them very convincing, while he might overlook the very quality that offers itself automatically as the true one, insofar as the concept that

would offer him a context for that proper meaning is unavailable to him. These basic concepts, however, are determined by the place that each deity occupies in the general system of gods; thus whoever does not know at least the basic traits of this system is only able to venture a guess and to proceed by trial and error but never achieving certainty about the way to avoid a host of errors. Hence when Bochart explains the name Axieros on the basis of the Hebrew ארץ אחז׳, Achsi-Eres, "Mine is the Earth," his derivation comes easily enough; yet at bottom we are no wiser than when the Greek seeks in his Δημήτηρ a Γημήτηρ, that is, an "Earth Mother." Ceres is of course also Mother Earth, yet this is a derivative concept, not the original one. If one is altogether satisfied with general concepts such as *magnipotens*, "very powerful," *perfecte sapiens*, "all-knowing," and so on, where will we ever find an explanation we can be sure of; where will we find a trace of that firm outline and the aptness that we perceive in all the concepts of antiquity? It may be taken as self-evident that the language in which we are seeking etymologies is known not simply on the basis of dictionaries but in and through the original sources and the very roots of the language. Yet even that is insufficient if we do not possess the highly nuanced form of knowledge that grammarians call the *proprietatem verborum*; for to more than a few words meanings accrue quite accidentally; or perhaps the proper meanings do not show themselves in the particular relations that the contemporary explanation grants to the word. It is useful, and indeed necessary, for the etymologist of divine names to pay heed to the analogy of proper names in the language from which he is seeking an explanation. To what extent I myself, in the following attempts to explain by way of etymology, am equal to these presuppositions and demands, the experts will have to judge.

|377| 30. Bochart, *Sacred Geography*, 1:12, explains this word in terms of the Hebrew אחז; what speaks in his favor is the fact that this word is actually used only when names are being contracted, as in Achasias, 1 Kings, 22:40. If it were a matter of a single name, this explanation would pass, but for three names the concept is too limited. Far more genuine seems to be the word אחש, which occurs in connection with the name of that Old Testament king of the Persians, Achas-Weros, in the Book of Esther, 1:1, but also in other contractions, such as in the word אחשדרפנים in Esther, 8:9; there too, in verse 10, we find the word אחשתרנים, where it merely designates an office, a dignity, or some excellence in general. One therefore appeals to the Persian word آخش, *dignitas, majestas*. For the moment we can leave it at that.

31. The Hebrew root ירש, to be sure, generally has the sense of possession (especially through inheritance); there is no need to cast aspersions on that general sense. However, the passages in Proverbs 20:13 and 30:9, where it constitutes the opposite of satiety, and Genesis 45:11, where the passive voice has the sense of being consumed by a lack, are adequate evidence that the word participates in the meaning of the related root רוש, from which the word ריש derives, namely, *paupertas* ("poverty"), *egestas* ("squalor"); the concept of lack or hunger comes first, only to be followed by the senses of appropriation, acquisition, taking possession. Written in Hebrew, the name would accordingly be אהשירוש, which, in the way proper nouns are transposed, as we observe, and pronounced in a somewhat milder form, would literally turn out to be *Achsieros*. And so, in the end, it would be the very name Achas-Weros, merely in a different dialect. Ludwig de Dieu, in *Annotations on Esther 1:1*, wanted to explain this in terms of the Persian word referred to above, اخش, along with the little word ور, which in Persian means what the Arabic means by ذو, namely, *dominus majestatis* ("lord of majesty"); perhaps at that moment he forgot he was dealing with a Hebrew word; for to take up the final syllable -*os*, as does Thomas Hyde's *On the Ancient Religion of the Persians* (Oxford, second edition, 1760), 43, which is the Greek ending, into Hebrew is something one should be scarcely inclined to do. One will find other equally unsatisfactory |378| explanations in Johann Simonis, *Onomasticon of the Old Testament*, 579. The syllable -*os* indubitably belongs to the root, which can only be רוש, identical to the Arabic ورش, *concupivit, avidus fuit, avide voravit aliquid de cibo*, "he craved, he was avid for, eagerly he devoured some foodstuff." The other meaning of ירש, "he possesses," is found after a very common division in another corresponding root, ورز. Thus the two names mean the same, and ירוש is the same form as ורוש. A third form that is indicative of the root רוש is the abbreviation אשרש, in Esther 10:1. If the word were the name of a deity, it could readily have become the name of a Persian king without making reference to its meaning, inasmuch as the Persian kings often took their names from those of the gods; see Jacob Golius, *On the Astronomical Treatise of Al-Farghani* [*Ad Alfergani Elementa Astronomica*], 21, and Barthélemy d'Herbelot, *Bibliothèque Orientale*, on the lemma *Bahram*. But how is this? A king's name, masculine, taken from a female divinity? Why not! This is not surprising, first of all, because of the gender ambiguity of all deities, such that the female deities can also be thought of as masculine. Recall the Cyprian name Ἀφρόδιτος, in Creuzer, 1:350; recall also the ancient Italian *Almus Venus*, in

Creuzer, 2:431; recall too a name not foreign to numismatists, namely, *Deus Lunus*, and finally, a name most relevant to our own considerations here, the *Cerus manus* of the Saliarian poems, whom we assuredly recognize as the masculine counterpart of the feminine Ceres. Flavius Josephus, *Against Apion*, 1:449 in the Sigebert Havercamp edition, when listing the kings of Tyre, records a certain *Astartus,* which cannot merely be a form of the name *Abdastartus,* since a king by the latter name appears immediately before *Astartus.* And yet how could a divine name employed in the Cabirian mysteries have become a Persian king's name? That question belongs to another sort of inquiry altogether. Meanwhile, see endnote 113, below.

32. Certainly remarkable in this respect is the following genealogy of concepts in the Hebrew language: אבה, *desideravit, concupivit,* "he desired, he craved," אב, *pater,* hence, the paternal or initiating force, אביון, *pauper, egenus*, "pauper," "wretch." The fact that in the explanation we have offered with regard to Axieros we moved from the concept of hunger directly to that of (a languishing) languor will not seem remarkable to anyone who knows that our German word *Schmachten*, which now has a more refined sense, originally (and today still in Low German and in |379| several word combinations) meant nothing other than "to starve," and that *Schmacht* (an ancient word) is itself "hunger." See Adelung.

33. See Hugo Grotius, *On the Truth of the Christian Religion*, Book 1, §16, note 15. Apart from the peoples of the Near East, among the nations in question were the ancient Germans, the Gauls, and the Slavic tribes. Concerning the Athenians, see Aulus Gellius, *Grammaticus Latinus*, 3:2.

34. Pausanias, *Description of Greece*, "Arcadia," 8:9, 216: Μαντινεῦσι δέ ἐστι... καὶ Δήμητρος καὶ Κόρης ἱερόν. πῦρ δε ἐνταῦθα καίουσι, ποιούμενοι φροντίδα, μὴ λάθη σφίσιν ἀποσβεσθέν. "Among the Mantineans ... there is also a sanctuary ... of Demeter and the Maid; they keep a fire burning there and take great care never to let it go out." Pindar, *Nemian Odes*, 11:7, calls Hestia πρώταν Θεῶν, "the first among the gods," yet only in relation to the order of libations, this in accord with the scholiast's appended Sophoclean fragment, ὦ πρῶρα (πρῶτα) λοιβῆς Ἑστία, "O Hestia, first in the order of libations," to which one should compare Cicero, *On the Nature of the Gods*, 2:27, along with the scholiast to Aristophanes, *The Wasps,* line 842, Ἐν ταῖς σπονδαῖς ἀφ' Ἑστίας ἄρχονται, "When making libations they begin with the one to

Hestia." Yet precisely this, the fact that in the centers of government and also elsewhere the libations to her were poured first, along with the general turn of phrase ἀφ' Ἑστίας, meaning "from the first beginnings," indicates that the concept of Hestia was commingled with that of the most primeval nature.

35. *Hymn to Demeter*, line 122, where Wolf, based on an intuition that is surely correct, now reconfirms the name Δηώ. No cheerful name such as Δωρίς ("she who gives"), suggested by David Ruhnkenius, or the similarly construed Δώς, which some scholars have suggested, can be understood as pertinent here. Just as little can it be a totally familiar name, or a name entirely imagined. Δεώ was the secret name of Ceres, the name that was concealed in Demeter. That *Deo* stands for *Devo*, like *Dia* for *Diva*, we can assume with assurance.

36. From the word דוה, *languit*, "to languish," from which we get דות (the sibilant pronunciation of the final ת would produce exactly the same sound as Δώς, if only the latter form were attested), *languor, praesertim muliebris*, "I languish, predicated principally of women," and דוי, *languor ex morbo*, "I languish with illness." This is in complete accord with our German word *Sucht*, "obsession," concerning which we read in Wachter's *German Glossary*, under *Sucht*: (a) *morbus* verbi causa: *Mondsucht, Fallsucht* ["illness," for example, "lunacy": literally "obsession with the moon"; "epilepsy": literally, the tendency to fall or collapse]; (b) *affectus gravior totum hominem instar morbi occupans. Tales sunt omnes cupiditates*, ["a grave affection of the whole human being, meaning to be beset with illness. Such are all the concupiscible passions"]. Ceres, who is deprived of her daughter, in the *Hymn to Demeter*, line 304, is said to be Πόθῳ μινύθουσα, she who is |380| wasting away in languor; for *schmachten*, "to languish," again according to Wachter, is *consumi, tabescere, sive inedia, sive siti, sive desiderio*, "to be consumed, to wither away, whether through starvation or thirst or craving." The etymology of טוב as "good," which Nicola Ignarra tries to establish in *On the Hymn*, 122, is deprived of all plausibility in the light of our own endnote 35, above.

37. Herodotus, *Histories*, 2:123.

38. Τοὺς νεκροὺς Ἀθηναῖοι Δημητρείους ἐκάλουν τὸ παλαιόν. "The ancient Athenians called their dead *Demetrians*," writes Plutarch in his *Moralia*, "Concerning the Face That Appears in the Orb of the Moon," *Works*, 4:546.

39. Namely, אבות, a meaning that may be added to what was said above in endnote 32 concerning the genealogy of concepts.

40. Ovid, *Metamorphoses*, 8:785: . . . *neque enim Cereremque Famemque / Fata coire sinunt.* "For Fate has not permitted / That starvation should accompany Ceres."

41. Aeschylus, *The Eumenides*, line 145: γραῖαι δαίμονες, "the hoary spirits," as opposed to τῷ νέῳ θεῷ, "the new god," namely, Apollo, and τοῖς νεωτέροις θεοῖς (l. 157), "the new gods" in general.

42. Callimachus, *Hymn to Ceres*, line 103: βούβρωστις ("ravenous appetite"). See *Iliad*, 24:532, which Heyne (8:707) renders as *Famem suum fanum habuisse memini lectum.* "He knows starvation as his bedmate on this sacred earth." We would not even dare to suggest that the name Erysichthon is itself quite significant and that it may in fact remind us of the identical root we find in Axieros.

43. Zenobius, in no. 106 of his *Proverbs* (*Paroemiographi*, II, 6), writes: ἄπληστος πίθος λέγεται οὗτος ἐν ᾅδου εἶναι οὐδέποτε πληρούμενος, πάσχουσι δὲ περὶ αὐτὸν αἱ τῶν ἀμυήτων ψυχαί. "It is said that in Hades the souls of the uninitiated are forever trying to fill a leaky jar, and that they are made to suffer in this way." The daughters of Danaus are said to have brought the Thesmophoriai from Egypt and to have instructed the Pelasgian women in them. See Herodotus, *Histories*, 2:171.

44. [Translators' note: Karl Schelling, the editor of his father's works, enters the following footnote, the only footnote in the *Samothrace* lecture: "In the author's handwritten copy, *die schmachtende Sehnsucht*, 'a languishing longing,' is altered to *das sehnsüchtige Schmachten*, 'a desirous languishing.' A number of insignificant alterations in style, along with a few minor addenda, have been taken up into the body of the text without being noted." F. W. J. Schelling's own endnote 44 reads as follows:] Excerpted from Damascius, *Difficulties and Solutions of First Principles*, in Johann Christoph Wolf's *Greek Anecdotes* [*Anecdota Graeca: sacra et profana*], 3:259: Σιδώνιοι δὲ κατὰ τὸν αὐτὸν συγγραφέα (Εὔδημον) πρὸ πάντων Χρόνον ὑποτίθενται, καὶ ΠΟΘΟΝ καὶ Ὀμίχλην. "The people of Sidon, according to their own account by Eudemon, subordinate everything to Time, both LANGUISHING and Gloom." *Time* here has the same meaning as *Zeruané akherené*, time without limits,

in the Parsee system. Because the gods come to the fore in sequence, they themselves are but the children of all-ruling time. Likewise, a fragment from Damascius (as quoted above) tells us that such limitless time was held to be |381| undifferentiated (hence to be the indifferent), precisely because it was everything, although grasped as indifferent merely by the intellect, purely in thinking. (That is the sense of the phrase τὸ νοητὸν ἅπαν καὶ τὸ ἡνωμένον, "the universe as thought and taken to be one," which is explained fully by the following phrase, ἡ ἀδιάκριτος φύσις, "undivided nature." Yet this same time, in its effects, is the positing of all difference, or, as an ancient Persian text has it, "The true creator is *Time*, which knows no bounds and has nothing prevailing over it, no root, for it always was and will be." See the *Zend-Avesta* in the translation by Johann Friedrich Kleuker at 3:55n. In our language, therefore, we would say that time without limits is that in which, according to the ancient Persian doctrine, both unity and difference are posited as themselves one. Accordingly, what has to be explained, if in that passage the emergence of difference is accounted for in terms of διάκρισις, is this: ἐξ οὗ (τοῦ ἡνωμένου) διακριθῆναι (φασὶ) καὶ θεὸν ἀγαθὸν καὶ δαίμονα κακὸν ἢ φῶς καὶ σκότος πρὸ τούτων (scil. δαιμόνων ὄντα). "Out of what prior [unity] are [they said] to be differentiated, the good god and the evil spirit, light and darkness, and so on (that is to say, all the spirits that are)?" That such time without borders is no *summus Deus* ("supreme God") everyone who understands the concept will assert along with Thomas Christian Tychsen, *Comments of the Göttingen Royal Academy of Sciences*, 11:13, against Anquetil and Kleuker. It cannot even be called a *principium superius*, because it permeates all things. Yet neither is it sheer eternity, whatever one means when one uses this term in the current Scholastic sense, nor does the statement, "Both Ormuzd and Ahriman were granted by boundless Time," simply mean as much as "Both are, or were, from all eternity."

45. Cited by Eusebius Caesariensis, *Preparation for the Gospel*, 2:10. Σύγκρασις, if translated as "mixture," easily awakens a false conception. I translate it as "contraction," in the sense of two vowels eliding. "Fusion" would also be a good translation; the word in general means an amalgamation in which one element is tempered by another, *temperamentum*. As to whether Πόθος ("languishing") may be taken to be the same as Ἔρως ("eros, love"), see endnote 47, below. In Phoenician the word was surely no form of אהב, which merely means "to love," but rather a word derived from either את

or אבה, here expressed by the word Πόθος. On the proper meaning of this word, see endnote 36, above.

|382| 46. *Is fecit Venerem et POTHON et Phaëthontem, qui Samothrace sanctissimis caerimoniis coluntur.* "He [Skopas] made a Venus, a POTHOS, and a Phaethon, all of which were revered on Samothrace in the holiest ceremonies." Pliny, *Natural History*, 36:4, at 727.

47. Because Varro views the duality that grounds the Cabirian system as *Coelum et Terra*, "Heaven and Earth," Sainte-Croix, as cited in *Recherches sur les mystères du paganisme*, 29, believes he can turn Phaethon into "Heaven," or (and this is not exactly the same) *la lumière, qui l'éclaire*, "the light that illuminates it"; he also believes (but why?) that this is Axieros, that Venus is Axiokersa, and that Pothon (Pothos) or Cupid is the young Cadmillus. Creuzer expresses himself more cautiously in this respect (2:303): "In any case, Phaethon was none other than the bringer of light, Axieros (Phthas, Hephaistos), and Pothos was the ministrant daimon Eros, known also to Plato." Even if we presupposed that Pothos were Eros, he [Pothos] would be always more naturally sought under the name [Axieros] than under the name Kadmilos, since Ἔρως, or, in his more archaic form, Ἔρος, ultimately might well be of the same provenance as Ἀξίερος. To this extent, the meaning of Ἔρως, Cupid, merely corroborates our explanation concerning the meaning of Ἀξίερος. The concepts of languor, longing, and craving are the only ones that can account for the homophony of the names of these gods, which are otherwise so different. However, according to linguistic usage, Πόθος is quite assuredly distinct from Ἔρως. The earlier references to the Homeric *Hymn to Ceres* and an even greater number of references in Creuzer, *Concerning Plotinus's "On Beauty,"* 213, indicate the proper concept of Πόθος. Πόθος is languor felt toward some good that has been lost or in any case is now absent. As Πόθος relates to the past, Ἵμερος (desire) relates to the present in time or space (as Plato tells us in *Cratylus* at 304 of the Zweibrücken edition [Stephanus 420a]). Ἔρως is the first kindling of fire, the craving that precedes possession and that therefore strives after what is still futural; see the choice of language in Plato's *Symposium* at 208 of the Zweibrücken edition [Stephanus 192e 5-6], ὁρᾶτε εἰ τούτου ἐρᾶτε, "Now see if this is what you would love." For this reason, the concept of Πόθος suits only Ceres among the Samothracian gods, for she alone languishes, longing for someone who has been lost, whether this be her daughter or, more likely, the god whom she, like Isis, is seeking.

All languor of any kind, including this first, primordial languor, according to ancient lore, points back to a prior |383| having been united with the one now longed for. (See Creuzer's reference also to the words of Aristophanes in Plato's *Symposium* at 204.) That primal nature too finds itself transported into solitude, lack, and destitution, whereby it appears now as languor, only after a prior separation. Yet art too made a distinction between the concepts of Πόθος and Ἔρως. Even if, as Creuzer notes (*Concerning Plotinus*, 214), later linguistic usage seems to have observed the distinction less rigorously, the Samothracian Pothos by Skopas took its name from the original sense, a sense that understood Pothos to be bound up with a very different artistic concept than Eros. Proof of this is the account of Pausanias, *Description of Greece*, "Attica," 1:43, 105; in Megara one could find three works by the hand of this same Skopas, namely, an Eros, a Himeros, and a Pothos, concerning which it was said: εἴδη διαφορά ἐστι κατὰ ταῦτὰ τοῖς ὀνόμασι καὶ τὰ ἔργα σφίσιν, an elliptical expression that can be unraveled only in the following way: "They are forms, various (in shape), appropriate to each particular work; they all have their own name and thus are the same in their (different) modes of comportment." The progression that is thought in these three configurations can therefore be nothing other than the one expressed above. Sufficient proof that the three figures were not mere representations of Eros or Cupid, which a prudish taste sees everywhere, even there where they are not. The third figure, Pothos, the languor that languishes over a lost object, here too can scarcely be thought otherwise than as feminine. Yet, however that may be, it remains true that the two series of works were different. The Pothos referred to by Pliny formed a sculptural trilogy with the Phaethon and the Venus, precisely in the way that the series referred to by Pausanias, with Himeros and Eros, constitutes a coherent whole. Pliny's Pothos is defined by the notions of Venus and Phaethon, the Samothracian deities with which it forms a whole; Pausanias's is defined by Himeros and Eros, with which it forms a complete artistic cycle. Pausanias's trilogy appears to have been the result of the free artistic play of the spirit of a master, although perhaps not of the hairsplitting thought that the cycle was to have represented three gradations of one particular sensibility; rather, |384| the cycle was inspired by something more poetic, something more symbolic. In the other series, the artist voluntarily limited himself to something given: he did not want to produce a Venus in general but a Venus that accorded with a specifically Samothracian representation—and likewise not a Pothos in general but the specific deity that was revered in Samothrace as languor. To this extent, therefore, but surely no farther, the two representations of Pothos were different.

48. For Ceres is the Hebrew חרש; *Kersa* is merely the Chaldean חרשא. One can hardly doubt that Ceres is nothing other than the Hebrew *Cheres*, if one is familiar at all with the usual meaning of this word and the words derived from it: חָרַשׁ, *aravit* ("he or she cultivated"), חֲרַשׁ, *sata* (Isaiah 17:9, "sown, planted fields"), the Arabic حَرَثْ, *cultura, fundi, aratio, satio, ager, satum*, "cultivation, lands, plowing, sowing, field, planted." Whoever wants to go in search of other possible derivatives will find them in Jean-Baptiste Villoison, *Clarifications of Sainte-Croix*, 523; Nicola Ignarra, *On the Hymn to Demeter*, 122; and also in Creuzer, 4:338. Creuzer speculates that there is a Near Eastern root for Ceres, as there is for the old word *cereo*, which Varro used in the sense of *creo*, "I create"; from *cereo* one can explain the expression *Cerus manus*, "the hand of Cerus," which Festus interprets as *creator bonus*, "the good creator."

49. Ezekiel Spanheim, "*On Callimachus's Hymn to Demeter*," 113. Creuzer, 4:10, 236, 253. Euripides, in *The Phoenician Women*, line 689, calls Ceres and Proserpina the διώνυμοι θεαί, "the double-named goddesses."

50. This entirely normal meaning of the word חרש in the Aramaic dialects has been overlooked by prior attempts to apply it to an explanation of the name *Ceres*, perhaps because it is rarer in Hebrew although certainly not altogether lacking; see Isaiah 3:3 and the name of the Valley of Charasim, in Nehemiah 11:35 and 1 Chronicles 4:14, where the text adds, "For they were Charasim," (i.e., magicians, somewhat like the famous citizens of Telmessos, who were renowned for their gift of prophecy, and the men and women of Thessaly, who were infamous for their sorcery). See Johann Simonis, *Onomasticon of the Old Testament*, 166. From Ezra 2:59 and Nehemiah 7:61, we learn the name of a place called חל חרשא in Chaldea, where we find the name that is homophonous with Axerios (Daniel 9:1). One usually |385| defines *Tumulus arationis*, "a hilly field," quite vapidly; yet I do not doubt that חרשא here is a proper name and that it names a deity. The way in which the concepts of agriculture and magic are connected in this word and in the notion of Ceres needs to be researched much more thoroughly.

51. Ovid, *Festivals*, 6:295ff. Also in a temple on the Peloponnese; see Pausanias, *Description of Greece*, "Corinth," 2:35 at the end. This did not prevent images of the Vesta from appearing outside their temple, however.

52. Creuzer, 3:455ff., 533ff., 4:247, and elsewhere.

53. The original meaning of the word *magia, magus* is lost to us. The Persian language itself has no word from which its مغ or موغ could derive; this induces Thomas Hyde to consider it a radical. Yet we might just as easily conclude that it was originally a foreign word imported into the Persian. The Arabic may have derived its مَجَّس, *magum effecit*, from an unknown source; however, it is clear how readily in Near Eastern languages the root letters of foreign words can change. The Hindu *Maja*, which is quite clearly nothing other than "sorceress" (*praestigiatrix*), indeed, precisely in the sense in which Persephone is a sorceress, is written in Persian as مایه. See the *Notes* of Louis-Mathieu Langlès, *Recherches Asiatiatiques*, 1:219. Here is where a reference to the true meaning of the word could lie concealed.

54. Creuzer, 4:13.

55. Demonstration of this will have to wait upon another occasion.

56. Troels Arnkiel's *Cimbrian Heathen Religion*, 1:62 has, "All sorcery in the northern world has its source in him (Othin), etc." In Snorri Sturluson, *Heimskringla* (in Arnkiel, 1:61), we read: "When his people were in need or in danger, whether on water or on land, they called out his name and they believed that he helped them; thus he was their entire solace." With regard to Freja, *frie, fri*, we scarcely need to be reminded of the Persian *Peri* (پری) or "fairies."

57. The identity of Osiris and Dionysos is known to all because of the references in |386| Herodotus and Plutarch. The similarity of traits in tales concerning Osiris and Odin becomes conspicuous to anyone who reads even the beginning of Plutarch's *On Isis and Osiris*, chapter 13: "It is told how Osiris at the very outset liberated the Egyptians from their animal-like existence by showing them how to cultivate their fruits, by giving them laws, and by teaching them how to revere the gods. He thereupon traveled throughout the land, teaching the people how to become less violent, not by using weapons himself but by persuasion, in most cases making the people milder through words and through every kind of song and music." Concerning Odin, Arnkiel, 1:63 and 62, writes, "He did all of this by means of rhymes and poems that are called *Galdrer* or *Schaldrer*. From that word the Asiatic 'Schald master' and 'rune master' receive their names ... Whatever he spoke he said in rhyme, practicing the art of the poets, so that people would listen to

him with pleasure." In order to avoid misunderstanding, I note that Odin and Wodan are not one and the same. The latter is rightly designated as Mercury by Tacitus, who is the most credible of authorities when it comes to the most remote antiquity of our own nation.

58. Ἄιδης καὶ Διόνυσος ὁ αὐτός. "Hades and Dionysos are the same." See also Plutarch, *On Isis and Osiris*, 28:333.

59. Ibid., chapter 79: ἄρχει (Herodotus, *Histories*, 2:123: ἀρχηγετεύει) καὶ βασιλεύει τῶν τεθνηκότων. "He rules over and is king of the dead."

60. Plutarch, *On Isis and Osiris*, 28:333: "Even that which the current priests utter in sacred awe, veiledly and with caution, namely, that this god is the ruler of the dead and precisely the one whom the Greeks call Hades and Pluto, disturbs the majority of believers, since they do not understand the matter fully and take it to mean that their holy Osiris truly dwells beneath the earth. For their Osiris is far removed from the earth, is unpolluted, is entirely purified of every form of nature that undergoes decline and death."

61. Εὐψύχει μετὰ τοῦ Ὀσίριδος, "May your soul rejoice in Osiris." See Georg Zoëga, *De origine et usu obeliscorum*, 305. By way of contrast, "Go to Odin!" is a curse among the northern peoples. See Arnkiel, 1:66.

62. Creuzer, 3:396.

63. Plutarch, *On Isis and Osiris*, 27:333.

64. This last is, to be sure, my own view of the matter. Axiokersa |387| and Axiokersos together construct the universe by means of a dual magic, inasmuch as the later form does not cancel or annihilate the earlier form but merely overcomes it. This would be the case even if the name merely expressed the general concept of the sorcerer. Yet we may suppose that the original name was not Kersos but Kersor, just as the name Amilcar in Greek is Ἀμίλκας, and Barthélemy, in his "Reflections on Certain Phoenician Monuments" (*Mémoires de l'Académie des Inscriptions*, 30:410), writes, "The Greeks appear to have ended in *-os* the Phoenician names that end in *-or*, for the same reason that the Lacedemonian words that end in *-or* elsewhere in Greece have the ending *-os*, Τιμόθεορ = Τιμόθεος, Μιλήσιορ = Μιλήσιος, etc." However, the name Κέρσορ, or Κέρσωρ, would be reminiscent of Sanchuniathon's Χρυσώρ, who is said to be Hephaistos. See Eusebius, *Preparation*

for the Gospel, 1:35c. This last assertion should not deceive us, however. For the first Cabirian deities are all Hephaistoi. (See §13 of my text and the endnotes pertaining to it.) We find appended to Eusebius's account the following: λόγους ἀσκῆσαι (τὸν Χρυσώρ) καὶ ἐπῳδὰς καὶ μαντείας. "He, Chrysor, pronounced incantations and uttered prophecies," which suggests that he is a sorcerer and thereby possesses properties that are not usually ascribed to the Hephaistos we know by that name. The fact that Chrysor is nonetheless explained in terms of Hephaistos shows us the true meaning. He is the fire god, since at all events he has to do with fire. He, like the Egyptian Phthas, is called Hephaistos by Eusebius (III, 11:115) and by Suidas (3:615) in the vocative form Φθᾶς. He is proclaimed Vulcan, even though this same Suidas (1:396), with reference to the vocative Ἀφθάς, says more correctly and even indisputably, on the basis of some ancient source, Ἀφθάς = Ὁ Διόνυσος. τὸ ἀ ἐπιτατικόν . . . καὶ παροιμία. Ὁ Ἀφθάς σοι λελάληκεν. ἦν δὲ χρησμολόγος, "Aphthas = Dionysos. The intensive . . . proverbial form. Aphthas has spoken to you, but he conceals himself in oracular sayings." He (Phthas) is also merely Hephaistos to the extent that he is the masculine fire that opens up and discloses. We should therefore pay even more heed, in spite of Johan David Akerblad's objection, to what Sylvestre de Sacy writes in his "Letter on the Subject of the Egyptian Inscription on the Monument at Rosetta," at 22ff., namely, that the inscription distinguishes between Hephaistos and Phthas: the latter name does not pertain to Vulcan |388| specifically but is a designation of all the gods (or at least many of them); and if, according to the observation of that same acute scholar, the letter sigma at the end of the name does not belong to the ancient Egyptian name, and if the true name, as in the Greek part of the inscription, is ΦΘΑ, we may perhaps offer—instead of the unsuccessful derivation of the name from Egyptian etymologies offered by Daniel Ernst Jablonski and Mathurin de la Croze—a derivation from the Hebrew. Accordingly, φθά would be the instigator, פתה, a meaning that would be in accord with all his properties. Another reason would be that Georg Zoëga believes he sees in Axieros, among other things, this putative supreme god of the Egyptian system! However that may be, the name Χρυσώρ refers to fire; thus Bochart, *Sacred Geography*, 2:2, was entirely right to translate it back into the Phoenician. According to him, Chrysor is חרש אור. Yet because חרש in the sense of *fabricare* has a transitive meaning and is actually the word for working in metals (Genesis 4:22), the words חרש אור could hardly mean anything else than the one who hammers things in the presence of fire. This is more probable than the words contained in this name that have another meaning, namely, conjuration. Yet in order to understand it even in the latter case, it would be necessary to have some knowledge of the doctrine of fire that was more related to the mysteries, a doctrine that was familiar also to the Hebrews. The word *Ur* (from which the German derives such words as *Ur-Bild*, the original or primal image) has an altogether more concealed sense. It is not external fire (which is called אש) but rather inner fire, the fire that is within fire, so to speak: in such a relation the words אור and אש cohere (see Isaiah 50:11). Yet if we take the word in the sense indicated, חרש אור can scarcely mean anything other than fire conjurer, he who tempers the fire, *incantator ignis*. Granted, I know of no instance of the transitive use of the word in this sense; however, שחר, which by way of metathesis, which itself is very common in the languages of the Near East, is the same as חרש, has at least the Arabic سحر in a transitive sense, as *incantare*. Thus in the *Geographia Nubiensis* in Samuel Bochart, *Hierozoïcon* 2:386: الحيوان الضار يسحرون, *incantant animalia noxia*. "They charmed the poisonous animals." See the passage in the Koran cited by Edmund Castell, *Lexicon Heptaglotton Hebraicum, Chaldaicum, Syriacum, Samaritanum, Aethiopicum, Arabicum, et Persicum* (1669), 2:1508. In that case, to be sure, Chores-Ur, Chrysor or Kersor would also be a name |389| that means the same as Oser-Es, Osiris; a name that, by way of explanations based on quite a few extremely general concepts, one could surely be inclined to explain as אסר אש, or in the more likely older notation אסר איש, that is, as the one who controls fire, the fire conjurer. For the Near Eastern words that have the sense of binding usually also have the sense of incantation. For the אסר, "to bind," see *Targum Jonathan on Deuteronomy* 18:11, where הבר חבר, "caster of spells," is translated as מחברין ואסרין הוין, "magical knots and bindings." The Phoenician-Greek inscription from Malta, sensibly interpreted by Barthelémy, becomes useful to some extent for this explanation of the name Osiris. See the illustration in plate 1 of *Mémoires de l'Académie des Inscriptions*, 30:424. There, in line 2, the Phoenician עבד אסר corresponds to the Greek Διονύσιος, servant of Oser, more or less in the way that on the stone made famous by Akerblad, *Commentationes Societatis Regiae Scientiarum Gottingensis* 14 (1800), the name Heliodorus has the sense "servant of the sun." By contrast, a part of the explanation becomes more dubious on this account, inasmuch as the name Osiris is taken to be merely Oser, with *–is* being treated as a Greek ending. Another Phoenician inscription, the Carpentras bas-relief, contains three mentions of the name Osiris, each time as

אוסרי, Oseri, *cum Jod quasi gentilitio*, "with an iota, as though indicating a tribe," as here in the quite analogous ידעני. The supposition that what is written here is the word אזסירי is made by Johann Leonhard Hug alone. (See the inscription in *On the Myths of the Ancient World*, 62n.) Barthelémy will have nothing to do with this supposition. (See *Mémoires de l'Académie des Inscriptions*, 32:728.) This inscription too devolves upon Oser and merely prevents us from reading אסר, which would be uniform with *Kabir*. If we take *Oser, Oseri* as the correct form, nothing stands in the way of our explaining this word as also meaning conjuror, magician. This is especially the case if we may associate the name with the noun having the same root, and the complete expression could be אסר אסר, *ligans ligationem*, "tying the knot," this last word in the sense of the Greek κατάδεσμος, "binding by a magic spell," as in Deuteronomy 18:11, חבר חבר, which in fact is translated by the Samaritan expression אסר אסר. And if anyone brings this into connection with the Etruscan *Aesar, quod AESAR Etrusca lingua Deus vocaretur*, "that AESAR in the Etruscan language means god" (Suetonius, *The Deified Augustus*, from *The Twelve Caesars* in the edition by |390| Wolf, 229), we would not necessarily be permitted to chide him. Thus we may be satisfied to render Ἀξιόκερσος with the unadorned expression חרש. This would mean almost literally the *Ceres manus*, cited in endnote 31, above, or *Creator bonus*. חרש would retain its usual sense of fabricator (demiurge), which, however, would now not exclude the sense of *magus*, just as little as חרשה in the sense of *maga, praestigiatrix* excludes the sense of *fabricatrix* (*rerum natura*, "of the things of nature": Lactantius, *The Epitome*, 68). One may pose the question as to how much confidence we may place in these two inscriptions. With the inscription from Malta, part of the response would depend on whether it was native Tyrians whose names had been translated into Greek or native Greeks whose names had been translated into Phoenician. Various circumstances speak in favor of the first alternative. Then it would merely be the Greek translator who would have explained the name Abdasar in terms of Διονύσιος. The case of the Carpentras bas-relief is quite different. There the name Oseri undoubtedly refers to the god Osiris. The bas-relief as a whole refers to a number of Egyptian conceptions, among them those concerning Osiris. Its provenance, whether from Egypt itself or from some other Phoenician settlement, is unknown to us, as is its age. Yet no matter what its date, it does go to show that during that age one felt entirely at ease in expressing the name Osiris as Oseri. If one were to grant the authenticity of this way of writing the god's name, one would have to grant the same thing for its derivation from אסר , such that Oser or Oseri would in the end be merely abbreviated forms of the name, the more complete names being Χρυσώρ and Κερσώρ. For what sustains the probability of the first of the two explanations is another name, Χουσωρός, found in the cosmogony of the Phoenician author Mochos, a name that either he himself or Damascius explains as "the primal instigator," ἀνοιγέα πρῶτον. (See Wolf, *Greek Anecdotes*, 3:260.) Here we would have a third instance of that significant syllable *Or*. The oddest sort of contingency must rule if this word only accidentally means "the one who binds fire," from the Chaldean חוס, which actually means *propitium, clementem esse*, "to be propitious, merciful," from which we have חאס, which serves as the Chaldean translation of the Hebrew מכבה in this important passage from Jeremiah 4:4: "In order that my |391| wrath not be kindled when there is no one there to assuage it," ולא יהי חאס, and in that same sense, Jeremiah 7:20 and Isaiah 1:30–31. See Johannes Buxtorf, *Lexicon Chaldaicum, Talmudicum, et Rabbinicum*, 721. It would make matters even more uncanny if the name Dionysos were finally to have the same meaning and thus join the company of Χρυσώρ, Κερσώρ, Χουσώρ! Yet no more of that for the present. Creuzer (in a note to 4:75) has already sought to associate Χουσωρός with Χρυσώρ, and with the Hesiodic Chrysaor and the adjective χρυσάορος, which is an epithet of Ceres. See line 4 of the *Hymn to Demeter*, where Wolf too retains this word and where one should by no means be so quick to follow Ruhnkenius and others who reject it. The usual Greek etymology, "the one with the golden sword," does not suit Ceres nor even Apollo (see *The Iliad*, 5:509; 15:256), to whom it is more often applied, and who has so much in common with Dionysos, nor does it suit Orpheus. (See Pindar, in Jean-Baptiste Villoison, *Scholia to Homer's Iliad [Homeri Ilias: ad veteris codicis veneti fidem recensita. Scholia in eam antiquissima ex eodem codice]*, to which I am here alluding.) This is one of those ancient words that came to the Greeks without their having a sense of its true meaning, and in times to follow, it was associated with particular deities due to tradition alone. Yet enough of these linguistic investigations. Let us now finally pose the question as to how Dionysos or Osiris can be called the fire conjuror, or the one who assuages fire, and how this quality goes together with that of the first instigator. We forgo every profound philosophical elucidation in favor of the following primordial doctrine: Κόσμος . . . πῦρ ἀείζωον, ἁπτόμενον μέτρα (Eusebius: μέτρῳ) καὶ ἀποσβεννύμενον μέτρα (Heraclitus, cited by Clement of Alexandria, *Stromata*, 5:711 in the Potter edition): "The world, an ever-living fire, is ignited and is extinguished in periods of pause." (This is the way I understand μέτρα, with an implied κατά.) Hence, a force that kindles the world (that is Ceres, Isis, Persephone, or however else one designates the primal nature) and a force that subdues the fire (compare endnote 66, below) and thus assuages it, thereby becoming the primal instigator of nature, disclosing it in gentle life and tender corporality, this being Osiris or Dionysos. Both Heraclitus and Hippasos (in Plutarch, "On the Opinions of the Philosophers," *Works*, 4:355; Eusebius, *Preparation for the Gospel*, 749) said, Τοῦ πυρὸς κατασβεννυμένου κοσμοποιεῖσθαι τὰ πάντα, "All things that come forth in the world are precipitates of fire," and for that reason Dionysos too was demiurge. See endnote 80, below.

65. Plutarch, 317, calls Osiris εὐεργέτης, ἀγαθοποιός, "the skillful worker, the maker of the good." |392| He also says (in chapter 42) that although Osiris means many things, his main characteristic is that he is κράτος εὐεργετοῦν (following Markland's correction) καὶ ἀγαθοποιόν, "skilled in effecting the good, and one who produces the good."

66. Plutarch, chapter 33. According to Eusebius, at 35, Sanchuniathon says, καλεῖσθαι αὐτὸν καὶ Διαμίχιον, which Creuzer (4:75) renders as *Jovem penetralem*, "the inner Jupiter." Hellanicus claims to have heard the name Ὕσιρις, related to moistening, and Hyes is said to have been called Dionysos. Plutarch (in chapter 34) in this regard refers to ὡς κύριος τῆς ὑγρᾶς φύσεως, "the lord of moist nature." Precisely this office of extinguishing the fire is what he fulfills in the next life. Hence the pious wish expressed on gravestones, "May Osiris give you cool water!" See Lucian, 16:24. There too Osiris is the beneficent god, inasmuch as he quells the fire of the inextinguishable obsession that saturates the souls of the uninitiated.

67. Sainte-Croix, at 27–28, writes, "A fourth deity, Cadmillus, assumed his place among them, but it was at the lowest rank." Another scholar, Nicolas Fréret, expresses it more strongly in *Mémoires de l'Académie des Inscriptions*, 27:14, "Who was given the office of merely carrying out the orders of the other three." Because Creuzer sees Axieros as the supreme deity, he has to agree with Sainte-Croix on the whole; yet he searches for other connections (2:297ff.) that almost seem to give Kadmilos another meaning altogether than that of Hermes (see 2:317), and this would indeed have to be the case if Kadmilos were to be made subordinate to the three others.

68. *Homeric Hymn to Demeter*, line 336.

69. *Casmillus nominatur in Samothraces mysteriis Dius quidam administer Diis magneis*. "In the Samothracian mysteries, the god who was to serve the Great Gods was called Casmillus." Varro, *On the Latin Language*, 6:88 in the Zweibrücken edition.

70. Horace, *Odes*, book I, poem 10: *superis Deorum / Gratus et imis*, "pleasing to the highest and deepest gods."

71. Bochart's explanation (*Sacred Geography*, 1:395) of the meaning, based on רזם and a derivation from the Arabic word for *ministrare*, is simply unnecessary. Κάδμιλος is quite straightforwardly קדמיאל, derived from קדמי, "prior, antecedent." The name Kadmiel, in this orthography, occurs in the *later* books of the Old Testament, indeed as the name for a priest, |393| a Levite. See Esra 2:40, 3:9, Nehemiah 7:43, and elsewhere. It assuredly does not mean what the usual explanation implies (see Johann Simonis, *Onomasticon of the Old Testament*, 509; Matthaeus Hiller, *Onomasticon sacrum*, was unfortunately unavailable to me during my work on this project), namely, *quem Deus beneficiis praevenit*, "to whom God dispenses his blessings"; rather, the reference is to one who "stands before God" (since that is the sense of the concept *ministrare*, for example in Genesis 18:8, where Abraham stands before the three men as a true Camillus; see Nehemiah 12:44, Jeremiah 52:12, and the Roman use of *praeminister* [*Deorum Macrobius, Saturnalia* 1:8], which employs this related concept). Or it refers to one "who is the herald, messenger, or announcer of God" (see endnote 72, below) or one "who sees the face of God," inasmuch as the *Ministri* (and also the kings) were generally designated by these expressions. For the etymology of this word, see the not unimportant passage in Esther 1:10. The Chaldean translation of the Old Testament expresses the word more energetically as מן קדם יי, whereas the Hebrew merely has מיהוה. See Buxtorf's *Lexicon Chaldaicum, Talmudicum, et Rabbinicum*, 1970. Even the Etruscan contraction (Camillus) is Hebrew, pertaining especially to the Hierosolymitanian dialect of the Chaldean. There the words קדם and קדמי are generally expressed merely as קם and קמי. (See Buxtorf, 1971.) The contraction is Hebraic, for it is found in the name *Kemuel* (Genesis 22:21; 1 Chronicles 27:17), which is rendered—surely incorrectly (see Simonis, 509)—as *grex Dei*, "the company of God"; *Kemuel* appears in the place of *Kemiel*, as, in Genesis 32:31–32, *Peniel* and *Penuel* are confused with one another, and *Kemiel* assumes the place of *Kadmiel*.

72. Note the expression מלאך הפנים (Isaiah 63:9) and the unadorned מלאך יהוה (Exodus 23:20ff.). A detailed explanation of this concept may be found in the first part of *The Ages of the World* [Karl Schelling adds the editorial remark, "Compare SW I/8, 272ff."]. Who can fail to be astonished when he sees this relationship traced throughout sacred history: Aaron becomes the *mouthpiece* of Moses, hence Aaron is the very Mercury of Moses (Acts 14:12: ἡγούμενος τοῦ λόγου, "He who is the herald of the Word"); John the Baptist is the forerunner of Christ, paving the way for him. John is therefore designated by a church father (Tertullian, *De Oratione*, 1) who is probably alluding to the concept of Camillus (see endnote 71, above) as *praeminister domini*. What the Old Testament calls |394| "the angel of the visage," what the Greek mysteries call Kadmilos, the one who in Etruscan religion is called Hermes-Camillus, is what for later Jewish philosophy is called the *Metatron*—a most peculiar name, one to be discussed perhaps at some later opportunity! He is the preeminent angel and is superior to all the other angels, that is, to all other natures that serve as the messengers and minions of the supreme deity; precisely in this way, according to our view of things, Kadmilos is superior to the initial series of Cabiri. He is also called the messenger and the one who is sent, שליח, according to Eisenmenger's *Judaism Unmasked* (2:395), and the "prince of the visage," the one who constantly beholds the visage of the blessed king (ibid., 2:396). They say of him that he is זקן and נער, simultaneously old and young; as the one who sails across the sky to the illustrious throne, he is old; yet when he returns to the world that is taking shape, that is, when he performs his duties as Camillus, he is young (ibid., 2:397). The Etruscan Camillus, as we know, was a mere *boy*. "The Metatron," says a Jewish book, "is called a *Naar*, that is, a boy, because in the face of the Schechinah (divine majesty) he performs the services of a boy" (ibid.). The Etruscans do not derive their notion from this later Jewish concept, nor does the Jewish tradition borrow its notion from them. Their common source is Proverbs 8:30, if one correctly translates אמון. In the same way, at 8:22, the very basis of the Metatron is said to lie at "the commencement of God's path" (ibid.), precisely in the way that Hermes is the god of *paths*.

73. Not simply *interpres* but *augur, quasi divinator Dei*, "the seer, as it were, the diviner of God." At Ezra 3:2 the word קסם stands next to נביא. If that account is true (Plutarch, "On the Opinions of the Philosophers," at the end of book 2), which says that Pythagoras was the first to call all things κόσμος, then the usual explanation of this word *cosmos* can be taken in two ways. According to the primeval doctrine upon which Pythagoras drew, the entire world is but a

Kesem, an *augurium Dei,* "a preliminary sign of God." I observe that Kasmilos can also in another regard be called *augur Dei;* yet this requires more detailed research, and it does not alter the relationship of a going before. Already Bochart (*Hierozoïcon,* 2:36) derives the name Kasmilos from קסמיאל. However, even if Münter in the treatise referred to earlier [*A Samothracian Inscription*], opposes this Phoenician explanation of |395| Kasmilos and proposes the Egyptian explanation for the first three deities, there is no avoiding the conclusion that because Kadmilos, Kasmilos, and Camillus are undeniably and irrefutably all three Hebrew words, the other names that pertain to the same doctrine and the identical mystery cult have to be derived from this same language. To be sure, Münter avers, albeit for no good reason, that the first three Cabiri came out of Egypt and that only the fourth is introduced by the Phoenicians. By contrast, Sainte-Croix takes precisely Kadmilos to be Egyptian. What remains remarkable is the fact that among all the Greek peoples it is precisely the Boeotians who called Hermes Kadmilos; these are precisely the people among whom the posterity of Tyrian Kadmos and the Phoenicians who arrived with him dwelled. (See Pierre Henri Larcher's translation and commentary on Herodotus's *Histories,* 2:49.) Kadmilos is often called quite simply Kadmos.

74. Thus Creuzer explains the matter (*Symbolism and Mythology,* 2:333). It does not at all seem to be a positive trait of this otherwise exceptional work that it takes the emanation theory as the foundation stone for all its explanations—this is due to a very particular philosophical view that one finds fully developed at the conclusion of the fourth part of the work, a view that can be foisted upon both Christianity and antiquity only with violence. Yet one can simply set aside this view as something utterly foreign to the work itself, whose inestimable merit, which remains undiminished, is that it has struck out on a new path toward a more profound insight into all mythology, and this by bringing elevated ideas together with comprehensive scholarship. I find it especially appropriate here to mention something that should have been said earlier, to wit, that Creuzer, by means of the light he sheds on the lore surrounding Ceres and Proserpina, provided the very first materials for the view that is being developed in the present treatise. He has demonstrated irrefutably, especially in §39 of volume 4, that Ceres is the first of all essences; this axiom must be correctly understood, that is, not taking her (as Creuzer does) because she is admittedly the first among the essences to be at the same

time the uppermost, but understanding her as the very ground of all things, as the fundament on which this system of clarifications rests. When therefore this ingenious and learned man, explaining the Samothracian mysteries, concedes to Zoëga the assertion that |396| Axieros is the supreme deity of the Egyptian system, this goes against the grain of the analogy he establishes elsewhere with regard to the basic principles of mythology.

75. Hence the reservation he [Creuzer] makes in the work just mentioned [*Symbolism and Mythology*, 2:333]: "This emergence from and return to a single essence was doubtless something presented to the *more cultured* peoples as the fundamental doctrine, which was something the *uncultured Pelasgians* would simply not have been able to understand. One gave them instead a series of astral gods and βαιτύλια, "ensouled stones" or meteorites, corresponding to these gods, that is, idols possessing sidereal energy, with magical force, etc.

76. Creuzer, 2:321.

77. The possible objection that Dionysos, as a higher demiurge, is set in opposition to Hephaistos (Creuzer, 3:414), and yet, according the to the view expressed above, that Dionysos is a Hephaistos, will be answered in endnote 80, below.

78. Creuzer, at this same place.

79. Τὰς ἐγκοσμίους ἕδρας, "the intramundane seat [of the gods]." Creuzer (ibid.) cites the same phrase from Proclus, *Platonic Theology*, 6:22.

80. Yet Dionysos too is demiurge, indeed the demiurge who in some way overcomes the demiurge that is Hephaistos—Dionysos being the one who releases creation from the fetters of necessity and articulates creation in an unrestrained manifold. This apparent contradiction dissolves as soon as we make the general observation that an essence or principle that occupies a higher position than another and to that extent is its opposite (that which overcomes it) can nevertheless belong together with it with respect to a yet higher principle that would be their common genus. Let the following be said to those who can understand the whole by virtue of a few hints! Zeus too is Dionysos once again, as from time to time was expressly taught. (See Creuzer's observations at 3:397 and 416.) That is to say, Zeus relates to the first three potencies in precisely the same way that the second relates to the first. I say that Zeus relates himself to the first three, even though previously

we have counted four. For, viewed more deeply, Ceres is not an arithmetic number. She is the mother of numbers, the intelligible *Dyas* with whom, according to Pythagorean doctrine, the Monad generates all real numbers. Persephone is the first number (πρωτόγονος), the arithmetic One. Thus, Zeus relates to 1, 2, and 3 precisely in the way |397| that 2 relates to 1; and, the other way around, 2 relates itself to 1 in no other way than as 4 relates to 1, 2, and 3. Zeus's number is always the fourth number. But besides that, Dionysos recurs once again in a higher potency. Axiokersos is Dionysos in his most profound potency.

81. Ἐν δὲ τοῖς κατ' Ἐλευσῖνα μυστηρίοις ὁ μὲν Ἱεροφάντης εἰς εἰκόνα τοῦ Δημιουργοῦ ἐνσκευάζεται ... ὁ δὲ Ἱεροκῆρυξ Ἑρμοῦ. "In the mysteries practiced at Eleusis, the high-priest was dressed to be an image of the Demiurge ... which is to say, as a herald of Hermes" (Eusebius, *Preparation for the Gospel*, III, 117). Samothrace too had its hierophant. He was called Κόης, Κοίης. Bochart, *Sacred Geography*, 397, derives it, not improbably, from כהן. Yet because the hierophant of Eleusis was also called προφήτης, "prophet" (Eusebius too, as quoted above, 39c, seems to have spoken of τελετῶν κατάρχουσι προφήταις), I take it to be more probable that the word means as much as חזה, "seer," a word that was expressed in Greek only by the word Κόης or Κοίης. The word seems to be less universally used than נביא. The latter word denotes the quality, the former the office (see 2 Samuel 24, 11, along with 1 Chronicles 21, 9 and 25, 5), and here it is the office that is being referred to.

82. Plutarch, *Lives*, "Numa," chapter 7 has the following extract: τὸν ὑπηρετοῦντα τῷ ἱερῷ (but already Reiske corrects this as ἱερεῖ) τοῦ Διὸς ἀμφιθαλῆ παῖδα λέγεσθαι κάμιλλον, ὡς καὶ τὸν Ἑρμῆν οὕτως ἔνιοι τῶν Ἑλλήνων ἀπὸ τῆς διακονίας προσηγόρευον, "[the name Camillus], which the Romans give to the boy with both parents living who attends upon the priest of Jupiter, is the same as that which some of the Greeks give to Hermes, from his office of attendant." Macrobius, *Saturnalia* 3:8, agrees with this: *Romani pueros puellasqve nobiles et investes Camillos et Camillas appellant, flaminicarum et flaminum praeministros.* "The Romans called boys and girls of noble ancestry dressed as Camillus and Camilla ministers and acolytes of the flame." Festus, in *De verborum significatione*, 149, edited for the use of the *dauphin*, says, *Flaminius Camillus per dicebatur engenuus patrimus et matrimus, qui Flamini Diali ad sacra praeministrabat.* "Flaminius is one of those with a freeborn father and mother and called to be Camillus, that is, to

serve as minister of the rites of Jupiter the Flame." Festus is not to be taken as intending to clarify merely the attribution *Flaminius*. What he means is that the boy who served as an acolyte to the priests of Jupiter was called originally and preferably Camillus. The fact that he had to be ἀμφιθαλής, a boy whose two parents were still living, was no less significant.

83. As Claudian puts it in *The Rape of Proserpina*, 1:89ff.:

> ... commune profundis
> Et superis numen, qui fas per limen utrumque
> Solus habes geminoque facis commercia mundo.

> ... you alone
> have the right to cross either threshold,
> and are the intermediary between two worlds.

|398| 84. Remarkably enough, the historian Mnaseas breaks off his report with the mention of Dionysos, either because he had not been initiated into the higher mysteries or, more likely, because his awe in the face of the sacred held him back from revealing the ultimate mystery. The scholiast tells us that *several* commentators add the fourth to their number. Thus not everyone arrived at this number, which is the number of Kadmilos, with which the meaning of the whole is first revealed. No writer takes the sequence beyond this number; it is merely the case that outside of this order several figures are mentioned individually, namely, Zeus, Venus, Apollo, and others. It is all the more natural to continue following the thread of the ancient scholiast who broke off with Kadmilos, connecting that thread with other fragments that can be found among the ruins of Phoenician cosmogonies. It may be less necessary to take up the controversy concerning the authenticity or inauthenticity of these fragments, since in any case both sides of the argument have begun to seek a middle ground. But perhaps the following remark is appropriate here: Sanchuniathon declares himself to be the enemy of every deeper, or, as he calls it, "allegorical," or as one would say nowadays, "mystical" meaning, for he is a proponent of pristine literal-mindedness when it comes to the ancient tales of the gods, tales that seem to have run completely amok in his work. In his capricious chaos, the debris indeed drifts about as raw material devoid of any expectations that a more subtle mind would have. It is such debris that I want to talk about here. Sanchuniathon's remark, as Johann Lorenz von Mosheim thought, is a deception, inasmuch as no purpose

would be served by such insertions. Yet after Sanchuniathon has spoken of the Korybantes and Cabiri, he continues: "*At the same time as these*, a certain Eljun was born, named the Highest." With a slight change, the meaning could be: *After them*. . . . But it is unnecessary for our purposes to make that slight change; all the more so since this fragment, if no higher origin is conceded, could be rooted in the myth of the birth of Zeus guarded by the Kouretes and Korybantes—a myth itself so remarkable! Eljun is the real name of the highest god (Genesis 14:18), whose priest is Malki-Sedek (Melchizedek), who wonderfully emerges from the darkness of primeval times as the name of the god who possesses "heaven and earth" (this is how the Cabirian duality was also |399| expressed), that is, as the lord of the world, the demiurge. If one may apply the remark that was ably expressed by Creuzer, namely, that the priest represents the god and also probably bears his name, then Malki-Sedek is the name of the highest god himself, which is also supported by the fact that even the oldest Jewish texts, which certainly followed ancient lore in this regard, for example, the book of Zohar, Sefer Yetzirah, Bereshith Rabbah (see Bochart, *Sacred Geography*, 707), express the name Zeus by צדק, Sedek. Everyone who knows the Hebrew language knows that Malki-Sedek means nothing other than the perfect king, the perfect ruler, what 1 Timothy 6:15 calls ὁ μακάριος (this also in the sense of "perfect") καὶ μόνος δυνάστης, ὁ βασιλεὺς τῶν βασιλευόντων καὶ κύριος τῶν κυριευόντων, "The blessed [perfect] and only ruler, the king of kings and lord of lords." The others, the most perfect natures after him, also indeed rule, but only as factotums; they are like servants of an earthly king, not rulers themselves, not autocrats but representatives, deputies. To all this the following must be added: the seven sons of Sydyk (Damascius calls them Sadiks) are called the Cabiri by *Eusebius*, 39. The meaning here is the same as in the case of the first (the lowest) Cabiri, which are called sons of Hephaistos. That is to say, all of them taken together are Sydyk, the one perfect ruler who lives in them alone; they are, as it were, merely the individual members of the One, the forces realizing and making visible the father, forces that in this respect also precede him in revelation or visibility. Anyone who wished to conclude something in favor of the idea of emanation from this relationship would be mistaken; what matters is what the word χρησμός ("herald of oracles"), cited in Richard Bentley, *Letters to John Mill*, in *Historia Chronica Johannis Malalae*, 81, is said to mean in another regard: ὁ παλαιός νέος καὶ ὁ νέος αρχαίος, ὁ πατήρ γόνος καὶ ὁ γόνος πατήρ. "The old is new and the new is ancient; the father is the offspring and the offspring is the father." Hence, if the Cabiri are the sons of Sydyk and if the priest of that same Sydyk (or Sedek) was the king of Salem, we might be permitted to say that this Malki-Sedek was the first known Cabir—for that was also the name of their priests and votaries—which the system revealed up to the fourth number. In the course of time, the system was quite clearly expanded to the seventh number, and indeed to the eighth number. |400| Yet these oldest connections may be only hinted at, and only with doubts. Too obvious to be completely dismissed by the most prudent researcher, these indications are after all still too weak to base an actual assertion on them. A fuller investigation, conducted on a larger scale and viewed from other angles, might however strengthen the power of these assertions.

85. Such a system was referenced by those in antiquity who most likely did not think it through to the end or understand it, believing that it was *merely* nature philosophy. Hence Cicero, in *On the Nature of the Gods*, 1:42:

> ... praetereo Samothraciam eaque
> ———— quae Lemni
> Nocturno aditu occulta coluntur
> silvestribus saepibus densa.
> Quibus explicatis ad rationemque revocatis rerum magis natura cognoscitur quam Deorum.
>
> ... the solemnities on Samothrace,
> ———— like those on Lemnos,
> Secretly resorted to by night,
> and surrounded by thick and shady groves;
> Which solemnities, if they were properly explained and reduced to reasonable principles, would rather explain the nature of things than uncover knowledge of the gods.
>
> [Tr. C. D. Yonge, with minor changes.]

Sainte-Croix, 356: "Clement of Alexandria avows that the ἐποπτεία (*Epopteia*) was a kind of doctrine concerning nature [*physiologie*]." See Clement of Alexandria, *Stromata*, 4:164. But this passage says something entirely different, namely: "Those who see nature philosophy (physiology) as in accord with the canon of truth (of Christian doctrine), namely, as the transmission of a higher knowledge, a transmission which earlier on was called *Epopteia*, begin with the cosmogonic aspect of the inquiry and ascend from that point of view to the inquiry concerning divine matters."

86. Sainte-Croix, 355.

87. Supercilious explanations in terms of fraud, priestly deceptions, and so on, are certainly characteristic of the most recent times. One attributes a forcefulness to falsehood that one hardly ever attributes to truth. Antiquity was not so idiotic, however, even if it did not sniff out deceptions everywhere with the same supposed cunning. If there were not something very earnest in paganism, and, more than one supposes, something efficacious, why did monotheism need so much time to become its master? Advanced experience, which from time to time learns to grasp some things that formerly seemed ungraspable, already issued |401| enough warnings. The latest such experience concerns the sonorous Colossi of Memnon. Various facts, for example, the periodic ceasing and recurrence of tones, also the fact that apparently there were several such resonant colossi, which Christian Jacobs with perspicacious nimbleness recently gathered together in the treatise mentioned above ("On the Graves of Memnon," 1809), did not prevent critics from speculating about some sort of priestly establishment. Now the doubtless unsuspecting French arrive, confronting the granite blocks of the Theban Thaïs resonating at sunrise.

88. Οἶδα ἐγὼ καὶ Πλάτωνα προσμαρτυροῦντα Ἡρακλείτῳ, γράφοντι. Ἓν τὸ σοφὸν, μοῦνον λέγεσθαι οὐκ ἐθέλει, καὶ ἐθέλει Ζηνὸς ὄνομα. "I am aware that Plato agrees with Heraclitus, who writes: 'The wise is alone one, unwilling and yet willing to be called by the name of Zeus'" (Heraclitus, fragment B 32). Clement of Alexandria, *Stromata*, 5:718. Compare with Johann Heinrich Voß on Virgil's *Georgics*, 808. The form of monotheism that admits of only a *single personality* or that concedes only a wholly simple power to the name of God may well be called Mohammedan. That this is not in accord with the New Testament requires no proof; that the same denial holds for the Old Testament, see *The Ages of the World* [Karl Schelling adds a reference to SW I/8, 272ff].

89. Compare Creuzer's preface to his *Symbolism and Mythology*, 4:iv. This system has collapsed not so much for inherent reasons as for its outworn applications, by Pierre Daniel Huetius, for example.

90. I say, "of a scientific system," and not merely a system based on instinctive knowing, for instance, through visions or clairvoyance or other similar approaches that have been devised these days, where some renounce science outright and others would like to muster a knowing without science [*Wissen*

ohne Wissenschaft]. By the way, the text does not actually assert but rather posits only as a possibility the existence of such a primordial system, one that is older than all written documents and is the common source of all religious doctrines and ideas. I therefore permit myself to defer to future research that does not merely try to reconstruct a part but rather seeks to establish the primordial system in its entirety. Whoever does not believe that he can actually recognize it as the most probable assumption may declare himself against it only after such research is completed and has delivered its results.

91. In roughly the same way that all the power and glory of modern |402| Europe arises out of the Germanic peoples, with whom the Pelasgians overall have several traits in common; their migrations and the judgments offered by later historical researchers about both (see, among others, Pierre Henri Larcher's *Chronology*; Herodotus's *Histories*, 7:277) are not the strongest indications of this.

92. 2:52, *Extracts*.

93. Δοκέω δ' ὧν μάλιστα ἀπ' Αἰγύπτου ἀπῖχθαι, 2:50. "I believe that most of [the names of the gods] came from Egypt."

94. That the *names* of most of the gods came to Greece from Egypt cannot be taken literally in any case. Perhaps if Herodotus's knowledge had extended further, far from deriving the Greek names of the gods from Egypt he would have doubted whether the Egyptian names themselves were of Egyptian origin. Osiris has already been mentioned. Those who want to increase their certainty in these matters should consider the equally uncertain and shallow explanations of the Egyptian names of gods as deriving from the Coptic language, explanations that have been offered since Athanasius Kircher's time by Daniel Ernst Jablonski, Agostino Antonio Giorgi (in *The Tibetan Alphabet*), Georg Zoëga, and others. How pointless it must seem, then, to extend Egyptian etymologies even further, even to Greek names! The Orphic Erikapaios is but one example of this. At one time, by cabbalistic calculation, one wished to see in him the *schem hamphorasch* (the name of Jehovah); Richard Bentley (*Letters to Mill*, 4) rightly calls this *aniles Cabbalistarum fabulas* ("old wives' tales of the Cabbalists"). But then came the Egyptian prejudice. Friedrich Münter, in *A Samothracian Inscription* alone, at 34n., gives two explanations. Several more can be found in Creuzer, 3:388. Bentley, who cannot leave the name in peace, coming back to it a second time on page

90, is content to note that the syllable -κεπ- (reading Ἡρικεπαῖος) can never again be taken to be either Greek or Latin. That is why he did not follow the *ineptis plerumque et cassis Etymologiis*, the "mostly useless and specious etymologies," namely, from the Greek language; he swears that even Orpheus did not know how to designate any etymologies. Without being presumptuous, one could, by contrast, swear that this is mistaken and propose an etymology (admittedly not Greek) that the unparalleled |403| Bentley himself, if he returned from the dead, would recognize as the true one. But do not expect anything so extraordinary here—here it will merely be something uncomplicated and quite simple. The word Ἡρικαπαῖος is no more and no less than the Hebrew ארך אפים (Erec-Apaim) that Exodus 34:6 and other sources use as the name or the predicate of the true God, or, to make the name even more similar, according to the Chaldean form (see Buxtorf's *Lexicon Chaldaicum, Talmudicum, et Rabbinicum*, 216) אריך אפין (Erik-Apain), meaning the long-suffering one, the compassionate one, the one who has a generous heart. And this is the Erikepaios who has so much in common with Dionysos. (See endnote 65.) Proclus says, αὐτὸς δὲ ὁ Διόνυσος (cited from *On the Orphic Fragments [Orphica]*, ed. Johann Matthias Gesner = Gottfried Hermann, 466) καὶ Φάνης καὶ Ἡρικαπαῖος συνεχῶς ὀνομάζεται, "Dionysos and Phanes and Erikapaios are the same and they are named conjointly," precisely as the giver of life (ζωοδότηρ, Richard Bentley, *Historia Chronica Johannis Malalae*, 91), the god with a generous heart, in contrast to the petty god who rather closes off and hinders life. The Hellenists, always with Greek derivations in mind, are to be forgiven if they are not faithful to these etymologies; David Ruhnkenius too, and not only once, declares himself strongly about this. Yet one should not spurn all the etymologies in any given language; for it cannot be unimportant, either critically or historically, for example, to know that the Orphic Erikapaios is derived from the Hebrew or the Old Testament. But this name is simply Orphic and it proves nothing with respect to Egyptian etymologies! Let us now listen to Plutarch, *On Isis and Osiris*, 359: Τὸ δὲ ἕτερον ὄνομα τοῦ θεοῦ (τοῦ Ὀσίριδος) τὸν ΟΜΦΙΝ εὐεργέτην ὁ Ἑρμαῖος φησι δηλοῦν ἑρμηνευόμενον. "Yet a different name of the god (that is, of Osiris) is said to be Omphis the benefactor, whom we must interpret as being Hermes." Is Omphis therefore another name for Osiris? Even Jablonski does not know how to reply here. The passage must be botched; surely Plutarch wrote Ῥόμφιν, "Rhomphin," because only for such a word can the meaning of "the beneficent" be obtained from Coptic; see *Vocum Aegyptiacarum*, edited by Jona Willem te Water, 1:184. But if one knows that the same word from which Erikapaios was earlier explained was also (or rather originally) written as ארך אנפין (*erik-anphin*), then one will find not only the name but also the meaning explained by the very natural abbreviation: the beneficent. We could now go even further; for that |404| *Erik-appin* also demands its opposite, to wit, an ungenerous god; it does not seem to be difficult to say in which name this is to be found. Yet this may be enough for the time being, merely to draw attention to the problem. The doubt that has been expressed regarding the Egyptian names of the gods may well in time be extended to the Indian names—to be sure, only the most important ones. That a people do not dare to change the names of the gods they did not themselves invent is more likely than the opposite. Furthermore, magic was attached to these names, and the rules of incantation or superstition, which generally stipulate that they work only in the language in which they were handed down, probably apply also to the names of the gods. Thus Samothrace not only kept the old rites with their old names but also retained certain expressions of an ancient, original language (παλαιᾶς ἰδίας διαλέκτου) that was used in sacred customs up to the time of Diodorus of Sicily. Diodorus wants to derive these words from the indigenous peoples of the island (*The Library of History*, 5:357) but probably all of them held onto the word κοίης, "priest." (See endnote 81.) In this manner Eleusis kept the alien form of dismissal and the cult of Sabazios kept its *Hues Attes!*, "Go now, you of Attis!" But why assert even this, since the example of the agile Greeks alone is decisive. Even in creative poetic use, they retained the names concerning which Herodotus, who was far more certain of this than of their Egyptian origin, *convinced himself through his investigations* that with few exceptions, which are not even all of them exceptions, the Greeks received these names from barbarians.

95. Herodotus, *Histories*, 2:49, *Extracts*.

96. 2:51.

97. Friedrich Münter, *A Samothracian Inscription*, 30; Creuzer, 2:285ff.; Christian Jacobs "On the Graves of Memnon," note 63.

98. Herodotus, 3:37.

99. Eusebius, *Preparation for the Gospel*, 10:38: "Saturn gave Poseidon and the Cabiri the city of Berytus as a seat." This is the only passage known to me

where Poseidon and the Cabiri are named together, albeit |405| distinguished from each other. That is to say, Poseidon is the antithesis of the Cabiri, or rather the Cabiri are antithetical to Poseidon. Poseidon is the one who randomly wants to disperse, sever, and disjoin, while the Cabiri are the ones who hold things together. Hephaistos holds Poseidon under control, although he himself is overcome by another, who in this respect is κύριος τῆς ὑγρᾶς φύσεως, "the lord of moist nature" (see endnote 66), albeit overcome in an entirely different sense than that represented by the destructive Poseidon. The twenty-first book of the *Iliad* provides sufficient clues concerning this opposition. The connection made between Poseidon and the Cabiri in this passage is proof of the authenticity of the account. One must remember what Herodotus too said about Poseidon. In accordance with this insight, I permit myself a more penetrating interpretation of something mentioned in section five of my text. In this respect it seems to me that Bochart's explanation of the *Pataeci* is even more convincing if one accepts as the fundamental concept of בסת (which is surely not incorrect) *firmus fuit, firmiter innixus est*, "it was firm, firmly supported." The *Pataeci* would thus be those who provide firm, secure ground, which is the opposite of *instabilis tellus, innabilis unda*, "unstable ground, a swell in which one cannot swim."

100. Tobias Gutberleth, *Philological Dissertation on the Mysteries of the Cabirian Gods* [*Dissertatio philologica de mysteriis deorum Cabirorum*], Franeker, 1704; this opusculum is contained in Giovanni Poleni, *Supplements to the Roman and Greek Thesaurus*, 2:824. Poleni translates πυγμαίου ἀνδρὸς μίμησιν as *fortis et robusti viri imaginem*, "the image of a strong and robust man," a turn of phrase to which he is unable to adduce anything other than what we find in Ezekiel 27:11, in Aquila's Greek translation, which opines that in context πυγμαῖοι could only mean "strong men."

101. Creuzer, *Dionysos*, 133ff.

102. *Tu, genior, cape sacra manu patriosque Penates*. "Do you, father, take to hand our country's sacred domestic gods." *Aeneid*, book II, line 717.

103. See endnote 72.

104. Johann Georg Wachter, *Glossarium Germanicum*, 2:1989: *Zwerg*, "dwarf" (Old English *dwerg, dweorh*, French *duverch*), *Daemon silvestris montes et saxa inhabitans, vocem compellantibus reddens, et nescio quae arma fabricans*,

secundum Mythologiam Islandorum, cui nomen Edda. Verel. in Jnd. duergur et in plural. duergar, semidaemones, rupicolae, arte fabrili mirabiles. Gudmundo |406| *Andreae in explicatione Voluspæ Stroph. VII. dwergi sic dicuntur a* θεοῦ ἔργον, "According to Icelandic mythology, which is called the Edda, a wood sprite living in the mountains and in mineshafts, speaking with a loud voice and knowing how to fabricate weapons. Olof Verelius in his *Index linguae veteris scytho-scandicae sive gothicae* has *duergur* and in the plural *duergar*, half-demons, inhabitants of rocks, able to work wonders. Gudmundur Andrésson, explaining the seventh stanza of the *Vǫluspá*, calls the dwarfs 'a work of God'"; but why not dare to say that it derives from θεουργός, "a maker of gods"? Our stalwart Georgius Agricola (concerning him, see Goethe's *Theory of Colors*, 2:237) writes about the minuscule miners, tiny dwarfs, etc. in the treatise *De Animantibus subterraneis* (*De re metallica* 12:491): "Others call those (whom the Greeks call *Cobalos*) 'little miners,' in accord with their typical stature, for they appeared to be dwarfs about three spans [i.e., about 27 inches] high; that is to say, they were like old men (*seneciones*), dressed as miners, in a hooded shirt and with a leather apron hanging down from their loins (like the Cabiri we see on coins; nor are the hammer and pick missing in other descriptions). Those who dig for ore are not harmed by them, but the dwarfs roam the tunnels and corridors, seeming to be engaged in all kinds of work, although in fact they do no real work. Sometimes they throw small stones at the workers, but they never hurt them unless they are irritated and disturbed in their illusory work. Therefore, the miners are not deterred by them from working, but are cheered by them as a good sign, one that makes them work more quickly, more eagerly, and more diligently." Paracelsus too would have had a lot to say about the pygmies, which he did not simply invent but took from common folktales. Even if he often speaks ill of them, he also praises them as "our admonishers, guardians, and protectors in great need, often helping us to escape from captivity and aiding us in analogous situations." The Bohemian highlanders welcome them in their houses as true *lares familiares* ("protective spirits of the family") or *lemures* ("ghosts of the dead"), such that one can hear them hammering and forging underground; that is why both there and in the neighboring German lands, they are also called "domestic smiths" [*Hausschmiede*]; see Bohuslav Balbin, *Miscellanea Historica Regni Bohemiae*, 1:45. The *daemones* also mentioned by Agricola at 492 belong to the same class, *qui quotidie partem laboris perficiunt, curant jumenta, et quos, quia generi humano sunt aut saltem esse videntur amici, Germani*

Gutelos appellant, "who participate in everyday labors, caring for the work animals, and who otherwise are at least seen to be friends to the human race, called by the Germans 'the good little ones'" (Χρηστοί are also called |407| Cabiri: see Macrobius 3:4; perhaps also those Penates of the Old Testament, the Theraphim, after the Arabic ترف). Johann Georg Scherz, *A Glossary of Medieval German* (*Glossarium Germanicum Medii Aevi*), 2:2011, cites an old dictionary: *wichtelein, wichte, schretlein, penates*, "little gnomes, wights, elves, household gods." These gentle ones are preferably called *Kobeln, Kobolde*, "cobolds, pucks," a word that Agricola and after him Wachter derived from the Greek Κόβαλος, among other derivations. Now, Isaac Vossius, *Ad Hesychius*, explains the word Κάβαρνοι in note 12: "Κάβαρνοι, Κάβειροι, Κόβαροι, Κόβαλοι (probably also the κόβειρος that follows in Hesychius's *Lexicon* immediately after that) *ejusdem omnia videntur naturae* . . . which all seem to be of the same nature." Given the innumerable examples of the confusion between the letters *r* and *l*, there can be no doubt that κόβαλοι stands for κόβαροι, and that the latter word has the same etymon as κάβειρος is equally indubitable. Thus the connection demonstrated in the conceptions is also demonstrated in the names. Often enough in the course of this investigation the intimate and profound connection between the Cabiri and the Lares and Manes has presented itself to us (see Arnobius the Elder, *Against the Pagans*, Leiden edition, 3:124), but we were forced to limit ourselves to these few remarks.

105. One could find the trace of such a representation in the name *Anaces* (Ἄνακες). For, however it may be, the sole probable explanation of this word, later transformed into *Anactes* (see Cicero, *On the Names of the Gods*, 3:21), lies in the *Enakim* of prehistory (Deuteronomy 1:28). Wherever one finds giants in the Nordic fables and poems one also finds dwarfs. Who can fail to think of the "company of strong dwarfs," which, along with the gigantic warriors of the Nibelungen, guard the treasures and the fortresses, the company in which abide not only strength but also magical powers?

106. Πυγμαῖος, "pygmy," is explained by πυγμή, about fist high. Δάκτυλοι are fingers.

107. The sons of Sydyk (see endnote 84) and the Dios-Kouroi are one and the same name. But the same name is documented already in those בני האלהים (Genesis 6). (The fact that the sons of the highest God are meant here is shown by that emphatic ה before אלהים.) Concerning these, the oldest work

of our history tells us: "And the sons of God saw the daughters of men, saw that they were beautiful, and took as wives those that |408| pleased them." It goes on in the same context: "In those days there were Nephilim (giants) on earth, especially after the sons of God coupled with the daughters of men and begat children. They are the mighty ones, the men of name (that is, the renowned) from the earliest times of the world." There is something quite wondrous about this passage, whether it be a popular mythical fragment, as it is usually taken, or a piece of history. If one does not want to believe these outlandish Jewish fables, one can explain בני האלהים only as worshippers of the true God, who are presented as distinguished from the rest of humankind and a race all its own. Thus spoke the initiates of the first and oldest mysteries; from the very beginning, something was concealed and confided to only a part of the human race, something that was to spread only gradually outward as though from a center. Is it not worth noting that all higher and better faith appears from the very beginning in Greece and elsewhere under the form of mystery doctrine? Not always and everywhere is it possible to think of spontaneous and local causes, but the secret, the recondite seems to have been given at the same time and from the outset as faith itself. Those holders of the oldest mystery doctrine became the *sons* of the supreme God, just as the apparently original human twins became Dios-Kouroi, who themselves finally became a part of the Cabiri. From these higher natures are descended the first human heroes, the Nephilim (*Nibelungen*?), who were mighty as long as they lived and who are still great and renowned in the underworld (*Niflheim* in ancient Norse mythology?), as in Ezekiel 14:9. Everyone may seek to link these marvelous indications as best as they can, but it is quite natural to look for an explanation of such general forms of mystery already in the oldest times. What was the strict seclusion of the Jewish people other than an endeavor similar to that of the mysteries, except that it did not draw a line between people of the same nation but between one nation and all the others? The first to eliminate all the barriers was Christianity.

|409| 108. Namely, from the Hebrew כביר, "mighty, strong." A great number of people agree with this explanation: Josephus Justus Scaliger, *On Varro* [1565] and *On Eusebius's Chronicle*; Gerhard Vossius, *On Idolatry*, 173; Samuel Bochart, *Sacred Geography*; Hugo Grotius in *Scholion to Matthew*, 4:24; John Selden, *On the Gods of Syria*, 2:287, 361; John Marsham, *Chronicus Canon: Aegyptiacus, Ebraicus, Graecus et Disquisitiones*, 35; Gutberleth, *Dissertation*

on the *Mysteries of the Cabirian Gods*; and all the more recent commentators. The chief doubt that may be raised against this explanation is that the unconditional meaning "powerful" is not evident without at least calling upon the Arabic to help; overall it seems to indicate the concept of the mighty and the strong only by virtue of *excess*. See Job 8:2 and 31:25. More decisive is the missing *proprietas verbi*, "particularity of the word," which is never used with regard to divine might and greatness. One could seek help from the related גבר, in which גבור is used in a compound with אל. *Gebhurah* is one of the qualities of God (1 Chronicles 29:11) and one of the ten *sephirah*. In 2 Samuel 22:11, the *Targum Jonathan* translates the words "[Jehovah travels] on the Cherub" as בגבורותיה, either according to the meaning or as a result of the Syriac ܒܓܒܪ, which a dictionary explains as *fortis, validus*, "strong, firm." Yet the word *Gebhir*, which should actually correspond to *Kabir*, has no relation to divine force. John Spencer, *De legibus hebraeorum ritualibus*, 2:848, finds *cherubim* to be reminiscent of *Cabiri*. The connection seems to him to be *might*. Closer relationships, however, could be found. Whatever shape they may take, those enigmatic beings are described as figures over which the supreme God resides. See 1 Samuel 4:4. These are therefore subordinate beings, as Camilluses, if one were to take them in a human way, beings that nevertheless also possess powerful indwelling forces. No one will want to appeal to this approximate phonic equivalent, however; rather, it is reminiscent of the closest relation to the Cabiri, the Korybantes, a name that cannot easily be other than of Eastern origin.

109. *In Augurum libris Divi potes sunt, in Samothrace* θεοὶ δυνατοί. "In the *Books of the Augurs* they are 'the potent gods,' in Samothrace they are 'the mighty gods.'" Varro, *On the Latin Language*, 5:58. Compare with Cassius Hemina in Macrobius, *Saturnalia*, III, 4; there are many such inscriptions, some of which appear in Gutberleth.

|410| 110. In the *Aeneid*, book III, line 12, the conjunction is quite striking: *feror exul in altum / Cum sociis, natoque, Penatibus* et *Magnis Dis*. "An exile, I fare forth upon the deep, with my comrades and my son, my household gods *and* the Great Gods." The declarative *et* is not to be emphasized. Nothing remains for us but to take the Penates as those that go before the Great Gods (insofar as they are inseparable from them, albeit different from them), whereby the sole probable etymology (see endnote 72) is in accord with this.

111. The main proof for this claim is found in the names and in their succession from one to the other. That in general they were viewed as natures with magical powers is demonstrated by the following. Direct descendants of the Cabiri, Korybantes, or Samothracians (he takes these all to mean the same thing), are, according to Sanchuniathon (Eusebius, 36), the first to discover knowledge of medicinal herbs, remedies for poisonous bites, and *spells*. Strabo, *Geography*, 10:466, says that some people regard the Korybantes, Cabiri, Idaean Daktyloi, and Telchines as one and the same, while others see them as related and distinguishable from each other only by slight differences. But concerning the Idaean Daktyloi, the scholiast to Apollonius of Rhodes, Paris, 1:1131, says, γόητες δὲ ἦσαν καὶ φαρμακεῖς, "they were casters of spells and pharmacists." They were thus both sorcerers and countersorcerers. Namely, those on the left side, as Pherekydes of Syros taught, were the γόητες, the casters of spells or charms, who bound by magic. Those on the right, however, released from such magic. Some people taught that those on the right (the Daktyls or "fingers") were masculine, whereas those on the left were feminine. Concerning these, the euhemeristic Diodorus of Sicily, *The Library of History*, 5:392, says that since they were sorcerers, they were skilled at spells, initiations, and esoteric teachings; while dwelling on Samothrace, they astonished its inhabitants in no small measure, which is almost word for word identical with some of the narratives we have about Odin and his companions. On the magical powers of the Telchines, see Diodorus of Sicily, *The Library of History*, 5:55, Strabo, *Geography*, 14:653, *Extracts*, and the lemma in Hesychios, among others.

112. Because of this founding concept, which has been demonstrated (namely, the concept that these deities are by nature inseparable), one could |411| make no use of the ostensible discovery of various epochs in the history of the Samothracian cult. Sainte-Croix, *Historical and Critical Research on the Mysteries of Paganism*, 28ff. asserts that only two deities were worshipped on Samothrace, namely, heaven and earth; thereupon, he says, Egyptian and Phoenician notions accrued to them; on that basis, people began to confuse the ancient Samothracian deities with the Greek gods. From one of them came Ceres, from the other Proserpina; from the third came Pluto; from the fourth came, but only by way of Egypt, Mercury. Sainte-Croix wants to deduce a third epoch from the passage in Pliny. (See endnote 46.) The mildest thing one can say about all this is that it consists of purely arbitrary and

unproven notions. True, he assures us, "Diodorus tells us in clear terms that the cult of Samothrace was restored, but that the reasons for this happenstance remain unclear, known only to adepts," and he refers us to Diodorus of Sicily, *The Library of History*, 5:49. Probably he means section 48 (Δία— παραδεῖξαν αὐτῷ [τῷ Ἰασίονι] τὴν τῶν μυστηρίων τελετήν, πάλαι μὲν οὖσαν ἐν τῇ νήσῳ, τότε δέ πως παραδοθεῖσαν, ὧν [μυστηρίων] οὐ θέμις ἀκοῦσαι πλὴν τῶν μεμυημένων), where the Latin translation has *ritus antea quidem in insula receptos, sed tum traditione* renovatus, "rites that were received on the island earlier on but then, according to tradition, *renewed*." Equally unusable was the passage found by Christian Gottlob Heyne in his *Excursus IX to Aeneid Book II*: *quae, ut simpliciora, ita probabiliora habeo, haec sunt,* magnas *intercessisse* mutationes *harum religionum; ab initio fuisse Coelum et Terram; postea accessisse duos alios: nunc quatuor ista numina, domesticis nominibus insignita, interpretatione varia ad diversos Deos Graecorum referri coepisse: igitur in illis memorari videas Cererem et Proserpinam, Haden et Mercurum, ab aliis Bacchum et Jovem; etiam Vulcanum in iis quaesitum, item Cybelen; nec improbabile fit, adscita fuisse haec ipsa sacra seriori aetate.* "To simplify matters, I am probably correct in asserting that *great changes* were introduced to this religion: in the beginning there were but Heaven and Earth; afterwards, two others were added; now there were four, with unspecified indigenous names [and yet the scholiast to Apollonius of Rhodes designates them by their oldest names!]; various commentators make mention of sundry Greek gods, seeing in them reminiscences of Ceres and Proserpina, Hades and Mercury, according to others Bacchus and Jove; even Vulcan is adduced to them, and Kybele the same. And yet it is not improbable that these sacred rites were known to be of great antiquity." Basically, this is the same as what Sainte-Croix avers. This atomistic method of explaining something that does not seem comprehensible as a whole by breaking it up into component parts should at least always be based on thorough evidence. But if Athenion, for example, in the scholiast to Apollonius of Rhodes, which we have already cited, *Argonautica*, line 917, speaks of only two Cabiri, this happens in a way that shows he |412| is not referring to, or did not know, the matter in question. He calls the two cabirs Jasion and Dardanos. And yet Sainte-Croix cites him as a guarantor that there were only two deities. Are Jasion and Dardanos really to be taken as *Coelum* and *Terra*? Most instructive here, however, are Varro's remarks, on the basis of which, read superficially, or in any case misunderstood, the opinion was first voiced that on Samothrace, at the beginning, only two deities were worshipped. Thus the main passage in connection with Varro, *On the Latin Language*, 4:17, reads, *Immortalia et mortalia expediam, ita ut prius, quod ad Deos pertinet, dicam* (from this introduction it is clear that the words that follow are the philosophy of Varro himself) *Principes Dei Coelum et Terra. Hi Dei iidem, qui in Aegypto Serapis et Isis et iste Harpocrates digito (qui) significat* (here a third is added to the two; whether these words are from the verses of a poet, for instance Lucilius, or are Varro's own is irrelevant—*iidem*), *qui sunt Taautes et Astarte apud Phoenicas, ut îdem principes in Latio, Saturnus et Ops. Terra enim et Coelum, ut Samothracum initia* docent, *sunt Dei magni et hi, quos (modo) dixi multeis nominibus. Nam neque, quas Ambracia* (so reads the Roman manuscript; commonly known as *Samothracia*, obviously against the context, which also rejects Scaliger's *Imbrasia*) *ante portas statuit duas virileis species aheneas, Dei magni, neque, ut volgus putat, hi Samothraces Dii, qui Castor et Pollux; sed hi* (scil. *Samothraces Dii sunt*) *mas et femina* (thus different from the two male figures seen in Ambracia), *et hi* (see *iidem*), *quos augurum libri scriptos habent sic: Divi potes, et sunt* (scil. *hi, potes dicti*) *pro illeis, qui in Samothrace* θεοὶ δυνατοί. *Haec duo, coelum et terra, quod Anima et Corpus, Humidum et Frigidum.* "I shall explain those that deal with immortals and with mortals, in such a way that first I shall tell what pertains to the gods.... The first gods were Heaven and Earth. These gods are the same as those who in Egypt are called Serapis and Isis, and these are the ones Harpocrates pointed to . . ., and the Phoenicians called them Taautes und Astarte. The same first gods in Latium were called Saturn and Ops. For Earth and Heaven, as the mysteries of the Samothracians teach us, are Great Gods, and these whom I have (only now) mentioned under many names are not those Great Gods that the city of Ambracia . . . represents by two male statues of bronze which they have set up before the city-gates; nor are these, as people think, the Samothracian gods, who are really Castor and Pollux; but they [i.e., the Samothracian gods] are a male and a female; . . . these [again, the Samothracian gods] are those that the *Books of the Augurs* mention in writing as 'potent deities,' and these gods are, for them, what the Samothracians call 'powerful gods.' These two, Sky and Earth, are like soul and body, moist and cold." The passage, read correctly, obviously says only this: Heaven and Earth are the first, the incipient deities; they are represented in Egypt by Serapis and Isis, in Phoenicia by Taaut (the Egyptian Thoth) and Astarte, in Samothrace also by a male and a female deity. Varro, therefore, does not even say that the number two is the oldest form of the |413| doctrine (Creuzer, 2:291n.) but only that the *principes Dei* are two; supposing that it was really his intention to lead all the deities philosophically back to an underlying duality, there is a clear difference between *two primary* underlying deities and the *two at first assumed to be the sole deities*. That the explanation given of *principibus deis* (the initial deities) is not just an inflated version of this is made clear by the following passages, which are also memorable in themselves and which could be a salutary remedy for some of the misunderstandings that have recently seen the light of day. *Saturnus unus est de principibus Deis* (Augustine, *The City of God*, 7:13). "Saturn is one of the first gods." *Saturnus pater a Jove filio est* superatus (7:18). "Father Saturn is *superseded by* Jupiter the son." *Juppiter Deus est habens potestatem causarum, quibus aliquid fit in mundo. Ei* praeponitur *Janus, quoniam penes Janum sunt* prima, *penes Jovem* summa. *Merito ergo rex omnium Juppiter habetur. Prima enim* vincuntur *a* summis, *quia, licet* prima praecedant tempore, summa superant dignitate (7:9). "The god Jupiter possesses the power of the causes by which anything comes to be in the world. Janus is *placed before* him, because Janus has dominion over *first* things, Jupiter over the *highest* things. Therefore Jupiter is deservedly held to be the king of all things. For *highest* things are better than first things: for although *first things precede in time, highest things excel by dignity*." Compare the expression *Jovis consiliarii et principes*, "counselors and princes of Jupiter," in the words cited in endnote 115 below.

These last passages of the Roman scholar may also shed light on the extent to which *some*, like the scholiast to Apollonius of Rhodes, whom we have already cited, could say that there are primarily (this is how πρότερον must be translated, if one does not refer it to φασί) only two Cabiri, Zeus, the older one, and Dionysos, the younger (of the two); this is the only place one could mention where one finds the original number two, but not as *Coelum* and *Terra*. Those who argued this (there were only a few) had drawn from the deepest stratum. For here we cannot mean the first Dionysos (see endnote 80) but only the highest one, superseding even Zeus. So it could be said that there were actually only two Cabiri, for these two were the highest, back to whom all the others reverted, those who alone were left, as it were, *a quibus*, to speak with Varro, *reliqui omnes superabantur*. From the last-cited passages of Varro, it also follows, at least in the book from which they are taken (*On Select Gods*), that together with the *principibus* or *primis* |414| *Diis* they recognized the higher deities that would overcome them; thus it follows that even in his own philosophy, Varro believed that the series continued and did not stop at the number two. And yet such continuation could not prevent him from interpreting everything (i.e., the entire series) dualistically and reverting to the fundamental opposition of masculine and feminine. For all philosophy is led to such an underlying duality, without claiming that there are only two *beings*. Furthermore, Augustine elsewhere (*The City of God*, 7:28) calls *Coelum et Terram* only the *d u o p r i c i p i a Deorum*, and he says of Varro (in the same chapter) only this: *Vir doctissimus et acutissimus Varro hos omnes Deos in coelum et terram* redigere *ac* referre *conatur.* "That learned and perspicuous man Varro attempts to *reduce* all the gods and to *refer them back to* Heaven and Earth." However, it is probably based on a misunderstanding that Augustine reproaches him there (at 62 in the Paris edition) in the following way: *istum in libro selectorum Deorum rationem illam* trium (not *duorum*) *Deorum, quibus quasi cuncta complexus est, perdidisse* (7:28). "And certainly the same Varro, in the book concerning the *Select Gods*, forgot all about this relationship of the three (not two) gods, in which he actually lets everything be enclosed." This refers to the following view, which we also know through Augustine (cited above) as the Varronian view and which is even compatible with the idea of reducing everything to a duality. *Ducitur (Varro) quadam ratione verosimili, coelum esse quod faciat, terram quae patiatur, et ideo illi masculinam vim tribuit, huic femininam. - Hic etiam Samothracum nobilia mysteria in superiore libro sic interpretatur, eaque se, quae nec suis nota sunt, scribendo expositurum eisque missurum quasi religiosissime pollicetur. Dicit enim, se ibi multis indiciis collegisse in simulacris, aliud* significare *coelum, aliud terram, aliud exempla rerum, quas Plato appellat Ideas* (7:28). "By analogy he comes to assume that heaven is the efficacious principle, earth the passive one, and therefore he assigns to heaven the male role, to earth the female one.—On this principle he interprets in an earlier book the celebrated mysteries of the Samothracians, and promises, with an air of great devoutness, that he will by writing expound these mysteries, which have not been well known to his own people, and that he will send them his exposition. Then he says, on the basis of the many proofs he had gathered, that among the images in those mysteries one signifies heaven, another earth, another the patterns of things, which Plato calls ideas." Here Varro claims that the triad, not the dyad, was decisive for the Samothracian ideas. There is also no doubt that in order to develop the whole series from the given three basic concepts, or, vice versa, reinterpreting (*redigenda*, as expressed above) the whole sequence of numbers in terms of the triad, amounts to the same. Namely, all the Cabirian beings are but continuous augmentations, such that the same number or the same personality returns in different potencies, all the numbers thus returning to certain, undisputedly three, basic numbers. Thus |415| the trinity (as he expresses it) is the *de quo*, "from which," the *a quo*, "by which," and the *secundum quod aliquid fiat*, "that according to which something comes to be," apparently the series that actually shaped the first three Samothracian deities. Demeter-Persephone (in the true count both amount to one) is the *de quo*, Dionysos the *a quo*, Kadmilos the *secundum quod aliquid fit*, and the unbiased researcher will happily admit that the Varronian interpretation is no small confirmation of our entire view. That underlying trinity can, however, be repeated progressively, and just as the three can be Persephone, Dionysos, Kadmilos, so can they be Juno, Jupiter, Minerva, as explained by Varro immediately after the passage just mentioned. Varro's remarks probably deserved this extensive discussion of ours. What such a man, the most learned not only of his nation but of many ages, a man who had researched everything in detail *on the spot* while still in Samothrace and who had heeded the meaning and significance of it all, is probably still decisive today. At the same time, this is sufficient to prove that the statement that there were only two Cabiri in the beginning and that the others were added by chance only later lacks any historical basis; therefore, it is not even necessary to remind ourselves of the very probable fact that not all the numbers (or degrees) were communicated to everyone and that many of the initiates knew of only two personalities. But whoever first possessed the system had to possess it completely; it could never have been created piecemeal. The Cabirian series is an indissoluble sequence; it is by its nature an indivisible system.

113. The root of this is חבר, *consociavit, conjunxit se*, "they accompanied one another, they joined one another." Concerning which, חברים, *socii*, with the specific notion that several persons are as one. Thus the decisive passage at Judges 20:11, אחד חברים כאיש ("knit together as one man"). This is the usual formula. But חבירים also occurs, in a passage that equally deserves to be cited. The two formulae seem to correspond to the *double* Greek spelling, κάβειροι (*Cabe[i]ri*—in printed books you can probably also see καβήρους) and κάβιροι. That would be sufficient, but the following passage in a Jewish |416| text proves in an especially powerful way the authenticity of the expression: the Metatron, which we already know as the kabbalistic Kadmilos, is called (Johann Andreas Eisenmenger, *Judaism Unmasked*, 2:401) הנער מטטרון שהוא גבוה מחביריו הק שנה, "the

boy Metatron, who is 500 years higher (this expression, too, is not insignificant) than his *Chabbirim*, i.e., elevated above his comrades or companions." One can hardly resist thinking about the Saxon abjuration in Johann Georg Eckart, *Monumenta Catechetica*, 78: *end eo forsacho*—Woden *end* Saxn-Ote, *end allen unholdum, the hira* genotas *sint*, meaning "all the ill-tempered sprites who are their comrades." I do not know what opinion is accepted in the textbooks or other writings on Jewish philosophy or the kabbalah that are based on the prevailing views, but I may be so bold as to try to demonstrate, from a rather superficial acquaintance with it, that it contains fragments and remnants, very distorted ones if you like, but remnants nonetheless, of the primal system that is the key to all religious systems and that the Jews are *not* entirely untruthful when they proffer the kabbalah as the transmission of a teaching that, in addition to the revealed (and therefore manifest) system in the written documents, was present as a more comprehensive yet secret system not generally shared or communicated. The announcement of a Hebrew-Rabbinical work, which has recently arrived from Vienna, must therefore appear very desirable to the connoisseur, promising to collect all the doctrines of Ben Jochoi, the author of the equally renowned and important work, the *Zohar*, on the basis of the sources. I hope some Jewish or other scholar will be encouraged to publish the entire *Zohar* and open up other sources as well! It is almost sad to see how even in this area of research one has so completely turned away from the true sources. One has long sought the key to ancient religions in Egypt's own obscure and undecipherable hieroglyphics, and nowadays there is talk of nothing else than India's language and wisdom. Yet the Hebrew language and scriptures, especially those of the Old Testament, in which the roots of the teaching and even the language of all the ancient religious systems are clearly |417| discernible in detail, lie unexplored. It is very much to be hoped that these most venerable monuments will soon pass from the hands of mere theologians to those of pure historians, since they may hope to receive there the same unbiased appreciation and to be considered as sources at least as much as the Homeric poems or Herodotus's tales. This is not to say that the pure historian and the theologian cannot be united in one person. In the end, everything must come together in this person. But for the time being, it will be difficult to persevere, although we are beginning to understand generally that dogmas explain things by force, namely, by reading into the sources or by weeding things out, and that in the true estimation of things, there is no difference between such readings except that the latter, like all merely negative procedures, leads to much more intolerance and shallowness than the former, which is at least a positive endeavor that seeks to make connections. The name *Kabir*, or actually *Chabir*, is a word in the Old Testament that expresses both an indivisible connection and a magical concatenation. The well-known חבר חבר, Deuteronomy 18:11, means, translated literally, if only for the Gentiles, *nectens nexum, consocians consociationem*, "sealing the bond, forming the association"; yet the meaning is *magicam exercens artem, incantator*, "exercising the art of magic, the enchanter," hence also straightforwardly חברים, *incantationes*, "the incantations," Isaiah 47:9 and 47:12. This meaning, connected with the word חבר־חבר, cannot be thought without an idea that is similar to or identical with the ideas that underlie the Cabirian system. In the many efforts to unravel the meaning of the name *Cabiri*, one or more of those ideas must have derived from that root. The first to recognize this, as far as I know, was Antonius Astorius in his *Dissertation on the Cabirian Gods* (Venice, 1703), printed in Giovanni Poleni, *Supplements to the Roman and Greek Thesaurus* [*Utriusque thesauri antiquitatum Romanarum Graecarumque nova supplementa*], 2:873–904. Yet Astorius contented himself in his eleventh paragraph with the meaning of the magicians called חברים, *quia se jungunt daemonibus*, "those who conjure demons"; he then demonstrated, by applying the literary sources given in endnote 111, not without some intricacy, that the Cabiri (neither the *Penates Dii*, nor demons, nor natural deities in the Varronian sense) were mere human magicians who first taught human beings the service of gods and demons, giving humans the means of winning them over and compelling them, but who |418| were then considered to be gods themselves. Adriaan Reland, in his *Dissertation on the Cabirian Gods*, published in his *Miscellany of Dissertations*, 1:191–206, while reading Astori's text, believed that *Cabiri* could also be translated according to that same Hebrew word by *juncti, socii*, whereby the *Dioskouroi*, Δίδυμοι, *Gemini, socialia sidera*, happily suggested themselves to him. But he was soon disturbed by the fact that, in addition to the Dioskouroi, Ceres, Proserpina, Pluto, and Mercury are also Cabiri. He therefore tried to find something in these too that makes them *socii*, and he discovered that they are all θεοὶ χθόνιοι or underworld gods and that all are occupied with the dead. Yet Zeus too, and also Apollo, are Cabiri, at least according to Dionysius of Halicarnassus, *Roman Antiquities*, 1:3. Here Reland's explanation comes to an end; concerning it, one must admit that it is valid only if one is willing to be content with an etymon that is at the same time suitable for both the Dioskouroi and the *Deos inferos* or underworld gods, all of them being גבירים, because that word expresses *Deos potes*, "powerful deities." It would be very natural to expect to find traces of the name *Cabiri* in other languages of the East. To list a few mentioned by Johannes Buxtorf, *Lexicon Chaldaicum, Talmudicum, et Rabbinicum*, at 704: *In Talmud saepe vocantur Sacerdotes Persarum* חברים, *vel Persae in genere ita vocantur, ut in Jevammoth fol. 63,2. Ad Psalms 14.* 'd*icit stultus in corde suo*' *R. Jochanan dixit* אלה חברים, *Isti sunt Chaverim. Gloss.* חברים, *i.e. Persae impii, qui non agnoscunt gloriam Israëlitarum.*— —*Dixit R. Immi ad R. Levi: Ostende mihi Persas; dixit: Similes sunt exercitibus* (? צבאות) *domus Israëlis: ostende mihi* חברין; *dixit: Similes sunt Angelis vastatoribus etc.; Baal Arach scribit: Persae vocabant Sacrificulos sive Sacerdotes* חברים *et fuerunt isti* חברים *pessimi graviterque affligentes Israëlem.* "In the Talmud, the priests of the Persians are often called חברים, or Persians in general are called such, as the treatise *Yevamot*, folium 63b confirms. To *Psalms* 14 'The fool says in his heart,' Rabbi Jochanan said אלה חברים, these are the Chaverim. The glossary states, for חברים, that these are the godless Persians, who do not acknowledge the glory of the Israelites——Rabbi Immi said to Rabbi Levi: Show me the Persians; he said, they are similar to the armies (? צבאות) of the house Israel: show me חברין; he said, they are similar to angels and destroyers etc.; Baal Arach writes: Persians called the sacrifices or priests חברים and these were חברים of the worst kind that severely afflicted Israel." In exact accord with the latter is what Thomas Hyde, *On the Religion of the Persians*, 365, adds: *Origenes contra Celsum meminit* Περσῶν ἡ Καβείρων. "Origen's *Against Celsus* reminds us that the Persians were called Cabiri." Just as one cannot help but recognize the so-called ghebers in those *Chabherin* whom the Persians themselves and their priests are said to be, so this name must also be one and the same as the name *Cabiri*. Creuzer is quite specific at 2:287, referring to Paul Foucher, "Historical Treatise on the Religion of the Persians," |419| in *Memoirs of the Royal Academy of Inscriptions and Belles Lettres* 29, translated in Johann Friedrich Kleuker, *Appendix to the Zend Avesta*, 1:217, that the Cabiri are nothing but *gabirim*, strong men; humans or gods who are involved in forging and working metals. According to the Parsee religion of fire, the blacksmiths were impure because they desecrated fire. *Hence* the scornful term associated with the word *Ghebr*, which continues to this day throughout the Orient. *Gheber* are actually blacksmiths who defile the fire, yet this very name is given to those who, according to the ancient Parsee doctrine, faithfully keep the fire holy and worship it, and the ones who add this despicable epithet to them are the Muslim Persians, who probably regard fire as holy! Or are the worshippers of the pure fire called blacksmiths just to annoy them? What choice malice! Hyde's view is easier to accept: *Alterum a Mahommedanis (et ante eos ab aliis) huic populo (veterum Persarum reliquiis) impingitur Epitheton Ghebr sive Guebr, i.e. in genere Infideles, in specie Ignicolae.* "The other epithet imposed on this nation (the descendants of the old Persians) by the Mohammedans (and prior to them by others) is *Ghebr* or *Guebr*, which means in general *infidels*, but specifically *fire worshipers*." He seems to assume that the ancient faithful Parsees did not receive the name from the Mohammedans. But because the word has a disparaging meaning today, he believes that it has always been used as a mark of contempt. But since according to Mohammedan-Persian dictionaries the word گبر means nothing else but *ignicola*, it can be scornful in the mouths of the Mohammedans yet still be honorable to the Parsees themselves alone. It is indisputably their ancient name, which in the Persian language has the little word مغ as an etymon; that is to say, it indicates a foreign judgment that is found nowhere but in חבר. Cabirism too is a religion of fire and fire magic that underwent various transformations in Persia until the final transformation, undertaken by Zoroaster, caused it to vanish in Ormuzd's law of light and fire. The name *Gaur*, which is otherwise common among the Turks, yet also a word for Jews and Christians, has nothing in common with that of the *Ghebern*; it is a corruption of *Kafur*, the plural of كافر, *infidelis*, "the unbelievers"; see Louis-Mathieu Langlès, *The Travels of Sir John Chardin in Persia*, 8:356n. Among the manuscripts of the Borgia Museum, there is a translation |420| of an Indian book titled *Mulpanci*, which the translator, Father Marco a Tumba, explains as *Book of the Root* or *Book of the Fundament*, which is said to contain the particular doctrinal concept of the Indian *cabirist* sect; see Paulinus of St. Bartholomew, *Manuscripts of the Borgia Museum*, 158. A German translation of the first song, communicated to us by Bishop Münter, can be found in volume III of *The Treasures of the Orient*. But there is not much more to take from it than what Agostino Antonio Giorgi, in *The Tibetan Alphabet*, 98, says: *Brahmanes Cabiritarum* Verbo *vim creandi tribuunt*, "The priests of the Cabiri attribute creative power to the *Word*," and Father Marco, in Paulinus of St. Bartholomew, *Manuscripts of the Borgia Museum*, 161: "The Cabiristi do not believe in any other God than the generative virtue, which they say is within everything in the world." Not a trace of the theses that attest to a special relationship with the Cabirian system! Because we have recently heard also from Paulinus of St. Bartholomew, *Manuscripts of the Borgia Museum*, 159, that the Hindi name is expressed by the word *Cabì vel Cavì*, only a scholar of Hindi can tell us in what way a *Cabirit* or a Cabirian sect in India can be deduced from it. The Sanscredamian *Cavì* or *Cabì* means, according to Father Paulinus, as much as *homo doctus, poëta*, "a learned man, a poet," and furthermore *theologus, sapiens*, "a theologian, a wise man." With this, the Talmudic meaning of חבר would correspond; see Johannes Buxtorf, *Lexicon Chaldaicum, Talmudicum, et Rabbinicum*, 703–4: *Doctoribus Hebraeorum priscis dicebatur* חבר *Magister sive Rabbi recens creatus—sed generaliter etiam idem quod* תלמיד חכם, *Doctor sive sapiens. Hinc in libro Cosri sapiens ille, qui Regi Persarum interroganti respondet, vocatur* חבר. "The venerable learned men of the Hebrews are called *newly appointed master* or *rabbi*—but generally this means as much as *doctor* or *sage*. Thus in the *Book Kuzari* the wise man who responded to the questions of the Persian king is called חבר." Consider also the Arabic خبر *scivit, cognovit*, "he knew, he was aware," concerning which خبير *sciens, gnarus*, "knowing, being informed," even in the sense of *omniscius, qui et praeterita et futura novit*, "the omniscient one who knows past and future," he who knows all things *in their interconnectedness*, which is an epithet of God. Scholars of Hindi may provide an indication of the extent to which the Indian *Cabì* or *Cavì* has a genuine connection with this word.

114. It is at least clear from this how uncertain it is to see this *senatores Deorum*, "council of the gods," as the Twelve Gods of Ennius's well-known verse (Apuleius, *On the God of Socrates*, 225), as they are also named in Martianus Capella, *On the Marriage of Philology and Mercury*, 1:16.

115. Arnobius the Elder, *Against the Pagans*, 3:123: *Varro, qui sunt introrsus atque in intimis penetralibus coeli, Deos esse censet, quos loquimur* |421| (namely, Penates, because the Penates constitute the entire context), *nec eorum numerum nec nomina sciri. Hos Consentes et Complices Etrusci ajunt et nominant, quod unâ oriantur et occidant unâ; sex mares et totidem feminas, nominibus ignotis et memorationis parcissimae; sed eos summi Jovis consiliarios et principes existimari.* "Varro thinks that they are the gods of whom we speak, gods who are within, and in the inmost recesses of heaven, and that neither their number nor their names are known. The Etruscans say that these are the *Consentes* and *Complices*, and name them thus because they rise and set as one, six of them being male, and as many female, with unknown names and of whom very little mention is made, but they are considered the counsellors

and princes of Jove supreme." The meaning of *complices* is clear, as is the sense of *consentes*, whether one relates this to *consentire* or derives it from *consum*, after the manner of *praesentes* from *praesum*. The reading "*memorationis parcissimae*" has a manuscript in support of it. See Geverhart Elmenhorst, *Collectanea Variarum Lectionum*, appended to the edition cited above. The *miserationis*, "regretful," from the Roman edition and the manuscript on which it is based makes no sense here. Otherwise the word *consentes* is found only in inscriptions, for example, in *Jovi Optimo Maximo ceterisque Dis consentibus*, "to Jupiter, the most good, the greatest, and other consenting gods" and *Mercurio Consenti* "to the consenting Mercury," in Francesco Scipione Maffei, at 238. In the work, *Agricultural Topics in Three Books*, Varro distinguishes *Deos consentes urbanos, quorum imagines (Romae) ad forum auratae stant* from the *consentibus rusticis*, of which, however, there are five male and seven female. Yet these are clearly mere replicas of the original ones. That the *Dii Consentes* were not the same as the *Dii selectis* is made clear in Augustine's *City of God*, 4:23: *Quis enim ferat, quod neque inter Deos consentes, quos dicunt in consilium Jovis adhiberi, nec inter Deos, quos Selectos vocant, Felicitas constituta sit.* "How unfortunate that *Felicitas* was not ranked among the *Consentes*, who are made to form Jupiter's council, nor among the gods that were called the Select." Also, for the concept *Senatores, consiliari*, חברים is the actual expression. On Hebrew-Samaritan coins, the members of the high council (of the *Synedrii*) attached to the high priest are called his חברים. See among others Thomas Christian Tychsen in *Commentationes Societatis Regiae Scientiarum Gottingensis*, 11:155 (1793).

116. Compare endnote 31, above.

117. In this way Jupiter must be thought in a double relationship: on the one hand, he must be thought insofar as he himself is one of the seven; on the other hand, he must be thought, as the Orphics say, insofar as he is Zeus the beginning, Zeus the middle, and Zeus the end.

118. Hence, basically, if one thinks about the pertinent distinction, it accords with the fact that Elohim in the plural is conjoined with a verb in the singular. [Karl Schelling adds the editorial remark: "Compare *The Ages of the World* (SW I/8, 273)."]

|422| 119. Ἧς στρατιῆς εἷς εἰμι, λαχὼν θεὸν ἡγεμονῆα, "I join forces with this throng because I was guided by god." See Münter, *A Samothracian Inscription*, 8.

For that reason, the Samothracian Mysteries were chiefly called ἄρρηκτα, "the indestructible." See the *Argonautica Orphica* of Apollonius of Rhodes, lines 464–65:

ζαθεὴν Σαμοθρήκην
Ἔνθα καὶ ὅρκια φρικτὰ θεῶν ἄρρηκτα βροτοῖσιν,

Thither to most holy Samothrace
To swear to the gods an awful oath that no mortal dare break,

where Richard François Philippe Brunck, in his commentary on Apollonius of Rhodes, and after him Gottfried Hermann, introduce two changes: first of all, they quite unnecessarily convert ὅρκια, "oath," into the customary ὄργια, "secret rites," and, secondly, they change ἄρρηκτα, "break," to ἄρρητα, "ineffable," with the result that the peculiar coloring of these passages is blurred. They should have preserved the original reading because it is less customary and therefore the more demanding reading. What copyist would have been ignorant enough to have come up with ὄργια for ὅρκια and ἄρρητα for ἄρρηκτα; what copyist would have been sufficiently learned to come up with the opposite? Ὅρκια understood as ἱερά, "holy," designates the Cabirian devotions with reference to their particular nature. They were taken up into the *covenant* of the gods (think only of the Old and New Testament concept of this word, *Berith*, "covenant," which had its most ancient seat in Phoenician. The bands (ταινίαι), the insignia of the initiated, also pointed to a covenant; see the scholiast to Apollonius of Rhodes, as cited. As here so also in Apollonius of Rhodes, *Argonautica*, 1:917, where ἄρρηκτα is the particular word.

120. Plato, *Phaedo*, 77 [Stephanus 77e–78a]; in the Zweibrücken edition, 177.

121. The souls of the dead are divided into two parties,
    One that wanders restlessly over the earth, the other
    That begins to dance with the scintillant stars of heaven;
    Because God was my guide, I am welcome among the latter host.
    —*A Samothracian Inscription*, [8–9], after Münter

122. Joseph Eckhel, *Doctrina numorum veterum*, 3:375ff.

The "Sacred Rock" of blue-green porphyry; at top left is the base of the Rotunda of Arsinoë II.

Schelling's Afterword

|423| The preceding treatise, as originally conceived, pertains to a series of works that have as their common midpoint *The Ages of the World*. The fact that the treatise is appearing earlier is due to an extrinsic circumstance and could not be said to alter the original conception. As a supplement to that work [i.e., *The Ages of the World*], the treatise will therefore appear in a larger context of work to be distributed by the book trade. The treatise's being appended to another work does not cancel its autonomy, since, as I hope, one will grant it its right to exist entirely for itself and without relation to anything else. It is not inherently, but merely by dint of the author's intention, supplemental to another work. It is at the same time a beginning and a transition to a range of works, all of which intend to bring to light and to develop in a scientific fashion, proceeding wherever possible along the path of history, the properly primordial system of humanity, a system that has long been cloaked in obscurity. For science, once it has reached a certain point, is inseparable from history; almost necessarily, the one is in transition to the other. It is no accident that the more general investigation is here being preceded by the particular examination of the Samothracian system; establishing this system as the very basis of the more general investigation was always my intention. For it almost seems as though the doctrine of the Cabiri, by virtue of its antiquity and the clarity and simplicity of its outline, was made to be the key to all other systems. So much, therefore, concerning the broader context of this treatise, which otherwise must be taken entirely on its own terms and which would like to be examined on its own merits, in accord with its special content.

Detail of the marble frieze from the Hall of the Choral Dancers, ca. 340 BCE.

2

Explanatory Notes on Schelling's Lecture

13 *the Euxine Sea.* Today called the Black Sea, the Euxine Sea is the ancient Pontus or Pontus Euxinus, which flows into the Aegean Sea by way of the Bosporus, the Sea of Marmora, and the Dardanelles, in this way connecting Asia and Europe. The expression *Euxine Sea* was common among English writers of the eighteenth century. In the nineteenth century, George Eliot, in *Middlemarch* (8:83), refers to an ancient people located "on the shores of the Euxine," although her reference is ironic, intended merely to mock the rarefied learning of her heroine's deceased husband, Casaubon. The name *Euxine* has by now disappeared from the standard reference works.

13 *such cataclysmic memories.* Schelling's speculations on the tumultuous beginnings of the isle of Samothrace reflect the battle that raged among paleontologists during the eighteenth century—the battle between the neptunists and the vulcanists. The neptunists, influenced by the biblical account of the flood, emphasized the role of rainfall and the seas on geological history, whereas the vulcanists focused on volcanic activity. The battle remained unresolved until the research and theories of Abraham Gottlob Werner (1750–1817), Alexander von Humboldt (1769–1859), and Georges Cuvier (1769–1832) tipped the balance toward the vulcanists. In any case, the early geological history of the island of Samothrace, like that of Santorini (the Greek Thera) far to the south, to which Schelling also refers in considerable detail in his notes, reflects the early history of the world-forming deities in Schelling's conception: both histories involve turbulence and subterranean or submarine fury.

13   *Poseidon... the Danaean ships.* In the thirteenth song of the *Iliad* (13:10–26), which recounts the battle for the Greek ships, Homer tells of Zeus leading the Trojans to those beached ships and so abandoning the Greeks to their fate. Lines 10–14 record Poseidon's witnessing the event:

> Yet not in vain the earth-shattering ruler observed,
> For he sat, astonished by the war and its battles,
> High on the uppermost peak of the wooded Thracian isle
> Of Samos; beyond it jutted Mount Ida with all the other heights,
> And the city of Priam too, and the Achaean ships.
> For Poseidon had quit the briny flood and watched with horror
> As Trojans slaughtered Greeks. His anger against Zeus ignited.

14   *a man whom all held to be divine.* Pythagoras of Samos, who lived during the sixth cenutry BCE, founded a renowned religious and learned brotherhood and sisterhood. A philosopher, mathematician, musician, and mystic, Pythagoras was particularly influential in Sicily and southern Italy (Magna Graecia).

14   *Iasion and Dardanos, Orpheus and the Argonauts, but also Hercules and Ulysses.* Iasion is said to have been a consort of Demeter, or Kybele; he desecrated the image of the goddess, however, and was destroyed by one of Zeus's lightning bolts. Iasion was himself a son of Zeus (note the parallel with Tantalos) by Elektryone, or Elektra, and was, by ἱερὸς γάμος (sacred marriage), associated with the sowing of wheat. Dardanos was a brother of Iasion, and Harmonia, who later married Kadmos, was their sister. All of these figures were closely associated with Samothrace in remote antiquity; some accounts even designate Iasion as one of the Cabiri. Herakles (Hercules), the son of Zeus (disguised as Amphitryon) and Alkmene, and the most renowned of the Greek heroes, was one of the Argonauts; he too therefore would have been initiated in the Samothracian mysteries. Later the archetypal hero, the original Herakles was often associated with vegetation rites, hence with Demeter and Dionysos, themselves among the Great Gods of Samothrace. The story of Odysseus, however, is the most dramatic of the entire set of figures. It brings the fifth song of the *Odyssey* to a close (5:333–462). Odysseus (the Roman Ulysses), adrift on the sea and clinging to his wreck of a raft, is about to drown in the Poseidon-whipped waves.

> But then Cadmus's daughter saw him, she of the shapely ankles, Ino
> Leukothea. She was once a mortal and spoke with a mortal voice,

Until she received godlike honors in the waves of the salt sea.
She felt pity for Odysseus now, for he was wretchedly tossed about.
(*Odyssey*, 5:333–336)

Ino, now Leukothea, "the radiant goddess," tells Odysseus to strip the rags from his body and wear only a purple sash, "the immortal girdle," which she gives him. She instructs him to abandon the raft, which Poseidon will soon smash to bits, and leap into the sea protected only by the sash. Commentators on this story largely agree that this is the purple sash worn by all the initiates at Samothrace: "Take this immortal veil [κρήδεμνον...ἄμβροτον] and tie it about your breast, / So that you will never have to fear suffering and death" (*Odyssey* 13:346–47). Before she becomes the shining goddess Leukothea, however, Ino is a daughter of Kadmos of Tyre, the Phoenician founder of Greek Thebes in Boeotia. His marriage to Harmonia is sometimes said to have been held on Samothrace, not in Thebes. Kadmos himself (as Kasmilos?), the maternal grandfather of Dionysos, is often acclaimed as one of the Cabiri. His daughter Ino responds to that hope shared by all Phoenician and other mariners—not to perish in the waters they must ply. Strangely, Ino Leukothea is yet another of those figures who earlier on in their lives desecrate and even murder the god Dionysos, then are driven mad and leap to their deaths in the sea—in order then to become themselves gods. (Compare the story of Lykurgos, recounted by Sophocles in the fourth stasimon, or fifth choral ode, of *Antigone*, lines 955–63.) Statues of Leukothea (sometimes called Halia) portray her as a Madonna-like figure with the infant Bacchus on her left arm. She is, then, a nurse of Dionysos but also a wicked stepsister of the god's mother, Semele, and the murderess of infant boys. One cannot but think of Melanie Klein's good breast / bad breast. Euripides, in the *Bacchai*, calls one of Semele's sisters Ino; she is one of the three sisters—Agave, the mother of Pentheus, and Autonoë being the others—who mock Semele by saying that her pregnancy is not by Zeus but the result of a mere adolescent escapade. The *Bacchai* tells the story of Dionysos's revenge on his aunts and his cousin Pentheus. Euripides does not tell the story of Semele's sister Ino, who, once she has plunged into the sea and drowned there, is transmuted into the divine Leukothea who rescues others from a similar death.

14   *the last Macedonian king.* According to Livy's *Histories*, King Perseus of Macedonia tried to take refuge on Samothrace after he was defeated by the

Romans in the battle of Pydna. Yet because he had committed a blood crime, the priests drove him out of the sanctuary.

14   *Noble Germanicus.* The most decorated of Tiberius's generals, Germanicus (ca. 15 BCE–19 CE) was active in Gaul and Germany. He later became proconsul of the eastern provinces. It was presumably during the last two years of his life, when he visited Athens, Lesbos, and the oracle of Apollo at Colophon, that he also made his unsuccessful effort to land on Samothrace. (See Tacitus, *Histories*, Book Two.)

15   *that unforgettable find from Aegina.* The "Aeginetan friezes" from the second temple of Aphaia on Aegina, preserved today in the Munich Glyptothek, show scenes from the battles at Troy. Schelling added detailed notes and observations about the Aeginetan friezes in a treatise written by Johann Martin von Wagner. See von Wagner's *Report on the Aeginetan Sculptures*, tr. Louis A. Ruprecht (Albany, NY: SUNY Press, 2017); the *Report*, with Schelling's "art-historical observations," was first published in 1817. There Schelling argues "that Aeginetan art led Attic art on the way to its true perfection."

15   *Mnaseas.* Mnaseas of Patara (a city on the southern coast of Anatolia) was a student of Eratosthenes during the third century of the ancient era; he wrote a series of books on myths and wonders arranged by geographical area (Europe, Asia, Libya). The single most important source for the names of the Cabiri, he is cited by Diodorus Siculus (that is, Diodorus of Sicily), an important source for Schelling's lecture and endnotes.

15   *Axieros, Axiokersa, Axiokersos, Kasmilos.* Mnaseas identifies the first three with Demeter, Persephone, and Hades, respectively. Kasmilos, he identifies as Hermes. These Greek equivalents, while to be taken seriously, as Schelling certainly does, seem to depend on the shaky reed of Mnaseas's surmise. The three non-Greek names (three or four, since Cadmus too was a Phoenician) are still not identified with anything like certainty by linguists, classicists, and archaeologists today. Nevertheless, one should not simply dismiss Schelling's argument that the man who knew the names of the Cabiri must have known at least something about their essential characteristics when he supplied those Greek equivalents.

15   *Kasmilos by name.* See the note on Kasmilos for page 22, below.

16   *Zoëga.* Georg Zoëga (1755–1809), Danish consul general in Rome from 1798 until his death, was an enthusiastic researcher of antiquities. His

best-known work, *Bassrilievi antichi di Roma*, was published in 1809; his other works, including his researches on Egypt, were edited and published by Friedrich Gottlieb Welcker in 1817.

16   *a path opened by earlier researchers.* Schelling probably means Samuel Bochart and Gerhard Vossius, whom he mentions elsewhere in his address (see the relevant note for page 27), but he might also be thinking of Joseph Justus Scaliger (1540–1609). It is at least often reported in the literature that Scaliger was influential in tracing aspects of Roman and Greek culture back to Egyptian and Near Eastern roots. He was especially important for integrating Jewish history, beyond Old Testament studies, into historical studies in general. Some scholars have argued that Scaliger's research and speculations on the ancient Hebrew and Phoenician languages may have unduly influenced Schelling and other German scholars in this respect.

16   *the Phoenicians.* A maritime people occupying the eastern Mediterranean (Syrian) coast from at least the second millennium BCE to the age of Alexander, with Tyre and Sidon as the principal cities. The very name *Phoenician* testifies to one of their most important exports, namely, purple dye and purple cloth (φοινός = blood-red); the geographical designation *Canaan* derives from *kinahhu*, "purple"; one recalls the purple sash worn by initiates at Samothrace. Such cloth, along with other trade goods, the Phoenicians carried from the eastern Mediterranean to Egypt, Crete, mainland Greece, and their own most important colony, Carthage, in North Africa. Their language seems to have been closely related to ancient Hebrew, and their consonantal script became the basis of written Greek. Astarte, as the Great Mother of Asia, and Adonis, the dying god of vegetation, played central roles in their religion. Schelling speculates, not unreasonably albeit controversially, that at some point very early on Phoenician sailors settled on Samothrace, bringing their cults—and the perduring *language* of their cults—to the island.

17   *Axieros can {initially} mean nothing else in the Phoenician dialect than "hunger," "poverty," and as a consequence, "languishing" and "obsession."* Schelling does not justify his assertion concerning this (initial?) sense of *Axieros* in the Phoenician or ancient Hebrew languages, for which no direct archaeological or literary evidence survives. Linguists today are far more cautious. Nevertheless, or precisely for this reason, Schelling's thesis concerning languor, languishing, and obsession or even addiction (*Sehnsucht, Schmachten, Sucht*) is the boldest step in his reflection. A word, therefore, about this set of very

strong expressions. *Sehnsucht* is a conjunction of two words, *Sehnen*, which means to long or yearn for someone or something, and *die Sucht*, which means obsession and even addiction. The verb *suchen*, "to seek," is at least morphologically suggested in the noun *Sucht*, although Schelling himself, while conceding that the goddess Demeter is *searching* for her daughter, appears to emphasize the more dire senses of the word: related to *Sucht*, and perhaps at its very origin, is *die Seuche*, initially referring to hoof-and-mouth disease but eventually taken to mean a "contagion" or an "epidemic" of any kind. A second word that Schelling uses to characterize *Sehnsucht* is *Schmachten*, "to waste away, to languish." The adjective *schmächtig* means delicate to the point of fragility. We have tried to render with some consistency *Sehnsucht* as "languor," *Schmachten* as "languishing," and *Sucht* as "obsession." This last word may be excessively "psychologizing," but the word *addiction* seems too closely related to substance abuse, and so, after considerable debate, we have settled for "obsession." At all events, for Schelling, the figure of Axieros is either "a languishing languor" or "a languorous languishing," a craving or yearning and seeking to the point of obsession.

Schelling's claim is surely the keenest and farthest reaching of his claims in terms of its consequences: for him, the Cabiri, who represent the most ancient religious and philosophical system of humankind, are not—at least initially—gods of power and majesty. The Great Gods, at least at the outset, are not emblems of glory, nor are they the rescuers and saviors that sailors and other endangered species expect them to be; they are figures of penury and destitution, hunger and search, languor and languishing. Indeed, the Platonic myth of Penia, the mother of Eros, as recounted in Socrates's (or rather Diotima's) speech in *Symposium*, becomes central to Schelling's meditation, as does the mourning of Isis and Demeter for their lost children and their vanished lovers. In terms of Schelling's philosophy as a whole, it would be worthwhile to trace the development of the notion of *Sehnsucht* from the 1809 treatise on human freedom through the 1811–1815 *Ages of the World* to the present text and then on into the final works. Arguably, that development leaves behind every hope that what Schelling in 1809 called "the will of love" can fulfill or even assuage or simply supplant languor and languishing—or that it can ever put an end to search and obsession. See also the note on "a languishing longing," for page 18, below.

17   *Plato's figure of Penia, who, having mated with Poros, becomes the mother of Eros.* Poros (Πόρος) and Penia (Πενία), which one might translate as

superfluity or resourcefulness and poverty or penury, respectively, are, according to Plato, the parents of Eros, who is conceived during a festival of the gods celebrating the birth of Aphrodite. (Eros is therefore not the child of divine beauty, as Western art generally represents him, although he is conceived the instant beauty is born.) The priestess Diotima tells the story in *Symposium* at 203a–204c. It is a particularly comic story, in its own way as rich as Aristophanes's tale concerning the three genders of humankind, because it is not superfluity or resource, the drunken and unconscious father-to-be of Eros, who sees to the god's conception, but the far more resourceful Penia, putatively helpless poverty herself. (Some say there is a life lesson in this comic account.) If necessity is the mother of invention, then Πενία is Ἀνάγκη or necessity herself, and Schelling is acutely aware of the divinity at work in what he is about to call *Sehnsucht*. To repeat, in earlier texts of his, such as the 1809 treatise on human freedom and the 1811–1815 *Ages of the World*, Schelling had already made *Sehnsucht*, "languor," "longing," "yearning," "craving," etc., a central—perhaps *the* central—notion of his thought.

18   *the night that bears the egg*. Schelling is thinking here not so much about Hesiod's *Theogony*, for which night is associated principally with Erebus, sleep and death, that is, with the murky, gloomy, and even evil aspects of life; rather, he is thinking of Orphic stories and perhaps the teachings of Pherekydes of Syros. See Kirk, Raven, and Schofield, *The Presocratic Philosophers*, 2nd ed. (Cambridge, England: Cambridge University Press, 1983), 17–33, for accounts of night and the cosmic egg. For Pherekydes, see esp. KRS 59–62.

18   *Hestia*. Ἑστία, goddess of the hearth and hence of domestic fire, is later represented by the Vesta. See Plato, *Laws* 5:745b, 8:848d, and 9:855e but also *Phaedrus* 247a, and especially *Cratylus* 401c, where she is associated with "the essence [οὐσία, ἐσσία] of things." She is at times also a figure derived from Gaia, the earth. Her character as the virginal Great Goddess (related to the Phrygian-Phoenician Kybele and Astarte) is the object of worship throughout the ancient Near East, most notably among the Persians and Scythians. Nor should the virginal character of the Mother cause confusion, even if it does have to evoke wonder. W. K. C. Guthrie explains:

> The Great Mother not only bears the crops for the husbandman, but also the flocks and herds for pastoral peoples and even the wild creatures whose abundance is necessary for men at a still earlier stage of culture, who live by

hunting and fishing. She may in fact be one of the oldest religious representations of all, and her presence an indication that the idea of personal divinity has been in man's mind for as long as we can trace his history, and at least as long as belief in the efficacy of magic or in a vague animism, such as have often been thought to precede the religious conception of divinity.

Parthenos, "virgin," has, at least for the earliest goddesses, a meaning more circumscribed than moderns might assume: the goddess was simply unmarried and she chose her consort year by year; moreover, annual lustrations (such as Plynteria in Athens) restored the goddess's "virginity" periodically. See W. K. C. Guthrie, *The Greeks and Their Gods* (Boston: Beacon, 1950), 58–59 and 102–103.

18   *the concepts of languor and a languishing longing.* The word *Sehnsucht*, discussed above in the note on Axieros as "languishing" and "obsession," is, to repeat, a key word for Schelling's thinking ever since the 1809 *Treatise on the Essence of Human Freedom*. The word *Sehnsucht* may be translated variously as "languor," "languishing," "longing," "nostalgia," "yearning," "desire," "craving," and so on; when the second half of the word, *Sucht*, is stressed, as Schelling often does in his lecture, the meaning becomes closer to "addiction," "obsession," "illness," or "epidemic." Schelling is aware that this second half of the word is reminiscent of, though not etymologically related to, *Suchen*, "to seek," yet he stresses the relation to illness and contagion, *Seuche*, a theme (namely, *illness*) that had fascinated him since the time of his medical studies. Likewise, the word *Schmachten* means a withering or wasting away—perhaps after the manner of Erysichthon but also of Demeter herself, who is pining for her missing daughter. It implies a malady or malaise resulting in utter languishing and a feeling of powerlessness. When languor gnaws at an individual—as in the case of Goethe's young Werther—it instigates a languishing. To say the least, we are unaccustomed to thinking of either languor or languishing in connection with deity, to say nothing of addiction, compulsion, obsession, or illness of any kind, which is precisely why Schelling's account of Demeter as Penia is so startling. For further discussion see Krell, *The Tragic Absolute: German Idealism and the Languishing of God* (Bloomington: Indiana University Press, 2005), esp. chapter 4, 135–44.

18   —*I am Deo.* The Homeric *Hymn to Demeter*, which Schelling is citing, has the goddess actually saying, "My name is Δωσώ [or Δώς]," which would

suggest that she announces herself as "the one who gives." The *Hymn* later does grant her the name "queenly Δηώ." Schelling understands the name Δηώ to derive from δέω in the sense of "I am far from, I want, I lack" and especially the deponent δέομαι, "I am in want or need, I require, I beg a favor." A second verb, homologous with the first, and listed first in Liddell-Scott, means "to bind, tie, enchain." From such binding comes the important impersonal verb δεῖ, "it is necessary or binding that" something is the case. Classicists and mythographers today are more inclined to associate Demeter, the Earth Mother, with such necessity, figured as Ἀνάγκη (Ananke), cited above in connection with penury and *Sehnsucht*, languor and languishing. Schelling, to be sure, would reply to his critics that what is necessary, the needful, and the needy are not so far apart; his vision of Demeter is of the goddess precisely as we see her in the Homeric *Hymn*, desperately mourning the loss of Persephone and furious with both gods and mortals for concealing from her Persephone's fate. Her fury reflects both necessity and neediness, and Schelling would insist that neediness—indeed a kind of compulsion or obsession (*Sucht*)—precedes and forever accompanies the more honorific necessity. Guthrie argues that the name Demeter, according to the evidence provided by the Homeric *Hymn*, comes from either Δώς or Δηώ and therefore has to do either with "giving" or with one or both senses of the latter word, "to bind," "to be destitute, distraught." "What *exactly* the name was, is uncertain," he concludes (283n 1). See in this regard Roberto Calasso, *The Marriage of Cadmus and Harmony*, tr. Tim Parks (New York: Alfred A. Knopf, 1993), 97–98, which cites Robert Onians's reminder of the direful phrase, "It was *bound* to happen," a phrase that captures the two senses of δέω, both "I give" and "I lack," as though these two were bound by necessity. On Demeter, see also Schelling's late *Philosophy of Mythology*, especially lecture 27 (SW II/2, 626–33).

18   *the daughters of Celeus*. The four daughters of Κελεός, a king of Eleusis, invite the wandering and mournful Demeter, who is in search of her daughter, to their father's palace. There the goddess becomes the nurse of the king's newborn son, who thrives under her care. After some time she reveals her identity to the four daughters and commands that an altar and a temple be constructed in her honor. Thus the famous cult site of Eleusis comes to be. See once again the Homeric *Hymn to Demeter* and the account in Carl Kerényi, *The Gods of the Greeks* (London: Thames and Hudson, 1951), 234–38, cited henceforth as CK with page number.

19   *avaricious Dis or Amenthes*. *Dis*, in the expression *dis manibus*, refers to the souls—or to the gods—of the dead and also to a gloomy place where the shades drift under the severe governance of Hades (Pluto) and Persephone (Proserpina). The *amenthes* are presumably those drifting shades who are in fact lifeless, the dead, who are senseless, drugged, beside themselves, insane, or without mind—*amens, amentis*. On *Dis*, see the discussion of the *Di Manes* in Friedrich Hölderlin, *The Death of Empedocles: A Mourning-Play*, tr. D. F. Krell (Albany, NY: SUNY Press, 2008), 268–69.

19   *Demetrians*. That is to say, those who have followed Demeter and are now themselves objects of mourning, languishing, and obsession in the underworld.

19   *the Manes*. See the earlier note on *avaricious Dis*. Manes is the name that Schelling's friend Hölderlin chooses for the Egyptian priest who dominates the third and final fragment of *The Death of Empedocles*. There is perhaps some justice in thinking of Manes as an alter ego of Empedocles himself, and a great deal of justice in thinking that Schelling had discussed the figure(s) of Manes with Hölderlin.

19   *a Ceres who is Erinyes*. Demeter becomes the Roman Ceres, the goddess of cereals and all vegetative life. Yet her first figure is not that of the generous goddess, the goddess of cornucopia, but the *furious* goddess. The *Erinyes* are the Furies. Demeter is, in fact, after the abduction of her daughter, a Fury and a Fatality for both gods and humankind.

19   *Erysichthon*. When Erysichthon, the "earth-ravager," began to chop down trees in a grove sacred to Demeter—and then threatened her with his axe when she intervened—she condemned him to unending, insatiable hunger. Divine punishment is the origin of irony.

20   *a Pothos*. Πόθος, not to be confused with the more common Greek word πάθος, means "mourning," or a kind of desire that longs for a lost object. The Homeric *Hymn to Demeter* uses this word repeatedly to describe both Demeter and her abducted daughter Persephone. They yearn for one another and they mourn one another's absence. Schelling associates the figure of Pothos with a languor that looks back—in memory—to a vanished loved one. In Plato's *Cratylus*, at 420a 5, Socrates perhaps not so playfully defines πόθος

as a yearning, mourning, or languishing that pertains "not to that which is present [for that would be ἵμερος, "desire" or "craving"], but to that which is elsewhere and absent [τοῦ ἄλλοθί που ὄντος καὶ ἀπόντος]." This is precisely the sense that Schelling is arguing for, even if the distinctions between Eros, Himeros, and Pothos were often blurred among the ancient Greeks themselves. Finally, πόθος is the name of a pallid flower the ancient Greeks often planted at gravesites, and the name of the flower became associated with a mournful yearning for a deceased person.

20   Kersa *is actually the same name transmuted into a different dialect*—. Classical philologists today would respond to Schelling merely by stressing the non-Greek language of which the names Axiokersa and Axiokersos are a part. It is doubtless a long journey from the Phoenician –*kersa* to the Latin *Ceres*. Whether Ceres is in some way bound up with the Greek kobolds or sprites called the κῆρες is an intriguing question. To be sure, Demeter has her dark side, the furious side that seeks and becomes Persephone, or even Erinyes, a Fury. One might also ask—although this is highly speculative—whether Ceres's troubles, her *cares*, have come all the way down to us in the selfsame phoneme. Surely, this is a philological fantasy, and yet any reader of Heidegger's *Being and Time*, with its notion of *Sorge*, or care (*cura*), and any reader of his earlier lecture courses at Marburg where he uses the words *Kummer* and *Bekümmerung*, "trouble" and "taking-trouble," as names for the very existence of mortals—who are always accompanied by cares and woes—is sorely tempted to hear a continuity there. Sorely tempted, in other words, to be bolder than Schelling himself and draw a possible line of descent from remote Phoenicia to our own places and times. On the Greek κῆρ, or troublesome sprite, a daimon that may be equated with doom itself, see the fourth and final part of Krell, "Kalypso: Homeric Concealments after Nietzsche, Heidegger, Derrida, and Lacan," in *The Presocratics after Heidegger*, ed. David C. Jacobs (Albany, NY: SUNY Press, 1999), 101–34. However, one can hear the linguists and the classical philologists howling in distress and rage, and so this note must be brought to a humbled close.

20   *Creuzer.* Friedrich C. Creuzer (1771–1858), classical philologist and mythographer at the University of Heidelberg from 1807 to 1845, was the renowned author of *Symbolik und Mythologie der alten Völker* ("Symbolism and Mythology of the Nations of Antiquity"), the third edition published

between 1836 and 1843. The correspondence between Schelling and Creuzer exhibits their respect for and influence on one another. For more details, see the essay by Alexander Bilda in the present volume.

21   *Maja.* The nymph who, through Zeus, becomes the mother of Hermes. Her name means "mother," which suggests that she is more than merely one nymph among others. She is, in fact, a local form of Gaia, the Earth Mother. She is perhaps related to an Indian goddess of the same name. For Schopenhauer's *World as Will and Representation,* the Indian Maja famously represents the illusion and deceit that entangle humankind. Schelling sees in her name a reference to *magic.* Maja appears at least to be related to two words in Greek, first, Μαῖα, and second, μάγος. Whereas the first is the mother of Hermes, the more general ἡ μαῖα is any "good mother." In the *Odyssey* the word is always used in the vocative and is usually addressed to Eurycleia, the nurse of Odysseus. Other senses of the word are foster mother, birth mother, nurturer, Mother Earth (ἰὼ γαῖα μαῖα, exclaims line 44 of Aeschylus's *Libation Bearers*), midwife, female physician, and grandmother; ἡ μαιάς is "midwifery," μαιόομαι is "to practice midwifery," "give birth," or "suckle." Μάιος is the month of May. A Μάγος, from the Old Persian *magus,* is a Magian or Mede, usually a priest of Zoroaster who tends the sacred fire, interprets dreams, and practices wizardry. As an adjective, μάγος means "magical." The German word for magic, *der Zauber,* is "of obscure origin" (Hermann Paul), although Grimm cites the old Nordic word *taufra* as meaning the "Phoenician color, *röthel,*" related to dried blood and later to ocher. The English words *magus* and *magic* have a long history. (Readers who enjoy adventures in and with the *Oxford English Dictionary* will relish the long and very rich article on *magic.*) *Magus* corresponds to the Greek μάγος, *magic* to the Greek τέχνη μαγική or μαγεία, "the pretended art of influencing the course of events, and of producing marvelous physical phenomena, by processes supposed to owe their efficacy to their power of compelling the intervention of spiritual beings, or of bringing into operation some occult controlling principle of nature; sorcery, witchcraft" (*OED*). As the clearly enlightened (or skeptical) lexicographer does not fail to point out, however, the crucial matter is that one be able to contrast "black" magic, necromancy, or goety (derived from the Greek γοητεία, itself derived from γοάω, "to wail"), which with maleficent intent conjures demons, with "white" or "natural" magic, θεουργία, which originally has the sense of divine work, sacramental rite, or mystery.

Natural magic eventually takes on the sense of harmless legerdemain, sleight of hand, or illusionism. It is necessary to dwell on this subject and engage in serious research on it because of the pervasive importance of magic—otherwise known as *theurgy*—in Schelling's account of the Cabiri. See the note for page 30, on the German word *Zwerg*, "dwarf," which also pertains to magic.

21 *Artemis... also refers to a sorceress.* Mistress of the animals, virgin patroness of birth, huntress, giver and taker of life, Artemis (the sister of Apollo, with whom she shares the bow and arrow) is a form of the pre-Hellenic "Potnia," or Earth goddess, although there is some evidence (see *Pauly-Wissowa* 1:623a) that, especially in Thessaly, she is also associated with Hekate and herbal magic. In ancient Ephesus, Artemis is the all-nurturing, many-breasted Mother and mural-crowned protectress of the city.

21 *Freya allied herself with Odin.* Freya, or Freyja, is the Scandinavian goddess of love. Odin, Odhin, or Wotan is the supreme god of the northern Germans, as portrayed in the Icelandic *Edda*. He is the god of war and victory, the god of the dead, lord of Valhalla, and the god of writing, saga, and magic.

21 *the Egyptian Osiris, the Greek Dionysos, and the German Odin.* Osiris, identified by Schelling as the Egyptian Dionysos, is originally a local sun god. He is the consort of Isis and, like Odin, lord of the dead.

21 *Hades and Dionysos are the same.* Heraclitus's fragment (Diels-Kranz B 15) reads: "For if it were not to Dionysos that they made their procession and intoned their hymn to the shameful parts [αἰδοίοισιν], the deed would be utterly shameless [ἀναιδέστατα]; but Hades and Dionysos, for whom they rave, singing the Lenaean rites, are the selfsame [ὡυτὸς δε...]." Heraclitus is referring to processions in honor of Dionysos during which the image of a gigantic phallus was carried—he seems to be suggesting that such an image might also be taken to be a corpse, its very rigor betraying rigor mortis. Another way to interpret the putative identity of Dionysos, who loosens cares, and Hades, who tightens his grip on the dead, is to think of the Greater Dionysia and the Lenaean rites, both celebrating the return of life in the spring yet sung in the dead of winter—in the full knowledge that other winters are bound to follow the spring and summer of one's hopes. Schelling's identification of Hades with Dionysos, relying principally on this fragment of Heraclitus, is an essential step in his interpretation of the ascendant sequence of the Cabiri.

21 *Persephone, as Kore and Libera.* Liber, Libera, and Liberalia all refer to an Italo-Roman deity identified with Dionysos or with Ariadne, the mortal consort of the god, and with their cult festival—a vegetation festival itself associated with the mystery religions devoted to Ceres and Proserpina. Hence Schelling's identifying Liber with Kore, the maid Persephone.

22 *the Tyrrhenian sailors.* Carl Kerényi tells the story of Dionysos and the Tyrrhenian (= Etruscan) pirates:

> The god first appeared upon a promontory in the shape of a youth in his first bloom. Beautifully hung the dark locks around his head, purple raiment covered his strong shoulders. At that moment Etruscan pirates were swiftly approaching over the wine-dark sea in their many-oared ship. It was their ill-fortune that brought them. When the pirates espied the youth, they nodded one to the other. Swiftly they sprang ashore, at once seized him and joyfully set him in their ship. They supposed that he was a king's son, and they sought to bind him with strong bonds. But no willow-bark cords could hold the youth; the bonds fell from his hands and feet. He sat there with a smile in his dark eyes. The helmsman perceived this and called out to his shipmates: "Unhappy wretches! Who is this strong god whom you have seized and made captive? This sturdy ship cannot support his weight. He is either Zeus, or Apollo with the silver bow, or Poseidon. He is like unto no mortal man, but to the gods who dwell on Olympus. Let us set him free at once, here on land! Let none lay a hand upon him, or in wrath he will send us adverse winds and storm!" But the captain sternly rebuked the helmsman. ... The sail was hoisted, the wind blew into the middle of it, the sheets grew taut. For the crew this alone was almost a miracle. And now wine began to purl through the swift, black ship, sweet to drink and sweetly smelling: it was a divine fragrance. Astonishment seized the crew. Near the top of the sail a vine suddenly sprouted forth, and the grapes hung down in great number. Ivy twined blooming around the mast, and even began to put forth its agreeable fruit. Wreaths appeared on all the rowlocks. When the oarsmen saw this, they soon enough began calling to the helmsman to put the ship back to land! Meanwhile they saw the youth turn into a lion, there on the ship, a lion that stood threateningly on the deck above them and roared mightily. The god caused a shaggy bear to appear in their midst. The bear stood on its hind legs, and the lion glowered dreadfully down from the deck. The crew fled to the stern and stood trembling by the helmsman, the only one of them who was still in his right mind. The lion sprang and seized the captain. The rest of the crew, in mortal terror, hurled themselves from the ship into the sea, and

turned into dolphins. The helmsman was held back by the god, who took compassion on him and comforted him. (CK 266–67)

Note that the Tyrrhenians, identified as Etruscans, of Tyrian-Phoenician origin, are said to have settled on Lemnos, one of Samothrace's neighboring islands, where they worshipped Hephaistos.

22   *Kasmilos by name, more usually called Kadmilos and Camillus.* The last form of the name is the Latin word for an acolyte or altar boy, a ministrant of the god. The name Kasmilos or Kadmilos is surely related to Kadmos, the legendary founder of Greek Thebes and the father of both Ino Leukothea and Semele, the mother of Dionysos. According to Robert Graves, the name Kadmos means "from the East," and Kadmos, as we know, is identified as a Phoenician from Tyre. In search of his sister Europa, who was abducted by Zeus, Kadmos is said to have sailed to Rhodes, to Thera (today's Santorini), and then on to mainland Thrace. After having sown the famous "dragon's teeth" at the Castalian font of Delphi, and after marrying Harmony, Kadmos founded Boeotian Thebes—but only after having been initiated into the Cabirian rites at Samothrace. All twelve Olympians attended the marriage of Kadmos and Harmony on Samothrace: it was the first and last time that gods and mortals shared a meal at the same table. See Roberto Calasso, *Marriage*, chapter 12.

22   *Varro.* M. Terentius Varro (116–27 BCE) was a Roman polymath particularly noted for his interest in ancient Roman history and culture, mythology, and language. Varro's *On the Latin Language* is an especially important source for Schelling.

23   *Angel of the Visage.* According to the *Oxford Annotated Bible*, the Angel of the Visage is the Lord Yahweh himself as he shows himself to mortals. For Schelling, Kadmilos is the *herald* of the god Zeus, going before him, announcing him.

24   *Xenophon.* Xenophon of Athens (ca. 430–354 BCE) belonged as a young man to the circle surrounding Socrates. He was a member of the aristocratic class, friendly to Sparta, and is remembered best for his *Memories of Socrates* and his *Symposium* and *Apology.*

24   *El.* A western-Semitic appellative of God, the proto-Semitic *'il (u)*, contrasted with Baal in that El is not a local deity, hence better suited to

monotheistic, universalist notions. A pre-Mosaic Canaanite religion dedicated to a henotheistic El rather than any figure in the Old Testament (Elohim and Elijah notwithstanding) seems to be the origin of the word as such. The most familiar epithet of El—and this is crucial for Schelling's use of the word here—is "creator of heaven and earth." Even if he is part of a polytheistic pantheon, El, often equated by the Greeks with Kronos, the son of Ouranos and the father of Zeus, is taken to be both the demiurge and the father of humankind.

25   *to the numbers seven and eight.* Karl Schelling's edition has "seven or eight," but the new critical edition by Arnold and Danz argues that the "or" was originally an "and" in Schelling's text.

25   *are called Hephaistoi.* The Cabirian deities, like the Daktyloi, have important relations to metallurgy, and while Hephaistos is more closely associated with the isle of Lemnos, it is not surprising, at least to Schelling, to find Hephaistos and all his retinue also on Samothrace. On the long-lasting tradition of these Hephaistoi, see Mircea Eliade, *The Forge and the Crucible: The Origins and Structures of Alchemy* (New York: HarperCollins, 2000), throughout.

25   *Parmenio too was Alexander.* Parmenion was the most celebrated general of both Philip II and Alexander of Macedonia. He was famous for his independent campaigns, especially in Persia, on Alexander's behalf. Parmenion was the force that held together the sprawling empire of Alexander, at least for a time, so in that sense Parmenion *was* Alexander. And yet because of Parmenion's more conservative politics and his eventually outspoken opposition to the king, Alexander had him assassinated by his own officers.

25   *the cycle of the days of the week.* Sketches of Schelling's efforts to connect the days of the week with the structure and order of the gods can be found in F. W. J. Schelling, *Philosophische Entwürfe und Tagebücher 1814–1816, Die Weltalter II—Über die Gottheiten von Samothrake*, ed. Lothar Knatz, Hans Jörg Sandkühler, and Martin Schraven (Hamburg: Felix Meiner, 2002), 70–71.

25   *the demiurge.* Schelling had long been fascinated by the figure of the demiurge (craftsman, maker) of the universe, a figure developed principally in Plato's *Timaeus*. Schelling wrote a detailed commentary on Plato's dialogue during his university years at Tübingen, now published as F. W. J. Schelling, *Timaeus (1794)*, ed. Hartmut Buchner, "Schellingiana vol. 4" (Stuttgart-Bad

Canstatt: Fromman-Holzboog, 1994), with an excellent explanatory essay by Hermann Krings. Schelling was particularly struck by the fact that the eponymous spokesman of *Timaeus* always combines the words *craftsman* or *maker* with the word *father*, so that the vocabularies of creation and procreation are interwoven from the start. However, Schelling is alert to the fact that in Timaeus's account not only the "father" but also the "mother [and nurse] of all things," namely, Ἀνάγκη (*Ananke*, "necessity"), plays a crucial role in the genesis of the universe. For she is the receptacle of all things—a receptacle that sometimes appears to be "space" and at other times "materiality" as such (55). Timaeus gives the name χώρα (*chora*) to this mysterious "third kind" of being, which communicates in some mysterious way with both ideas and material things. Schelling accepts Timaeus's (and therefore Plato's?) judgment that this "mother" and "nurse" of the universe is, as Schelling too writes, "difficult to grasp" or even "inconceivable" (58–59), as though everything we might say about it—or her—is "illegitimate," spoken "as though we were dreaming" (74). As a young theology student, Schelling was understandably gripped by the "kingly soul" of the "uppermost ruler" of the universe, the powerful demiurge (66), to which mere mortals must "ascend." If the Cabirian deities represent an "ascending sequence," as Schelling insists several times during his Samothrace lecture, he is simply repeating what he once said of Plato's *Timaeus*: "Everywhere here one observes an *ascent*—the continuous progression from the lower to the higher, from the subordinate to the dominating" (64). One may wonder, however, whether the more mature devotee of Samothrace and later the philosopher of mythology is forced to confront Ananke, in the figures of Demeter and Persephone, with greater persistence. The teleologist, trained in ascent, may turn out to be an archaeologist, excavating the ever deeper strata of necessity.

26   *Warburton*. The author of *The Divine Legation of Moses*, published between 1737 and 1741, William Warburton (1698–1779) was an English cleric and writer, an apologist for Alexander Pope (recall Pope's "Essay on Man") but also a proponent of the view that all polytheistic religions were stumbling and failed attempts to achieve the monotheism of the Old Testament. Warburton is an important figure in Jacques Derrida's analysis of what he calls a "crisis of the European consciousness," a crisis that occurs when the phonetic alphabet of the West confronts the Chinese ideogram and the Egyptian hieroglyphic. From the mid-eighteenth century onward, something like a

"grammatology," a reflection on "scripture" and on *logos* in general, becomes unavoidable. See Derrida, *De la grammatologie* (Paris: Minuit, 1968), 112–21.

26 *Sainte-Croix*. Guillaume de Sainte-Croix (1746–1809) wrote a well-known work on the Indian *Veda* (1778) and a series of studies (ca. 1784) on the religious history of pre-Christian antiquity, emphasizing the importance of the mystery cults.

26 *the esoteric or acroamatic presentations of the philosophers*. Both Plato and Aristotle are said to have had esoteric or secret doctrines taught only to the most advanced students in the Academy and Lyceum and never written down. The "indeterminate dyad" is usually held to be Plato's principal acroamatic teaching (that is, the supremely elevated doctrine, communicated by spoken word alone to the initiates). Schelling, who stresses the *dyas* over all monisms, was surely keen to pursue these esoteric doctrines even if here he seems to be downplaying their importance.

27 *a saying of Heraclitus*. Schelling translates Heraclitus's fragment (Diels-Kranz B 32) in a very strange yet revealing way. The saying is usually rendered as follows: "The One, which alone is wise, will not and yet will be called by the name Zeus." Schelling shifts the word μοῦνον ("alone") to a key position in the fragment. Zeus is now the One who both wills and yet is repulsed by his aloneness: he contracts and thus excludes the other, yet at the same time he becomes expansive and yearns for the other. Schelling's translation is even more daring than Heidegger's (in his "Logos" essay): in Schelling's view, the One does not merely *gather* the many, letting all beings lie before us in presence; rather, the One, as Zeus, *languishes* in his craving for many, many others. Schelling was fond of comparing the *life* of Zeus to the throne that Phidias sculpted for him at Olympia: myriad life-forms, plants and animals of all kinds, decorated that throne, which therefore seemed to be "teeming with life." See Krell, *The Tragic Absolute*, chapter 5, especially 170–72.

27 *Gerhard Vossius, Samuel Bochart, and other worthy researchers*. These scholars are not much studied today, except by historians of biblical hermeneutics. Gerardus Vossius (1577–1649) was a Dutch theologian and classicist noteworthy for his treatment of antiquity from a historical rather than theological point of view. Samuel Bochart (1599–1667), a French Huguenot biblical scholar writing in the 1640s, is noteworthy for his support of a hermeneutics of history that tries to establish historical context without

religious bias of any kind. Bochart's *Sacred Geography* is an important source for Schelling. While both scholars are admirable researchers for their time, they can no longer be accepted as authorities when they (like Schelling after them, however!) proclaim the Phoenicians to be the universal source of Western culture. Vossius, whatever else we may discover about him, is cited by the not always reverent Laurence Sterne in volume 2 of *Tristram Shandy* as one of many experts . . . on ancient Roman trousers.

28   *the Pelasgians*. A name the Greeks often used to designate their ancestors, but a people very difficult if not impossible to trace in the space-time of antiquity. The "Pelasgian Creation Myth," which opens Robert Graves's *The Greek Myths*, is quite eclectic, with Orphic stories as its chief component. Pelasgus is said to have been the first human being, born (but from whom?) in Arcadia during the reign of Eurynome, the far-wandering lunar goddess of all things. The term *Pelasgians* is often used to designate the earliest natives of Samothrace—concerning whom, however, we know next to nothing. This may change, however, as archaeologists uncover a growing number of prehistoric sites on Samothrace to the south and east of the Sanctuary of the Great Gods.

28   *the priestesses of Dodona*. The oracle at Dodona, devoted to Zeus, located in a remote corner of northwestern Attica, is said to be as ancient as Apollo's Delphi and Demeter's Eleusis. It was known already to Homer. The mythical king Croesus is said to have consulted the oracle there. Plato's *Phaedrus* (at 244a–b) cites both the Pythoness of Delphi and the priestesses of Dodona in its account of divine μανία or madness: "The greatest blessings come by way of madness, indeed, madness that is heaven-sent. It was when they were mad that the prophetess at Delphi and the priestesses at Dodona achieved so much for which both states and individuals in Greece are thankful." Schelling, however, in the present case doubts the word of those priestesses—one of whom is Diotima, famous for her speech in Plato's *Symposium*—who presumably were quite sane when they spoke to Herodotus about Egypt and the Cabiri.

28   *these ancient Hebrew documents*. Schelling is referring to ancient Near Eastern texts associated with Phoenicia—not, presumably, with Old Testament texts, or at least not *merely* with these biblical texts. Unfortunately, he is not precise here.

28   *those Phoenicians who had settled in Boeotia with Tyrian Kadmos.* As noted earlier, Kadmos was a native of Tyre, the capital city of a small island 750 meters off the coast of Phoenicia—today's Syria. Tyre dominated Phoenicia from 1198 BCE, that is, from the time of the fall of Troy until the Alexandrian age. On the general tendency in Schelling to emphasize the importance of Phoenicia, and especially the Phoenician language, for the entire cultural development of the ancient world, one should note the debate among historians since Schelling's time. Eduard Meyer, in his monumental *Geschichte des Altertums* (1884–1902), criticizes the "fantastic etymologies" of earlier scholars and their general tendency to overestimate Phoenician influence in the Mediterranean area. Meyer argues that due to the lack of physical and literary evidence we have to be agnostic about Phoenicia. That said, even he does not doubt the extent of the Phoenician trading network, which extended from the eastern Mediterranean to Greece, Crete, Egypt, North Africa (Carthage was a colony from the mid-ninth century onward), and Spain (2/2:85–86). The more recent *Fischer Weltgeschichte*, by contrast, not only confirms the importance of the Phoenician trade routes but also reasserts, against Meyer, the universal cultural importance of Phoenicia for antiquity—a cultural influence "that can hardly be overestimated" (4:168). While the absence of adequate archaeological and literary evidence no doubt compels a kind of agnosticism, Schelling's surmise that Phoenicia is essential to the development of the Cabirian system seems at least plausible, even if scholars nowadays emphasize the importance of Anatolian Phrygia rather than Phoenicia for the Cabirian system. See the earlier note (for page 22) on Kasmilos.

28   *Kambyses.* The son of Cyrus, the Persian king Kambyses (who ruled from 529 to 522 BCE) conquered Egypt, thus expanding the great Persian empire throughout the Mediterranean world. The desecration reported by Herodotus occurred during Kambyses's long but eventually successful siege of Memphis in 525. The Aramaic papyri of Elephantine confirm Herodotus's account of this desecration.

28   *the dwarflike figures on the prows of the Phoenician ships.* The entire phrase translates Schelling's *die phönikischen Patäken*. The Πάταικοι were dwarflike apotropaic ornaments on the prows of Phoenician triremes. Herodotus identifies these foreboding dwarflike figures with the Hephaistoi, the sons of Hephaistos, and with the Cabiri. The Greeks had long been fascinated by

these Phoenician figures and soon came to use the word *pátaikoi* to designate any type of dwarf.

30   *our German word* Zwerg. Hermann Paul notes the Old and Middle High German form *twërc* but otherwise says nothing that would confirm Schelling's bold etymology, which identifies *Zwerg* ("dwarf"), via *Tuwerg*, to the Greek θεουργός, "divine worker," or, more radically, "maker of gods." Paul proposes instead that the word may derive from *Trug*, "deception," "fraud," which would have pleased Hölderlin, for whom the sense of betrayal and deception is crucial to the relations between immortals and mortals. Grimm defines the word *Zwerg* as the Latin *homunculus vel nanus*, citing many sources that refer to the presence of dwarfs at royal courts and among "great men" generally, the dwarfs acting as their servants or jesters, but it does not confirm Schelling's surmise about theurgy. J. C. Adelung (1732–1806) remarks in the 1793 edition of his *Wörterbuch der hochdeutschen Mundart*: "By all appearances it is a very old word; hence the uncertainty and obscurity of its lineage." Adelung notes that Gudmund Andreä derives it from "the Greek θεδυργον"—surely a typo for θεουργός. One may therefore take it that Schelling has the derivation from Andreä, as cited by Adelung, to whose dictionary Schelling often repairs. Every classicist, including, for example, Roberto Calasso, has puzzled over these dwarflike creatures who pursue metallurgy and who also assist at the birth of gods, yet perhaps no one before or after Schelling has so persistently pursued the *divinity* of the dwarf and pygmy. See also the note (for page 21) above on Maja and magic.

30   *Georg Agricola*. Georg Bauer (1494–1555), called Agricola (the Latin equivalent of *Bauer*, "farmer"), was a geologist and mineralogist who promoted the mining and metallurgy industries of sixteenth-century Germany. In so doing he preserved much of the lore concerning the dwarfs, trolls, gnomes, and kobolds that were said to occupy the mineshafts and caves in the mountains.

30   *the Idaean Daktyloi*. Greek sprites given the name "finger men," the Daktyloi served as smiths and workers in metals. Mount Ida refers to both the mountain near Troy and the sacred mountain of Zeus in Crete. The Daktyloi are thus associated with the mountain cults of both Kybele-Astarte-Adrasteia in the Near East and Rhea in Greece. On Crete, Rhea gave birth to Zeus and had the Daktyloi serve as guardians of the endangered child. They are often said to be ten in number, having sprung from the earth at that

cave in the mountain where Rhea, in the throes of her labor, braced herself by digging her fingers into the soil. Thinking of women gripping or merely touching the soil, one might also think of the Maenads, who extract not ores but milk and honey from the earth, and of Demeter, who fructifies the fields during the marriage of Cadmus and Harmony.

30   *the Dioskouroi.* The familiar story of the twin brothers Castor and Pollux (the Greek Kastor and Polydeukes) takes on greater depth when considered in the light of the Cabirian mysteries. The familiar account says that the twins, "sons of Zeus" as their shared name implies, were born from a single egg gestated by Leda. They were thus brothers of Helen and Klytaimestra, and they performed many heroic deeds—Kastor as a tamer of horses, Polydeukes as a boxer. They were said to have been Argonauts and thus initiates in the Samothracian cult. Kastor, a mortal, unlike his more fortunate brother, fell in battle, whereupon Polydeukes convinced their father to allow the two to remain united in death. Zeus, unable to frustrate the Moirai or Fates entirely by agreeing to Polydeukes's request, arranged for them to alternate between heaven and the underworld. As the stars of Gemini, the Dioskouroi are said to aid mariners; they are the "candles" or "corposants" that Melville writes about so eloquently in chapter 119 of *Moby-Dick*, the Saint Elmo's fire that promises rescue to storm-tossed mariners. Their cult did not disappear even with Christianity, as the twin saints Cosmas and Damian testify. Yet the origins of the Dioskouroi extend far back to pre-Greek lore. Again, Carl Kerényi tells the story movingly, wearing the narrative mask of a classical Greek man, and his story begins in Thrace with an account of the Cabiri:

> The Kabeiroi, too, were servants of the Great Mother. It was known in ancient times that they were called Kabeiroi after Mount Kabeiros in the country of Berekyntia, which belonged to the Phrygian Great Mother, and came thence to Samothrace, their sacred island. Their name always sounded foreign to us, and must have belonged to the same barbarian language as was preserved in Samothrace as the language of the religion and mysteries of the Kabeiroi. It was perhaps akin to the language of the ancient inhabitants of Lemnos, the foreign-speaking worshippers of Hephaistos. It was said of the Kabeiroi that they were the Idaioi Daktyloi, who had come westwards from Phrygia and whose magical practices had made the inhabitants of Samothrace the first converts to their secret cult. It was also believed that Orpheus had been one of their pupils at that time. It is said that the Mother of the Gods herself had

settled her sons, the Korybantes, on Samothrace; but nobody was allowed to reveal who their father was, since this was told only in the secret cult. In these stories the Daktyloi, the Kouretes, the Korybantes and the Telchines are sometimes only a few [of the] primitive beings and sometimes entire primitive peoples—who, in comparison with the great size of the Mother, were, as I have said, of dwarfish stature.

Nevertheless the Kabeiroi were called amongst us *megaloi theoi*, "great gods." This was how our seamen invoked them, as rescuing gods in moments of danger. They were also called Kouretes and Korybantes, and in Lemnos also Hephaistoi, in the plural. . . . Kabeiro, mother of the Kabeiroi, she whose name was translated in our language as Rhea, Demeter, Hekate, or Aphrodite, was a daughter of Proteus: or so, at least, it was said in Lemnos. Kabeiro bore to Hephaistos the boy Kadmilos. The latter begat three Kabeiroi and three Cabirian Nymphs. This genealogy makes no special mention of two brothers. In Samothrace, on the other hand, there stood on both sides of the entrance to the All-Holiest two brazen phallic statues like our statues of Hermes. They were said [by Varro] to be twin brothers, sons of Zeus, the Dioskouroi. In the All-Holiest itself stood—so much even an uninitiate can guess—the third brother, who was worshipped both as a small and as a great Kabeiros, as a small Kadmilos and as the great and mysterious Korybas. His relationship with the Great Mother was kept secret. But it has been said that the father of the Korybantes was also kept secret, and yet it was revealed in the genealogy that the Kabeiroi and their Nymphs were descended from Kadmilos. "Korybantes" and "Kabeiroi" are well known to be two names for the same beings. The boy Kadmilos and the father of the Kabeiroi seem to have been one and the same person. You here recognize an identification by which the Great Mother is doubly connected with her youngest son: he is both her husband and her child. This relation between the two is often to be found in tales concerning our mysteries. The four names of divinities that reached us from Samothrace—Axieros, Axiokersa, Axiokersos and Kadmilos—were said to be identical with Demeter, Persephone, Hades and Hermes respectively. (CK 86–87)

Kerényi's suggestion that the Cabiri are the *children* of Kadmilos adds a strange dimension to Schelling's interpretation of Kadmilos as a herald of the demiurge. But let us add one more dimension to the connection of the Dioskouroi or Gemini to *seafaring*. It is as though Melville's Captain Ahab has studied Schelling's "Samothrace" essay, perhaps communicated to Melville, if only indirectly, by Samuel Taylor Coleridge. In chapter 119 of *Moby-Dick*,

Ahab broods on the dangers that mortals face at sea, broods in his own furiously defiant Persian-Promethean way, addressing "the candles," that is, the "corpusants" or flaming masts, of the *Pequod* thus:

> "Oh! thou clear spirit of clear fire, whom on these seas I as Persian once did worship, till in the sacramental act so burned by thee, that to this hour I bear the scar; I now know thee, thou clear spirit, and I now know that thy right worship is defiance. To neither love nor reverence wilt thou be kind; and e'en for hate thou canst but kill; and all are killed. No fearless fool now fronts thee. I own thy speechless, placeless power; but to the last gasp of my earthquake life will dispute its unconditional, unintegral mastery in me. In the midst of the personified impersonal, a personality stands here. Though but a point at best; whencesoe'er I came; wheresoe'er I go; yet while I earthly live, the queenly personality lives in me, and feels her royal rights. But war is pain, and hate is woe. Come in thy lowest form of love, and I will kneel and kiss thee; but at thy highest, come as mere supernal power; and though thou launchest navies of full-freighted worlds, there's that in here that still remains indifferent. Oh, thou clear spirit, of thy fire thou madest me, and like a true child of fire, I breathe it back to thee."
>
> *(Sudden, repeated flashes of lightning; the nine flames leap lengthwise to thrice their previous height; Ahab, with the rest, closes his eyes, his right hand pressed hard upon them.)*
>
> "... Light though thou be, thou leapest out of darkness; but I am darkness leaping out of light, leaping out of thee! ... Oh, thou magnanimous! now I do glory in my genealogy. But thou art but my fiery father; my sweet mother, I know not. Oh, cruel! what has thou done with her? There lies my puzzle; but thine is greater. Thou knowest not how came ye, hence callest thyself unbegotten; certainly knowest not thy beginning, hence callest thyself unbegun. I know that of me, which thou knowest not of thyself, oh, thou omnipotent. There is some unsuffusing thing beyond thee, thou clear spirit, to whom all thy eternity is but time, all thy creativeness mechanical. Through thee, thy flaming self, my scorched eyes do dimly see it. Oh, thou foundling fire, thou hermit immemorial, thou too hast thy incommunicable riddle, thy unparticipated grief. Here again with haughty agony, I read my sire. Leap! leap up, and lick the sky! I leap with thee; I burn with thee; would fain be welded with thee; defyingly I worship thee!"

Schelling as Ahab, defiant? Probably not. Yet the old forms of piety are withering in Schelling after the 1809 *Essay on Human Freedom*, and the deity, as it searches for the deepest strata of love and languor, is assuming unaccountable forms: "Thou knowest not how came ye." If Albert Camus was right to praise *Moby-Dick* as the only truly absurd novel, perhaps Schelling's "Samothrace" lecture may be called the first truly absurd theology, or a truly absurd *genealogy* of the heretofore untraced origins of spirit. And the two Dioskouroi? Starbuck and Stubb, to be sure.

31   *a chain of enchantment.* This is surely a reference to the famous chain of Plato's *Ion*, 533d–535a. Socrates emphasizes the divine force (θεία δὲ δύναμις) that binds the rhapsode to his or her art, comparing that dynamism to a magnet (Μαγνῆτις) or Stone of Herakles (Ἡρακλεία λίθος) that energizes an entire iron chain. The muse causes the poet or rhapsode to be filled with divine enthusiasm (ἡ Μοῦσα ἐνθέους), and the magnetic attraction works through the inspired artist to enthuse all who are in his or her vicinity (διὰ δὲ τῶν ἐνθέων ἄλλων ἐνθουσιζόντων). Socrates sees such magnetic power at work in the dancing Korybantes (533e 8) and in the Bacchai (534a 4), who are able to cause milk and honey to flow from the earth at the touch of an inspired and inspiriting hand. All of this is *theurgy* in Schelling's sense— which is precisely Plato's sense as well. Socrates does not shy from calling it θείᾳ μοίρᾳ (534c 1), "the godly portion" and θείᾳ δυνάμει (534c 6), "divinity at work." The efficacy of the chain of inspiration, the magnetic chain, is of ὁ θεὸς αὐτός (534d 3–4), "the divine as such," θεῖα καὶ θεῶν (534e 4), "divinity and the gods themselves." Schelling had long considered magnetism to be the essential mystery in the physics of nature, as that which binds the organic and the inorganic, and perhaps even freedom and necessity. (See his *First Sketch toward a Philosophy of Nature*, 1799, and the discussion of it in the second section of Krell, *Contagion: Sexuality, Disease, and Death in German Idealism and Romanticism* (Bloomington: Indiana University Press, 1998), esp. 85–88 and 112–14.) In this respect Schelling follows a tradition as old as Democritus, Empedocles, and even Thales, all of whom observed the magic of magnetism. Alexander of Aphrodisias, the second-century commentator on Aristotle, devoted an entire treatise to the phenomenon, which was of central interest to physicists and physicians alike. For magnetism is a force that works its effects on both macrocosm and microcosm, whether the latter be animal or animator, beast or poet, illusionist or enlightener, quack or scientist.

31   *the Hebrew* Kābbir. See the commentary on Schelling's endnote 113.

31   Consentes *and* Complices. Although the word *consentes* was later taken to derive from *consentire* and *consilium*, it originally comes from *consum*, "to be with, to accompany." The *con-sen-tes* are those whose very being (*ens, entis, Sein, Wesen*) is marked by companionship. The *consentes dei* ("the company of gods") played a role in the Etruscan fulguration system, that is, in the lore and the cult by means of which lightning strikes were interpreted. According to Pauly-Wissowa, the *consentes* were not the supreme Etruscan gods, not "the concealed," but lesser gods who served as counselors to Tinia, or Jupiter. Not only the Etruscan connection points back to the Lydians, Phrygians, and Phoenicians, however; it may also be significant that the *consentes dei*, as the circle of twelve Olympian divinities, were introduced into Rome in 217 BCE, at the time of the second Punic War. This was of course a time of intense contact—and conflict—with that principal Phoenician colony, Carthage, and also the time of the defeat of the Roman armies near Lake Trasimeno by Hannibal. The priests of Rome were clearly in search of new divine confederates, accomplices, or *complices*, at this critical juncture.

31   *the Tuscians.* Yet another name for the Etruscans.

31   *Lavinium.* Lavinia, the daughter of Latinus and Amata, was Aeneas's wife, and Aeneas named his newly founded city Lavinium, close to the spot where his ship first touched Italy, in her honor. The Romans celebrated this "return" of the Penates or household gods to Italy, inasmuch as it was believed that long before the Trojan War the Pelasgians carried the Penates to Etruria (today's Umbria and Tuscany). The founding of Rome is thus held to be a homecoming of the Phoenician-Trojan-Pelasgian deities. According to some ancient legends, the Penates originally stood at the harbor of Samothrace and were thus in service to the Great Gods. At all events, the allegiance of the Romans to Samothrace and the Cabiri remained remarkably strong throughout the periods of the Republic and the Empire.

32   *the child in us.* See Plato, *Phaedo*, 77e–78a, in the (here slightly altered) translation by Hugh Tredennick. The context is as follows: Socrates has only now teased Simmias and Cebes that they are afraid—as little children are afraid—that were they to die on a windy day their expired souls would be gone with the wind.

> Cebes laughed. Suppose that we are afraid, Socrates, he said, and try to convince us. Or rather don't suppose that it is we who are afraid. Probably even in

us there is a little boy who has these childish terrors. Try to persuade him not to be afraid of death as though it were a bogy.

What you should do, said Socrates, is to utter a magic spell [ἐπᾴδειν] over him every day until his fears have been charmed away [ἐξεπᾴσηται].

But, Socrates, said Simmias, where shall we find an enchanter [ἐπῳδός] who understands these spells, now that you ... are leaving us?

Greece is a large country, Cebes, he replied, which must have good men in it, and there are many foreign races too. You must ransack all of them in your search for this enchanter, without sparing money or trouble, because you could not spend your money more opportunely on any other object. And you must search also by your own united efforts, because it is probable that you would not easily find anyone better fitted for the task.

Schelling would doubtless have stressed Socrates's reference to the "many foreign races" in Greece that are knowledgeable when it comes to incantations to charm away the fear of death.

33 *Today's celebration.* October 12 was the birthday of the King of Bavaria, Maximilian I. Joseph, who reigned from 1806 to 1825. In the year 1815, Schelling was invited to address a public session of the Bavarian Academy of Sciences in honor of its royal patron, who was in attendance. In 1806 Schelling had been appointed the first director of the Bavarian Academy of Fine Arts, a division of the academy that he was now addressing.

33 *to riddle on the riddle of a belief that comes to us from the elevated past.* What makes the entire riddle of the Cabirian system so riddlesome, in Schelling's view, is that we are aware of it at all. In his *Ages of the World*, he had expressed that riddle on the very first page of his first attempt to write "The Past": after beginning with the words, "How sweet is the sound of the narratives that come from the holy dawn of the world," he only a few lines later writes, "No sagas have come down to us from those times." No sagas or legends, he adds, but only "divinely revealed discourses," or *Reden*, "flash like lightning bolts that pierce the primordial darkness." See F. W. J. Schelling, *Die Weltalter Fragmente: In den Urfassungen von 1811 und 1813*. Nachlaßband to the Münchner Jubiläumsdruck (Munich: Biederstein and Leibniz, 1946), 10.

33 *that Cabirian confederation by which the ancient tyranny was first broken ... a truly Typhonian empire.* Typhon was the last of the Titans to be subdued by the Olympian Zeus. A gigantic serpent, Typhon, the last child of Kronos

and Rhea, was blasted by a lightning bolt and compelled to dwell in the underworld. He lives beneath Mount Etna in Sicily and from time to time he still vomits forth the fires of his rage. Although Schelling is careful not to specify the modern equivalent of this "truly Typhonian empire," he seems to be referring to the Napoleonic Empire and its armies, recently defeated at Waterloo. Yet because Bavaria despised Austria and Brandenburg-Prussia, both of them allied with the coalition forces against Napoleon, it is quite possible that Schelling is taking the view that Maximilian himself would prefer to have taken: the Typhonian empire in question may in fact be the *ancien régime* precisely as it survives in the three hundred petty German principalities—such as Brandenburg-Prussia far to the north. Upon reflection, however, it is far more likely that Schelling is wisely following the lead of his sovereign, who had only recently, in 1813, dropped his support of the Napoleonic Rhine Confederation and joined the fight against the French armies. Napoleon was the new Typhon, only recently blasted by coalition lightning and soon to be buried—if not on the island of Elba—then finally on St. Helena.

One of the many libation sites at the sanctuary; offerings were poured onto the bedrock below. The marble cover stone dates from the Roman period.

3

Explanatory Notes on Schelling's Endnotes

The following comments by the translators are preceded by the *endnote* number, not the book page number. Not every challenging argument by Schelling has received comment here nor every reference to the now often obscure linguistic and historical sources.

1   *the Gulf of Saros.* See the map at the outset of the Translators' Preface. A wide peninsula on the western coast of Turkey separates the Gulf of Saros from the Dardanelles and the Bosporus, the waterways to the north leading to the Black Sea.

1   *the later name Samos.* One of the ancient legends said to have had an influence on the name of the island tells of Saon, a son of Zeus by a nymph, or a son of Hermes and Rhene. Saon (a name closer to the Saos mountain chain and Mount Saokis on Samothrace than to the island itself) is said to have gathered the Samothracians into villages and cities, dividing them into five tribes, named after his five sons, and giving them laws. As for the earlier names *Elektr(i)a* and *Leukosia*, the latter is surely related to the name of the "radiant goddess," Ino Leukothea, who is closely associated with the island. This connection is made more probable by Schelling's reference to the "doubtless similar" case of Malta, named after Melite, the Babylonian "Mylitta," the goddess who, for Schelling, exhibits the necessary "becoming female of god" (SW II/2, 195). The accepted interpretation today of the name *Samothrace* understands *samos* as "height." Thrace too is quite mountainous, so that Thracian Heights would hardly seem to distinguish the island from the rest of the mainland. Yet when one approaches the island from the sea,

"height" is perhaps the overwhelming sensation—as one sees five thousand feet of rock suddenly emerging from the sea.

3   With regard to Schelling's close attention to the volcanic history not only of Samothrace but also of that famous Cycladic island far to the south, Thera or Santorini, just north of Crete, we should note how important every aspect of *nature* was to him: during the 1790s he published three remarkable books on the philosophy of nature, culminating in his interpretation of *organic* nature in the 1799 *First Projection of a Philosophy of Nature*. Two aspects of his philosophy of nature, which in Schelling's view always runs parallel to a philosophy of mythology, seem particularly relevant for his "Deities of Samothrace": (1) the importance of *magnetism* for both the inorganic and organic realms of nature and (2) the overwhelming force of *fire*, including subterranean fire and magma, the source of volcanic activity. A massive volcanic eruption around 1650 BCE (more than a millennium earlier than 237 BCE), perhaps the most devastating in human history, caused about three-quarters of the Cycladic island of Thera to collapse into the sea. Schelling mentions in his first endnote the accounts he has read of the two most recent volcanic eruptions at Santorini, forming the *Cammenies* or "chimneys," today called *Palia Kameni* and *Nea Kameni*, the "ancient" and "new" volcanic islets still visible in the bay or caldera of Santorini—one of the most spectacular geological sites, and sights, in the world. Perhaps it is matched by a traveler's first view of Samothrace and its Mountain of the Moon looming out of the North Aegean.

6   *no one would think of calling them "compasses" or "magnetic needles."* "Magnetic needles" here translates *Die Boussole*, a magnet needle with its housing; from the French *boussole*, itself from the German *Büchse*, meaning tin box or container, the Dutch *Boxel*, in which the magnetic needle was housed—hence, what we today call a compass. See the German dictionary by Adelung, GKW 1:1140. See also Walter E. Ehrhardt, "Samothrake: '(an Boussolen wird niemand denken)' (SW VIII, 373)," *Schelling-Studien* 3 (2015), 149–159.

13   *the Klodonian and Mimallonian sects.* Plutarch, in his account of Alexander, attests to the cult practices of the Thracian-Macedonian Κλώδωνες-Μιμαλόνες, Dionysian sects noted for their wild enthusiasm, their prophecy by fire (reminiscent perhaps of the epiphany of Zeus to Semele but also of

the many associations of fire with magic), and their Maenadic rites. The first name may be derived from Κλονᾶς, a priest associated with both Thebes and Arcadia at the outset of the seventh century BCE who composed sacred songs with flute accompaniment. Schelling suggests that such wild enthusiasm, inherited from his mother Olympia, may have induced Alexander to overreach himself by attempting the conquest of India—at which point his troops balked, the conquest failed, and Alexander himself soon died.

15 *cut off only by the sea and by his sacrilege.* The German text has *nur vom Meer und der Entweichung ihn abgeschnitten. Entweichung* would of course mean "feint" or "evasion," but from the context one may take it to be a typo for *Entweihung,* "pollution" or "sacrilege," since the king is said to have polluted himself by committing a murder. In cases like this, one particularly regrets the absence of Schelling's holograph.

19 *Theodosius.* Presumably Theodosius I ("the Great," an epithet granted him by the bishops of the Eastern Church), Roman Emperor from 379 to 395 CE. Under pressure from the bishops, Theodosius proscribed all pagan rites in 391–392, including the games at Olympia and the rites at Samothrace. Yet Schelling may be referring to his son, Theodosius II, who in 426 sacked the temples at Olympia and removed the cult statue of Zeus—the famous statue of gold and ivory sculpted and erected by Phidias—from Olympia to the Eastern imperial capital of Constantinople. The statue, one of the wonders of the ancient world, was destroyed in a fire in Constantinople only fifty years later.

29 *the experts will have to judge.* This very important note initiates Schelling's investigation into the names of the Cabiri. He will focus on the roots *axio-* and *-kers.* He stresses here that only an expert in the ancient languages can have much to say about the etymology of these roots, but he speculates that their meaning has little to do with the usual understanding of divine names like *Ceres* or *Demeter* as "Mother Earth" or "Mine is the Earth." The general concepts of omnipotence and omniscience that scholars apply to deity will in fact not automatically apply here. Rather, Schelling will argue—astonishingly—that the roots of the Cabirian names point in the direction of hunger, poverty, solitude, obsession, languor, and languishing.

31 *the sense of being consumed by a lack... "poverty"... "squalor."* In this complex note, Schelling tries to find etymological evidence for the preeminent

quality of deity as hunger, need, poverty, and even squalor. To be sure, this flies in the face of the almost universal claim by religionists that their deity is a figure of omnipotence. In Schelling's view, the phrase "he craved, he was avid for" describes the condition of deity long before anything like "possession" and "power" can apply to it, even if the etymologies of the sundry Hebrew, Persian, and Arabic words seem to combine in a baffling way the senses of both "possessing" and "craving." Also striking in the note is the parallel thesis that "gender ambiguity" or, more specifically, "gender doubling" applies to all deities. Endnotes 32, 35, 36, 45, and 47 continue to emphasize the proximity of a double-gendered deity—at least in its initial state—to poverty, hunger, and loneliness, to *Sehnsucht* and *Schmachten*, longing and languishing.

35   *That Deo stands for Devo, like Dia for Diva, we can assume with assurance.* Schelling's meaning here is not clear. That *divus* is an older form of *deus* is clear. Yet he is surely not making a mere reference to the divinity of Demeter, at least not divinity in the sense of majesty. Rather, Schelling is everywhere bent on showing the derivation of divinity from poverty and lack. The *Oxford English Dictionary* has an intriguing article on the Indo-Iranian word *div*, which may be the origin of *divus, deus*, which means both god and evil spirit; this is hardly surprising when one thinks of the *dev*il or the *dia*bolical. Yet nothing in that article confirms Schelling's interpretation of languishing and neediness. As endnote 36 goes on to show, Schelling takes the name Δηώ or Δεώ to mean not ironclad necessity but neediness, poverty, hunger. And, as he has already argued, languor, languishing, and obsession. There is much evidence of this in the *Hymn to Demeter*, which repeatedly refers to the goddess as mourning or languishing for her daughter. The word πόθος, discussed in detail in later endnotes, is used to express such languishing (πόθῳ μινύθουσα, in lines 201 and 304 of the *Hymn*). Likewise, Demeter's daughter Persephone is said to have pined for her mother (μητρὸς πόθῳ, line 344). These phrases are perfectly rendered by Schelling's words *Sehnsucht* and *Schmachten*. In fact, one may take the Homeric *Hymn to Demeter* to be a principal source for Schelling's thesis concerning Axieros. For the hymn also shows how Demeter's yearning eventually turns into rage against the other gods and the mortals, and it also tells us why Hölderlin's name for Demeter was "the Impenetrable," even though human beings continuously work the earth: "Then she caused a most dreadful and cruel year for humankind over

the all-nourishing earth: the ground would not make the seed sprout, for rich-crowned Demeter kept it hidden in the earth. In the fields the oxen drew many a curved plow in vain, and much white barley was cast upon the land without avail." (Translation of lines 305–309 by H. G. Evelyn-White, with minor changes.) An angry Demeter is indeed "impenetrable."

43   *The daughters of Danaus are said to have brought the Thesmophoriai from Egypt.* The Thesmophoria, an important fertility festival throughout Greece in antiquity, conducted by married women usually at seedtime in late October, had as its central mytheme the story of Ceres (Demeter) and her daughter Proserpina (Persephone). In Egypt, according to Herodotus, it was also a women's festival, but celebrating the passion of Osiris. Why Schelling refers to the festival here, where he is talking about Demeter's punishment of Erysichthon, is unclear. It seems to be merely an addition to the account of Ceres—unless the punishment of Erysichthon is somehow reminiscent of the passion of Osiris, hence a reference to ritual. Perhaps the most important source on the festival is Aristophanes's comedy *Thesmophoriazusae.*

44   *Karl Schelling.* Because this is the only substantive footnote entered by Karl Schelling into the text of his father's lecture, one may take it that he recognizes the importance of both *Schmachten,* "languishing," and *Sehnsucht,* "languor" or "longing." Perhaps it is less useful to subordinate one term to the other as a modifier than to see the two in synergy with one another across time. Schelling's thesis seems to be nothing short of revolutionary; it is surely fair to say that languor and languishing offer an idea of deity that challenges every familiar traditional concept.

44   *Zeruané akherené.* Schelling's reference to "time without limits" in the Persian cosmogonies touches on a persistent question in his philosophy: How can the original unity of being have been sundered into pairs of opposites such as light and dark, good and evil, health and illness, female and male—by what sort of scission or crisis can this have occurred? Or can it be that duality, the *Dyas,* is primordial?

47   ὁρᾶτε εἰ τούτου ἐρᾶτε. "Now, see if this is what you would love." This proposal is made by Hephaistos in Aristophanes's tale of the lovers who want to be joined together—as though by a kind of welding—in life and in death. It is the first line on page 208 of the Zweibrücken edition, having the now commonly used Stephanus number 192e 5. There is an important reference

A head attributed to Skopas from about 340 BCE, presumably from the Hall of the Choral Dancers.

to the future in Hephaistos's proposal, a future that chance or luck may or may not bring: ἂν τούτου τύχητε, which Ficino translates using the word *futurum: videte, an hoc sit, quod ardetis, satisque futurum sit vobis.* ("See if this would be what you are ardent for, and what would satisfy you, were it to be your future.")

With regard to the three statues by Skopas at Megara, namely, "Eros," "Himeros," and "Pothos," Schelling is at pains to distinguish carefully between them. The usual translations of Pausanias's *Guide to Greece* have him saying, "Skopas made [the statues of] Eros and Desire and Sex, if the names differ in the same way as the statues." This last cryptic or elliptical if-clause, according to Schelling, means that each statue in fact expresses a "unique mode of comportment." Schelling is concerned above all to show that Pothos is not "sex" but languor and languishing, even a form of mourning, at all events a response to a love that has gone missing and now belongs to the irretrievable past. Here too we find the parallel thought that "the languor that languishes over a lost object . . . can scarcely be thought otherwise than as feminine," assuredly an allusion to Axieros or Demeter. Our thanks to Sean Kirkland and Michael Naas for help with this reference.

48   The first three Hebrew words in this note seem to be identical due to missing diacritical marks; they are in fact three slightly different words. Schelling claims that the central syllable in both the second and third Cabirian names, Axio*kers*a and Axio*kers*os, derives from the Latin form of Demeter, namely, Ceres, related to cultivated fields but also to the practice of magic and to fire. How all of that relates to the languor and languishing that Schelling has thus far emphasized for the figure of Demeter remains an essential question.

53   Here and in the following notes Schelling is drawn to the figure of Persephone as sorceress and as a bright—even fiery—light.

58   *"Hades and Dionysos are the same."* Once again, this is a reference to Heraclitus's fragment B 15 in the collection by Diels-Kranz.

64   *reminiscent of the Χρυσώρ of Sanchuniathon, who is said to be Hephaistos.* Sanchuniathon is reputed to have been a Phoenician writer of the ninth century BCE who lived in either Beirut, Tyre, or Sidon. He wrote a cosmogony and a zoogony, listed the various generations of gods, testified to the divinity

of serpents, and reported on the practice of human sacrifice. Fragments of his writings were preserved by Eusebius and Philo of Byblos. One can hardly be surprised if the "gold" that is attached to his name is associated with or even called *Hephaistos*, the god of metallurgy, associated with fire and the forge. Schelling's abstruse and wide-ranging note on the root *kers-* in the second and third names of the Cabiri, tries to connect the theme of magic (and theurgy) to the taming of fire by a fire that is also moisture, the pyrotechnic magic that would be "the primal instigator of nature." Once again, at the end of the long endnote, Schelling alludes to Heraclitus, the philosopher of "ever-living fire" and "the changes of fire." The goal seems to be to think of the transition from Persephone-Axiokersa to Dionysos-Axiokersos, whom Schelling, invoking now the supreme form of Dionysos, feels he can also call the demiurge. Later in his lecture, he will identify Dionysos as "the god of the spirit-world," although by *spirit* he means not what one might think of as the "immaterial world" but "gentle life and tender corporality." In the 1811 draft of *The Ages of the World*, searching for a kind of materiality that is to an equal degree spiritual, he takes as his examples gold, oil, and "balsam," the last meaning the moisturizing ethereal oils of plants that support the health and beauty of animals and human beings. For the 1811 and 1813 drafts of *The Ages of the World*, see F. W. J. Schelling, *Die Weltalter Fragmente: In den Urfassungen von 1811 und 1813*, Nachlaßband to the Münchner Jubiläumsdruck (Munich: Biederstein und Leibniz, 1946), here at I 60–61.

64   *Oseri, cum Jod quasi gentilitio, "with an iota, as though indicating a tribe."* The meaning here is mysterious, the translation perforce speculative. The word *Jod* normally means—and is the symbol of—iodine, but the reference could also be to the tenth letter of the Hebrew alphabet, *Yodh*. This letter, the smallest of all, "scarcely worth an iota," as we say, is nonetheless important in the name *Adonai*, which is a name for God and also indicates the number ten. More probable is the explanation that Schelling is merely adding an *i* to *Oser*, indicating the genitive case, as in *puer, pueri*, thus suggesting "the people of Oser." *Gentilitio*, usually written as *gentilicius, -io*, the origin of the word *Gentile*, refers to membership in a particular *tribe* or *clan*. The translators, with the help of Lena Rudolph (to whom our thanks), have settled for this particular sense—but not without misgivings. In truth, misgivings arise almost everywhere as one reads and attempts to understand Schelling's notes.

64   *metathesis.* Metathesis is a term in linguistics indicating the transposition of letters or syllables in a word. Children practice it when they ask for *pasghetti* instead of *spaghetti.* As Schelling suggests, metathesis is quite common in Hebrew. In the present case, Schelling is concerned with the Hebrew word or words for *fire.* Philosophers today will doubtless find it difficult to follow Schelling's thinking of magic, incantation, and the subduing of fire. Yet they might recall the culmination of Jacques Derrida's *Of Spirit,* which is driven to reflect on the Hebrew word *ruah,* usually rendered as "spirit," in the context of Heidegger's interpretation of Trakl's "flame of spirit." Derrida argues that Heidegger would have done well to open himself to certain Jewish traditions that think *ruah* precisely as fire, perhaps even as "the fire in fire," as Schelling says, rather than shutting himself up within an unreflected Greek-Latin-German interpretation of *pneuma-spiritus-Geist.* In Derrida's view, what is at stake is not merely a matter of understanding "spirit," which would be important enough for any philosopher, but of coming to see the *foreclosure* in Heidegger's thinking of the *epochs* of being, a foreclosure that threatens Heidegger's entire project of a "history of being." It is no accident that Schelling plays an important role in Derrida's reflections here and that even the island of Samothrace is mentioned, albeit by way of Hegel. (See *De l'esprit* [Paris: Galilée, 1987], 161n. 1.) In Schelling's lecture and notes, the *movement* from Axieros as languor, hunger, and obsession to Axiokersa as sorceress to Axiokersos as the tamer of fire is both clearly traceable and utterly mysterious.

64   Lactantius's *The Epitome.* This work is an appendix to Lucius Caecilius Firmianus Lactantius's (ca. 250–ca. 325 CE) major work, *Institutiones Divinae, The Divine Institutes.* To repeat, this extraordinary endnote, perhaps the longest and most complex of the entire series, moves from an interpretation of Demeter (Ceres) and Persephone as sorceresses to Axiokersos or Dionysos as *Cerus manus,* the fire tamer and fabricator, that is, the demiurge as such.

72   *in the first part of* The Ages of the World. Karl Schelling introduces here an editorial note, citing particular pages in the *third* version of *The Ages of the World* to which he says his father is referring. (In the edition of his father's collected works, the reference is to SW I/8, 272ff.) There Schelling emphasizes the importance of the Old Testament, which devotees of the New Testament are often tempted to ignore: "The beginnings are what is essential; whoever is ignorant of them can never arrive at the whole" (SW I/8, 271).

Schelling focuses on the apparently *dual* figure of Elohim/Jehovah, with *Elohim* itself being a plural. He interprets Elohim as the *expressed* name of Jehovah. Another expression or communication of Elohim is "the angel of the visage," which appears to Moses as the fire of the burning bush. The figure of fire soon (SW I/8, 275ff.) leads Schelling to reintroduce the theme of *Sehnsucht*, the languor and all-consuming languishing that lie at the very basis of the Samothracian system. See also endnote 88.

72 "*The Metatron.*" Metatron or Mattatron is said to be one of the highest of the angels in certain Jewish, Christian, and Islamic traditions. The etymology and origin of the name is obscure and has been much debated since ancient times. (One interpretation is that it derives from *Mitra* or *Mithra* and thus represents a dualistic strain in an otherwise monotheistic system; such an interpretation would have been of particular interest to Schelling.) It is often understood to be "the angel of the visage" or "the messenger or herald who goes before the throne."

73 *see Larcher on Herodotus.* The reference is to Pierre Henri Larcher, 1726–1812, a classical scholar and archaeologist whose translation of Herodotus contained a great deal of useful commentary. In *Larcher's Notes on Herodotus*, we find a chronology of the ancient world derived from the information and data Herodotus gives in the *Histories*.

74 *Thus Creuzer explains the matter.* Schelling here expresses his two most important objections to a scholar he otherwise admires: he rejects Friedrich Creuzer's use of the idea of *emanation* of lower gods from a single divine source, along with Creuzer's assertion that the initial and deepest deity (Axieros-Demeter) is the uppermost god. It has to be admitted that at least on the second point, the preeminence of the goddess, contemporary archaeologists and students of the mystery cults almost universally side with Creuzer. On the Schelling-Creuzer relationship, see the essay by Alexander Bilda in this volume.

80 *Ceres is . . . the mother of numbers.* Schelling here seems to be thinking back to *Zeruané akherené*, the Persian figure of "time without limits," discussed in endnote 44. In his later lectures on *Philosophy of Mythology*, Schelling will stress the feminine nature of this figure—which might represent the maternal source of both Ormuzd and Ahriman, the principles of light and darkness, respectively. Yet Schelling may also be reflecting on the

Pythagorean *tetractys of the decad*, seeking to relate it to Demeter or Ceres as "the intelligible *Dyas*." The *tetractys* represents the very concrete way in which the Greeks represent the first four natural numbers as forming a kind of triangle, expressing the relation of 1, 2, 3, and 4 to 10, or the decad:

•

• •

• • •

• • • •

With 2, the entire figure is expressed in microcosm; the figure is repeated with 3; with 4, the series is completed on all sides and the middle point of 3 becomes the only point (the One) not exposed to any side of the triangle, as though it were an intrauterine unit. Perhaps this is what Schelling means when he writes that Persephone is the first number, the arithmetic One, and that Zeus, always the fourth number, "relates to 1, 2, and 3 precisely in the way that 2 relates to 1; and, the other way around, 2 relates itself to 1 in no other way than 4 relates to 1, 2, and 3."

84   *the forces realizing and making visible the father.* With the growing emphasis on "the father," El, Eljun, or Malki-Sedek, all of them having Kadmilos as their herald or forerunner, Schelling at least appears to be leaving Axieros-Demeter behind: instead of hunger, languor, and languishing, figures of kingship and dynasty as powers of the demiurge are now emphasized as Schelling advances upward in his ascensional system. Yet the note ends with caution, with "doubts," and calls for further research.

85   *Clement of Alexandria avows that the* ἐποπτεία. The *epopteia* is the "showing" of a sacred object, a showing that occurs as a higher and perhaps the final event in the Eleusinian and Samothracian mysteries. Note that the word *physiology* in Clement's context means "a natural object," such as a wheat stalk or an ear of corn. Schelling takes the word to mean a "philosophy of nature" in general. Such a "philosophy of nature," Schelling always believed, would be the royal road to knowledge concerning the gods and the history of consciousness as such.

87   *the sonorous Colossi of Memnon.* Schelling is here referring to a phenomenon that captured Hegel's imagination as well, namely, the massive twin statues of the enthroned Pharaoh Amenhotep III from 1350 BCE. After an earthquake in 27 BCE severely damaged the northern Colossus, it began to emit a sound—usually soon after sunrise. Such "speaking" or "singing" earned it the name "the Vocal Memnon." At the very end of note 87, Schelling refers to "the doubtless unsuspecting French" who were forced to confront such strange phenomena; the reference is presumably to Napoleon's campaigns in Egypt and Syria during the years 1798–1801. At all events, the note makes clear Schelling's resistance to the "enlightened" skepticism of his time, which seeks to demystify the wonders of both nature and culture by interpreting them as a fraud perpetrated by priests. Likewise, Schelling's contemporaries generally view the myths and mysteries of polytheism as bubbles the skeptic's needle is keen to burst. Regarding the skeptic's "enlightened" *monotheism*, however, Schelling will later say that it is most often the proud boast of people who have not yet *heard of* the other gods—and goddesses—so that the boast is based on sheer ignorance (II/1:127; see also Krell, *The Tragic Absolute*, 394 and 406n, 12).

88   *see* The Ages of the World *(SW I/8, 272ff.)*. Schelling is most likely referring to the following passage in his 1815 version (the third version) of *Die Weltalter*:

> Hence that unity in duality and duality in unity that we have recognized as what is essential in divine individuality. The two names for God, often occurring separated and often occurring connected, have always attracted the attention of all researchers. One explained in the good old times that the word "Elohim," which indicates the plural, is as a rule conjoined with a verb in the singular because the three persons should be indicated in a single essence. This view was long ago abandoned. Indeed, all arguments of analogy fight against it.
>
>   But what would there be to object to in the interpretation that, through Elohim, the divine substance, that (first of all One, but then) the Totality of the primordial forces, would be indicated? That it would indicate that which is for itself inexpressible but which is what is actually expressed through the pure, spiritual Godhead? Jehovah was in an equally originary way posited as Elohim in this relationship of the expressing of the *name* or the word. "What should I answer the children of Israel," asks Moses, "when I say to them, 'The Elohim of your fathers sends me to you' and they ask me: 'What is his

name?'" And Jehovah answered, "Hence you should say, 'Jehovah, the Elohim of your fathers, sends me to you. *That is my name* for eternity'" (*Exodus* 3:15). Here it is obvious that Jehovah should be the name of Elohim. Yet Elohim is what is addressed and so receives the name. Hence Jehovah is simply called *the name* (the expressing), as in *Leviticus* 24:11, "One of the *names* was blasphemed against," and *Deuteronomy* 28:58, "If you will not fear the *glorious name*," where, added to this in an explanatory fashion, is "and this terrible one, Jehovah, your Elohim."

With regard to Schelling's controversial way of reading Heraclitus B 32, see the explanatory note for page 27 of Schelling's lecture, above. By contrast, the translation we have offered here in endnote 88 is the one that scholars today generally accept.

91   Unfortunately, Schelling here, with his note on "the power and glory of modern Europe" arising "out of the Germanic peoples," participates in a widespread tradition among German thinkers and writers of the eighteenth and nineteenth centuries. Even though one denies that this is nationalism, much less chauvinism, there is arguably a persistent need among German philosophers from the eighteenth century through Heidegger to identify Germany as *the* nation of thinkers and poets, *the* inheritor of the Greek (or, in Schelling's case, the Pelasgian) mantle. Marx would point out that the hoped for compensations of "the German ideology" in fact mirrored the political backwardness of the petty fiefdoms throughout Germany at the time.

94   *that* Erik-appin *also demands its opposite, to wit, an ungenerous god.* Schelling does not identify this "ungenerous god," but he had been speculating for years about a primal deity that is entirely self-centered, resistant to all others and all otherness. Such a centripetal deity, as it were, is needed if the god is to *be*; yet that self-centered, ungenerous phase is bound to pass—in the direction of a yearning and eventually loving god, a personality and an existence open to the other.

94   *Hues Attes!* The meaning of this exclamation is not clear. Already in the ancient world it was a mysterious expression used in manifold contexts, for example—only one among others—it was an epithet or perhaps an invocation of Dionysos. The context suggests something like a command to set forth to do the god's bidding, perhaps something like the Roman Catholic *ite, missa est*, meaning not merely "go, the mass is over," but "go, you are sent!" On "Hues Attes!" see the comment in Theophilus Gale, *The Court of*

the Gentiles, or, a Discourse Touching the Original of Human Literature, Both Philologie and Philosophie, from the Scriptures and Jewish Church (Oxford: Hall, 1672), 2:26–27.

99 ... *the name of Berytus*. Berytus is the ancient name of what is now Beirut, Lebanon, originally the ancient Phoenician village of Biruta. Although the Greeks called it *Laodicea*, the Romans, after conquering it in 64 BCE, called it Berytus, thus reviving its former Phoenician name.

99 *Poseidon is the antithesis of the Cabiri*. Poseidon's wrath against Odysseus and his effort to destroy Odysseus's raft are discussed in song 5 of *The Odyssey*. Odysseus's rescue by the goddess Ino Leukothea is a story important to the rites on Samothrace. But here Schelling refers to song 21 of *The Iliad*. Presumably, he means lines 436–60, where Poseidon urges Apollo to join the fight against the Trojans and to annihilate men, women, and children without mercy.

99 *One must remember what Herodotus also said about Poseidon*. Schelling here returns to the discussion in endnote 94 about the putative Egyptian origin—or at least the foreign, non-Greek origin—of the names of the Greek gods. In the same passage (book II, "Euterpe," section 46 of the *Histories*), Herodotus claimed "that the Egyptians say that they do not know the names either of Poseidon or of the Dioscouroi, nor have these been accepted by them as gods among the other gods" (G. C. Macauley translation).

99 *Bochart's explanation of the* Patäken. The Πάταικοι were dwarflike apotropaic figures used as ornaments on the prows of the Phoenician triremes. Intriguing in this endnote is the opposition between Poseidon, the unruly ruler of the sea, and the Cabirian figures attached to the prows of ships—perhaps in hopes of holding the boards of these ships together against the onslaught of the waves.

104 *a wood sprite living in the mountains and in mineshafts*. Schelling now moves into the oddest part of his discourse on "the oldest system of humanity." Having begun with the hunger and neediness of the goddess and then identifying Dionysos as the principle of moisture and the tamer of Persephone's fire, such that Dionysos himself may be identified with the demiurge, Schelling now returns to those Hephaistoi or intramundane gods who forge metals—dwarflike creatures, pygmies, small of stature but great in

power—identifying those gods as *kobolds* and hence *Kabeiroi*. A recent writer on mythology, Roberto Calasso, says this about the age-old tradition of the little people or gods who have magic powers:

> In the solitude of the primordial world, the affairs of the gods took place on an empty stage, with no watching eyes to mirror them. There was a rustling, but no clamor of voices. Then, from a certain point on (but at what point? and why?), the backdrop began to flicker, the air was invaded by a golden sprinkling of new beings, the shrill, high-pitched cry of scores of raised voices. Dactyls, Curetes, Corybants, Telchines, Silens, Cabiri, Satyrs, Maenads, Bacchants, Lenaeans, Thyiads, Bassarides, Mimallones, Naiads, Nymphs, Titires: who were all these beings? To evoke one of their names is to evoke them all. They are the helpers, ministers, guardians, nurses, tutors, and spectators of the gods.... We don't even know whether they are gods, *daímones*, or human beings. But what is it that unites them, what makes them a single group, even when different and distant from one another? They are the initiated, the ones who have seen. They are those who let themselves be touched by the divine. (Roberto Calasso, *The Marriage of Cadmus and Harmony*, 302)

107 *that all higher and better faith appears . . . under the form of mystery doctrine?* Schelling's argument throughout this endnote is in tension with his initial claim that no major discrepancy between the mystery cults and the publicly supported myths and cults of the Greeks would have been tolerated. True, Schelling adds that the "best" people of antiquity, such as Xenophon, gravitated toward a monotheism, and his general thesis is that the mystery religions, especially the cult of the Great Gods on Samothrace, constitute the oldest and most noteworthy and exceptional system in history. Perhaps the tension noted here runs parallel to that between *Schmachten* and *Stärke* in deity as such, Schelling sometimes stressing the languishing of deity, at other times celebrating the strength and supernatural power of the Cabirian gods and the demiurge they serve.

108 With regard to *excess*, Schelling cites the following sources: Job 31:25 reads: "If I have rejoiced over my *great* wealth, the fortune my hand had gained" (NIT). Job 8:2 reads: "How long will you say such things? Your words are a *blustering* wind" (NIT). *Gebhurah*, גבורה, "strength," is also the fifth *sephirah* of the cabalistic Tree of Life. The *Targum Jonathan* is the Aramaic translation of the *Nevi'im*, or Prophets. Samuel 4:4 reads as follows: "So the people sent men to Shiloh, and they brought back the ark of the covenant of

the Lord Almighty, who is enthroned between the cherubim. And Eli's two sons, Hophni and Phinehas, were there with the ark of the covenant of God" (NIV). As for the figures Schelling identifies as most proximate to the Cabiri, or Kabeiroi, the Korybantes, here is W. K. C. Guthrie's account:

> The Great Mother of Phrygia had a train of attendant daemons called Korybantes, and since from the earliest times of which we have record Thracian and Phrygian religion are closely akin the Korybantes are brought into relation with Dionysos also, whose home (though we cannot be certain) was probably Thrace. That they were the servants of a cult of ecstatic or orgiastic type is made plain, to take a single example, by the way in which the Greeks formed a verb from their name. "To korybant" (κορυβαντιᾶν) meant to be in a state of divine madness in which hallucinations occurred. It was known to the medical writers of Greece as a pathological condition. (Guthrie, *The Greeks and Their Gods*, 154)

Guthrie goes on to mention the identification of the Thracian-Phrygian Korybantes with the Kouretes of Crete, who protected Zeus at his birth, dancing around the infant and clashing their spears against their shields, drowning out the infant's cries so that the all-devouring Kronos would not hear them.

109   The translation from Varro's *On the Latin Language* is by Ronald G. Kent (Cambridge: Harvard University Press, 1938), 55, here slightly altered.

110   The translation from Vergil's *Aeneid* is by H. R. Fairclough, with some alterations.

111   *the Idaean Daktyloi, and Telchines*. These are among the dwarflike figures that populate Greek mythology generally. The Daktyloi were said to have arisen from the cave on Mount Ida in Crete, where Rhea gave birth to Zeus: her fingers gripped the earth in her birth pangs, and on that spot, these helpmates suddenly appeared. They are thus often conflated with the Kouretes and the Korybantes. Yet they first seem to appear in Phrygia, playing a role in the rites of Kybele, the Great Mother of Asia. The Telchines are said to be dwarflike smiths who worked principally on the island of Rhodes. Called "sons of the sea," they have technical skills that allow them to form the earliest images of the gods. Since antiquity, these figures, among many others, are often associated with the Cabiri.

112   *Coelum et Terram*. The Roman historian Varro initially interprets—or at least *seems* to interpret—the Samothracian system in terms of *two*

principal deities, namely, Heaven and Earth. As Schelling reads Augustine's account of Varro in book VII of *The City of God*, however, he is at pains to suggest that Varro in fact recognizes both a *duality* of gods *and* a *threefold* deity in the Samothracian system. For Schelling, such a trinity would consist of (1) Demeter-Persephone, here considered a unity, (2) the highest form of Dionysos, which supersedes even Zeus, and (3) Kadmilos, as a forerunner of the demiurge. He interprets these, as Augustine does, in terms perhaps derived from or at least related to Plato's *Timaeus*, as (1) the "from out of which," (2) the "by means of which," and (3) the "according to which" of creation. Schelling sometimes emphasizes *duality*, especially the twofold of masculine/feminine, "which underlies all philosophy as its ground," but also the dual figures of father/son and of twins (the *Dios-kouroi* or Gemini); here he particularly stresses the threefold Cabirian system, but in both cases it is a matter of an "indissoluble sequence" and an "indivisible system." Note that Schelling's chapter references to passages in *The City of God* are often incorrect, even in comparison with contemporary editions of Augustine's text; it may well be, of course, that—as in so many cases—the typesetter jumbled the references. We have altered Schelling's references according to modern editions of *The City of God*.

113   *traces of the name* Cabiri *in other languages of the East*. The web of references that follows this phrase is difficult to unravel, to say the least. The gist of these references seems to be that in various Hebrew texts, the name *Chaverim*, which Schellings links to the Cabiri, is associated with Persian hierophants or priests, or with the Persians in general. The tendency of the note is to assert the essential sense of the Cabiri as a *company* of gods, as associates or *socii*, closely bonded to and bound up with one another. The figure of a magnetically charged chain seems to supplant that of a ladder one must ascend.

114   Apuleius (ca. 124–ca. 170 CE) cited the "twelve gods" whose visage nature has denied us, gods who are therefore accessible only to the "eye of the mind," from a verse by the early Latin writer Quintus Ennius (ca. 239–ca. 169 BCE): "Juno, Vesta, Minerva, Ceres, Diana, Venus, Mars, Mercury, Jove, Neptune, Vulcan, and Apollo."

115   *Dii Consentes*. The *Dii Consentes* are the twelve major Roman deities, consisting of the six goddesses Juno, Minerva, Vesta, Ceres, Diana, and Venus, along with the gods Mars, Mercury, Neptune, Vulcan, and Apollo, with

Jupiter as the leader of them all. When it comes to the etymology of con-*sentes*, it is important to stress Schelling's clear preference for *con-sum*, "to be together with," rather than *con-sentire*, "to take counsel with or to agree with one another." The *socii* are bound to one another by the strongest possible bond—a bond of *being*, as it were. They are born together, work their magic and communicate their magnetism together, and die together. They come to presence together and can absent themselves only in company with all the others. Perhaps it is not too fanciful to suggest that "presence" and "absence" here have to be written as pre-*sen*-ce and ab-*sen*-ce, stressing the root *sen* as meaning *Sein* or a metathetical form of *ens*, "being." The translation from Arnobius is taken from *Ante-Nicene Christian Library: Translations of the Writings of the Fathers Down to AD 325*, volume XIX, *The Seven Books of Arnobius Adversus Gentes*, ed. Alexander Roberts and James Donaldson (Edinburgh: T. & T. Clark, 1871), 178–79. Schelling, of course, is using a different text for his Arnobius citation; the translation has been altered to take into account Schelling's reading "memorationis parcissimae" instead of "miserationis parcissimae." Not long after completing the *Deities*, Schelling, in 1818, tried to improve the edition of the texts of Arnobius; see *Spicilegium observationum in novissimam Arnobii editionem*, SW I/9, 253–303. For the relevant passage here, see 285.

118   Karl Schelling's reference to *The Ages of the World* is to the page that contains the following lines:

> From this it was concluded that it indicated that the Godhead was pure breath, pure spirit. This is, as the Jews express it, the name of the essence, while Elohim is the name of the divine effects.... Presupposing this [i.e., the Pythagorean tetractys of the decad, discussed in the commentary to endnote 80], the doctrine of the unity in duality of the divine nature is deeply woven into the innermost meaning of things, even in the language of the Old Testament. First of all in the way that the plural Elohim is bound up with a verb in the singular.

120   The passage from Plato's *Phaedo* to which Schelling refers here appears in the explanatory note for page 26 of Schelling's lecture, above, concerning "*the child in us*." At the risk of repetition, let us note once again that the passage (77d–78a) does not involve a "proof for the immortality of the soul" nor is it that famous passage (64a) concerning philosophy as "preparation for dying and being dead"; rather, this passage involves Socrates's urging that Simmias

and Cebes search throughout Greece—and perhaps especially among the groups of foreigners who live in Greece—for sorcerers who are expert in charms and incantations. Such magicians, says Socrates, may charm away the fear that obsesses the "child in us," namely, the fear of death. For Schelling, the Cabirian cult, or the cult of the Great Gods on Samothrace, provides humankind with its oldest and most reliable charms of this kind. Under the influence of such incantations, initiates in the mysteries will be "better prepared to live and to die, and happier in both their living and their dying."

The Afterword. Schelling's predicament is clear. He is dedicated to the insights his research into the Samothracian system have granted him, and he places the highest value on his research and argumentation in both the lecture and its copious notes. Yet the relation of *On the Deities of Samothrace* to the major work he had been struggling to write during the five preceding years, *The Ages of the World*, is a recalcitrant one. Not long after delivering the Samothrace lecture, he decided to call it and all the notes pertaining to it a "supplement" (*Beilage*) to *The Ages of the World*. Yet not even the first volume of that work, "The Past," had appeared in print. How then can he supplement a work that has not been published and not even completed, after three attempts—indeed, a work that appears to have faltered at its initial stage? Would not *The Ages of the World* have to be the eventual supplement and *Samothrace* the principal text? Anyone who has studied Jacques Derrida's *Of Grammatology*, which has a great deal to say about "the logic of the supplement," will immediately see the knot of problems concealed here. To repeat, Schelling made three attempts to formulate "The Past," in 1811, 1813, and 1815. Yet on each occasion he refused to allow his texts—each remarkably different from the others—to appear in print. It was as though he had underestimated the problem of his *access* to what he called "the elevated past," almost as though his problem was not getting out of the past and putting it behind him but getting *into* the past. This is not the place to discuss *The Ages of the World* in detail. Yet it is safe to say that in the Cabirian system of ancient Samothrace and its Great Gods, Schelling believed he had found one of the "oldest narratives" (*älteste Erzählungen*) that could tell him and us about the ages of world, serving perhaps as "the key" to those ages. He calls his meditation on the Samothracian system "a beginning and a transition to several other works." Yet this "supplement," this "beginning" and "transition," is the last book he himself published—even though he had three more very active decades of work ahead of him. One final note: in the last two pages of his *Phenomenology of Spirit* (1807), Hegel envisages a transition from history to science; Schelling appears to suggest the opposite, namely, that science is in transition to history. Could one say that *On the Deities of Samothrace* marks Schelling's transition to history but also to story—since the German word *Geschichte* means both story and history—and to a conception of philosophy as pure dynamism, unending hermeneutical development, and even infinite "story"?

Either sunlight or the Cabirian deities alighting on the Phoniás River of Samothrace.

PART TWO

Three Essays on Schelling's *Deities of Samothrace*

4

Schelling *archaeologicus*

DAVID FARRELL KRELL

The north Aegean isle of Samothrace and its "Great Gods," Schelling's Cabirian deities, play an important role in Goethe's *Faust II*, completed sixteen years after Schelling's lecture "On the Deities of Samothrace." At the culmination of the second act, in a scene that takes place in a "Rocky Cove of the Aegean Sea," the Tritons and Nereids prove that they are more than mere fish by swimming off to Samothrace in order to fetch the Cabiri. Why? They hope that these ancient gods will be able to help one of the central figures of the *Klassische Walpurgisnacht*, namely, Homunculus, the "little human" or the "seed of humankind." For Homunculus, who is all spirit and no body, hovers ghostly in an alchemist's retort. Yet he (she? it?) would love to become embodied and thus fully human. The Sirens comment, as the mythical sea creatures depart for Samothrace and the Cabiri:

> They're gone in a trice!
> Heading straight for Samothrace,
> Vanished on a favorable wind.
> What do they think they will attain
> In the realm of the exalted Cabiri?
> These are gods! themselves quite marvelous,
> Recreating themselves on and on,
> And never knowing what they are. (lines 8070–77)

If Goethe's Sirens are right and the Cabirian deities remake themselves so regularly that they do not know what they are, the chances of the archaeologists and philosophers of later centuries knowing what they are seem slight.

When the Tritons and Nereids return, balancing the tiny Cabiri on a shield, the skeptical Sirens are unimpressed by the pygmy-like size of the gods but amazed by their power to rescue those who are in peril at sea:

> Small in form,
> Great in power,
> Rescuers of the shipwrecked,
> Gods honored since time immemorial. (lines 8174–77)

The Nereids and Tritons announce that they have brought these gods to the rocky cove not only to incarnate Homunculus, however, but also to help celebrate the perilous sea in a festival of peace. They have brought only three of the Cabiri (presumably, although Goethe does not name them, these would be Axieros-Demeter, Axiokersa-Persephone, and Axiokersos-Hades or Dionysos, the first three of the series) since the fourth (presumably, Kasmilos-Hermes) refused to come. His reason? Hermes claims to be the "proper" Cabirian deity, the "real" one, *der Rechte*, who does the thinking for the other three—a gentle slap, perhaps, at Schelling's preferential treatment of the fourth god as the acolyte and avatar of the demiurge. There is also some confusion about the *number* of the Cabiri. Actually, they are seven, say the sea creatures, but the other three (or four, if one includes Hermes) have meanwhile relocated to Olympus. Even an eighth Cabiri dwells there, although few have thought of him as a Cabiri, and that would be Zeus, if not the demiurge as such. Yet what the Nereids and Tritons emphasize about this confusion concerning their number is that the Cabiri are fundamentally unfinished, *Doch alle noch nicht fertig*. Why unfinished? Why regularly recreating themselves?

> These incomparable ones
> Want to go ever farther,
> Full of longing, they suffer hunger
> For the unattainable. (lines 8202–5)

Here Goethe is surely alluding to, and perhaps ironizing—although perhaps also paying his respects to the first interesting theological idea to arise in the past two millennia—Schelling's emphasis on *die schmachtende Sehnsucht* or *das sehnsüchtige Schmachten*, the deleterious languor and languishing, the wasting away in longing that characterizes the very provenance of the Cabiri in the sufferings of Axieros-Demeter. Homunculus, meanwhile, is underwhelmed. How could such languorous deities, consumed by their own yearning and apparently powerless to help themselves, help him get a body?

> They're all ill-shapen, seems to me,
> Botched clay pots is all I see,
> And now the wisemen gather round,
> Crack their pates on what they've found. (lines 8219–22)

Friedrich Creuzer and F. W. J. Schelling would be two of those *harte Köpfe*, at least from the point of view of an impatient spirit in a bottle, a spirit that itself, amoeba-like, looks ill-shapen. When Proteus first espies Homunculus, he cries, "A little dwarf that glows in the dark!" (line 8245), and the word *Zwerglein* is perhaps the clue to Goethe's motivation for calling on the minuscule Cabiri to help with his homunculean task. The Telchines come from Rhodes, the Daktyls from Mount Ida in Crete, to join the Cabiri of Samothrace—all the dwarfish smithy gods who guard the secrets of technology. Yet in the end the wisdom of Thales the neptunist prevails: the only way for Homunculus to get a body is to immerse himself (herself? itself?) in the celebrated sea, to assume and pass through all the myriad forms of organic life, to evolve after eons of time in the direction of a still remote humankind. One must make one's peace with the seductive sea. The beauty of Galatea, who suddenly appears on Venus's half shell, captivates the spirit of humankind, who is now all afire, himself (herself? itself?) all *Sehnen* or longing. All the elements, melting now in the elemental brine, combine to provide Homunculus, the spiritual seed of humanity, the body that it craves. "For thus rules Eros, who began it all!" (line 8479).

If Schelling turned to the Cabiri to find the oldest cult devoted to the immortality of the soul, it is Goethe who sees what Schelling in fact always desired. From the period of his philosophy of nature through the *Weltalter* project, Schelling determined to follow the path of deity that culminates in erotic, mortal embodiment.

More than once in his "Deities of Samothrace," Schelling insists—although he sometimes strikes these lines as though he is uncertain—that the earliest is not the highest, the aboriginal not the supreme, the humble beginning not the exalted end. The end seems almost everywhere to excel over its meager beginnings. To that extent, Schelling often seems to be a teleologist rather than an archaeologist, a thinker of end results rather than remote beginnings.

He seems to dedicate himself to the demiurge at the top of the divine ladder rather than to the goddesses down below "where all the ladders start." And yet he wonders about the humble beginnings of the demiurge "himself."

Schelling loves Samothrace because it is the birthplace of the "oldest system of humankind." What sort of system? Philosophical? Theological? Mythological? Difficult to say, precisely because it is so archaic. Like any archaeologist, Schelling digs for the gold of origins, the gold of the Golden Age, way back when. Why? Because the highest must still bear traces of the deepest, in which it is grounded, traces of the oldest, which contains the seed of everything to follow. Had Schelling been given the chance to visit the sanctuary of the Great Gods on Samothrace, he would not have left his spade behind—he would have dug into ever deeper strata, sifting through the powdery earth and brushing off with loving care every object he found. He would have become what in fact he always wanted to be: Schelling *archaeologicus*.

Let us therefore pursue the archaeologist in Schelling, and in seven respects, paying heed to (1) the literary sources for the ancient cult at Samothrace; (2) the material sources, that is, recent archaeological finds at the excavations on the site of the Great Gods, virtually none of these available to Schelling and his contemporaries; (3) the enigma of the *language* spoken and written at the Samothracian sanctuary throughout the centuries when the mystery cult was active; (4) the apparently dual origin of the Samothracian cult, involving as it does both (a) the rescue of endangered sailors from storms at sea and (b) the more familiar sorts of agricultural or fertility cults of the mysteries throughout Greece, especially the cult of Demeter at Eleusis; (5) the problem of the identities of the Great Gods themselves and their questionable relation to the Cabirian deities to which Schelling is so strongly drawn—for here contemporary archaeologists are far more skeptical about this relation than Schelling was. Perhaps skepticism should not be the final word, however, so that one might envisage something like a "return" of the Cabiri to Samothrace, a return that contemporary archaeology may only grudgingly accept. Let us therefore (6) try to follow "the path of initiation" for someone who comes to Samothrace to be initiated into the mysteries, after which we will add (7) a brief concluding word.

No doubt each of these topics encroaches on all the others, so that some repetition will be unavoidable. In the course of these analyses and speculations, I will try to state as straightforwardly and concisely as I can the impact of all this archaeology on the *philosophical speculation* we find in Schelling's quite astonishing lecture and notes, indeed with respect to some of his most remarkable claims, namely, (1) the importance of *goddesses* for "the oldest system," whether they are enraged or caught up in suffering, mourning, and longing; (2) the importance of poverty, hunger, and powerlessness rather than majesty, might, and glory for the character of the original deities of Samothrace and, in Schelling's view, for deity "as such"; and finally, expanding the scope of the inquiry beyond Schelling himself, (3) the importance of at least some aspects of Schelling's "Deities of Samothrace" for discussions among philosophers today—whether or not they have ever heard of Samothrace or its great gods and goddesses.

It is necessary to begin with a caveat. It is extremely rare to find classicists and archaeologists agreeing about anything, rarer still to find such agreement persisting over the centuries from antiquity to the present day. Yet about Samothrace almost all agree, and they almost always have done so. The agreement, unfortunately, is a Socratic one, namely, the concession that we know almost nothing about the ancient mysteries on the island. In the early 1890s, archaeologist Otto Rubensohn spoke for everyone before and after him—with the possible exception of Schelling—when he wrote, "Concerning the cult of this site, next to Eleusis the most significant site of the mystery cults in Greece, we know to all intents and purposes nothing at all; we cannot be completely certain of a single point with regard to it, and much here will have to remain hypothesis" (OR 125). The literary basis for our understanding of the cult is "confused," says Rubensohn, if only because ancient authors, fearing sacrilege, were careful not to betray too much about the mysteries. The Homeric *Hymn to Demeter* alludes to these "awful mysteries that no one may in any way transgress or pry into or utter, for deep awe of the gods checks the voice" (lines 478–79). If the very root of *mystery* is μύω, to close or shut—said especially of the eyes and mouth—it is little wonder that so much about the mysteries lies concealed. For that reason we must, says Rubensohn, place our confidence in "monuments" alone. Yet the history of the archaeological digs on the island seems to consist principally of each generation denying the antiquity and cultic significance of virtually every find uncovered by the previous generation. It is difficult not to agree with Walter Burkert when he asserts that the archaeological evidence on Samothrace remains so much in dispute that willy-nilly we are cast back upon those confusing and often cryptic literary sources of antiquity (B93 178–91). This is not to deny Rubensohn's central argument about the source of the confusion in the literary testimonies. Ancient authors, as he says, in addition to the secrecy they had to respect, were always anxious to compare the unknown with what was known. Because, for example, they were familiar with the Cabirian deities of Boeotian Thebes and Egyptian Memphis, and because the Korybantes, Kouretes, Telchines, Daktyls, and other such ancillary deities were familiar to them from the worship of Phrygian Kybele and Cretan Rhea, they assumed that Samothrace must have been home to the similarly ancillary Cabiri, even though not a single surviving inscription on the island refers to the Cabiri as such. The surviving inscriptions refer instead only to "the Great Gods," the Θεοὶ Μεγάλοι.

The origin of the very name *Cabiri* is likewise obscure. Carl Kerényi confirms the generally accepted view that the *Kabeiroi* are more closely associated with the island of Lemnos than they are with Samothrace (CK 189). One cannot even be sure that κάβειροι is a Greek name, although Kerényi cites a possible Greek derivation: when Rhea hid her infant son Poseidon on the isle of Rhodes, which is the isle of the dwarflike Telchines, she appointed as his nurse Kapheira, a daughter of Okeanos (CK 180). "On the more northerly islands of the Mediterranean she was also called Hekate, Kabeiro, or Demeter Kabeiria, and was thought to be the mother of the Kabeiroi" (CK 184).

Some sixty years after Otto Rubensohn recorded his doubts, Bengt Hemberg expressed even more skepticism about the presence of Cabirian divinities on Samothrace. From the archaeologist's point of view, Hemberg insisted, Schelling's entire effort is spurious—although in fairness one would have to remember that Schelling himself expresses doubts (in his lecture, immediately prior to note 110) about whether the Cabiri *and* the Great Gods occur on that island. Only one thing seems to be certain about the Great Gods of Samothrace, in Hemberg's view, and that is that initially some form of the Anatolian Mother-Goddess is the principal figure of worship there and that therefore the gods of Samothrace are chthonic deities (BH 29). Despite Schelling's insistence that the deepest is not the uppermost, contemporary archaeologists would assert that the Mother is at both the bottom and the top of the ascendant sequence, if sequence and ascent there be. Not only is a Kybele-like figure chief among the deities on Samothrace, argues Hemberg, but also the enigmatic figure of Kasmilos cannot be identified with the Olympian Hermes, the herald of Zeus (BH 100–103). Although everything here remains hypothetical, the hypothesis that Kasmilos is both Hermes and the Old Testament Angel of the Visage, hence the project supervisor of the demiurge himself, is one that no archaeologist today could ever accept. Given those caveats, perhaps we can begin our analyses and speculations.

1. The Ancient Literary Sources

There are some 243 references to Samothrace in the ancient literary tradition (AG 231). Antiphon of Athens, who flourished in the fifth century BCE, offers the most ancient testimony: "For those who originally settled the island were Samians, and from them we are descended. They settled by necessity, not by desire of the island; for they were expelled from Samos by tyrants and experienced this misfortune; after seizing booty from Thrace, they arrived at the island" (AG 232). A fragment from Aristotle's *Constitution of Samothrace* records: "Samothrace was originally called Leukania because of being white [or "radiant," "shining"], but later, when Thracians occupied it, it was called Thrakia. When the Thracians had left it, Samians settled it seven hundred years later, after having been expelled from their own country, and they called it Samothrace" (ibid.). Aristotle's account gives rise to the question as to whether the island was unoccupied when the Samians colonized it—a most unlikely scenario, archaeologists agree, inasmuch as they have uncovered Neolithic settlements there.

Another ancient testimony (from Pseudo-Scymnus) adds Trojans into the mix of settlers on Samothrace: Samothrace is "a Trojan island, which has mixed inhabitants" (AG 232–33). Pseudo-Scymnus elaborates: "The Samothracians, being Trojan by race, although called Thracians due to their geographical position, stayed in the place because of piety. But once during a time of famine the Samians supplied them; at that time they received some settlers from Samos and had them as fellow-inhabitants" (AG 233). Herodotus, who visited Samothrace and was initiated into the mysteries, refers to the ancient dwellers on the island as Pelasgians, a common term in ancient Greek literature unfortunately without any specific ethnic or geographical reference (AG 234). Pelasgians seem to constitute any given indigenous population (AG 248n. 103). Herodotus writes: "Anyone who has been initiated into the secret rites of the Cabiri, which the Samothracians derived from the Pelasgians and now practice, knows what I mean. Samothrace was formerly inhabited by those Pelasgians who used to dwell among the Athenians, and it is from them that the Samothracians derive their secret rites. Thus the Athenians, who learned from the Pelasgians, were the first of the Greeks to make ithyphallic statues of Hermes. The Pelasgians told a kind of sacred story about this, and it is disclosed in the mysteries at Samothrace (*Histories* 2:51, 2–4). The reference to the archaic mix of Pelasgians and Athenians is puzzling, yet the mention of Hermes as a Pelasgian chthonic deity, symbolized by ithyphallic statues, is noteworthy.

Strabo, on whom Schelling often depends, is, according to Graham, the only ancient author to contest in a serious way the Samian colonization of Samothrace (AG 235–36). For Strabo, Samothrace is the Thracian Σάμος only in the sense that it is a "lofty place," a summit from which a god might survey everything down below. In this context, Strabo alludes to Homer, who, speaking of Mount Phengari on Samothrace, says, "For from thence all Ida was plain to see, and plain to see were the city of Priam and the ships of the Achaeans," lines from the *Iliad* (13:10–14) that Schelling cites in his *Deities*. Graham takes some pains to discredit Strabo's ancient sources, Demetrios of Skepsis and Apollodoros, arguing instead for the prevailing ancient view that Samothrace was indeed colonized by Samians. His thesis is that ancient literary and contemporary archaeological evidence alike suggest that the Ionian Greeks of Samos colonized Samothrace in the first half of the sixth century BCE. This is not to say, however, that the island was unpopulated at the time. To repeat, archaeologists have confirmed that the island was richly settled already in Neolithic times, over four thousand years prior to the Samian settlement (MB 25–28).

Against Karl Lehmann, the leading archaeologist at the Samothracian site for most of the twentieth century, who argues for *Aeolian* Greek colonization, perhaps because of the proximity of Troy to Aeolia, Graham argues for the Ionian-Samian colonization with a *terminus ante quem* of 550 BCE (AG 239). Graham also contests Lehmann's claims about the antiquity of certain finds in the sanctuary by citing Lehmann's successor, archaeologist James R. McCredie, who concedes that he "had found no stratum anywhere, in more than a dozen years of digging, that is earlier than the middle of the fifth century B.C."[1] The range of possible dates for the Samian colonization

---

1. AG 243. McCredie's revisions of Karl and Phyllis Lehmann's findings, especially their dating, are summarized by the most detailed scholarly account in English of the Samothracian mysteries: Susan Guettel Cole, *Theoi Megaloi: The Cult of the Great Gods at Samothrace* (Leiden, Belgium: E. J. Brill, 1984), cited henceforth as SC with page number. Cole's first three chapters, especially the third, are important for my account throughout.

of Samothrace would therefore be from 550 to 450 BCE (AG 245–48). Current archaeological excavation of the cemeteries near the sanctuary may be able to push this dating back to a higher range, but because cremation was the prevailing custom among the Greek settlers, the remains in the *nekropoloi* offer scanty evidence. What does seem clear is that Samothrace was continuously populated (whether by an autochthonous race, by Pelasgians, or by Thracians remains unclear) from Neolithic times onward (i.e., from the fifth millennium BCE) through the middle Bronze Age in the second millennium and into the current era. One is forced to concede that so far none of this supports Schelling's thesis, criticized already by his contemporaries, that it was the Phoenicians who introduced the Great Gods to Samothrace.

Graham notes that the cult of the Cabiri was practiced on the neighboring islands of Lemnos and Imbros, the former island populated by the Tyrrhenians, a non-Hellenic people with their own language (AG 249). Whether Samothrace itself was a site of the Cabirian cult remains uncertain. Many of the inscriptions on Samothrace (none of which, to repeat, refer to the Cabiri by that name), while written in the Greek script, are not Greek but reflect some barbarian tongue. Whether that language can be called "Thracian," as Karl Lehmann assumes, is uncertain; linguists concede that it could well be an Indo-European language, *perhaps* Thracian (AG 250–51). This non-Greek language may have been adopted by the colonizing Samians themselves as a liturgical language, and this would account for its survival. Graham writes:

> The simplest conclusion to be drawn from the above discussion is that a non-Greek language was in use on Samothrace for a very long period after the Greek colony had been established. There are two possible users of this language: a non-Greek people, who used Greek letters to write their own language, or the Greeks using their own alphabet but a foreign language. The latter possibility must be admitted, since Diodorus [of Sicily] (5.47.3) states that many words of the earlier autochthonous language were used as a *lingua sacra* in the Samothracian cult down to his own day. (AG 254)

More on the language of the cult—Indo-European? Western Semitic?—in a moment. Meanwhile, if Graham's surmise is correct, it seems likely that the Greek colonizers from Samos mixed with a native non-Greek population that continued to live on the island. The hypothesis that these aboriginal inhabitants abandoned the island when the Greeks arrived is unlikely to be correct. Graham concludes that "before the Greek colonists came to Samothrace, it was occupied by a population who were probably Thracians, worshiped the Cabiri, and maintained close contacts with the neighboring islands of Lemnos and Imbros"; the mystery of those indigenous peoples who occupied the island some four thousand years before the Greeks colonized it—were they Thracian? Tyrrhenian? Phoenician?—remains closely guarded up to the present day (AG 255).

Returning to the ancient literary sources, Apollonius of Rhodes, born in Alexandria in the first half of the third century BCE, tells us at least something, albeit precious little (in book I, lines 913ff. of his *Argonautica*) about Samothrace and its gods. Jason and his crew are escaping from Lemnos, where they have been laboring away at repopulating the island—the Lemnian women, prior to Jason's arrival, having murdered their husbands for reasons that are disputed but in each case gripping. Jason addresses his farewell to Hypsipyle of Lemnos in the way that Odysseus addresses Kalypso, and the Argonauts set sail for Samothrace—called here *Electra*, perhaps in recollection of the name *Leukania*, the "shining" isle: "Whereupon they mightily smote the water with their long oars, and in the evening, accompanied by the injunctions of Orpheus, they touched at the island of Electra, daughter of Atlas, in order that by gentle initiation they might learn the rites that may not be uttered, and so with greater safety sail of the chilling sea. Of these rites I will make no further mention; but I bid farewell to the island itself and the indwelling deities to whom belong those mysteries, which it is not lawful for me to sing."

The invocation pronounced by Orpheus as they approach the isle of Electra at eventide, ἑσπέριοι (line 915), suggests that they are approaching sacred land just as the nocturnal rites are about to begin, rites concerning which it is forbidden to speak. And so it has been down through the ages. We know very little about ancient Electra, or Leukania, or Samothrace. And about that enticing "gentle initiation," ἀγανῇσι τελεσφορίῃσι, we know next to nothing.

Yet why "gentle"? Robert Graves, in his account of the voyage of the Argonauts, confirms that "they sailed for Samothrace, where they were duly initiated into the mysteries of Persephone and her servants, the Cabeiri" (RG 2:225). But again, why "gentle"? Schelling's friend Hölderlin calls Persephone *zornigmitleidig... ein Licht*, a light that is "furiously compassionate."[2]

---

2. See Hölderlin's translation of Sophocles's *Antigone*, line 926, in *Friedrich Hölderlin Sämtliche Werke und Briefe*, 3 vols., ed. Michael Knaupp (Munich: Carl Hanser, 1992), 2:351; 3:439. Cited from hence as CHV by volume and page.

Schelling himself thinks of Persephone as both a magician, not far removed from Hekate, and a tender maid, Κόρη. The word ἀγανός means "tender, gentle," and is often used to designate traits of Artemis and Apollo when these gods grant mortals a peaceful death. Some speculate that the word derives from ἄγαμαι, "to marvel at, to be astonished, to admire" but also "to be jealous or envious" of someone, hence to be "irritated" by the sight of them. In this latter sense, it would be related to ἀγανακτέω, an important word for Plato's *Timaeus*, in which the effects of Aphrodite and the erotic in general are described as "irritating." Another possibility is that ἀγανός derives from the negation of γανός, "sparkling, shining," said of a face radiating joy. One would hardly desire its negation, unless perhaps dying is conceived of as a gradual, peaceful dulling of the senses and evanescence of life. In any case, the adjective is most likely related to peace and gentle repose. "Initiation" here translates τελεσφορίῃσι, derived from τελεσφορία but in its literal sense, as τελεσφόρησις, referring to "the power to bring to term, to bring to maturity and perfection." One hears in the word a reminiscence of τέλος as end in the sense of "accomplishment" but also "consummation," that is, death (RC 244). "Gentle initiation" into the mystery religions, including that on Samothrace, perhaps means initiation—with the least possible pain—into the mortal condition as such. There are reasons to suppose that Schelling thought of it precisely in this way.

What exactly did Jason and his fellow heroes experience that night on Samothrace? The Laurentian scholiast to Apollonius of Rhodes (at 1:917), following the account of the Alexandrian scholar Mnaseas of Patara, lists the names of the four gods identified as Cabirian. If Schelling is right, Jason and the Argonauts would have learned about this divine fourfold during their initiation. The following table shows the Samothracian (Thracian-Phrygian? Phoenician?) names with what the scholiast and Mnaseas claim to be their Greek equivalents:

Ἀξίερος, Axieros	=	Δημήτηρ, Demeter
Ἀξιοκέρσα, Axiokersa	=	Περσεφόνη, Persephone
Ἀξιόκερσος, Axiokersos	=	Ἅιδης, Hades
Κασμῖλος, Kasmilos	=	Ἑρμῆς, Hermes.[3]

---

3. For a dizzying account of the debate surrounding the names of the Cabirian deities, see the article "Kabeiroi" in *Pauly-Wissowa* (KP 3:34–38).

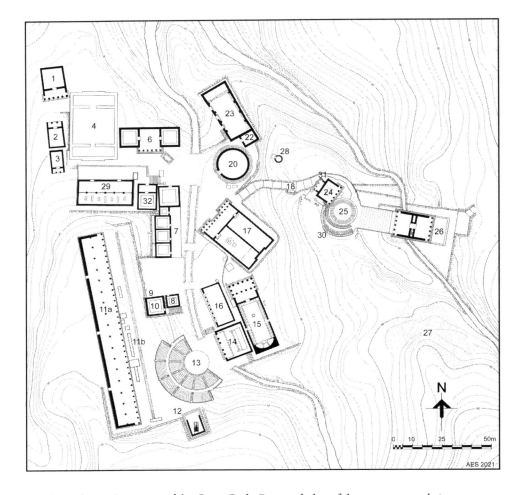

Samothrace. Sanctuary of the Great Gods. Restored plan of the sanctuary early in first century of the current era. 1, 2, 3: unidentified Late Hellenistic buildings; 4: unfinished Early Hellenistic building (Building A); 6: Milesian Dedication; 7, 8, 10: dining rooms; 9: Archaistic niche; 11: Stoa; 12: Nike monument; 13: theater; 14: Altar Court; 15: Hieron; 16: Hall of Votive Gifts; 17: Hall of Choral Dancers; 18: Sacred Way; 20: Rotunda of Arsinoë II; 22: Sacristy; 23: Anaktoron; 24: Dedication of Philip III and Alexander IV; 25: theatral circle; 26: Propylon of Ptolemy II; 27: South Necropolis: 28: Doric rotunda; 29: Neorion; 30: stepped retaining wall; 31: Ionic porch; 32: Hestiatorion (© American Excavations Samothrace, used with permission).

But again, what would Jason and his crew have experienced that night? For this we have to turn to the insights that recent archaeologists have attained by excavation and study. Karl Lehmann's many articles on the sanctuary, along with his detailed guide to the site, is perhaps the place to begin.[4]

2. Recent Archaeological Finds

Lehmann, the head archaeologist at the Samothracian excavations from the late 1930s until the end of the 1960s, himself begins with a brief summary of the early excavations on Samothrace, which were in fact fewer and far less fruitful than one might have imagined:

> The island of Samothrace, the "Delos" of the northern Aegean, is today less accessible than any of the larger Greek islands. This inaccessibility has contributed perhaps to the comparative absence of methodical investigation, which began only after the casual discovery of the famous Victory,[5] with

---

4. See now, in addition to other sources cited below, Sandra Blakely, "Kadmos, Jason, and the Great Gods of Samothrace: Initiation as Mediation in a Northern Aegean Context," in *Electronic Antiquity: Communicating the Classics*, 11:1 (November 2007), cited as SB.

5. The famous statue of Nike that today dominates the grand staircase of the Denon Wing of the Louvre is a Hellenistic monument, erected early in the second century BCE, which is quite late in the history of the Samothracian cult of the Great Gods. Yet various aspects of the statue—analyzed by Heiner Knell as an extraordinary work of art in its own right but also as crucial for the cult site as a whole—point back to an archaic history. Whereas the citizens of Rhodes appear to have erected the statue in honor of their recent victory over the Seleucid dynasty, the theme of a winged Victory landing on the prow of a ship is an ancient one. The very fact that Victory is landing safely on the prow of a warship (the so-called *prora*, itself mounted at the rear of a fountain high above the cult site) recalls the story of Leukothea and the early reputation of Samothrace as a site of rescue for endangered mariners. The erotic aspect of the statue calls to mind both the Roman dedication to Venus Victrix and much older connections with the goddesses Kybele, Astarte, Urania, Demeter, and eventually Aphrodite. This is not the Aphrodite whom Diomedes can wound on the hand and whom the other gods can therefore ridicule but the Aphrodite who instigates wars and brings peace among both gods and mortals. Especially helpful in the present context of the deities of Samothrace is Knell's chapter, "The Samothracian Sanctuary of the Cabiri," which is richly illustrated and gives the reader an excellent

A view of the cult site from the top of the theater where the "Winged Victory" once stood: the columns of the Hieron are on the right; to the left are the Altar Court and the Hall of the Votive Gifts; beyond the Hieron are the Hall of the Choral Dancers and the Rotunda of Arsinoë II.

a subsequent French expedition in the sixties of the past century [i.e., the nineteenth], and the two Austrian excavations in the following decade.... With the exception of a few fruitless trial digs in the ancient town by the first French expedition, methodical work has been confined to the sanctuary of

---

impression of the splendor of the cult site during Hellenistic and Roman times. When one views Knell's reconstruction of the position of the statue, which dominates the theater and the entire cult site (see his illustration 62 at 76–77), one has the uncanny sense that the setting of the statue today, atop one of the grand staircases of the Louvre, is actually quite fitting. See Heiner Knell, *Die Nike von Samothrake: Typus, Form, Bedeutung und Wirkungsgeschichte eines rhodischen Sieges-Anathems im Kabierenheiligtum von Samothrake* (Stuttgart: Theiss, 1997). My thanks to Professor Lore Hühn of Freiburg University, who presented me with a copy of Knell's fine study.

the Kabeiroi, which is situated near the town to the southwest. There, too, former excavations have left large areas untouched, without uncovering earlier strata. This situation is very striking in view of the general fame of the sanctuary in Greek and Roman times and the considerable importance of the town in at least some periods of antiquity. Methodical excavation, which in recent years has been repeatedly urged by prominent scholars, seemed, on the other hand, to offer promise, in view of the deserted character of the whole main archaeological area. (L39 133)

Lehmann goes on to stress the importance of more recent excavation and archaeological investigation for the history of the sanctuary: "The once world famous sanctuary of the Kabeiroi ranked among the Greek mystery sanctuaries next to that of Demeter of Eleusis, with which it constitutes the principal source for Greek mystery religion and its related art. Furthermore, the enigmatic character of the religion of the Great Gods of Samothrace, discussed for centuries, is more obscured by the written sources than any other of the mystery cults. The nature of the cult can be revealed only by excavation" (ibid.). As I noted earlier, because ancient authors, some of them initiates, were forbidden to betray the secrets of the cult, very little is actually known of liturgical practices, general beliefs, and the personalities of the Great Gods themselves. However, because excavation has up to now revealed nothing older than items from the fifth century BCE, it is also difficult to ascertain much about the origins and precise nature of the ancient cult from the archaeological finds.

Lehmann's principal discovery during the 1939 dig was the "Anaktoron," a rectangular building located to the south of the junction of the two rivers, about twenty-five meters north of the later "Arsinoeion." Lehmann dates the Anaktoron at about 500 BCE.[6] Referring to a stone that bears the bilingual

---

6. As noted earlier, most of Lehmann's dates have been revised: McCredie and Cole (see SC 12–13) suggest the third century, if not later, as a more likely date for the construction of the Anaktoron. That said, for this and all architectural and archaeological references, the essential source is still Karl Lehmann, *Samothrace: A Guide to the Excavations and the Museum*, 6th revised and enlarged edition (Thessaloniki: Institute of Fine Arts, New York University, 1998), here at 56–61. James R. McCredie has revised portions of the guide over the years, especially the third chapter, on the sanctuary of the Great Gods. Professor Bonna D. Wescoat of Emory University is now the chief archaeologist at the excavation; she and her students have produced a remarkable 3-D reconstruction and an interactive view of the entire cult site that can be found online at

warning, DEORUM SACRA QUI NON ACCEPERUNT NON INTRANT • ΑΜΥΤΟΝ ΜΗ ΕΙΣΙΕΝΑΙ, "Sacred to the gods; noninitiates shall not enter," found in the vicinity of the Anaktoron, Lehmann writes,

> Originally standing at the passage from the main to the higher rear part of our building, it [i.e., the inscription] is documentary evidence that the building was used for very important and final stages of the initiation. In other words, our building is a Telesterion [i.e., the building where a higher, concluding rite of some kind was conducted], which was in use from very early times down to the late pagan period. Furthermore, the inscription explains the division into two parts: the main part was used for the μύησις [i.e., the first part of the initiation], the rear part for the ἔποψις [the *showing* of a secret cult object]. In the older periods the stage-like layout without a permanent partition may have reflected consecutive action before the community, to which at the end, much as at Eleusis, something was revealed from the rear of the stage. (L39 138)

Added to the stone that bears the incised warning to noninitiates is the so-called *kerykeion* (κηρύκειον, the heraldic staff or insignia of Hermes, the origin of the physician's caduceus), which, along with the two snakes accompanying it, testifies to the chthonic nature of the cult and the importance of Hermes Kadmilos for it.[7] Concerning the Anaktoron, Lehmann writes,

> From Hellenistic times the main part was used as a *Theatron* for the *Dromena* and *Logoi* [i.e., as a place to witness the deeds and hear the words of the liturgy] and then the initiated *mystai* were allowed to enter the Adyton and to see there something not visible before. Of great interest, too, are the incised symbols at the end of the inscription. The *kerykeion* of Hermes Kadmilos,

---

http://samothrace.emory.edu. (Readers should be advised that the Lehmann-McCredie *Guide* is fairly difficult to find either in the United States or in Thessaloniki; one is well advised to search the various deposit libraries in the United States and Europe in order to locate a copy. The Library of Congress catalogue card number is 55–8563.) A second very useful guide, easier to come by, is D. Matsas and A. Bakirtzis, *Samothrace: A Short Cultural Guide*, 2nd revised and enlarged edition, tr. Dimitris Matsas and Bill Phelps (Athens: Ephorate of Prehistoric and Classical Antiquities, 2001), on the Anaktoron at 51–55. Finally, readers who are close to the city of Chicago should visit the School of the Art Institute to see the magnificent drawings by John Kurtich of reconstructions of many of the Samothracian buildings. My thanks to David Matthew Krell for the reference to Kurtich's drawings at the school.

7. The *Cultural Guide* cited above has fine photographs of both the Anaktoron, the warning stone, and its *kerykeion*: see figures 27 and 29.

The upper half of an engraved marble stele from the entrance to the Anaktoron, with a text in both Latin and Greek prohibiting entry to noninitiates. On the lower right, one can make out something like a caduceus (the wand of Hermes) with, to the left and right, two additional snakes.

who is the *administer* of the Great Gods of Samothrace in the ancient sources, shows him as guarding the entrance of their Abaton [i.e., the inviolable sacred space of the sanctuary]. The two snakes symbolize the διφθεῖς Κάβειροι [i.e., the twice-born, dual-natured, or twin Cabiri], who are mentioned in an Orphic hymn as assuming the form of snakes. They again point to the chthonic element of this cult. (Ibid.)

The third-century Church Father, Hippolytos, in his *Refutation of All Heresies* (5:8, 9), refers to a building of this type, an Anaktoron, where, as Lehmann says, "two famous bronze images of the Kabeiroi stood." Even if no *inscription* testifies to the presence of the Cabiri on Samothrace, Lehmann argues, these symbols and the statuary are testimony enough.[8]

---

8. The sole mention of the *Kabeiroi* in the *Cultural Guide* is to these statues. The inner sanctuary of the Anaktoron, reserved for initiates, is cut off from the larger room by a support wall, itself interrupted by two doors being "flanked by

An orange clay oil lamp carried by hand during the nocturnal initiation into the mysteries.

Many undecorated eating and drinking utensils—undecorated probably due to some cult restriction—are found throughout the site, suggesting that eating and drinking were an important part of ritual practices.[9] In a later report, Lehmann stresses the importance of these finds: "The mass of accumulated ceramics from various strata allow us to ascertain now that in

---

two bronze statues of the *Kabeiroi* with raised hands" (55). See also the Lehmann *Guide*, 60. As for the snakes that frame the *kerykeion*, W. K. C. Guthrie notes: "There are many ancient references to snake-handling in ecstatic cults, e.g. Olympias the mother of Alexander the Great is said by Plutarch to have indulged in it 'to the dismay of the menfolk'" (WG 148n 2).

9. On ritual dining as a part of the rites of Demeter and Kore on Acrocorinth, see Nancy Bookidis, "Ritual Dining at Corinth," in Marinatos and Hägg, *Greek Sanctuaries: New Approaches* (London and New York: Routledge, 1993), 45–61. On ceramic objects found at the Kabeirion near Boeotian Thebes, see Kirsten Madeleine Bedigan, "Boeotian Kabeiric Ware: The Significance of the Ceramic Offerings at the Theban Kabeiron in Boeotia" (PhD diss, University of Glasgow, March 2008).

all periods from the archaic through the Hellenistic age clay vessels were ritually used by the worshippers and afterwards dedicated or broken up and dumped in the sanctuary. In all periods, too, the mystae evidently had a lamp, a drinking vessel, and an eating dish. It is evident that drinking and participation in meals were an integral part of this as of other mystery cults, and that in Samothrace these rites go back to the archaic beginnings of the Greek cult" (L50 18).

Triangular clay votive objects found at the site may have symbolized the female genitalia (L39 140), although they may also have been supports for use in pottery kilns (SC 29), a confusion one might otherwise have thought unlikely. A faience pendant representing a Silenos head (Lehmann's fig. 11 in L39), dating from the classical period, testifies to the presence of Dionysos at the site (L39 142), as Schelling certainly anticipated. By contrast, the presence of Jupiter-Zeus and Minerva-Athena at the site seems to be a late (Roman?) recognition of the *political* powers that rule alongside the Cabirian divinities. One renders unto Athena the things that are hers and to Axieros-Demeter the fundamental things that are god's (L39 145).

Excavations at the sanctuary site resumed in 1948, after a great deal of destruction during World War II. Lehmann once again argues that investigation of the ancient sanctuary, "whose fame in antiquity almost equaled that of Eleusis," has to rely on archaeological rather than written evidence because of the enforced silence that surrounds the mystery rites (L50 2). The most important new find of the postwar excavations? In the New Temple, the Hieron or "Holy Place," Lehmann and the New York University team of archaeologists uncovered two *eskharai* (ἡ ἐσχάρα, a sacrificial hearth or ἑστία in the form of a "shallow rectangular pit" covered by a metal grill) similar to ones dating from the seventh century BCE in Crete. Such hearths remained in use for centuries, "an example of the tenacious preservation of very archaic rites in the Samothracian mysteries" (L50 5–6). Burnt sacrifices (sheep bones, according to later testimony, have been found there) are followed by libations poured into hollow shafts or *bothroi* (ὁ βόθρος) that allow the liquids to flow over sacred rocks to the gods who dwell beneath the surface of the earth. The dating of these finds, it has to be said again, is still unsettled. What seems uncontroversial, however, is Lehmann's hypothesis that at least by the Hellenistic period the Samothracian rites involved a series of nocturnal processions advancing "through a series of monumental buildings," with sundry buildings reserved for specific aspects of the ritual (L50 7).

The base of the two-story Rotunda of Arsinoë II, dating from 288–270 BCE; beneath it is the "Orthostate Structure" from the first half of the fourth century BCE, used for the first part of the initiation, the *myesis*.

The most important archaic finds, Lehmann reports, are from the Anaktoron and the "Orthostate Structure" beneath the Arsinoeion and the Anaktoron. A "Cyclopean" terrace wall of gigantic, roughly hewn stone appears to date from the late Bronze or early Iron Age. Potsherds in the vicinity resemble the type found at Troy VI–VII. "At its present northern end, this terrace includes huge boulders of a colorful variety of rock not otherwise found in this region and evidently deposited here by natural forces long before any building began" (L50 8). That would mean, presumably, long before any Hellenistic building and perhaps even prior to all Greek Ionian-Samian influence. At one end of the terrace, a crude stairway leads up to a large boulder with a flattened surface. Another upended boulder serves as a sort of parapet; a channel runs along the ground beneath the area. "These curious features and the fact that . . . the earliest Greek settlers selected this place for religious worship, point to a religious function for the structure" (ibid.). The flattened boulder with the stairway leading up to it "recalls the 'rock altars' of the Phrygian region [of central Anatolia]. The channel beneath the rock could find its natural explanation as a libation channel connected with sacrifices" (ibid.). Lehmann draws the following conclusions, some of which, to repeat, have been contested or at least questioned and challenged by later archaeologists working at the site: "The Phrygian rock altars are affiliated with the cult of the great mother goddess, Kybele. Her name occurs persistently in ancient literary sources apropos of the origin and rites of the Samothracian mysteries. And while the Mother of the Samothracian mysteries, Axieros, was also identified with the Greek Demeter, her image, enthroned and flanked by lions, appears on the reverse of later coins of Samothrace where she, the main deity of the mystery sanctuary, is coupled with an image on the obverse of Athena, patroness of the political community" (L50 8–9).

In a footnote, Lehmann once again cautions that the presence of Athena and Zeus has more to do with the town than the sanctuary precinct itself: they represent the political arm of the deities of Samothrace, as it were. What he wishes to emphasize, however, is the remarkably autonomous and very powerful religious arm, for it extends over quite a stretch of space and time. To repeat, Axieros, flanked by lions, is surely a local form of the Anatolian Mother Goddess, whose most common name is Kybele: "The Kabeiroi of Samothrace were often identified with the [Phrygian] Korybantes of Kybele or the [Cretan] Kouretes of Rhea, while later popular belief identified them with the Hellenic Dioskouroi. And in Samothrace, Hermes-Kadmilos was attached to this circle as, in the Phrygian cult, he so frequently appears as the companion of Kybele" (L50 9).

I interrupt Lehmann's report to state the obvious about the "Hermes" we are seeing so often invoked here. This is not the Hermes who, equipped with talaria at his heels, delivers flowers to one's beloved. Hermes is an ancient figure associated with the Mother Goddess, one of whose names is Aphrodite. Hermes and Aphrodite unite in Hermaphroditos, notes Carl Kerényi (CK 171). The images erected in honor of Hermes "were either in the 'Cyllenian' style, in which the image was a phallus of wood or stone, or else in that related style in which the image was a rectangular pillar with a head and an erect phallus—an image which in our [Greek] language is called a *herma*" (ibid.). "This form of image," Kerényi continues, "is said to have come from the Mysteries of the Kabeiroi—that is to say, from northern Greece, where Thessaly lies.... We are always confronted with the same Great Goddess, to whom Hermes—in that form of his ancient religious images which was connected with the Daktyloi—was both husband and son" (ibid.). Hermes's son was said, at least in some cities of the Hellespont, to be Priapos: the relation between the two corresponds precisely "to the relation between the Great Mother and her male partner, whom she bore, took to husband and bore again" (CK 175). To those who may be shocked by this double function of the male consort—as both son and lover and son again in turn—Guthrie offers a convincing explanation: "No contradiction was involved in imagining the spirit now as a babe and now as a virile youth. Owing to his connexion with the cycle of vegetation, the fertility-spirit must be born, grow to maturity and die within a single year, and it is natural therefore that his development should proceed with miraculous speed" (WG 61). Needless to say, these more recent accounts of Hermes Kadmilos as the son and consort of Axieros differ radically from Schelling's account of Hermes as a ministrant of Zeus or the demiurge.

But to return to Lehmann's "Third Preliminary Report" of 1950. Lehmann comments on the presence of those "two statues of nude young men" found outside the doors of the *adyton* in the Anaktoron, where the *lex sacra* warning stone stood. He identifies these figures, "undoubtedly," as Hermes and Kadmilos. The two snakes on the incised stone *kerykeion* represent the Dioskouroi, he argues, which are elsewhere represented by paired stars. Lehmann does not hesitate to conjoin "the Dioskouroi-Kabeiroi" in his text and he proceeds now to his conclusion: "The ancient legends of Dardanos and the legendary connection of Samothrace with the [Anatolian] Idaean Great Mother thus seem to be rooted in the facts of religious history. It may also be mentioned that prehistoric potsherds found so far, alas, only included in later strata, show definite connection with the ceramics of the late Bronze and early Iron Ages of northwestern Asia Minor and Lesbos" (L50 9). Lehmann, noting that no item of Greek manufacture dated earlier than the seventh century BCE has been found on Samothrace, affirms that no Greeks were present on the island prior to that century. The Greek settlers, wherever they came from, presumably "mingled peacefully with the natives and carried on their [that is, the natives'] old worship of the Mother and her acolytes [that is, the Cabiri]" (L50 11).

Alongside a sacrificial pit and a beehive oven, excavators uncovered "a narrow open vertical shaft" down which libations may have been poured; this seventh-century *bothros* was uncovered in the northern precinct of the Anaktoron (L50 12). At the lower end of the shaft, a "sacred stone" received the poured libations. The presence of sheep bones in the area once again

A possible *bothros*, or sacrificial pit, in the Neorion on the western hill of the cult site.

suggests that animal as the sacrificial victim. Lehmann argues that such *bothroi* containing sacred stones represent a constant component of Samothracian rites in later times; likewise, the antiquity of the hearth suggests that a similar ritual extends back to earliest times. Such *bothroi*, "into which the blood of sacrificial animals was evidently poured," are reminiscent of Homer's *Nékyia* and Odysseus's sacrifice of a ram above the gateway to the underworld (ibid.; see *Odyssey*, 11:24–36). With regard to those sheep bones and sacrificial blood, however, it is noteworthy that the *dating* of such ritual practices is difficult—as are virtually all the specifics of the rites themselves. There is no reason not to think that the rituals evolved over centuries and were subject to various refinements. For example, it is difficult to assess whether, when Pythagoras and Empedocles demanded an end to blood sacrifice, they were crying in the wilderness or merely reflecting contemporary enlightened practice. And it is worth remembering that on Thera, a thousand years before the epoch Lehmann is describing, what the Mother demanded of her worshippers was not blood or even honeyed wine but only crocus petals and precious saffron.

After citing the "key passage" for the "Samothracian Pantheon," namely, the passage from the Laurentian scholiast to Apollonius of Rhodes (*Argonautica*, 1:917–18, cited above), which lists the four Cabiri by name, Lehmann wrestles with the difficult question concerning the continuity of the tradition of the Great Mother, presumably here "the Queen of the Rocks," and the Samothracian deities, the Cabiri proper. Whereas earlier on (L50 9) he stresses the common identification of the Kabeiroi with the Korybantes of Kybele and the Kouretes of Rhea, with both Kybele and Rhea clearly associated with the Great Mother, Lehmann now prefers to speak of a "loose fusion" of "quite different" beliefs and practices. He writes,

> Furthermore, the Samothracian cycle of gods included a king and queen of the underworld, Axiokersos and Axiokersa [identified by both Schelling and his ancient sources as Hades and Persephone, respectively], representatives of a religious sphere quite different from that of the Queen of the Rocks and her entourage. We are, therefore, drawn to the conclusion that the southern section of the archaic precinct belonged to these underworld gods who, in a loose fusion with the Great Mother of the Rocks, the Kabeiroi and Kadmilos, were worshipped in separate, if successive rites in the seventh century BC in Samothrace. Gradually, out of varying religious concepts and rites, the complexity of a Greek mystery religion seems to develop here into what must have already been an elaborate theology a century later when, around 500 BC, the great initiation hall, the Anaktoron, was built over the northern part of the original northern Temenos [i.e., the consecrated space within the temple]. (L50 12)

And yet, however loose the fusion and eclectic the sources, there are decisive continuities here. "When the Arsinoeion was projected in the early third century BC, its builders took care to include within its circumference this old ritual area—the *bothros*, as yet undestroyed, the altar, and the 'rock throne'" (L50 13). Whereas the ritual areas remained concise, the stories surrounding them evidently expanded.

One of the most striking features of the initiation—recall that Jason and his Argonauts leave Lemnos in the evening and arrive at Samothrace during the night—is its nocturnal character. "The prevalence of nocturnal

Another view of the "Sacred Rock" of blue-green porphyry, near the Rotunda of Arsinoë II.

ceremonies in the mysteries of Samothrace is further borne out by the increasing number of lamps" uncovered at the site (L50 14). Some of these lamps have fixtures for suspension, presumably for sacrifices and prayers at fixed installations, while others are meant to be carried by the initiates in procession (L50 15). By the fifth century, artisans on the island are producing these simple, undecorated clay lamps for use in the sanctuary (L50 16). Ceramic manufacturing is evidence of the island's "economic life stimulated by a rich cult which, as Herodotus and Aristophanes attest, must have already been extremely popular in the Greek world" during the classical age (ibid.).

In his initial 1939 report, Lehmann refers to the discovery of a marble female head, presumably from the archaic period (L39 19). He cites Pliny's reference (cited by Schelling as well) to a statuary group by Skopas in the fourth century, a group featuring Aphrodite and Pothos, Pothos being an Eros who expresses "mourning" or "languishing." The badly corroded marble head seems to be from a statue of this kind, hence anticipating Skopas's work. The head is a further illustration of the "thorough Hellenization of Samothrace in the three centuries after the Greek settlers had begun to transform the 'barbarian' native cult into a Greek mystery religion" (ibid.). Whereas the peoples of Thrace and Macedonia were only superficially hellenized, that is not true of the indigenous folk on the isle of Samothrace, which itself became "one of the most conspicuous centers of the religious life of the ancient world" (L39 20).

Katherine Welch, writing in 1996, refers to a much later statuary head. Discovered in 1988, a "fine under-life-size head" from a votive statue of the Great Mother (Welch's plate 89) is probably from the Hellenistic period, from the third to the first centuries BCE. On each side of the head, a long plaited lock of hair, gathered about each side of the head and covering the upper half of the ears, extends from behind the ear to the shoulder. The hair is parted in the middle and pulled back into "narrow, shallowly chiseled" fillets, typical of statues representing "nurturing, motherly divinities" (KW 468). The eyebrows crowd the large, wide-set eyes. The bridge of the nose is long and delicate, carved "flat and with sharp edges." The mouth is small but full-lipped and slightly open. The closeness of the brows to the eyelids and the open, unsmiling mouth lend an attitude of seriousness and dignity, perhaps of august mourning. The underchin "is plump, and the neck has two 'Venus rings,'" suggesting maturity (ibid.). The head "turns slightly to the right and has an upward tilt," suggesting that the statue was in a seated position. The head is similar to representations of Demeter "in her capacity of earth goddess, with whom the Great Mother was sometimes conflated by the Greeks" (ibid.). She wears no mural crown, although such a crown is typical of representations of the Great Mother of Anatolia, the Phrygian Kybele, the Ephesian Artemis, and the Greek Rhea (KW 470). I will take up Welch's speculation on this head of the Mother in section 4, below, but here merely note that for the archaeologist in Schelling the discovery of such heads testifies to the persistence and preeminence of Demeter and Persephone in the cult. Whereas Schelling may hope to find Kadmilos heads so that he might scurry up the ladder to the demiurge, Axieros-Demeter keeps calling him back.

3. The Language of the Samothracian Cult

One may safely wager that no one has pursued the question of the *language* of Samothrace as doggedly and as daringly as Schelling has. If one takes only endnote 113 of his lecture as an example, the note in which he pursues the possible roots of the word κάβειροι, we find him taking up the possible relations of this word to other words in the Hebrew kabbalah (*Chabirim*), the Hebrew Sohar and Old Testament (*Kabir, Chabir, Chaverim*), Greek and Latin, Etruscan, Farsi (the Persian *Chabherin, Ghebern*), Hindu (*Gabirim, Cabi, Cavi*), Arabic (*Ghebr*), along with possible Old Saxon derivatives, to mention but a few. What would it take to unravel this entire skein of Cabirian names? What conscientious and well-trained linguist would dare try? Recent efforts have been far more modest than Schelling's. Let us begin once again with Karl Lehmann.

Lehmann notes that during the Hellenistic period the ritual lamps mentioned above bore a magical symbol on the bottom of their interior—precisely the symbol (the "open point") that for Jacob Böhme, Franz Baader, and Schelling himself (in the 1809 *Treatise on Human Freedom* [see SW I/7, 366–67n] but also in the 1811–1815 *Weltalter* fragments [see 1:63–66, on "the pulsating point"], the Erlangen lectures of the 1820s [see AA II, 10, 1, 519], and the 1842 *Philosophy of Mythology* [see SW II/2, 600]) had enormous cosmic significance, namely, a circle with a dot at its center:

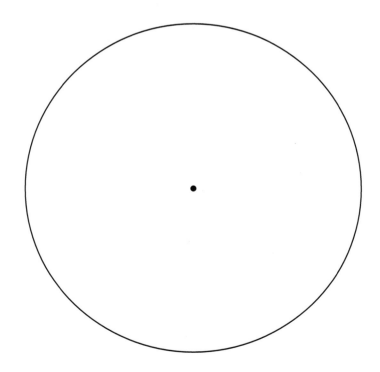

It is possible that this symbol, incised into the ceramic lamps, represents a dedication "to the gods" (Θεοῖς, whereby the theta often appears simply as a dot within an oval or a circle); often a kappa is incised into the bowl, suggesting a dedication to the Καβείροις or to Καδμίλῳ; similarly, an alpha (or an aleph) may refer to Axieros, Axiokersos, and/or Axiokersa. An archaic vase incised with the letters ΔΙΝ probably refers to a "barbarian" proper name, perhaps Thracian, in hellenized form, Δίνων (L50 17–18). Although Lehmann does not speculate on this, one may wonder whether the name might refer to the Thracian Dionysos. And if the archaic Thracians are indeed closely related to the ancient Phrygians, as most scholars agree, one may wonder whether Schelling's speculations on the Phoenician origins of the Cabiri lie so far afield. For, presuming that Phrygian traders relied on maritime transport, at least on occasion, would they not have come into close contact with the Phoenicians of Tyre and Sidon? With regard to the letters ΔΙΝ, they are more likely, in Alexander Bilda's view, to be referring to the "whirling" (διν-εύω, δίν-η) of initiates in circle dances. To be sure, none of the archaeological evidence amassed thus far attests to any of these speculations, although the linguistic analysis of the extant inscriptions argues for an Indo-European, not a Western Semitic, language as the aboriginal language of Samothrace.[10]

When Diodorus of Sicily says of the archaic Samothracians that they are earthborn, meaning that the island was "inhabited by men who sprang from the soil itself," we are reminded of the earthborn race of humankind during the reign of Kronos, as recounted in the Platonic myth in *Statesman* (L55 93). Diodorus asserts that these autochthonous people spoke "an ancient language that was peculiar to them, of which a good deal is preserved to this day in their sacrificial rituals" (DS 5:47). Lehmann presents the forty words that have been transmitted, largely in dedicatory inscriptions on clay ritual vessels found on Samothrace. He dates them from the sixth and fifth centuries of the archaic era, although later researchers, led by James R. McCredie,

---

10. Alexander Bilda has recorded the most recent discussions by linguists who are now generally in agreement that the ancient language of the Samothracian cult was Phrygian, not Phoenician or Western Semitic, as Schelling maintains. See Bilda's chapter in the present book, along with his "'Wahre Namen' oder 'Wurzelphantasmagorien'? Schellings Philosophie der Götternamen," in Christian Danz, ed., *Schellings Gottheiten von Samothrake im Kontext* (Vienna and Göttingen: Vienna University Press and Vandenhoeck & Ruprecht, 2021), 162–69, esp. 163n. 24.

down date them by at least a hundred years.[11] The word *Thursday* seems to be the only word in this aboriginal language that we can understand; other scholars, while uncertain, speculate on the Samothracian word for *bread*. In any case, Lehman draws several suggestive conclusions concerning the *lingua sacra* of Samothrace:

> The indications are that it was actually to some extent a living language in the archaic age and gradually declined as such only in the 5th century until it disappeared in the 4th century. But in what sense the language remained alive centuries after the foundation of a Greek polis on Samothrace (around 700 [probably closer to 550—D.F.K.] BC) remains a problem. Were these dedications written by descendants of the pre-Greek inhabitants who still used their old language? Or are they—like Latin in the Middle Ages—documents of the continued if, in this case, religiously restricted use of a dying language by both natives and Greeks? The latter seems more probable. The stele seems to indicate the official liturgical existence of this language around 400 BC (L55 95)

Dedications "to the gods," ΘΕΟΙΣ, are perhaps abbreviated to the letters ΘΕ, or, as noted above, simply Θ. Lehmann suspects that the letters ΔΙΝ or ΔΙ may be short forms for "the gods" and that the letters ΔΚ may refer either to the Divine Kabeiroi as a whole or to Kadmilos in particular, the former as ΔΙΝ ΚΑΒΕΙΡΟΙΣ, the latter as ΔΙ ΚΑΔΜΙΛΩΙ. Although neither Lehmann nor the linguists would go so far, one can hardly help but think of the Latin *Di Manes*, the Greek δαίμονες, and the declension of Zeus in the form δι-. One must stress that not all the letters found on Samothrace are recognizably Greek. One particular letter found on Samothrace, for example, has been found only much farther south, on Thera, the present-day Santorini, where "the gods of Samothrace" were also worshipped (L55 96).

"Very little can be said about the texts found in Samothrace," begins linguist Giuliano Bonfante in his reply to Lehmann (GB 101). Yet he ventures to say that the aboriginal language of the island is Indo-European, perhaps a dialect of Thracian, as Lehmann supposes. That dialect differs from the language spoken on nearby Lemnos, however, which is related to Etruscan. Because of the frequency of vowels and diphthongs (in comparison with the frequency of consonants), one can argue for the Indo-European basis of the Samothracian tongue (GB 102). True, the only Samothracian word

---

11. See L55, "Documents," 97–100 for the catalogue of inscriptions, with illustrative plates at 101–102.

that looks familiar to linguists is βεκα, which may be related to a Phrygian word cited by Herodotus, namely, βέκος, meaning "bread." Possibly, and remarkably—even incredibly—this word may be the origin of, or at least be related to, the German *backen* and the English *bake* (GB 105). It is surely not too farfetched to speculate that bread, the gift of Demeter, was involved in ritual performances at the sanctuary (GB 106).

Concerning the root that is common to the first three Cabirian deities, and which is so important for Schelling, Bonfante wonders if it may have to do with the river Ἄξιος. This is unlikely, however, as the deities "do not seem to be river gods" (GB 107). The fact that the sanctuary is encompassed by two rivers, however, or by two branches of the same river, may make the association with river gods more plausible, especially when one thinks of the maritime background of the rite and the proximity of the sea to the sanctuary. Concerning the root common to the second and third deities, -κερσ-, which Schelling takes to be an early form of *Ceres*, Bonfante wonders whether it might derive from the Sanskrit *kársati*, "to furrow," a name that would befit that other tradition, to wit, the chthonic deities as vegetation goddesses and gods. The name of the fourth deity, Κασμῖλος or Καδμῖλος, is likely to be an Indo-European diminutive of Κάδμος, the famous Illyrian hero Cadmus, said to have been Phoenician in origin, who married Harmony on Samothrace and then founded Greek Thebes, the city of Dionysos, and who, if Roberto Calasso is right, also founded much of Greek mythology.[12]

A speculation on the name *Adam* leads Bonfante to discuss the possible Phrygian origins of the Cabirian cult. He writes, "Another conceivably Samothracian name appears in a prayer quoted by St. Hippolytus which seems to come from Anatolia: σὲ καλοῦσι ... Σαμοθράικες Ἄδαμ(να) σεβάσμιον" (GB 108). The name Adam or Adamna, which may be a taboo name, is said by Hesychios to be related in meaning to the Greek φίλος, "friend" or "beloved." Bonfante recalls the association of the Phrygian Κορύβαντες with Samothrace and concludes by observing, "We know that Thracians and Phrygians were closely related peoples" (ibid.).

---

12. The very mention of Cadmus in the context of Samothrace intimates that the Samothracian cult will be important for Calasso's entire account of Greek mythology. See esp. RC 9, 98–99, 197, 203, 210–11, 214, and, in effect, the entire final chapter, 375–91. It is also important to recall that Cadmus's Thebes itself had an important Kabeirion.

As we have seen, the absence on Samothrace of preserved inscriptions of great antiquity prohibits confident speculation on the origins and identity of the Samothracian language. And yet one can hardly avoid the tempting thought that Samothrace may have played a mediating role between the two most ancient systems of written language that we know, namely, that of the south-Balkan Vinča civilization, by far the oldest system of writing (dating from the seventh to the fifth millennia BCE), and that of ancient Sumer. Both were essentially hieratic scripts used in rituals for the dead, for magic, and in ancestor worship. Samothrace is of course quite close to the southernmost extent of the Vinča civilization, and it is not unlikely that its original population was of that same pre-Indo-Germanic stock that occupied the Balkans. Furthermore, the proximity to the Dardanelles and the Bosporus, hence to Anatolia, makes contact with the civilizations of the Golden Crescent quite likely. In the cases of both the Vinča and ancient Near Eastern civilizations, the importance of female deities—goddesses of water, earth, and underworld—is central, and Samothrace certainly conforms to this profile as well. Finally, the striking similarity of the Cretan Linear A script to both the ancient Sumerian and Old-European (Vinča) systems of writing suggests at least the possibility of contact among these peoples—and what was possible for Crete would have been readily possible for Samothrace. No such inscribed cult objects from the archaic period have been found on the island, however, and so, even though classical literary sources attest to the antiquity of the cult site of the Great Gods, speculation in this area has to be curtailed.[13]

Interlude

By this time I can imagine my readers' objecting: What do all these detailed observations about recent archaeological finds—the cult site, the sacrificial vessels, the disputed *language* of the rites, and so on—have to do with

---

13. On the Vinča and Sumerian scripts and their relation to cult practices, see HH 70–81 and 94–100. On Linear A in relation to Old-European scripts, see HH 85. Schelling would have been intrigued by the fact that one of the most famous linguists and philologists of antiquity, Aristarchos (220–140 BCE), was born and raised on Samothrace. Aristarchos later became the head of the library at Alexandria. Perhaps it was the rich linguistic and cultural tradition of Samothrace that gave him his start?

Schelling? After all, he could have known nothing of these matters, so that they can scarcely have influenced his speculations. My first reply will seem capricious: I believe that Schelling would have been intrigued by all these details, with the result that, if I may say so, his archaeological drive continues to feed my own, and my own drive feeds these materials back to him. My second reply would be that much in and about the current archaeological investigations sometimes confirms and sometimes challenges Schelling's theses on Samothrace, but always in philosophically interesting ways. For example, if the Mother Goddess *remains* at the heart of the cult, what impact does this have on Schelling's assertion that the Cabiri form an ascendant sequence, with Demeter and Persephone at the bottom and the demiurge at the top, and with Hermes serving as the demiurge's male herald? In his 1842 lectures on mythology, Schelling himself is fascinated by the importance of female figures and the feminine features of all the *higher* forms of deity in the myths and mysteries of every culture he investigates—indeed, one could argue that the development of deity in the direction of the feminine stands at the very center of his inquiry into mythology and the mysteries in which mythology culminates. Looking back from the vantage point of the mythology course to the Samothrace lecture, in which Schelling sometimes seems to be willing to leave the goddesses behind in order to ascend to the traditional "father" and "maker" of the universe, one might again say that Schelling's archaeology and teleology are struggling against one another. My own suspicion is that Schelling's archaeology constantly calls him back to the oldest, the earliest, the immemorial ἀρχή that leaves its mark on all that comes later—up to the end, if there is one. The earliest, the "unprethinkable," leaves its mark on the very names of the second and third Cabiri, which begin with *Axio-* and continue with the very name of Ceres or Demeter: Ceres is originally *Keres*, such that in both Axiokersa and Axiokersos, in both daughter and son, as it were, the mark of the Mother survives. Will not that mark survive in Hermes too, whose very name longs to join that of Aphrodite? Will it not survive in the face of the Angel of the Lord? As Schelling says concerning Samothrace, and here contemporary archaeologists would agree with him, "Everything points to a cult and a doctrine at the center of which stands Ceres." Ceres as cornucopia, to be sure, but also Ceres-Demeter as rage and "debilitating languor," languishing, and obsession, Ceres in desperate search of Proserpina. The very least one can say, and Schelling says it in his endnote 112, is that the entire series of deities at Samothrace reflects "the fundamental opposition of masculine and feminine," the irreducible *dyas*. "For all philosophy is led

A fifth-century BCE image of the enthroned Mother, Demeter, or perhaps Persephone, on Samothrace.

to such an underlying duality," insists Schelling in that same note, doubtless, some would say, because of the "Dyas in his machina."[14]

For the remainder of the present essay, I want to pay particular attention to the question of the feminine side of the dyad, mother and maid, as figures of both fury *and* compassion, potency *and* poverty, longing *and* languishing. As we have seen, at the very end of his lecture on the deities of Samothrace, Schelling comes to stress, not the ascensional sequence of the deities but their companionship, their sociality, their interwoven *being* as *con*-sen-*tes*. Born together, dying together, they are *commourans*, as Montaigne said of all us mortal animals. Schelling, as archaeologist, is gathering evidence concerning the shared *mortality* of the great gods and goddesses. Why the feminine quality of deity should provide decisive insight into divine *materialization*, divine *embodiment*, and divine *mortality* is, at least for me, the mystery of all mysteries. In Schelling's view, *hers* is the "ineradicable sorcery," *hers* the "magic" that "underlies *every* female deity," and perhaps every male deity as well. Schelling calls her "the artist-goddess."

4. Mortal Mysteries: For Sowers or Sailors?

If we ask whether the mystery cult on Samothrace was intended for the rescue of mariners or the fertility of flocks and fields, we know already that the answer has to be both. Let us turn first to the fields and flocks, nurtured by

---

14. The phrase "because of Dyas in his machina" appears in James Joyce, *Finnegans Wake* (New York: Viking, twelfth printing, 1971), 55. The omnivorous Joyce must at some point have devoured all of Schelling to know of this *dyas*, which appears to be nothing less than *deus*, the *deus* in every *machina*. Joyce continues: "*isce et ille* equals of opposites, evolved by a onesame power of nature or of spirit, *iste*, as the sole condition and means of its himundher manifestation and polarised for reunion by the symphysis of their antipathies. Distinctly different were their duasdestinies" (92). And then, much later, emphatically, "*Zweispaltung as Fundemaintalish of Wiederherstellung*" (296). And then, still later, "egotum sabcunsciously senses upers the deprofundity of multimathematical immaterieealities wherebejubers in the pancosmic urge the allimmanence of that which Itself is Itself Alone (hear. O hear, Caller Errin!) exteriorises on this ourherenow plane in disunited solod, likeward and gushious bodies with (science, say!) perlwhitened passionpanting pugnoplangent intuitions of reunited selfdom (murky whey, abstrew adim!) in the higherdimissional selfless Allself" (394–95), which, admittedly, leaves little more to be uttered.

the Great Mother and her consort, and then to the sailors rescued by one of her incarnations, namely, Ino Leukothea, whose very name reflects one of the earliest names of the island of Samothrace itself. Whereas one is tempted to say that the protectress of fields and flocks is the older figure, one has to remember how long human beings have been plying and plowing the waves. We have no idea, really, which of the two strands of culture is older. Let us consider them equiprimordial until proven otherwise.

Katherine Welch cites Lucian (*De Dea Syria* 15) regarding Rhea and Attis, whose fertility rites occur also on Samothrace, albeit under different names. Early on, those rites assume a more drastic form than any we—although not the later Schelling—have so far contemplated: "Attis was Lydian in origin, and was the first to teach the secret rites devoted to Rhea. The rites performed by the Phrygians, the Lydians, and the Samothracians were all learned from Attis; for when Rhea castrated him, he left off the masculine form of life, took on a feminine appearance, put on women's garments and, traveling into every land, performed secret rites, related what he had suffered, and sang the praises of Rhea" (KW 470). We remember that sometime during the second millennium BCE Thracian tribes moved east to Phrygian Anatolia, passing through the vicinity of Samothrace. Welch elaborates the astonishing consequence of this migration: "By Hellenistic times the Samothracians felt entitled to claim that the rites of the Phrygian mother had actually originated on their island and had been exported from it to Asia Minor by Dardanos. Dionysius of Halicarnassus (*Antiquitates romanae* 1.61.2–4) tells us that Dardanos founded Samothrace and subsequently emigrated from the island to Asia with his son Idaios, 'who occupied the mountains which are now called after him the Idaean mountains, and there founded a sanctuary to the Mother of the Gods and instituted secret and initiatory rites which are observed to this day throughout Phrygia'" (KW 471).

Perhaps the Great Mother, on Samothrace, was called by the name Axieros. Yet Welch too emphasizes the fact that neither stone nor ceramic inscriptions cite the individual names of the quaternity of goddesses and gods recorded by Mnaseas of Patara (KP 3:1370), names passed on to us by the *Scholia Laurentiana* to Apollonius of Rhodes. Rather, the archaeological evidence offered by votive dedications gives us simply the collective name "the gods" or "the Great Gods" (KW 472). Perhaps this is because the individual names were sacred and not to be uttered. Welch cites the Emperor Julian ("the Apostate," nephew of Constantine) in *On the Mother of the Gods* (8.5) in this respect. In what follows, I offer a more complete version of Julian's account. As we will see, Julian's questions and speculations take us well beyond the sorts of material evidence that archaeologists prize; yet they may bring us closer to the character of at least some of the very early fertility rites at Samothrace.

"Shall I write about things not to be spoken of and thus divulge what ought not to be divulged? Shall I utter the unutterable? Who is Attis or Gallus? Who then is the Mother of the Gods, and what is the manner of their purification rituals?" (EJ 1:442–43). Julian identifies the Mother with "that very Deo" whom the Romans worship and with Rhea and Demeter (ibid.). Her origins are Phrygian, yet even the pythoness at Delphi is her advocate (EJ 444–45). Julian's central narrative involves the descent of Attis from the ether or upper air and his passionate love affair with moisture and matter, that is, his lovemaking with "the nymph of the cavern." In order to restrain Attis, limit his power, and bring him back home, the Mother has him castrated; she then takes him back to her bosom, crowning him with a tiara of stars. Julian repeats his question, "Who then is the Mother of the Gods?" and he replies, at 166a–b:

> She is the source of the knowing and creating [i.e., the demiurgic] gods who in their turn guide the visible gods [τῶν κυβερνώντων τοὺς ἐμφανεῖς νοερῶν καὶ δημιουργικῶν θεῶν]; she is both the mother and the spouse of great Zeus; she came into being next to, and together with, the great creator; she is the queen of every form of life, the cause of all generation; she easily brings to perfection all things that are made; without pain she brings to birth and through the father creates all the things that are; she is the motherless virgin [παρθένος ἀμήτωρ] enthroned at the side of Zeus, and in truth the Mother of all the Gods. (EJ 1:60–63; KW 472)

Like Kybele and Metis before her and Athena after her, Julian's Mother of the Gods is πρόνοια, forethought. She loves Attis "with a passionless eros [ἔρως . . . ἀπαθής]," and she desires that he should requite her love in this way alone. Yet Attis, although himself a god of intellect, is impelled by a wayward or downward desire to mix with matter—he descends "even to its lowest limits" (167b) and visits the cave of the nymph, as Odysseus was later to visit Kalypso and Aeneas Dido. The Mother thereupon sends the lion of fire to contend against the nymph of moisture and her lover, instigating the latter's castration.

By whom and precisely how Julian does not say, although he implies, at 168b, that it may have been the very companions of Attis, the Korybants, who performed the deed. "What is the meaning of this castration?" asks Julian, and he replies, as though remembering the teaching of Anaximander, "It is the checking [or suspending, i.e., holding in suspense] of the unlimited," ἐποχὴ τῆς ἀπειρίας (167c, 175b). The ritual castration is a constraining of the forms, or a restraining of the force behind the forms, from an otherwise limitless, boundless trajectory.[15] The castration occurs on the third day after the spring equinox, in our calendar on March 24 or 25; on the following day, the feast of the Hilaria is held (168d). By contrast, notes Julian, the Eleusinian mysteries, which recall Demeter's desperate search for her vanished daughter, are celebrated as the year declines (173a–b).[16] Yet Attis is the rays of the sun, and his ritual castration expresses the secret of the sun's curbed and harnessed power—reminiscent of Schelling's claim that Dionysos-Axiokersos tames the fire of Persephone-Axiokersa. "For what could be more blessed, what more joyful than a soul that has escaped from limitlessness and generation and the inner tempest [ἀπειρίαν ... γένεσιν ... καὶ τὸν ἐν αὐτῇ κλύδωνα], and has been translated up to the very gods?" (169d). What could give greater joy than the story of a god who, for a time quite out of his mind (179c: ἄφρων), is recalled to glory? It is no accident that the time of the celebration of Attis and his mother coincides with the festivals in Athens in honor of Dionysos (179a, 180a). And it is no accident that Athena and Zeus are likewise honored at such a time. Nor should we be surprised by the appearance of Hermes Epaphroditos, Hermes "favored" and even "touched" by Aphrodite, at such festivals (179b).

Julian, however, like Schelling long after him, is not unaware of the central ontological puzzle of these myths and the remembered rituals of a descent, κατάβασις, into moisture, followed by a purification through fire. For even though the Mother demands exclusive devotion and even though she

---

15. In his early philosophy of nature, Schelling invoked what he called the force of inhibition, *Hemmung*, a less drastic force than Rhea's but no less consequential. See the discussion in chapters 5 and 6 of Krell, *Contagion: Sexuality, Disease, and Death in German Idealism and Romanticism* (Bloomington: Indiana University Press, 1998), esp. 94–96.

16. W. K. C. Guthrie, citing Aristotle and others, confirms the widespread belief in Greece that the spirits of fertility were most active in winter, after which, of course, comes the burgeoning of spring (WG 69).

commands the castration of her wayward son, one cannot say that the descent of Attis to the cavern of the nymph occurs against the will of the gods or even against the will of the Mother: the descent is absolutely essential for the creation of the universe by a "self-materializing god," as Schelling himself will later say (SW II/2, 501); equally as necessary is the Mother's periodic "anger" or "fretful irritation" (171b: ἀγανάκτησις) over that descent. And yet her fury always abates. Each year Attis "yearns passionately for generation" and each year he descends, but then his descent is cut short, as it were; and each year, once the Mother's irritation abates, his scepter (σκῆπτρον) is returned to him (171d). The only matter that needs to be thought through is the periodic upsurgence of anger in a goddess who otherwise is celebrated for her apathy, her lack of passion. For one could easily confuse that very fretfulness or fury of hers with the driving force behind her son's descent into "the unlimited." If Demeter is the preeminent name for the Mother in Greece, then one has to recall Carl Kerényi's claim concerning her: the central mystery of Demeter has to do with her fertility and her ability to rejuvenate herself and even give birth to herself ever anew. "In her marital alliance with Zeus, Demeter was predominantly the *alter ego* of Mother Rhea, who bore Persephone to her own son, and in so doing bore her own self anew—a mystery of which little was publicly told" (CK 185).

The importance of the Mother Goddess, however, in the view of many scholars, implies the relative unimportance—or even absence—of the Cabirian deities on Samothrace. Bengt Hemberg, whose study *Die Kabiren* appeared over seventy years ago, is surely the leading skeptic in this regard.[17] Readers should not be fooled by the date of the book's publication: Hemberg's work is still an essential source because of its careful treatment of the literary sources for the Cabiri. Hemberg is particularly concerned with distinguishing the many cults that appear to have gathered about this name in the complex history of the Samothracian and neighboring gods. His epigram

---

17. Bengt Hemberg, *Die Kabiren* (Uppsala: Almqvist & Wiksells, 1950), cited as BH with page number. Of particular value are the appendices (303–57), which offer detailed bibliographies for the discussion of (1) the names of the deities of Samothrace, (2) the names of the heroes associated with the island, (3) the names Καδμίλος and Camillus or Camilla, (4) the derivation of the word κάβειροι and the names Κοάλεμοι, κόβαλοι, and κόβειροι as possible sources of that word, and (5) the most common properties of the Cabiri and related figures.

(from Goethe's *Faust II*, lines 8075–77), which appears at the outset of the present essay, says it all: "These are gods! themselves quite marvelous, / Recreating themselves on and on, / And never knowing what they are."

In Hemberg's view, one may safely assume that Schelling takes over from the renowned sixteenth-century philologist Joseph Scaliger the theory that the names of the Cabirian deities derive from the Phoenician language. The Romantics, Hemberg adds, were convinced "that the covert wisdom of Greek religion" as a whole "was contained in the teachings of the mysteries on Samothrace" (BH 11). By "Romantics," namely, those who developed "fantasy-laden systems" around Samothrace, Hemberg means preeminently Schelling and his most important source, Friedrich Creuzer (BH 12). The thesis of Hemberg's study is that we have no justification, either through the testimonies of ancient literature or through contemporary archaeology, for assuming that the Great Gods of Samothrace are Cabiri or that the latter name has an identifiable content at all. Hemberg cites the skepticism of the French archaeologist Chapouthier, who worked at the dig early in the twentieth century: "Les Kabires de Samothrace, c'est un grand nom, mais une insaississable matière" (BH 13). In much of the ancient literature, the Cabiri are associated with other groups of "lesser divinities," mysterious figures identified as giants, titans, cyclopes, hundred-handed monsters, centaurs, satyrs, *dioskouroi, kouretes, korybantes,* erotic gods, dactyls, telchines, and pygmies—among many others (BH 17). These are the daimonic "gangs" that cause Roberto Calasso such befuddlement but also offer him many tantalizing tales (RC 302). Concerning which more in a moment.

Whereas Joseph Scaliger assumed that the Greek expression Θεοὶ Μεγάλοι was a direct allusion to the Κάβειροι and that the latter name derived from the Phoenician word *kabirim*, a name for otherwise unknown Phoenician gods brought to Samothrace in the ninth century of the ancient era (BH 27–28), the expression "great gods" most likely derives from still more ancient references to "the great goddess" or "great mother," identified as the Phrygian Kybele (BH 29). It is of interest to note that the local goddess Bendis, from the nearby island of Lemnos—the Bendis who is so important for the opening of Plato's *Republic*—is related to, if not identical with, Kybele (ibid.).[18]

---

18. Do we as yet have a reading of *Republic* that keeps at the very center of its interpretation Socrates's desire—confessed at the very outset of the dialogue—to learn more about Bendis? Perhaps the most stalwart effort in this regard is

However, to repeat, no surviving inscription to date cites the Cabiri as having been present on Samothrace—inscriptions there invoke only the "Great Gods" (BH 73). Herodotus associates the Cabiri with Egyptian Memphis and thus assumes that the Greeks had the name—and the gods themselves, though not their ithyphallic herms—from the Egyptians (BH 77–78).[19]

Hemberg casts doubt on the significance of Mnaseas's account of the Cabirian quaternity for Samothrace; he follows the Roman historian Varro's insistence that the Cabiri are gods of an uncertain nature, *dii incerti* (BH 80–81).[20] What Hemberg does accept are the sundry names of the maternal goddess: "That a goddess stands at the center of the cult is indisputable" (BH 82). The goddess displays two aspects: first, she is the mother of all the gods, surrounded by those swarms of minor deities or daimons, such as the Korybants; second, she is the beloved consort of a god, or, reversing matters, it is *she* who has a consort or companion, one whom she changes year by year. The importance of the goddess is confirmed on Samothrace by the presence of the Venus-Pothos statuary group (BH 85). However, Hemberg, like Carl

---

John Sallis, *Being and Logos: The Way of Platonic Dialogue*, 3d ed. (Bloomington: Indiana University Press, 1996). Schelling would have agreed with Socrates: one must try to learn a great deal more about that goddess.

19. Much of the critical reception of Schelling's "Deities of Samothrace" during the nineteenth century involves the various claims for an *Indian* or an *Egyptian* or perhaps most likely a *Phrygian* background, as opposed to a *Phoenician* or ancient *Hebrew* one, to the Samothracian cult. For a detailed account of this matter, see the essay by Alexander Bilda in the present volume.

20. Countering Hemberg's skepticism concerning the Cabiri, Sandra Blakely attempts to reaffirm the Semitic origins of Cadmus, hence of the Cabirian cult on Samothrace, thus by indirection supporting Schelling's arguments concerning the Phoenician or Old Hebrew *language* of the Cabirian cult. She writes, "Those working in Indo-European linguistics, however, have seen another route through this term [i.e., *kabeiroi*] to unlock the identity of the gods. Kadmos' Phoenician origins, and his intimate connection with the rites, recommended reading *Kabeiroi* in terms of Semitic *kbr*, meaning 'great.' The term *Theoi Megaloi*, 'great gods,' thus became a Greek calque on a Semitic term—and the legend of Kadmos a signal of the derivation of the gods, and the cult, from the Levant." Yet in the end Blakely too urges caution: "The etymological arguments for a Levantine origin have long been challenged, and caution advanced regarding arguments which rely on etymological evidence to the exclusion of other categories." See SB 2–3. *Dii incerti*, at all events, seems to be the proper appellation.

Kerényi, argues that the initial three Cabirian deities may well consist of a single goddess, Axiokersa, and two male deities, Axieros and Axiokersos; furthermore, he takes these three to be not proper names but general epithets or *epikleses*, that is, forms of apostrophe (BH 88). *Axios* would mean "powerful, worthy," and the root *kers-* would mean "spouse" or "consort." The two male figures, often represented by the two lions who flank the goddess, would be related to the *Dioskouroi*, and the original figures on Samothrace would be the brothers Iasion and Dardanos, who accompany their sister, Harmonia (BH 89).

Diverging from this account, to be sure, would be the myth associated with Eleusis, namely, the myth of the mother and the ravished maid, which has overriding importance for Schelling. If we try to integrate the conflicting interpretations of the myths by Hemberg and Schelling, we might assert that the maid, Kore or Persephone, is closer to the center of the story than the mother: Kore or Persephone, raped by Hades, draws the languishing Demeter in her train, as it were. On Samothrace, one is reminded of the importance of Demeter's foray (or is it Persephone's foray?) into the fields and her lovemaking with Iasion during the marriage of Kadmos and Harmonia, as a result of which the Samothracian fields are fertilized (BH 91).

In any case, Hemberg is also less skeptical when it comes to Hermes. Hermes is the ithyphallic deity known already to Herodotus. As the consort of the Mother, Hermes represents Zeus. It is always in any case a matter of the ἱερὸς γάμος, sacred marriage or ritual mating (BH 93). Nor can we doubt that Pliny's *Pothos* and Lukian's and Julian's *Attis* represent this selfsame ithyphallic Hermes (BH 94).[21] As for the implication that Hermes is some sort of acolyte or servant at the ritual, the *Kadmiloi* of Samothrace remind Hemberg of the Hermai at Trophonios in Lebadeia, a group of thirteen-year-old boys who perform various ceremonial functions at the sanctuary (BH 95). Yet one has the feeling that such an acolyte is more crucial to the story than any priest can be. Schelling, at least, strongly has that feeling.

Hemberg is least skeptical when it comes to the expectations of the initiates, as eclectic and even contradictory as these expectations may have been during any given period. Because Homer tells us nothing about the mysteries

---

21. Walter Burkert explains the presence and condition of these statues with uncanny directness: the *hermai* are erect, he writes, because they have seen Kore (B93 182).

at Samothrace and because the uninitiated Greeks themselves could only riddle on their meaning, nothing but contradictory accounts survive (BH 100). In any case, even if little else is known, the mother of the gods and her consort doubtless stand at the center. The only general characteristic of these gods is that they are helpmates to humankind "in every sort of calamity" (BH 101), humankind as a whole, whether sower or sailor, tinker or tailor. Indeed, Hemberg adds to the range of possibilities of such assistance. Whereas most accounts stress rescue of sailors and aid to the fertility of fields, flocks, and humans, Hemberg argues that the ithyphallic nature of the consort suggests that the fishery (inasmuch as fish, like Aphrodite herself, spawn in the foam of the sea), agriculture, and even viniculture turned to these gods for assistance (BH 102). The original goddess of the mountain in Samothrace, continues Hemberg, was the Thracian Aphrodite Zerynthia, later identified with the earlier figures of Kybele or Rhea (BH 103). Under these latter guises, it is easy to take even Artemis to be an Aphrodite.[22]

As for the cult practices themselves, Hemberg stresses the importance of "hieratic dances" and the "nocturnal character" of the rite (BH 107–08). He interprets the purple sash made famous by Homer's Odysseus as a reminiscence of the flow of cleansing blood, sacrificial blood, and also of the rivers, which flowed more generously down the Samothracian mountainside in ancient times, as sources of purifying lustration (BH 110). Most intriguing is the fact that Hemberg the skeptic agrees with Farnell (and also with Schelling, it must again be said) that the Samothracian cult promised its initiates "a better lot in the other world"; otherwise no one would have sought to land on such a remote island, where docking a ship is often a very hazardous undertaking (BH 116–17).

We may now, in our search for the mortal mysteries of Samothrace, turn to a far gentler skeptic, the formidably learned classicist and historian of philosophy W. K. C. Guthrie. Although he does not discuss Samothrace in

---

22. Carl Kerényi and Roberto Calasso both remind us of the myth concerning Artemis, the story of the nymph Aura, who teases the goddess about her full breasts, more worthy of Aphrodite than of a virgin goddess. However wrathful Artemis becomes over the nymph's insolence and however disastrous the consequences for Aura, one cannot entirely suppress thoughts of the many-breasted Mother of Ephesus, Artemis, who is both the Great Mother of Asia and a goddess of "strong hemaphroditic characteristics" (CK 145; RC 27–34).

detail, his reflections on Greek mystery cults in general are insightful—they will help us to understand Schelling's fascination with the Cabiri. Guthrie, in his introductory chapter on the history of religion, "Our Predecessors," poses what might readily be taken as the weightiest objection to Schelling's "Samothrace" lecture and related writings. Guthrie writes,

> It is sometimes said that the history of religion, as a science, was born in the early years of the nineteenth century. This is a partial truth, and we may add to it another partial truth, that comparative philology was its parent. Philology did indeed draw attention to the value of the comparative method for the study of mythology, a method which has kept its place at the centre of the whole science of religious history. The positive lesson which comparative philology taught was that the various names of a number of gods occurring in the myths of different peoples speaking Indo-Germanic tongues could be shown to have a common origin. (WG 5)

I interrupt to note that Schelling goes far beyond the limits of Indo-European languages, extending his etymological researches into ancient Persian (an Indo-European language using a cuneiform and later a quasi-Arabic script), Arabic, and (in order to approach the Phoenician) ancient Hebrew. Nevertheless, early in his lecture Schelling warns us about the temptation of etymologists "to mix everything with everything else." But to let Guthrie continue:

> But if the names of gods in use in various tribes and nations were only different versions of the same name, they must originally have referred to one god, and by comparing the stories told and the beliefs held about them, it must be possible to reconstruct the religion of the original Indo-Europeans. The philological studies on which these conclusions were based were in their early youth. This meant, first, that the actual identifications were sometimes wrong, and secondly that in the first flush of discovery they were regarded as a kind of magic key and forced into locks which they did not really fit. (Ibid.)

The "first flush of discovery" and the "magic key" certainly seem to be fitting characterizations of Schelling's very exciting and very excited text. Whether and in which cases the implied criticism holds true is a matter far beyond my competence to judge. What puts Schelling in a more positive light, however, is his objection to William Warburton and others who were quick to reduce all the varieties of ancient polytheism to a single grand Christian narrative. Schelling is actually quite nervous about any such claim to a "magic key."

What makes the subject of Greek religion and mythology so complex, argues Guthrie, is its "blending" of northern, especially Thracian, with Mediterranean elements, especially the Phrygian and Cretan (WG 6). Moreover, "One of the most remarkable things about the Greek genius, at least as manifested in religion, is the way in which it preserved the old alongside of the new. Not only was it capable of astonishingly rapid development to some of the highest forms of religious experience; it was also loth to let even the oldest and crudest forms of worship disappear without a trace" (WG 28). Exemplary in this regard is the story of Dionysos. His double provenance, from both the north (Thrace) and the east (Lydia, Phrygia), is less a problem than one might think, however. Guthrie confirms what Bonfante, Welch, and Pauly-Wissowa all tell us, namely, that these two peoples were originally one:

> Dionysiac religion, though known to Homer, had no place in the society which he describes. It descended upon Greece from Thrace in post-Homeric times as a foreign intrusion, and was met with considerable hostility. It was an orgiastic religion involving a belief in possession by the god whereby for a fleeting instant, under the influence of torches, wine, heady music and dancing, the worshipper felt lifted out of himself and exalted to the plane of the divine. Its natural affinities seem to be all with the fertility-cults of the Mediterranean basin, and have nothing in common with the prosaic Achaean religion. Yet Dionysos is the god of a Northern people, the Thracians, speaking an Indo-European tongue, and whatever accretions his cult may have acquired from the lands through which it spread, ecstasy and immortality are the gifts of the native Thracian religion. (WG 31–32)

In a note, however, Guthrie immediately adds that the *eastern* origins of Dionysos, his Phrygian-Lydian origins, in some sense remain "northern": as we have mentioned more than once, the Phrygians were originally a Thracian tribe that migrated eastward early on, perhaps at about 1200 BCE. It therefore becomes very difficult to sort out what sorts of "Asiatic" elements entered into the Dionysiac cult, and even more difficult to know in what language these elements expressed themselves, whether in the Indo-European or Semitic language groups. Guthrie is nevertheless able to solve the mystery of Dionysos's double origin, that is, of his having been both northern, hailing from Thrace, and eastern, invading Greece from Lydia or Phrygia. Semele herself, the mother of Dionysos, is not merely a princess of Boeotian Thebes, but, as a daughter of Kadmos, she is originally a Phrygian goddess "whose name can be recognized in the *Zemelō* of Phrygian inscriptions and who seems to have been a form of the Anatolian Earth-mother" (WG 154).[23] Yet Thrace is also relevant, inasmuch as, to repeat, "Thracians and Phrygians were of the same race, since some time in the second millennium BC there was a movement of tribes from Thrace across the Hellespont to settle in Asia Minor" (ibid.). Semele, Dionysos, and Kybele are therefore blood relatives. The *Korybantes* of the Phrygian mother, like the Kouretes of Cretan Rhea, are likewise related to the Dionysian satyrs and the Maenadic sisterhood. Guthrie cites lines 119–34 of Euripides's *The Bacchae*, setting in italic type the Phrygian, Thracian, and Cretan elements of this "one gloriously catholic stanza":

> O cave of the *Kuretes* and sacred haunts of *Crete*, birth-place of *Zeus*, where the *Korybantes* triple-helmed invented in thy grottoes this my circlet of stretched hide [i.e., the tympanum]. In *Bacchic* rout they mingled it with the shrill sweet breath of *Phrygian* flutes and gave it into the hands of *Rhea* his mother, fit sound to accompany the cries of *Bacchic* women. And from the Mother Goddess did the frenzied *Satyrs* borrow it, and joined it to the dances of the three-year feasts [i.e., the winter festival on Mount Parnassos above the temple of Apollo], in which *Dionysos* rejoices.

The syncretism of Dionysian traits combines elements from Anatolia, Egypt, Crete, Thrace, and Greece, all of them represented in the names "Dionysos, Zalmoxis, Sabazios, Attis, Adonis, Thammuz, Osiris and many others" (WG 156).[24]

---

23. In an earlier note (55n. 2), Guthrie says this about Semele: "Semele is fairly certainly a name taken from Thraco-Phrygian religion, being related to the Phrygian *Zemelō*, the earth. If so, she must have been introduced at Thebes contemporaneously with the worship of Dionysos. Similarly, Dione, the consort of Zeus in the strange oracular cult at Dodona, whose name is simply a feminine form of Zeus-Dios himself, must, one would think, have ousted a pre-Greek earth-goddess on the spot."

24. The mention of the "three-year feasts" at Delphi hints at the perhaps unexpected relation of Apollo both to Dionysos and the Great Mother. Guthrie notes a series of stories about Delphic Apollo and the need to respect the Phrygian Great Mother (188–89). After all, the very name *Delphi* refers to one of the words for the womb. As for the linkage between these two sons of Zeus, Apollo and Dionysos, Guthrie writes: "Dionysos himself was buried at Delphi, or so said one account, linking the story with the general belief that the grave of Dionysos was in the temple of Apollo there" (170). Buried, no doubt, during

Guthrie is careful not to identify the Achaean religion of the Olympian gods as the more highly developed and the Mediterranean-chthonic strain as the more "primitive" sort of religion. Indeed, he turns the tables on the usual set of expectations in a way that is highly reminiscent of Schelling. The ideas of communion with the god, of Mother worship, and all such "southern" or "eastern" modes of worship, all of them quite foreign to the Homeric world, "contained, despite their crudeness, possibilities of spiritual development which were lacking to the religion of Homer" (WG 34). What lies at the core of such "spiritual development," even with regard to the dwarfish daimons who surround the Mother? To begin with, Guthrie cites Strabo on the identity or at least close affiliation of the Cretan Kouretes with the Phrygian Korybantes (along with the Daktyls and Telchines) and the Cabiri of Samothrace (ibid.). Although, to repeat, Guthrie rarely mentions Samothrace in his book, the identity of Zeus as both Achaean sky god and Cretan cave god, that is, as an identity split into planes of power and weakness, is crucial to Guthrie's account. For that account, it is Zeus on the plane of weakness—as the helpless infant either protected or assassinated by the circling *Kouretes* and *Korybantes*—and not Zeus on the plane of strength that is important for the mysteries and hence for Greek religiosity and spirituality in general. Zeus on the plane of weakness is surely reminiscent of Schelling's account of hunger, poverty, and languor in the life of the divine. Guthrie's entire book is constructed about "a central problem," which is whether kinship with the gods is possible for the weak and ephemeral mortals or whether such an aspiration is simply hubris:

> There seem to be two ways of regarding the relationship between man and god which at first sight are diametrically opposed, yet are both strongly represented in the Greek tradition. We become aware of the problem if we try to answer the question: Did the Greeks think it possible or desirable for man to emulate the gods? We probably think first of the many warnings against the folly of setting oneself up to vie with heaven, of "thinking high thoughts" and forgetting that, as Herodotus said, "the divine is jealous," a maxim which the

---

winter—coinciding with the reign of Persephone in the underworld—at the time when fertility spirits, as we have already heard, are most active. On the subject of Delphi, the Mother, and the words for womb, see Krell, "Female Parts in *Timaeus*," in *Arion*, New Series 2/3 (Boston University, 1975), 400–21.

whole of his history and many Greek myths seem designed to illustrate.... What are we to say to the conception of man's religious duty which we find in Plato, [however], namely that his aim should be "the completest possible assimilation to god," and the downright statement of his pupil Aristotle that man's chief end is "to put off mortality as far as possible"? (WG 113–14)

In short, when it comes to approaching deity, how do the Greeks balance "fine abandon" with "prudent counsel"? Zeus worshipped on the plane of weakness: Is this not quite close to Schelling's imprudent insistence on yearning, obsession, and languishing at the core of deity?

The plethora of Greek heroes and demigods spawned by the mating of immortals with mortals only complicates the problem. Guthrie avows quite soberly the truth that dazzled Schelling's friend Hölderlin from his high school years to the end of his life: "The gods were captivated by mortal beauty" (WG 120). And when a god was captivated by a beautiful mortal woman, she was certain to become pregnant. As one of the dead souls in the underworld tells Odysseus (11:251–2), "A god's embrace / Is never barren." Yet mortal women become pregnant with mortal children, not with a god. Guthrie notes, "They [the children] had blood, not ichor, in their veins. Curiously enough, this conception of the gods, linking them morally and physically so closely to mankind, is the one which bars the way most effectively to any aspirations after divinity in man" (ibid.). Herakles is one of the few exceptions to the rule. Yet the rule itself must have inspired ancient casuists to inquire closely after Zeus's "golden rain" or Aphrodite's golden rooms: How could they have failed to transmit to their progeny the ichor that was the elixir of their own life? Surely divine ichor would overpower mere mortal blood? Surely golden rain would flush away mere mortal seed? Mortality itself, it seems, is the great mystery that binds the worshipper to gods and goddesses alike.

Dionysos is the central figure of this mystery too. For it is he who promises that a human being can be filled with god. Dionysiac experience "rests on the possibility of obliterating the line between human and divine, and, whether for a long period or for a brief moment of ecstasy, blending the two natures in one" (WG 49). Thus Dionysos is the test case for the central question of Guthrie's inquiry: Did the Greeks believe in an absolute split between god and mortal, such that the mortal's desire to become godlike would be sheer hubris, or did they in fact believe that divinity served as the ideal and even the end and goal of a human being?

What happens when one poses this question to Schelling? It seems at first that Schelling is interested in "the oldest system of humanity" precisely because of its promise of "a future life," which one almost automatically understands as immortality or the enduring rescue of the human psyche from death. Such rescue would seem to depend on a deity of power, not of weakness. Yet what Schelling emphasizes is that the Samothracian system promises a "better" life *and a "better" dying.* As the lecture and its notes proceed, it becomes clear that he does not deny death—neither for mortals nor, remarkably, for the so-called immortals. The penultimate word of the lecture (immediately prior to note 120) invokes those incantations that are designed merely to soothe a child's fright in the face of death, the incantations to which Socrates refers in *Phaedo* (77e). Schelling's final word on the matter is that the *consentes* or *socii*, like the stars of a constellation, are born together and insist on dying together.²⁵

From the outset of his *Ages of the World* up to and including his *Philosophy of Mythology* (see especially SW II/2, 605), what Schelling emphasizes is the passion, the suffering, longing, and powerlessness of gods and goddesses, not their imputed might and immortality. In Guthrie's language, the deities of Samothrace exist as much "on the plane of weakness" as "on the plane of strength." Whereas divine Leukothea—to whom we will turn in the following section of this inquiry—may toss a *salvavida* to a drowning mariner, saving a life in a dire situation, she does not toss immortality. Every rescue is but a delay, every salvation a postponement of the inevitable. In some uncanny sense, Leukothea remains true to her own having drowned even as she appears to open the distance between mortal and immortal, both guarding and putting into question the difference between the mortal she once was and the deity she now is.²⁶ Demeter, mourning her lost daughter, may eventually

---

25. Sandra Blakely, who stresses the role of *mediation* in the Samothracian cult, says this about the assimilation of initiates into "the community of the gods," that is, the *complices* and *consentes* stressed by Schelling: "The gods of Samothrace are consistently understood as a group, even in those texts which provide individual names, in opposition to the individual Kabeiros on the Theban sherd, or the sacred child Kabeiro born in the Lemnian rites" (SB 10). What remains unclear is whether the group identity of the *socii* has anything to do with immortality in any traditional sense.

26. For the story of Leukothea, see "The Tears of Kronos," which is chapter 5 of Krell, *The Sea: A Philosophical Encounter* (London: Bloomsbury, 2018) and

come around to letting the rains fall once again so that the earth will bear fruit, but she does not erase the difference between the ephemeral beings that we are and the ever living gods. Even so, she is powerless to avert her own daughter's fate. When Zeus shares his golden rain with Danaë, neither she nor her offspring will find that their veins now contain ichor rather than blood. As for what one might have called "Thracian immortality," Guthrie emphasizes the passing nature of divine possession: "The *ekstasis* was temporary, as was emphasized by Socrates' remark in the *Ion* about the contrast between the Bacchae when they are 'possessed' and when they are 'in their minds,' and as it receded they felt that the god had left them and that they were human—*thnetoi*—once more" (WG 180). These are the oldest narratives, the narratives that seem to have had the greatest impact on Schelling during the period of *The Ages of the World* and "On the Deities of Samothrace." Even if he firmly believes in "the spirit world," the world of Dionysos, the aspect of said world that interests him is "self-materializing deity," a goddess and a god for whom the word *matter* is a verb, not a noun. Or, if a noun, then one that is certainly derived from *mater*. Perhaps Schelling thinks of his friend Hölderlin once again at the moment when the poet speaks of *reversing* Zeus's "eternal tendency," that is, his tendency to remain aloof from the affairs of mortals, indeed by "*compelling him more decisively to the Earth.*"[27]

What compels such a descent? For the Schelling of *The Ages of the World* and "Samothrace," the answer is clear: the primal condition of deity is not omnipotence but helpless solitude, loneliness, hunger, and longing. There is initially *nothing* out there for it. The loneliness of deity, loneliness to the point of languishing, is perhaps the most daring insight of both Schelling and his friend Hölderlin. In the "Fragment of *Hyperion*," published in Schiller's *Thalia* in 1794, Hölderlin has Hyperion lament as follows: "Ah, the god in us is always lonely and wretched. Where will he find all those who are akin to him? Those who once were there and who some day will be there again? When will

---

section 5 of the present essay. One detail that I have learned since writing that chapter is that John Milton cites "Leucothea" in *Paradise Lost* (11:135): there she is another name for Eos, the Dawn, "To resalute the World with sacred Light / Leucothea wak'd, and with fresh dews imbalmed / The Earth." The dew of morning is reminiscent of both Leukothea's watery demise ("imbalmed") and her transfiguration ("sacred Light").

27. See Hölderlin's "Notes on Sophocles," in CHV 2:373–74.

it convene, the magnificent rendez-vous of spirits? For once upon a time, as I believe, we were all united" (CHV 1:493). Schelling, in his conversations with his friend, may well have countered that the loneliness and wretchedness of deity would assuredly have been the spur to any dream of union.

Let me not abandon too quickly this question of the identity and difference of immortals and mortals. It is a vital question ever since Heraclitus raised it darkly in his fragment B 62: "Mortals immortals, immortals mortals—each living the death of the other and dying their life." Walter Burkert elaborates on Guthrie's insight into the "plane of weakness" with respect to the gods. In his *Ancient Mystery Cults*, Burkert emphasizes the importance of "personal needs in this life and after death" for the ancient mysteries. He notes that not only on Samothrace but also quite generally in the mysteries, protection during sea voyages, or rescue from drowning, is a common hope of initiates (B87 19–20). Diagoras the Atheist sheds indirect light on this hope when, after having viewed all the votive offerings at Samothrace donated by those who escaped drowning, he observes that there would have been many more such offerings if those who did indeed drown would have survived and been able to send them. Diagoras is doubtless thinking ahead to Herman Melville's *Pierre; or, The Ambiguities*, which observes that "the sea is the sea, and these drowning men do drown." Mortals and immortals alike, it seems, are caught up in Melvillean *Ambiguities*. "Thracian immortality" would be one of those ambiguities—for Schelling too, I suspect. Recall how he translates Heraclitus B 32: Zeus is the solitary one who is emphatically desirous, even languorous, and thus decisively compelled back to earth. Zeus is the one who cannot bear to be alone.

From the most ancient times through the Roman period, the relation of Dionysian orgiastic cults to death and dying (once again one hears echoes of Heraclitus concerning the identity of Dionysos and Hades in fragment B 15) is a constant in such cults. Yet Burkert touches on Guthrie's and Schelling's question when he stresses that in any case it is not a matter of "resurrection" from the dead. Rather, it is a matter of trying to reduce the terror human beings experience in the face of death. Burkert adds, as though remembering a thesis of Freud's, that cult is perhaps preeminently a matter of assuaging the anger of the already dead. Be that as it may, among the Greeks "there was no dogmatic faith in overcoming death in mysteries, as there was no devaluation of life. There was neither gospel nor revelation to immunize believers against the disasters of this life. Mysteries, like votive religion, remained to some extent an experimental form of religion. As such, they could at times disappoint the hopes of the believers" (B87 29). Even if Burkert's observation seems post-Nietzschean (and post-Melvillean), one can readily imagine Schelling affirming it—an amazing concession on the part of any scion of an eighteenth-century Pietist Protestant household. In neither Dionysiac nor Mithraic rites is there a word about resurrection or rebirth: "To sum up," writes Burkert, "there is a dynamic paradox of death and life in all the mysteries associated with the opposites of night and day, darkness and light, below and above, but there is nothing as explicit and resounding as the passages in the New Testament, especially in Saint Paul and in the Gospel of John, concerning dying with Christ and spiritual rebirth" (B87 101). What there *was*, concludes Burkert, was the "Extraordinary Experience." That is to say, what the mysteries offered the initiate was "a chance to break out of the enclosed and barren ways of predictable experience," and this by way of "an amazing event of *sympatheia*" (B87 114). Yet what is *sympatheia* if not shared suffering?

5. Turns and Returns of the Cabiri

In spite of all the skepticism of archaeologists after Schelling, is there a chance that the Cabirian deities may, as it were, return to Samothrace?[28] Carl Kerényi, writing at about the same time as Bengt Hemberg, often has his differences with Schelling, but he is less skeptical than Hemberg about the importance of the Cabiri for everything we have been discussing here. And yet Kerényi adds an important aspect to the difficulties we have in interpreting the Samothracian system. He repeatedly emphasizes a twofold ambiguity concerning the gods, a twofold we could call *synchronic* v. *diachronic*. The synchronic ambiguity involves the gender identity of gods and goddesses, an identity that is often either expressly hermaphroditic or in some way refers to a *pair* of female and male divinities. Schelling himself, as we have seen, refers to an Aphroditos and a Deus Lunus among the Greeks and Romans, and in general is well aware of this ambiguity. Kerényi confirms that in the city of Amathus, on Cyprus, Aphrodite was worshipped as Aphroditos (CK 172). For its part, the diachronic ambiguity has to do with the slippage of identity between generations, such that the goddess is often

---

28. Such a return is eloquently affirmed by Jason Wirth in the final essay of the present volume.

indistinguishably maid and mother, mother and daughter, her consort both august father and threatened infant boy, both the consort and the child of the mother. Schelling too is quite aware of the recurrent slippage among the divine generations. The fourfold Cabiri cited by Mnaseas are surely susceptible to such ambiguities.

Early on in his text, Kerényi, agreeing with Hemberg, suggests the likelihood, *contra* Mnaseas, that the Great Mother has only male consorts and is the mother of a boy: "Thus the Great Mother appears with her two companions and her little darling: with three sons, who together with her constitute a quaternity" (CK 10). If it is true that "Hesiod always mentions the female divinity first" (CK 22), that is because she is preeminent in the fourfold. However, to make matters still more confusing, goddesses almost always appear as a *trinity* of females, either as a group of three sisters or as a threefold or triune goddess (CK 31). The number three represents the tripartite lunar month, the month of the neap *and* the flood and ebb tides, with the waxing, waning, and new moon. Whether as Moirai, Furies, Erinyes, the "gray goddesses," the Parcae, Sirens, Graces, or Gorgons, these three sisters combine their skills to weave the tapestry of any given human or divine life. Eurybia, the "strong" goddess, baneful Styx, and Hekate form such a trinity, and we often meet them (as perhaps Oedipus did) at a *trivium* (CK 33–36). Much later in his account, Kerényi confirms the equal likelihood of three female deities and one male precisely on Samothrace. What speaks to the probability of three goddesses and one male consort and/or son, to repeat, is the prevalence of what Kerényi calls the "Threefold Goddess": "Three appears to have been their [the nymphs'] basic number, the number of the Graces and of the other well-known Trinities, all of which imaged the dispersed form of a great Threefold Goddess. The nymphs can also certainly be said to do this. Hermes, their constant companion—often in the presence of Pan—represented the male fourth beside the female Trinity" (CK 178).

Kerényi elaborates on the magic threefold. The female trinity, the Threefold Goddess, also implies a *male* trinity, the three in each case having to do with the cosmic realms of the sky, the earth, and the underworld. The universe was ruled initially "much more by a threefold goddess than by a male divinity—the latter being merely the husband of the former" (CK 230). Or it may be that "the oldest goddess, the Mother of the Gods, has always had three sons, two of them older, and more closely identified as brothers [the Dioskouroi], than the third, the youngest, who is destined to gain supremacy"

(CK 230–31). Kerényi recognizes here a "basic scheme," in which "either a female or a male trinity predominates," the former entertaining a male fourth, the latter a female fourth (CK 231). Such are the dizzyingly ambiguous turns of deity!

Like Hemberg, Kerényi is also willing to complicate the question of the initiates' expectations concerning the Samothracian rite. He stresses the importance of Hekate in the Cabirian system, whether at Samothrace or, more likely, on Lemnos. Hekate is said to have been purified by the Cabiri in the Acherusian Sea of the underworld (CK 61). If we wonder how deities who help seafarers in distress could become the objects of worship of a far deeper and broader significance and not merely for the fishery, Kerényi gives us a clue: "The sea-goddesses were also oracular goddesses," he writes, adding, "the oldest of them, Tethys, had an oracular shrine amongst the Etruscans. Her granddaughters, the daughters of Nereus, could often—or so it was believed—rescue seamen in danger of shipwreck. It was they, too, who revealed to men the mysteries of Dionysos and Persephone" (CK 66). Thus the sea goddesses may be linked to the great goddess of the land, Demeter, at least as the Orphics and the worshippers at Eleusis understood her, namely, as the mate of Dionysos and the mother of Persephone. It does not require too great a stretch of the imagination to connect Samothrace with Eleusis, as Schelling certainly does.

The mysteries of Samothrace are often compared to those of Eleusis, Kerényi notes, because of the preeminence of Demeter and Persephone—and the role of Kore's father Zeus—in each. In the Orphic stories told and the rites practiced at Eleusis (less is known about Samothrace), the mating of Zeus and Demeter (producing Persephone) as of Zeus and Persephone (producing Dionysos Zagreus) are the central events (CK 113). Zagreus means "mighty hunter," notes Kerényi, although he neglects to say that it also means "the hunted, the quarry." Both Zeus and Dionysos may both be called hunter and hunted alike, indeed, emphatically so, inasmuch as ζα- is the emphatic prefix. The root -γρευς is more difficult to interpret; perhaps it derives from γράω, "to gnaw, eat, devour." In any case, Dionysos often joins Zeus on that "plane of weakness" mentioned earlier. The fact that Persephone is both daughter and mate of Zeus and that Zeus and Dionysos can be identified by the same epithet is evidence of that slippage between generations mentioned earlier. Kerényi argues that "the stories of the Daktyloi and the Kabeiroi" should prepare us for such turnings and such slippage (CK 114).

A further instance of slippage, one not yet mentioned, is the status of those various pygmy-like creatures somewhere between deity and humanity. Kerényi argues that they are creatures of our own human ancestry, reminiscent of the birth of Protalaos ("the first man") at Thebes, or of Kabeiros and Pais ("child"). He writes,

> It will be remembered how she, the Great Mother, always had with her Daktyloi, Kouretes, Korybantes, or Kabeiroi, whom she had bred from within herself and with whom she also bred further. In the various tales these beings became entire primitive peoples, such as the Telchines, the aboriginal inhabitants of the island of Rhodes. All primordial gods of this kind were at the same time primordial men. The difference between their two qualities doubtless lay in the fact that as primordial men they ceased to be husbands of the Great Mother, and received other wives. On Lemnos there were tales of three Cabirian nymphs, *Nymphai Kabeirides*. They were the daughters of the Great Goddess and the Kabeiros who bred from her, and they had three brothers, with whom they formed three pairs, which can be described as the first primordial human couples. (CK 211)

The stories of the creation of the first woman by master craftsmen—whether by the Titan Prometheus or the Olympian Hephaistos—are also tales of Daktyloi and Kabeiroi. Even the Pygmalion who, with a boost from George Bernard Shaw, eventually winds up in *My Fair Lady* is originally *Pygmaion*, a Cypriot king, but also a craftsman-dwarf (CK 211). Perhaps here we may recall Roberto Calasso's account of these befuddling dwarflike figures, called by many different names but ubiquitous throughout Greece, "the helpers, ministers, guardians, nurses, tutors, and spectators of the gods" (RC 302). Calasso suggests that these figures, touched by deity, are "initiates" in the mysteries—either that, or they themselves are the objects of the mysteries. They are perhaps precisely what Schelling calls them, namely, the *Dii con-sen-tes*, whose common fate enfolds them as *complices*; they are the *socii*, the divine company, born together, working their effects together, dying together. In that case, the designation *con*-sen-*tes* does not derive from *consentio, consensio,* or *sentio* at all. It is not so much that these gods (these mortal gods?) take counsel together and are in agreement with one another. Rather, as Schelling avers, the sense of -*sen*- is much older.

Surprisingly, and seemingly out of nowhere, Martin Heidegger hits upon it in his research into "the grammar and etymology of the word *being*," or

Sein.²⁹ Basing his account on that of the linguist Ernst Fraenkel, Heidegger analyzes the three roots of the words for *being*, primarily (1) the third-person singular present tense *ist* (*is, es, est, está, è*, etc.); (2) the first-person singular *bin*, as in the English homophone *been*, both deriving from the Latin *fui, fuo*, and ultimately from the Indo-Germanic stem *bhû, bheu*; and (3) the Old German *wes* (compare the English *was*), related to the hearth (*vesta*, Hestia) and hence to dwelling, residing. Heidegger puts particular emphasis on the present participles *wesend, an-wesend*, and *ab-wesend*, coming to presence, being present, and being absent. The *-sen-* of ab*sen*ce and pre*sen*ce does not have to do with *Wesen* or essence as *quidditas*, the "what-it-is" of a thing but rather with some older sense, now lost, a sense that in Heidegger's view clearly relates to the meaning of being, *das Sein*, as such. True, *-sen-* is not *sein*, and it might also appear to be closer to a scrambled form of *ens* or a truncated form of *Wesen*, but in any case Heidegger takes the *-sen-* of *con-sen-tes* to be a reference to *being*. Then, out of the blue, and with no reference to Schelling, he concludes his discussion by asking this: "Does the expression *Dii con-sentes* mean the gods as coming to presence together [*die beisammen an-wesenden Götter*]?" (EM 55). The first root of *to be*, the "is," Heidegger relates to the Sanskrit *asus*, "life and the living"; the second root, the *bhû* of "been," he relates to "upsurgence" and "dominion" (*aufgehen, walten*), referring to the Greek φύω, related to birth, growth, and nature generally. *Life, upsurgence*, and *tarrying awhile in presence* (*verweilen*) would then designate the three roots of *being*—and of being *together*.

Schelling, whether cited or not, is not remote from all this: recall that he speaks of the divine company, the *socii*, as living and dying together as one. More than the Olympian *council* of the gods is meant here; more than divine *counsel* and *consensus* is intimated here. The claim made by Schelling, and the question posed by Heidegger, express the strongest possible *ontological* connection between the Cabirian deities and beings as a whole: these gods *are* together and together they are the *causes* of being as such. In his 1842 lectures

---

29. Martin Heidegger, *Einführung in die Metaphysik* (Tübingen: Max Niemeyer, 1953), 54–56. Hereinafter cited as EM, with page number. Heidegger (EM 40) cites as his source Ernst Fraenkel, "Das Sein und seine Modalitäten," in *Lexis: Studien zur Sprachphilosophie, Sprachgeschichte und Begriffsforschung*, ed. Johannes Lohmann (1949), 2:149 ff.

on *The Philosophy of Mythology*, Schelling emphasizes that the Cabiri are not mere drudges but the *formellen* gods, *formell* in the positive sense of *formative, causative*. They are the *Deorum Dii*, "the gods of gods," gods that "comport themselves as pure causes" (II/2:605), born together, dying together. Their story becomes quite dramatic, at least when they are called Korybants, Kouretes, or Dactyls, inasmuch as they have to do with the birth of Zeus. They are helpmates to Rhea as she gives birth and protectors of the infant Zeus, drowning out his cries so that Kronos will not devour him. And yet. With a flick of Apollo's cloak, a different story emerges. It is the story of Zeus's twofold secret on the "plane of weakness," here betrayed by Roberto Calasso: "The secret of Zeus was made up of two parts: his having killed Typhon [the last of the powerful Titans]; and his having been killed, as an infant, in the Cretan cave. Zeus transferred the first secret to Apollo: Apollo killed Python. And the second to Dionysos: the baby Zagreus was killed by the Titans.... Just as Dionysos is the tearer apart and the torn apart, so Apollo is both the hunter and the quarry" (RC 304).

It is here that one begins to sense that these ancient stories, the myths that arise from or perhaps institute the mysteries, have much in common with the story invented or intuited by Freud in *Totem and Tabu*. The dwarfish warriors dance around the infant Zeus. "Are they protecting him? Are they about to kill him? They save him with the terrifying clamor of their weapons, and they trick him with toys, before burying their knives in his flesh" (RC 305). No doubt, as with every violent sacrifice—for the murder is not committed out of random cruelty—they eat him. And eating is, as Calasso says, "the primordial crime" (RC 311). It is the source of the ἀδικία, the being "out of joint," that Anaximander and Empedocles alike decry: existents insist on devouring other existents, and their very existence depends on the disappearance—the killing and consuming—of the other. Thus, for a reader of Freud at least, the dwarfish warriors become the brotherhood that will later be crushed by guilt, the guilt that all initiates must be taught to share. For if the father of the gods has his twofold secret, the initiates at Samothrace come to share that secret. One has to wonder whether Schelling is on the trail of this more audacious secret? One suspects that the rage and grief of Demeter and the poverty and impotence of deity generally, its *Schmachten* or languishing, have everything to do with the following realization, expressed in Calasso's telling words: "For those not initiated in the mysteries, they seem to have to do with the immortality of human beings; for the initiates, the mysteries are a moment when the gods become tangled with death" (RC 315–16). Calasso cites Plutarch's *On the Failure of the Oracles* at 417e: "Many things related to death and mourning are to be found mixed together in the initiation ceremonies" (RC 316). Likewise, Clement of Alexandria's *Hortatory Address to the Greeks* (2:19, 2) proclaims: "The mysteries can be summed up in just two words—killings and burials" (ibid.). Clement was perhaps careful not to write "killings and *consumings*," lest the latter word remind him and his readers of the Christian love feast.

Schelling would not have been altogether unprepared for such a dire initiation—if one can be prepared for the thought that the causes of all things, the formative gods, are subject to sacrifice and death. Although he begins by citing the Samothracian hope for a better life *and* a better dying, which is not exactly the same thing as a hope for immortality, he surely ends by remembering the relation of the mysteries to *tragedy*. Late in his life, after 1845, Schelling composes a series of lectures designed to provide a "philosophical introduction to the philosophy of mythology, or the presentation of a purely rational philosophy." In the twentieth of these entirely rational lectures, Schelling writes, "The world's portion and the portion of humankind are *by nature* tragic portions. And every tragic event that unfolds in the world's course is but a variation on the one grand theme that renews itself continuously. The deed in accord with which all suffering is scripted did not happen once and for all; rather, that deed *is happening* always and eternally. For it is not, as one of our poets says, 'something that never ever was'; it is what always and eternally is—'that alone which never grows old'" (SW II/1, 485–86).

Schelling would certainly have been haunted by his friend Hölderlin's indication, mentioned earlier, that "the father of the earth or of time," namely, Zeus, finds his trajectory being turned about—away from the "eternal tendency" and back to the earth of Eros and Thanatos. Concludes Calasso, "Hence the vertigo of the mysteries" (RC 315).

Such vertigo may induce a feeling that it must be blasphemous to speak of Zeus's death. It must be some sort of sacrilege to drag Zeus from the sky back down to earth. Here a remark by Guthrie may help. He is discussing Dionysos, whose cult experienced violent opposition when it was first introduced. Yet, beyond that, violent resistance seems to be a part of the Dionysian cult itself. For example, Lykurgos is said to have thrashed the Maenads with an ox goad, but whether this was to punish them or fulfill a requirement of the cult is the question. Guthrie says, "The ox-goad in the hand of the persecutor recalls the

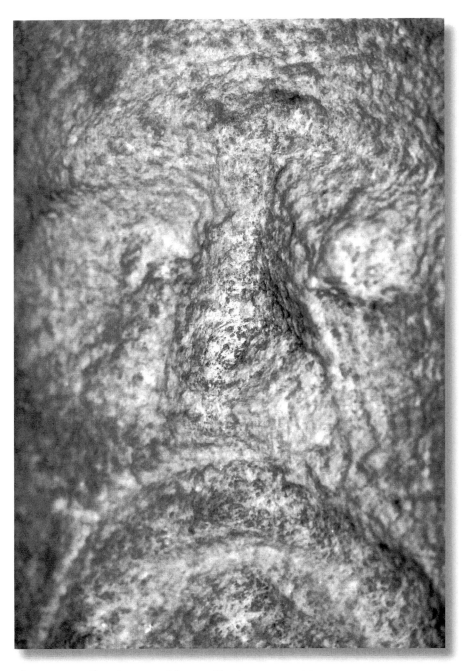

The unseeing, all-seeing eyes of the seer Tiresias, an essential character in Greek tragedy; detail of a marble statue at Samothrace dating from about 460 BCE by an unknown sculptor.

bovine form of the god, and may have been a ritual weapon. The scourging of women had its place in cult, being recorded by Pausanias of the biennial Dionysos-festival at Alea in Arcadia. At Orchomenos in Boeotia the maenads were pursued by the priest of Dionysos at the annual festival of the Agrionia, and the element of terror was very real, since if he caught one he put her to death, as happened once, says Plutarch, in his own lifetime" (WG 162).

The imbrication of violence and the sacred is of course present everywhere and is everywhere acknowledged, but one is always shocked to see it: the women worshippers of Dionysos are both his pursuers and his victims, and every prince, like Pentheus, would want to save the women from that treacherous immortal. This is the essence of scapegoating, where ugly is beautiful and friend is enemy, so that a noble prince would at least try to curtail it. And yet if King Pentheus violently opposes Dionysos and suffers violent death on account of his opposition, it is good to remember that Pentheus and Dionysos are first cousins and that Pentheus's fate closely resembles that of the god himself. Thinking of Pentheus perched high in his fir tree, spying on the women who will soon dismantle him, Guthrie notes: "It is therefore highly relevant to recall that in the ceremonies of mourning carried out for the Phrygian Attis, the body of the god was represented by a fir tree, which was wrapped in grave-clothes and decked with wreaths. Similarly Dionysos was known as δενδρίτης, the tree-god, and ἔνδενδρος, the god in the tree" (WG 62). Others will point out that the death of Christ resembles the violent deaths of Attis and Pentheus, killed on wood. The ultimate mystery of Dionysos is perhaps that in the end no living being *can* resist his or her shared destiny. Guthrie observes:

> Even the idea of opposition, with which the stories regularly start, was probably inherent in the ritual and comes into the myths primarily from that source and only secondarily, if at all, from the fact of historical opposition to his cult in Greece. It expresses indeed a deep and abiding truth about human nature as well as something inherent in Dionysiac religion, a truth which underlies a tragedy like the *Bacchae* and gives it its permanent and universal validity.... Every surrender to this power must have been preceded by opposition, which, at least among the Greeks, was sure to find imaginative expression in myth. (WG 172)

According to Hölderlin's "Notes on Antigone," it may well be that blasphemy and sacrilege alone open the space in which the god achieves epiphany.

As Antigone confronts her imminent death, she engages in a dialogue with the chorus. Hölderlin describes her words as "sublime mockery" and explains the need for such mockery in this way: "It is a great help to the secretly laboring soul that when it reaches the extremity of consciousness it evades consciousness, and before it actually grasps the god that is present it goes to meet that god with bold words—often, indeed, words of blasphemy—and in so doing it attains the holy and the living possibility of spirit" (CHV 2:371). Piety, otherwise known as obsequiousness and sycophancy, incites no theophany. The gods, it seems, like a challenge.

One of those challenges comes from Ino, one of Cadmus's four daughters, who has a special relation to the Samothracian cult. Ino finally brings us back to the importance of the Samothracian rites for sailors *and* for sowers. We know that the Dioskouri, who on Samothrace are called *Kabeiroi*, represent for all Greeks the twin stars that help guide the mariner at night. Yet the importance of Ino for seafarers goes back at least as far. Kerényi tells the story succinctly (CK 264). Ino, Semele's sister, is selected by Zeus to be the nurse of thigh-born Dionysos now that Semele has been blasted by Zeus's theophany. But the jealous Hera drives Ino mad. Ino, in her confusion, throws the infant god into a pot of seething water. She then, holding the dead god in her arms, plunges into the sea and drowns.

Details of Ino's subsequent elevation to divinity are vague. All we know is that after she drowns she becomes Leukothea, the shining goddess who is sometimes called Elektra and who gives both names to the isle that is later called Samothrace. It is Leukothea who lends Odysseus her purple veil, thus rescuing him from drowning, in one of the most dramatic scenes in all of Homer. Odysseus feels the raft beneath him breaking up in the fury of Poseidon's storm.

> But then Cadmus's daughter saw him, she of the shapely ankles, Ino
> Leukothea. She was once mortal and spoke with a mortal voice,
> Until she received godlike honors in the waves of the salt sea.
> She felt pity for Odysseus now, for he was wretchedly tossed about.
> She emerged from the depths and, swooping like a gull,
> Alighted on his raft and spoke these words to him:
> "Miserable man! Why is Poseidon so angry with you?
> Why does the Earth-shaker send you one ill after another?
> And yet he will not destroy you, though he would like to.
> Strip off your clothes and let your raft fly to the winds,

Whichever way they blow; you have hands to swim....
Take this immortal veil [κρήδεμνον ... ἄμβροτον] and tie it around
Your breast, so that you will never have to fear suffering and death.
Untie it as soon as your hands touch land beneath you,
Toss the veil far behind you into the winedark sea,
For it dare not touch the land. And then go your way."

(*Odyssey*, 5:333–350)

This is one of the original Samothracian stories: Odysseus, naked but for the goddess's purple sash, is the most famous of the initiates into the Samothracian rites. As for the infant Dionysos in Ino's arms, Guthrie would emphasize as much as Schelling does the importance of Dionysos in the Samothracian rite. He reminds us of the ubiquitous appearance of ships in the stories surrounding the god, and this in turn reminds us of the story of Ino Leukothea. There are multiple myths of Dionysos having been locked in a chest soon after his birth and the chest having been cast into the sea, so that his rebirth is an operation of the tides. The "arrival" of Dionysos is often by ship, the same sort of ship that carried his Tyrrhenian captors (WG 162). One of the most beautiful representations of the god is on the kylix by the sixth-century artist Exekias, "which depicts him reclining in a sailing-boat with dolphins playing around him and a vine growing out of the deck and overshadowing the sails" (WG 163).

Later initiates at Samothrace, under less dire circumstances than those suffered by either Dionysos or Odysseus, probably donned the purple sash at the outset of the ceremonies in the "theatral area" (B93 180) or "Holy Circle" on the eastern hill of the sanctuary. In the torchlit night, not far from the sea, as the initiates stood near the altar at the center of the circle, surrounded by observers who stood on five rows of stone stairs reminiscent of a theater, they must have felt the presence of Ino Leukothea and her infant charge. As the shining goddess, Leukothea was doubtless a figure of Persephone, herself a "Light ... furiously compassionate," and hence, by that metonymy or slippage across the generations, a figure of Mother Demeter herself (CK 264). What happens in such a night, the night of "gentle initiation," such that it gives birth to "an amazing event of *sympatheia*"?

6. On the Path of Initiation

Our young initiate—and let us assume that it is a she, although whether man or woman, slave or free, does not matter, at least on Samothrace—is alive

The "Holy Circle" on the eastern hill of the site. Built during the fifth century BCE, it became the place where, with initial instructions and sacrifices, the initiation began.

at the turn of the ancient millennium to the first millennium of the current era, when Caesar Augustus rules in Rome. By this time the glorious buildings of the Samothracian sanctuary of the Great Gods have been completed, gifts mainly of the Macedonian rulers and the Ptolemies over the past three centuries. A series of splendid temples now spreads across the hilly cult site.

Let us call our initiate Mnesarete. Her mother, initiated not two decades earlier when she learned that she was pregnant, has brought her daughter here from the Boeotian town of Thespiai. Mother and daughter are descendants of a long line of priestesses at the temple of Eros in Thespiai, one of them, Phryne by name, the most renowned courtesan of her time and the lover of the sculptor Praxiteles. Young Mnesarete has already climbed the hill from the port of Palaiopolis and is now passing through the monumental Propylon of Ptolemy II, the massive entry gate to the cult site. She feels very small as she passes through the narrow gateway of the immense Propylon and descends the ramp toward the Holy Circle. She can hear the torrent rushing below her, one of the two rivers that frame the sanctuary of the Great Gods before they converge and flow into the sea.

She stands with the small group of initiates—companions of every age and description—at the altar in the center of the circle. In the dazzling torchlight, she can see rows of past initiates standing on the periphery. She cannot make out her mother, but she knows she is standing there among the silent spectators. The priest of the Holy Circle speaks of the antiquity and holiness of the sanctuary, whose rites are older than anyone can remember. The language of those rites too is ancient, although the priest is fluent in both Latin and Aeolian Greek so that he is able to explain to the initiates the meaning of all the strange names involved in the mysteries. After he has given the initial instructions, he orders a group of boys and girls, the sanctuary's acolytes, to prepare the initiates. Two smiling girls gently strip Mnesarete, careful not to disturb the garland of wildflowers and ivy that her mother has woven for her hair; they cleanse her and robe her in white wool from shoulder to toe—for even in late July the night wind is chilly. Finally, she is given a shallow bowl and a cup that she holds in her left hand and an oil lamp that she holds in her right. The flame dances in the breeze coming off the sea.

Mnesarete's feet are bare, for these are sacred stones. She proceeds across a stepped ramp and down the Sacred Way along the eastern hill. To her left and right are the splendid buildings of the sanctuary, including the Rotunda of Arsinoë, which she will visit tomorrow. Mnesarete's group files to the Anaktoron, where the initiation proper begins. After instructions, lustrations, prayers, and libations by the priests in charge, the acolytes lead Mnesarete to a chair placed at the center of a raised circular platform. The silence of the night is broken by a chord struck on a stringed instrument. A slow and steady beat is sounded on the tympanum. An oboe murmurs a seductive phrase. A company of dancers, all of them women, surround Mnesarete in their ring dance, slow of step, the dancers smiling like brides. After the dance, two acolytes approach Mnesarete, who is now a proper initiate. The girls reach beneath her woolen robe, careful not to offend her modesty, and wrap about her waist the purple sash that all the initiates to the mysteries have worn since long before Homer's time. Mnesarete is then invited to enter the smaller area, the *adyton*, at the northwest end of the Anaktoron. She passes through the doorway flanked by the two bronze Dioskouroi or Kabeiroi, their arms raised high in the sacred gesture of epiphany. That gesture means "no!" to anyone who is not initiated, but now "yes!" to her. In the *adyton* of the Anaktoron something will be shown to her, something about heaven and earth, says Varro, but our initiate is not allowed to tell us what it is.

The rotunda may be the site of the next stage, although perhaps that magnificent building is reserved for the more public ceremonies that will take place tomorrow, so that Mnesarete's group merely passes it by tonight, all the initiates struck by its ornate marble facade decorated with rosettes and filleted bulls' heads, or bucrania. She processes with her small group toward the Hall of the Choral Dancers and the Hieron, the holiest of all the temples. The path from the Anaktoron first takes them downhill to the Sacred Stone, a huge pyramidal block of blue-green porphyry. It seems to Mnesarete a mountain in miniature. The green veins of the blue-black stone pulsate in the torchlight, as though stones too might be alive. The initiates stand on the smooth pavement that surrounds the stone; near by is another block of porphyry with a flattened surface, a trough carved into its side. Here each initiate pours a libation of honeyed wine; the precious liquid flows over the altar and down the incised trough to a narrow channel running along the ground. Mnesarete cannot see where the channel ends, but she knows that its destination is the deities of the world below.

The procession then ascends to the magnificent Hall of the Choral Dancers, a large temple designed by the sculptor Skopas and cladded with Thasian marble. It is decorated by an Ionic colonnade and a frieze of women dancers. The initiates will be asked to join the dance here, a wilder dance than the one back at the Anaktoron. For this dance is reminiscent of the tumultuous dances of whirling Korybants and Kouretes about the infant Zeus, as of the dances that took place at the marriage of Cadmus and Harmony, where mortals spun and twirled with the immortals and things got out of hand—dances inconceivable to us godless latecomers. Yet there might also be more restrained dances, commemorating Demeter's search for her vanished daughter, followed once again by joyful dances performed at the sacred marriage of Hades and Persephone. As she approaches the Hall of the Choral Dancers, Mnesarete can already hear the oboes and the tympani—oxhide shields beaten by spear shafts—resounding within.

Entering the hall, she sees Skopas's statues of Aphrodite, Eros, and Pothos. The mournful look of Pothos—his wings widespread for flight as though he were an Eros but his eyes gazing downward, distraught, to his left—reflects the grieving Demeter's search for her daughter and Ino Leukothea's grief over the role Hera forced her to play in the ritual death of Dionysos. Once the dances have been concluded—never did Mnesarete dance so gracefully and with so much inspiration, so that her entire cohort and even the priests were astonished—more libations are poured into a pit to the right of the entrance to the hall; a sacrifice to Cadmus the Founder is burned at the hearth in the opposite corner of the temple.

Our initiate is given one bite of the sacrificial lamb. It is barely cooked. She swallows it with difficulty. She will not eat a full meal until the ceremony is completed and the entire company crosses the bridge over the second torrent and ascends to the dining hall on the western slope. Higher up that hill, in the vast Stoa, a bed awaits her and her mounting exhaustion. For already here in the Hall of the Choral Dancers Mnesarete is being encouraged to drink freely of red wine, to imbibe what the uninitiated would surely condemn as "too much."

Mnesarete, elated by the wine, the music, and the dancing, and now by the night wind and the flickering torches outside the hall, proceeds up the slope on the eastern side of the nearby Hieron, the "Holy of Holies," the most splendid of all the buildings, with its Doric columns jutting high into the jet sky. There is a full moon, however, and she can see the outline of the mountains above the sanctuary, dominated by the Mountain of the Moon, Phengari, looming more than sixteen hundred meters above them. Before she is allowed to enter the Holy of Holies, she must stop at a place along the wall where two marble stepping stones have been placed. A huge torch, mounted on a slab between the stones, illuminates the entire area. Here there is nowhere to hide. One of the priests, the tiniest of them, no taller than she is but much heavier—she cannot suppress the thought that he looks like a dwarf—mounts one of the stones. He wears a richly embroidered white robe. A wide purple sash crosses his right shoulder and chest and is bound by a golden fibula over his left hip. Mnesarete mounts the other stone, as she has been instructed to do. She must now relate the worst deeds of her young life and she must swear never to reveal the rites and the mysteries. Earlier on, perhaps back at the Holy Circle, she has been told about the need for both this oath of secrecy and the disclosure of anything in her past that might pollute the sacred site, so that she has had ample time to reflect. The priest will decide, after hearing her confession, whether she may enter the Hieron. Unless she is guilty of a blood crime, however, it is unlikely that the priest will refuse her. She has thought long and hard. She mumbles her many faults, fearful that the night will overhear her. The dwarf smiles.

After her group enters the Hieron in formal procession, a sacrifice is made at the *eschara* or hearth in the center of the cella and a libation poured at its northwest corner. At that point a still higher level of initiation takes place; yet another *epopteia*, or "showing," is granted. What it is that gets shown our initiate is once again forbidden to reveal. Yet she has noticed that several of these otherwise magnificent buildings have earthen floors, more befitting a shepherd's hovel high in the mountains than glorious temples such as these, otherwise reminiscent of the temple dedicated to Eros in Thespiai, where she grew up. She is grateful for the smooth marble floor of the Hieron: all night long she has had to worry about her feet, for stones and boulders jut through the surface of the earth everywhere here, each one a reminder that all these buildings and all these rites are dedicated to the Mountain Mother, Our Lady of the Rocks. Perhaps the "showing" has been going on from the very moment she shuffled through the Propylon? Perhaps her eyes are in the soles of her feet?

As Mnesarete and her fellow initiates leave the Hieron, she sees the Hall of Votive Gifts and the Altar Court off to her right and beyond them the theater with its tiers of seats, white marble accented with red porphyry, rising up the hillside. Years ago her mother offered a gift to the Great Gods; tomorrow Mnesarete will present her own votive gift. And tomorrow, after further libations at the Altar Court and further ceremonies, sacrifices, and circle dances down at the Rotunda of Arsinoë, there will be performances at the theater, ritual plays involving local stories, among them the story of the infant Dionysos and the crazed Ino, now the goddess Leukothea, or the abduction of Persephone, ending with her marriage to Hades, or the marriage of Cadmus and Harmony, with all the mayhem that attended the wedding feast. Above the theater, awash in bright moonlight, she can make out

Magnetism seems to have played an important role in the Samothracian cult; pictured here are a magnetic stone and an iron ring, the latter probably given to every initiate.

the large fountain. There, at the rear of the fountain, alighting on the prow of a ship just as Leukothea alighted on Odysseus's raft, looms the Winged Victory, a gift from the citizens of Rhodes. Mnesarete, gazing up at the the Victory, her head tilted back as far as it can go, is suddenly beset by a bout of dizziness and bedazzlement.

In truth, by this time in the course of the long night, she remembers very little of what the priests have been saying. It is as though oblivion is helping her to keep her pledge of secrecy. But she does recall—not word for word but the gist of it—something that a handsome bearded priest in the Hieron has just now said about the sufferings of Demeter and Dionysos. His pale blue eyes were sparkling as he murmured the words.

—Loved one, love on! But know that heaven hath no roof. To know all is to be all. Beatitude there is none. And your only happiness is but exemption from great woes—no more. Great Love is sad; and heaven is Love. Sadness makes the silence throughout the realms of space; sadness is universal and eternal; but sadness is tranquillity; tranquillity the uttermost that souls may hope for.[30]

Precisely when Mnesarete receives her metal ring, fashioned of iron and sensitive to the magnetism of the Samothracian lodestone, we do not know. Perhaps the ring is given at the very end of the initiation, as though the initiate herself has been wedded to the mysteries?

7. Concluding Remark

Dare one dream that philosophers today—no doubt they would have to be young philosophers since the old ones have gone sclerotic—might discuss some of the themes touched on here? In a secular and skeptical age, deity doubtless does not draw. And yet. What if deity were now marked by two things we usually do not associate with the holy? What if deity were multisexual, more than bisexual, more than dual, and what if sexual activity itself were taken to be sacred? That might inspire comment, or at least a thought or two. And what if deity were not always majestic and never omniscient,

---

30. The priest, clearly a magician and hence clairvoyant, is reciting from future memory the words of a figure in Herman Melville's *Mardi, and a Voyage Thither* (Evanston and Chicago: Northwestern University Press and The Newberry Library, 1970), 636.

certainly by no means omnipotent, but sometimes consumed by hunger, languor, grief, and mourning? What if the holy, instead of being hale, whole, and wholesome, as we were always taught, were riven and torn? Recall the testimony of Crazy Jane, who, after talking to the Bishop, concludes,

> "For nothing can be sole or whole
> That has not been rent."[31]

It is as though Crazy Jane, not known for her bookishness, has absorbed a great deal of Schelling's philosophy. For, as both Alexander Bilda and Jason Wirth persuasively argue in the following two essays, Schelling is in search of a divine principle that no traditional, and certainly no orthodox, theology has uncovered heretofore. From *The Ages of the World* on, through the months devoted to "The Deities of Samothrace" and the years at Erlangen, and even during the final years in Berlin, Schelling is in search of what in *The Ages of the World* he calls "a barbaric principle" in the life of the godhead, a principle that hovers undecidably between freedom and necessity. Whether that principle be expressed in the Phoenician-Hebrew or Thracian-Phrygian language systems is surely less important than the fact that it expresses a mystery— perhaps *the* mystery, that of the *socii* and *consentes* in their "ring dance of stars."

Among the Orphic stories, but also in the teachings of Pherekydes of Syros, the most important cosmogonic myth is that of the egg hatched by night, the egg containing Eros, later called Phanes, "the shining one" (CK 114). These two names, Eros and Phanes, assume the highest philosophical significance in Plato's definition of *beauty* as superlatively radiant and most erotic. At 250d 8 in *Phaedrus*, Socrates says, "To beauty alone has it been allotted to be what shines most brightly and incites love most ardently." His two superlatives are τὸ ἐκφανέστατον and τὸ ἐρασμιώτατον. Schleiermacher translates these two superlatives, the first containing the name Phanes, the second the name Eros, quite beautifully: he calls Phanes *das hervorleuchtendste* and Eros *das liebreizendste*. Together, as beauty, they are that which shines forth most brilliantly and incites love most passionately.[32]

---

31. "Crazy Jane Talks with the Bishop," in William Butler Yeats, *Complete Poems* (New York: Macmillan, 1956), 255.

32. Schleiermacher himself presents these two superlative nouns in lowercase letters, as though they were action words, not names. It is precisely this passage in Plato's *Phaedrus* that Heidegger took to be the supreme moment of Plato's

Phanes and Eros, together with the Mother, or rather in and through the Mother herself, engender all that is beautiful. They inaugurate all the ages that the world has passed through so far. By now, in our own time, in "an age that in so many respects is accustomed to fraud," the reign of deities of any kind seems to have crumbled, although nothing has come to take their place. Never enough life insurance, never enough apparent progress, never enough sedation, as the night advances. Yet night in her oldest guise is both the mother and the mate of Phanes, "radiance," in the ring dance of generation. She is also the mother and the mate of Eros, "love," without whom where would we be?

Radiant creatures of languor and mourning, the Cabirian gods and goddesses of Samothrace, precisely where the "barbaric principle" is at home, testify to the love that suffers loss and endures on the plane of weakness, the plane of mortality. What did the priest of the Hieron say? "Sadness makes the silence throughout the realms of space." Even as figures of languor and languishing, however, Demeter and her daughter Persephone regularly recreate themselves and us, "weaving the raiment of mortality," as Schelling says, "and spinning the bedazzlement of the senses." They are more promise for the future than rage against the past. For it is they who in the sea of their divine bellies grant Homunculus a mortal body.

Key to the Main Sources Cited

AA   Friedrich Wilhelm Joseph Schelling, *Historisch-kritische Ausgabe im Auftrag der Schelling-Kommission der Bayerischen Akademie der Wissenschaften*. Ed. Hans Michael Baumgartner et al. (Stuttgart-Bad Cannstatt: Frommann-Holzboog, 1976–ongoing).

AG   A. J. Graham, "The Colonization of Samothrace," in *Hesperia*, 71:3 (July–September 2002), 231–60.

AR   "Apollonius of Rhodes," *The Argonautica*, tr. R. C. Seaton (Cambridge, Massachusetts: Harvard University Press, 1961).

---

thinking as a whole. It was this dialogue, rather than *Sophist* or *Parmenides*, both of which he also admired and studied, that he placed on the list of the essential works in the history of metaphysics. And it was precisely this passage in *Phaedrus* to which he devoted one of his most insightful lectures. See Martin Heidegger, *Nietzsche*, 2 vols. (Pfullignen: Günter Neske, 1961), 1:227–31; in English translation, *Nietzsche*, 4 vols. (San Francisco: HarperCollins, 1993), 1:195–99.

B87 Walter Burkert, *Ancient Mystery Cults* (Cambridge, MA: Harvard University Press, 1987).

B93 Walter Burkert, "Concordia discors: The Literary and the Archaeological Evidence on the Sanctuary of Samothrace," in Nanno Marinatos and Robin Hägg, *Greek Sanctuaries: New Approaches* (London and New York: Routledge, 1993), 178–91.

BH Bengt Hemberg, *Die Kabiren* (Uppsala: Almqvist & Wiksells, 1950).

CK Carl Kerényi, *The Gods of the Greeks* (London and New York: Thames & Hudson, 1951).

DK Hermann Diels and Walther Kranz, *Die Fragmente der Vorsokratiker*, 3 vols. 6th ed. (Zürich: Weidmann, 1951). I cite this text merely by fragment number (e.g., Heraclitus B 62).

DS Diodorus of Sicily, *The Library of History*, 12 vols., tr. C. H. Oldfather et al. Loeb Classical Library (Cambridge, MA: Harvard University Press, 1993).

EJ *The Works of the Emperor Julian*, 3 vols., tr. W. C. Wright. Loeb Classical Library (Cambridge, MA: Harvard University Press, 1962).

GB Giuliano Bonfante, "A Note on the Samothracian Language," *Hesperia*, 24:2 (April–June 1955): 101–109.

HH Harald Haarmann, *Universalgeschichte der Schrift* (Frankfurt am Main: Campus, 1990).

KP *Der Kleine Pauly: Lexikon der Antike*, 5 vols, ed. Konrat Ziegler and Walther Sontheimer (Munich: Deutscher Taschenbuch, 1979).

KW Katherine Welch, "A Statue Head of the 'Great Mother' Discovered in Samothrace," *Hesperia*, 65:4 (October–December 1996): 467–73.

L39 Karl Lehmann-Hartleben, "Excavations in Samothrace," *American Journal of Archaeology*, 43:1 (January–March 1939): 133–45.

L50 Karl Lehmann, "Samothrace: Third Preliminary Report," *Hesperia*, 19:1 (January–March 1950): 1–20.

L55 Karl Lehmann, "Documents of the Samothracian Language," *Hesperia*, 24:2 (April–June 1955): 93–100.

LG Karl Lehmann, *Samothrace: A Guide to the Excavations and the Museum*, sixth, revised, and enlarged edition (Thessaloniki: Institute of Fine Arts, New York University, 1998), Library of Congress catalogue card number 55–8563.

MB D. Matsas and A. Bakirtzis, *Samothrace: A Short Cultural Guide*, 2nd revised and enlarged ed., tr. Dimitris Matsas and Bill Phelps (Athens: Ephorate of Prehistoric and Classical Antiquities, 2001).

OR Otto Rubensohn, *Die Mysterienheiligtümer in Eleusis und Samothrake* (Berlin: R. Gaertner's Buchhandlung Hermann Heyfelder, 1892).
PF P. M. Fraser, *Samothrace: The Inscriptions on Stone* (New York: Bollingen Series LX, 2, 1; Pantheon, 1960).
RC Roberto Calasso, *The Marriage of Cadmus and Harmony*, tr. Tim Parks (New York: Alfred A. Knopf, 1993).
RG Robert Graves, *The Greek Myths*, 2 vols. (Harmondsworth: Penguin, 1955).
SB Sandra Blakely, "Kadmos, Jason, and the Great Gods of Samothrace: Initiation as Mediation in a Northern Aegean Context," in *Electronic Antiquity: Communicating the Classics*, ed. Terry Papillon, 11:1 (November 2007): 1–21.
SC Susan Guettel Cole, *Theoi Megaloi: The Cult of the Great Gods at Samothrace* (Leiden, Belgium: E. J. Brill, 1984).
SW F. W. J. Schelling, *Sämmtliche Werke*, ed. Karl Schelling (Stuttgart and Augsburg: J. G. Cotta'scher, 1859). Schelling's *Die Weltalter* is cited from the edition by Manfred Schröter: F. W. J. Schelling, *Die Weltalter Fragmente: In den Urfassungen von 1811 und 1813*. Nachlaßband to the Münchner Jubiläumsdruck (Munich: Biederstein and Leibniz, 1946). This volume presents the original versions of *Die Weltalter*, set in print but not released for publication in 1811 and 1813; I cite it without code by version (i.e., either 1 or 2) and page number in the body of my text.
WG W. K. C. Guthrie, *The Greeks and Their Gods* (Boston: Beacon, 1950).

One of the many pristine pools formed by the Phoniás River high in the mountains of Samothrace.

5

The Importance of Schelling's *Deities of Samothrace* for His Own Work and for His Contemporaries

ALEXANDER BILDA

The importance of the *Deities of Samothrace* for the development of Schelling's own work cannot be overestimated. This is all the more true as his final book publication is still today scarcely considered by current research into Schelling's philosophy. Certainly, this avoidance may be attributed to its design: it presents itself not only as a philosophical work but also as belonging to classical studies. It is supported by an impressive philological-historical framework of endnotes that far exceeds the main text in length. Given the breadth and depth of Schelling's knowledge and his language skills, we are often forced to confront our own ignorance and even our difficulty in following the argumentation. Today we lack the essentials, namely, a thorough knowledge of the ancient languages, the ancient sources, and the early modern literature that deals with these sources. Yet the hermetic notes themselves are saturated with philosophy. They pertain to a living philosophical core that rises from a seed planted in deep soil, coming to maturity in Schelling's *The Ages of the World* and *Erlangen Lecture Course* and finally flourishing in his late *Philosophy of Mythology*.

Today's readers may rest assured that the problem of understanding the *Deities* was already a problem for his contemporaries, a problem that concerns precisely the *philosophy* contained within this work. The core of the problem lies in the overlapping of philosophical aspects, on the one hand, and philological, historical, and archaeological aspects, on the other. In his *Introduction to the Philosophy of Mythology*, Schelling writes concerning his reflections in 1815 that "their philosophical content and relevance was little understood, or rather not understood at all, in Germany" (SW II/1, 196n1).

Schelling would have seen his opinion confirmed when reading reviews of the *Deities*, which, with the exception of those by Friedrich Creuzer, manifested scarcely any understanding at all of his historical-philosophical investigation. The *Philosophy of Mythology* is Schelling's last attempt to correct this lack of understanding. Many others preceded this last attempt, especially from Schelling's days at the University of Erlangen. These efforts were accompanied by solid scholarship in the classics, evident in several brief texts by Schelling. Both Schelling's philosophical-systematic undertakings and his research in classics can be traced back to their germ in the *"Deities."*[1]

The following report will indicate what role the *Deities* plays in Schelling's work as a whole (sect. 1). Just as the island of Samothrace situated in the North Aegean Sea, is remote, so also is Schelling's work on the *Deities* well hidden in his philosophy. From its distance and depth, however, that work unfolds enormous power. Although the book deals with a single phenomenon—the emergence of the Samothracian Cabiri—its philosophical content is central to Schelling's philosophy in general. Accordingly, various motifs crucial for his thinking, such as hunger and longing or the unity of the many, are worked out here. In what follows, I will review their presence in the *Essay on Human Freedom* and *The Ages of the World*, then in the *Erlangen Lecture Course*, and finally in Schelling's late philosophy. To put Schelling's development in a nutshell: the remarkable priority of the hunger motif gradually recedes in favor of the unity motif; in other words, Schelling's monotheistic aspirations increasingly prevail during his career of thought.

A second aspect of the present paper involves the *reviews* of Schelling's *Deities*, reviews that have not yet been taken into account in the literature on Schelling (sect. 2).[2] As a late scion of the *Querelle des Anciens et Modernes*,

---

1. A precise philological discussion and processing of all the relevant material cannot be carried out here. For such a thorough processing and discussion, see now the recently published historical-critical edition of Schelling's works (AA I, 19).

2. Only one monograph on the topic of Schelling's *Deities* is available today, and it does not treat the reviews at all: Volker Reinecke, *Der Wiederholungsprozess und die mythologischen Tatsachen in Schellings Spätphilosophie: Eine religionswissenschaftliche Studie unter der Voraussetzung des Verhältnisses der "Weltalter" zu den Abhandlungen "Über die Gottheiten von Samothrake"* (Rheinfelden: Schäuble, 1986). Christian Danz has recently mentioned four of the reviews, CD 182n4. For further, but still meager literature, see also CD 183n7 and the more detailed remarks in Martin Dönike, *Altertumskundliches Wissen in Weimar* (Berlin/

these reviews continue the debate about the right way to deal with antiquity. They bear witness not only to Schelling's daring and almost foolhardy plan to place the cult of Samothrace at the center of a new philosophy but also to the exuberant interest of contemporary scholars in his attempt. Only the *System of Transcendental Idealism* of 1800 seems to have received more reviews than the *Deities*.[3] With at least seven reviews in German and one in English, not counting mere announcements of the book,[4] they surpass the five known reviews of the *Essay on Human Freedom* (AA I/17, 73). Schelling's innovative approach to his subject is not least evident in the biting criticism his contemporaries direct at this work. Because no comprehensive treatment of the reviews has been presented to date, I trace their principal lines of criticism and reasoning, although their complex and extensive argumentation cannot be fully presented here. In their efforts to understand (or not understand) Schelling's text, the reviews commonly open it up precisely at points that cause particular difficulties for us as well. In order to understand the tendency of the reviews, I will first explain how Schelling's *Deities* is to be positioned against a philology shaped by the Enlightenment—personified in Johann Heinrich Voss—and succeeding upon the efforts of Christian Gottlob Heyne and his pupil Friedrich Creuzer, who was Schelling's contemporary. Finally, I will report on the significant impression the *Deities* made in England and France; indeed, the *Deities* became the first French

---

Boston: Walter de Gruyter, 2013), 187–191. Dönike, however, does not mention one of the few English commentators, namely, Kyriaki Goudeli, *Challenges to German Idealism: Schelling, Fichte and Kant* (London: Palgrave Macmillan, 2002). See also Kyriaki Goudeli, "In Quest of a Possible Re-Enchantment of the World: Reflections on Schelling's Study on *The Deities of Samothrace*," *European Journal of Social Theory* 4:3 (2001): 295–310. A new addition to these studies is Christian Danz, ed., *Schellings Gottheiten von Samothrake im Kontext* (Vienna: Vienna University Press, 2021). This volume arose from a workshop organized in 2020 by the editors of the historical-critical edition of Schelling's works. In the course of the workshop, we were able to provide the editors with additional information allowing for a full account of the reviews.

3. The *System of Transcendental Idealism* was discussed in twelve reviews. See the overview in AA I/9, 2, 24–26.

4. See, for example, the rather odd announcement in *Denkschriften der Königlichen Academie der Wissenschaft zu München für die Jahre 1814 und 1815*, vol. 5 (Munich, 1817), ix–x. See also note 32, below.

translation of a work by Schelling—and probably the first translation of any work by Schelling.

1. The Place of the *Deities* in Schelling's Work

Schelling's son Karl is the first who, after Schelling himself, assigns the *Deities of Samothrace* its systematically decisive place in his philosophy. In the foreword to the volume of his father's *Sämmtliche Werke* in which the *Deities* is republished with corrections and slight changes, Karl Schelling states,

> The book *On the Deities of Samothrace* was described at its appearance as a "Supplement to *The Ages of the World*," but with the explanation ... that this addition does not suspend their independence, as well as their connection with other works still in prospect. At least the edition of the first part of *The Ages of the World*, which is included here, is related to it only by rare references. However, it reveals that decisive progress has been made in the determination of the first foundation of philosophy, to which Schelling himself (SW II/1, 294) drew attention. (SW I/8, vi)

Karl Schelling takes this remark "Supplement to the '*Ages of the World*,'" which Schelling's *Deities* includes in the title, as a rather surprising opportunity to make the references to *The Ages of the World* seem as meager as possible. This assertion contrafact should make us suspicious. Karl Schelling is here certainly following his father's later intention, since Schelling's late philosophy sought to distance itself from the philosophy of *The Ages of the World*.[5] However, the *Deities* stands in close relation to *The Ages of the World*, a relation Schelling clearly indicates through the "supplement" subtitle. Yet to designate the work as a supplement is still rather an understatement. The *Deities* illustrates and proves, as it were, what *The Ages of the World* develops within an ontotheological context as languor or longing (*Sehnsucht*) and addiction or languishing (*Sucht, Schmachten*). The Samothracian deity Axieros

---

5. Such distancing becomes clear not least in Schelling's intellectual testament. See Horst Fuhrmans, "Dokumente zur Schellingforschung IV: Schellings Verfügung über seinen literarischen Nachlaß," *Kant-Studien*, 51:1 (1959/60): 14–26, esp. 14; see also SW II/3, 138–39n1. Perhaps Schelling's subsequent corrections to the text of the *Deities*, which go beyond the correction of mere errors (represented by square brackets in SW), can also be interpreted as a distancing.

in fact embodies this languishing and hunger.[6] In Axieros we find the figure depicting the "determination of the first foundation of philosophy," that is, the place where the foundation of Schelling's philosophy takes place. This "place" is essentially characterized by being perpetually in withdrawal—perpetually resituating itself *as* withdrawal.

Schelling's retrospective description, however, also refers to his later distinction between "negative" and "positive" philosophy by the position of the *Deities* as the *initial* basis of his philosophy. Another foundation is said to be given with his "positive" philosophy. While this prioritization, which at the same time involves a disempowerment of the *Deities*, is carried out only internally in 1815, Schelling's later approach merges the *Deities* with a so-called "negative philosophy," from which a "positive philosophy"one can then distinguish itself. Even if it would be wrong to dismiss Schelling's *Deities* as a specialized treatise, Schelling himself does not draw as much on the investigation of the Cabiri in later periods of his work as one would have expected. This is due not only to the fact that the panorama of his philosophy expands considerably but also to a philosophical reorientation that de-emphasizes precisely the moments of withdrawal and longing in favor of an ostensible overcoming of these traits.

A. The *Essay on Human Freedom* and *The Ages of the World*

The motif of hunger and longing that Schelling associates with the Samothracian deities has, as so often with Schelling, precursors of its own. The figure of longing can be read as a solution to the deficits of his identity philosophy, which did not seem to admit an adequate form of finitude vis-à-vis absolute identity. It is precisely the problem of the transition from identity to difference that is mediated through longing, inasmuch as in longing a unifying effort seeks to concretize itself, even if in the end it fails.

At the height of the identity philosophy, the first approaches to a Ceres project can be found. Indeed, Schelling announced such a project to August Wilhelm Schlegel in an 1802 letter.[7] I doubt that the basis for the much later

---

6. Goethe expressed in his *Faust II* the fact that the motif of hunger is central to Schelling's *Deities*. For a detailed development of the motif of longing, see David Farrell Krell, *The Tragic Absolute*, esp. 84–89 and 135–48.

7. Schelling to August Wilhelm Schlegel, dated November 29, 1802; Plitt I, 432.

Deities was actually already laid here, as Hans Kunz confirms, especially since Schelling's intentions with the Ceres project are more likely to have been literary in nature.[8] Even if remnants of the Ceres project can still be found in the conclusion of the essay "On the Relationship of the Philosophy of Nature to Philosophy in General," which was written at about the same time as the letter to Schlegel, the Ceres of 1802, who "arrives exhausted at *Eleusis*,"[9] is much more harmless than the powerful Ceres (or Demeter-Axieros) on Samothrace. Although the "indissoluble chain,"[10] which Schelling cites as early as 1802, is strongly reminiscent of the magic chain of Samothracian deities, the concatenation of 1815 goes much deeper than that of 1802. This deeper foundation is already reflected in the fact that Axieros is to Demeter what Demeter is to Ceres, taking us from a Roman to a Greek and then to a pre-Greek or archaic goddess. The concatenation of the finite and the infinite, for which the finite is flawed in a way that can be remedied only by a philosophy of absolute identity, stands in opposition to the concatenation of the Samothracian gods, who possess an irreducible eternity of their own. The more powerfully developed form of longing (*Sehnsucht*) is therefore a later addition, long after 1802.

It is in the *Essay on Human Freedom* that Schelling characterizes the "hunger of selfishness" (SW I/7, 390) as evil's quest to create a unity, a unity it destroys precisely in the endeavor to create it. This addiction or obsession, however, remains limited to the level of the human spirit, just as the whole essay represents only a certain part of the whole. Whereas the *Essay on Human Freedom* compresses the whole into a special part, insofar as it treats the person who is in the center of the ontotheological whole, the *Deities* itself is located at the very center of the whole of being, "special" only insofar as it is a historical example, albeit an archaic one.

One year after the freedom essay, in the *Stuttgart Private Lectures*, Schelling basically maintains the structures of the *Essay on Human Freedom*. He merely positions the "hunger for being" (SW I/7, 466) in the mind of spirit itself as an

---

8. See Hans Kunz, *Schellings Gedichte und dichterische Pläne* (Zürich: Juris, 1955), 68. My thanks to Christopher Arnold for this reference.

9. F. W. J. Schelling, "On the Relationship of the Philosophy of Nature to Philosophy in General," in *Between Kant and Hegel Texts in the Development of Post-Kantian Idealism*, trans. George Di Giovanni and H. S. Harris (Indianapolis: Hackett, 2000), 379; AA I/12, 2, 474, translation slightly altered.

10. Ibid., 380; AA I/12, 2, 474.

insatiable addiction, an obsessive desire and a lust for being, as it were, which distinguishes spirit in its deepest potency. All these considerations are no doubt radical for the concept of human freedom. Yet, however much human freedom is central here to the overarching scheme of the world, these reflections remain limited to the merely human. Indeed, Schelling's method of anthropological analogy is what lends these considerations their plausibility.

With the philosophy of *The Ages of the World*, Schelling reaches out more comprehensively to the whole of philosophy, where he measures nothing less than the relationship between time and eternity. When Karl Schelling restricts the few references between *The Ages of the World* and the *Deities* to the version of *The Ages* he published in 1814–15, he is arguably suggesting that the other versions better demonstrate these references. And in fact the earlier versions and fragments of *The Ages of the World* contain both stronger formulations of the figure of hunger and more apt references to this figure and its significance in antiquity.

Already in the earliest version (1811), the motif of hunger is depicted as consumption or the will to consume, a level that reaches beyond God to "the brilliance of the inaccessible light" in which "God dwells" (WA 16).[11] Schelling here already refers to this "devouring force of purity" that "consumes all being in itself as in a fire" (WA 16), attributing it equally to God and to man as a "lustrous radiance" (*Lauterkeit*) whose pristine purity surpasses and strains them both. Nevertheless, the dynamic initiated by this radiance remains largely underdetermined, especially in the contradictory descriptions of it as simultaneously starving and all-consuming. If the clearest and most fitting words for what Schelling describes are found right at the outset of this development, in 1811, it is only after a long process that their more detailed explication follows. In the 1813 version of *The Ages of the World*, a structure of longing, or *Sehnsucht*, is established that is decisive for the philosophy of that period: "The eternal will . . . posits itself as the mere *will* of eternity and

---

11. Schelling takes up these descriptions again and again. In addition to the passages to be explained in greater detail, there are many more, such as WA 173, 213, and 219; and from the 1814/15 fragment of *The Ages of the World* SW I/7, 230, 236, and 265. For the fragments of *The Ages of the World*, edited by Klaus Grotsch, which are still too little considered, see SG 1, 174, 193, 195–6, 248; 2, 34, 106–7, 165, 280, 302. Besides the abovementioned passages of the *Essay on Human Freedom*, see SW I/7, 381, and 391; also the *Stuttgart Private Lectures*, SW I/7, 438, 448, and 483.

in this respect as negated. But positing himself as negated, he is at the same time the self-negating will. He cannot deny himself... as being the being (*das Wesen seyend*) without positing himself as deprivation and, insofar he is at the same time effective, as hunger, as addiction [or obsession: *Sucht*], as craving for being" (WA 138). Exclusion from what eternity is traditionally taken to mean is understood here as negation because the will that wants eternity simply is not itself eternity. But this also means that a beginning is postulated in eternity as a rupture, as it were, in an otherwise flawless eternity. Eternity can claim reality only if it is opposed by something against which it can assert itself. Otherwise it would remain unconscious. In this respect, it is the will that establishes at least the possibility that eternity *is*—if not in itself, then in its desire, its hunger. Such longing becomes the beginning of the entire theogonic process that Schelling sketches out in *The Ages of the World*. An undated fragment brings this thought even closer to the *Deities* by describing this central idea as a thought of the earliest antiquity:

> This silent, germinating inward-turn is in itself still powerless and without deed; it is most comparable to hunger, which does nothing, yes, in a sense is nothing, and yet is the greatest agony. But precisely this hunger of nothingness becomes the mother of the deed and is the eternal and actual beginning, which, as the word suggests, cannot consist at all in giving, expressing, or sharing, but only in taking, robbing, drawing all toward itself. This hunger is the true all-attracting magnet, the first but also constantly continuing tension of the bow in whose image the remote antiquity of life already imagined itself. (WA 216)[12]

In well-nigh unsurpassed radicality, Schelling describes here the way in which the dynamics of life, the way in which vitality, and the most original movement of the living can be understood, namely, from an emptiness described as hunger, an almost absolute hunger, a craving that in its all-consuming and fundamental negation gives rise to all beginning. One is tempted to use an early formulation by Freud to designate it: according to Freud's 1895 "Project toward a Scientific Psychology," every newborn, its mouth already in search of the breast, confronts *die Not des Lebens*, "the exigency of life."[13]

---

12. See also WA 231, where Schelling refers to antiquity as a reference point of this thought.

13. I thank David Farrell Krell for bringing this thought to my attention. See his *Of Memory, Reminiscence, and Writing: On the Verge* (Bloomington: Indiana University Press, 1990), 110–118.

It only stands to reason that Schelling demonstrates the alleged proximity of the thought of hunger to antiquity. Certainly, the proximity of the archer's "bow" and "life" in the passage is not only a play on the Greek words βιός/ βίος but also an allusion to Heraclitus's saying according to which "the bow's name is... life, but its work is death."[14] The *Deities*, however, provides the full demonstration of this thought. By portraying the mystery rites of the Cabiri, Schelling is led to the fact that from this development of hunger, the collective forces of life arise. These forces are not detached from each other but are interlinked. As *socii* and *consentes*, they form together and in connection with each other the elemental forces of life. It is precisely this harmonizing aspect that is taken up again in the *Erlangen Lecture Course* of 1821, but it is not until the late philosophy that emphasis is placed most strongly on the harmonizing aspect.

B. The Erlangen Lecture Course

After presenting the *Deities* to the academic audience and its dignitaries in Munich, it would be more than five years until, at the beginning of 1821, Schelling appeared in public again. He no longer lived in Munich but in Erlangen; he no longer worked privately in the Academy of Sciences but taught at the university, moving from the metropolis of Munich to tranquil Erlangen in Lower Bavaria.[15] After the *Deities*, he would no longer publish a full-size book; work on the publication of *The Ages of the World* repeatedly ground to a halt shortly before its conclusion. With a new audience in Erlangen, Schelling undertook to present his philosophy in a different way. In this respect, Hegel's polemical remark that "Schelling worked out his philosophy in full public view"[16] is entirely correct, although Schelling's tireless work in the background, reflected in the countless fragments and drafts from that time, complicate Hegel's caricature. The diverse threads of Schelling's

---

14. For the allusion to Heraclitus, see *The Fragments of the Pre-Socratics*, DK 22 B 48; see also WA 224.

15. For the historical context of the *Erlangen Lecture Course*, see the editorial report in AA II/10, 1–3 (2020).

16. Georg Wilhelm Friedrich Hegel, *Lectures on the History of Philosophy: Medieval and Modern Philosophy*, vol. 3, trans. E. S. Haldane and Frances H. Simson (Lincoln: University of Nebraska Press, 1995), 513, translation slightly altered.

thinking are woven together in the first *Erlangen Lecture Course* to form a vast tapestry—an amazing attempt at systematization.[17] Based on the concept of capability (*Können*), Schelling once again tries to describe the world as a whole within a plausible system of knowledge. The conflicting tendencies of an elusive hunger, on the one hand, and a harmonizing systematization, on the other, are openly revealed here.

Schelling's altered and more dynamic system is based on a strong concept of capability. Such a theoretically explicated capability is made visible by the differentiations Schelling worked out in the *Deities*, involving a chain of deities in which all those gods are connected through an enchantment that Schelling understands as magic. The concept of magic, based on Friedrich Creuzer's *Symbolism and Mythology of the Ancients* (1:592–594), may be found right at the beginning of the *Erlangen Lecture Course* with the definition of capability as eternal freedom; it is both a pure magic that works without objects and an ensuing magic that, as it were, practically actualizes what wisdom is.[18] Taking recourse once again to "the Oriental languages," as he doubtless explains in more detail in the endnotes to the *Deities*, Schelling finds confirmation that "in the concept of magic we find the concept of knowledge," such that "all magic is knowledge" (AA II/10,1:189).

All the previously developed images of hunger and languishing (*Sehnsucht, Schmachten*) are still in force in the *Erlangen Lecture Course*. The concept of capability, *Können*, which has doubtless become more powerful, nevertheless goes hand in hand with a figure of hunger, which itself is radicalized: "Pure capability is essentially and by its nature nothing more than desire for being—it is *essential* hunger" (AA II/10,1:320). The "hunger for essence," as described above with reference to *The Ages of the World*, is upgraded to "essential hunger" in view of the category of "skill." In this context Schelling refers to "the fact that in the Hebrew language the word that means *capability* is precisely considered to be one and the same as the word that means *eating*

---

17. Schelling offered some less voluminous, still unpublished lectures on mythology, which I omit here. The title of the lecture *Initia philosophiae universae* in the *Erlangen Lectures* is therefore an improper generalization on my part, but it is acceptable as a general characterization of this period.

18. See for the earlier considerations of "Magia" and on the assumption of an etymological relationship of "Maja" and "magic" in relation to the Persian SW I/8, 355–56, 385, and other endnotes to the *Deities*.

and *consuming*" (AA II/10,1:320).[19] Schelling remarks in his notes to this passage that the Hebrew word *yakhol*, or יכל (AA II/10,1:325), "to be able to," shares two root consonants with the Hebrew word for "to eat," *akhal* (אָכַל). The elaboration of consumption in the *Deities* is nevertheless only a beginning.[20] A precise connection between capability and hunger is worked out only afterward. The essence of hunger consists precisely in not being separated from capability; the hunger inherent in capability consists precisely in not being a mere *quality* of capability. Rather, in capability itself we already find the essence of hunger.

Though the deity Axieros is not named explicitly by Schelling in the *Erlangen Lecture Course*, the highly speculative constructions previously worked out are concentrated in this deity:

"The name of the first among the Samothracian deities, I am convinced, expresses nothing other than this very concept of hunger, poverty, endurance in pure capability, dormant fire (for all capability is consuming, as it becomes active)—thus this inner, not articulated, consuming fire, *eternal capability* where only the purest souls are blessed . . . is the secret power that moves everything, the eternal magic (which merely says the same thing), the magnet[21] that draws everything, the eternal *inner* beginning" (AA II/10,1:377).

Two conceptions of hunger (or of poverty and languishing) are clearly at odds here, and Schelling tries to unite them by resorting to Axieros.[22] The

---

19. See Wilhelm Gesenius, *Hebräisch-deutsches Handwörterbuch über die Schriften des Alten Testaments mit Einschluss der geographischen Nahmen und der chaldäischen Wörter beim Daniel und Esra*, vol. 1 (Leipzig: Vogt, 1810), אָכַל, 382–3, 382: "to be able to (*können*)" and ibid., אָכַל, 37–38: "to eat, consume."

20. For the semantics of hunger and consumption in Hebrew and Persian, see SW I/8, 377–78.

21. Magnetism plays a major role in Schelling's early philosophy of nature in the 1790s and the theory of potency developed there, but it is expanded and strengthened in and around 1821. See, for example, the 1799 *Einleitung zu einem Entwurf eines Systems der Naturphilosophie*, in AA I/8, 72–75, 74–5: "Sensitivity is only the higher potency of magnetism. Irritability is only the higher potency of electricity, formative drive (*Bildungstrieb*) only the higher potency of the chemical process." On magnetism in Schelling's *First Projection*, see chapter 5 of David Farrell Krell, *Contagion: Sexuality, Disease, and Death in German Idealism and Romanticism* (Bloomington: Indiana University Press, 1998), esp. 85–86 and 112–13.

22. For the corresponding comments, see SW I/8, 351–52 and for the notes on this passage, see SW I/8, 377–379.

consumption that Schelling previously claimed for hunger is equated with nonconsuming, at least insofar as consumption does not articulate hunger in the form of its highest purity. Schelling thus goes beyond his original explanations of Axieros.[23] However, this development reflects a fundamental problem for Schelling's philosophy as a whole, namely, the relationship between unity and difference. The development of what Schelling understands as hunger and poverty, which in 1815 differentiates itself into several deities, is at the same time conceived of as an interconnected "magical chain."

This development also addresses another central matter brought to bear at several points in the 1821 system. The cosmic dimension of the Samothracian system of gods also colors the conception of the Erlangen system. It is no longer merely a self-contained whole that, as in the *System of Transcendental Idealism*, in the end leads back to its beginning. The system is vitalized so that Schelling, in analogy to the planetary system, interprets the formula "living and dying together" (AA II/10,1:171) as definitive for his 1821 system. The "chorus of gods," which, as Schelling wrote in 1815, presents itself "as the ringdance of the stars," thus involving gods who "can only have been born together and that can die only together and at one stroke!" (SW I/8, 368), is now also found in what Schelling formally expresses in 1821 with his theory of "potencies." Taking a step beyond the *Deities*, Schelling theorizes that the potencies gain a material dimension not least through the multifarious figures of the gods presented there, a dimension Schelling will further develop right into his late philosophy.

Schelling understands the theory of potencies as a dynamic of capability, one that steadily increases. He considers it to be "a chain reaching from the deepest to the highest" (AA II/10,1:527). The concept of the magical chain elaborated in the *Deities*, which is used to emphasize the intertwining of the individual deities, thus becomes the theory of potencies in Erlangen. The theory of potencies consists in the unfolding of an admittedly magical capability. If Schelling describes the Cabiri as a representation of "inalienable life itself as it advances in a series of enhancements from the deepest to the highest levels" (SW I/8, 368), the potencies are now for him merely

---

23. In a parallel passage in a fragment of *The Ages of the World* (NL 81), Schelling articulates the contradiction even more clearly as the "inner, consuming—but not an articulated consuming—strength, of which only the purest souls are capable" (SG, I, 174).

the formal expression of this burgeoning life. It is therefore only consistent when Schelling describes, substantiates, and renders his theory of potencies plausible, not only through the *Deities* but also by embracing the entirety of mythology. His later *Philosophy of Mythology* is the comprehensive and truly brilliant result of this endeavor.

C. The Late Philosophy

In Schelling's late philosophy, aspects of the philosophy of *The Ages of the World*, *The Deities of Samothrace*, and, above all, the *Erlangen Lecture Course* lead to a further unfolding and a more comprehensive systematization. This is not the place to trace in detail the many references to the *Deities* that can be found in this period. But Karl Schelling's claim about the *Philosophy of Mythology*, to the effect that "the preparatory work for it reaches back to the time when the treatise on the deities of Samothrace appeared" (SW II/2, v), can be demonstrated in greater detail as being perfectly apt.

From a systematic point of view, the two aspects that had already been further developed in the *Erlangen Lecture Course* are rearranged: on the one hand, an unrestricted *capability* that can be understood as hunger and, on the other hand, the joint *concatenation* of all potencies. This integration, however, sublimates what was still working powerfully and in a rather unshielded way in Schelling's philosophy up to the Erlangen period. It may therefore come as no surprise that Schelling no longer reverts to the Cabiri to explain the aspect of hunger (and the moments of withdrawal, such as longing and languishing, which he associated with it) but rather emphasizes the unifying moment of concatenation.[24]

Many considerations that Schelling had elaborated through his preoccupation with the Samothracian Cabiri are woven into a vast panorama of mythology in his late philosophy. The contrast between the secret mysteries

---

24. See, however, on the continuation of the figure of hunger as lack, Manfred Frank, *Der unendliche Mangel an Sein: Schellings Hegelkritik und die Anfänge der Marxschen Dialektik*, second, expanded edition (Munich: Wilhelm Fink, 1992). For another interpretation of the Cabiri in the late philosophy of Schelling, see Jason M. Wirth, "And Hence Everything Is Dionysus: Schelling and the Cabiri in Berlin," *Rethinking German Idealism*, ed. Sean J. McGrath and Joseph Carew (Hampshire, England: Palgrave Macmillan, 2016), 271–291. Jason Wirth's reflections are further developed in the concluding essay of this volume.

of Greek antiquity and the publicly propagated mythology, though still relevant, almost disappears in comparison with the development of the opposition between polytheism and monotheism, which Schelling focuses on in his later investigations. On the way to Schelling's goal of achieving a fortified monotheism precisely by passing through polytheism, the mysteries remain in the background. This is not contradicted by the fact that, even though Schelling draws on elements of the mysteries with unprecedented abundance, he often implicitly excludes the Samothracian mysteries. In his discussion of the philosophy of mythology in the second book of the first part of the *Philosophy of Revelation* (SW II/3), Schelling makes this exclusion explicit, especially when he deals more fundamentally with the content of the mysteries; he chooses to deal particularly with the "Attic mysteries . . ., so that the others, especially the Samothracian ones, are only occasionally discussed" (SW II/3, 443).

This marginalization of the *Deities* does not happen despite but precisely because of the great importance that the mysteries continue to have for Schelling's philosophy. This significance is summarized most trenchantly in the following sentence: "It is only in the mysteries . . . that the mythological process is truly ended" (SW II/3, 529). The result of Schelling's entire discussion of mythology, before he can move on to the philosophy of revelation in the narrower sense, is an apotheosis of the mysteries. The mysteries are what brings mythology to its proper conclusion. It is not a merely temporal or historical conclusion, however, but a logical one, a conclusion suited to the mysteries. They allow the necessary yet essentially unconscious process of mythology to become visible as such. Thus the mysteries point beyond the entirety of mythology to the advent of Christianity and the strengthened monotheism that emerges from polytheism. And yet the Cabirian deities of the Samothracian system are not so readily left behind: in Schelling's final lectures on mythology, indeed at their very culmination, it is precisely the Cabirian gods—Demeter, Persephone, and Dionysos—who reappear in their overwhelming power, namely, the power of their languor and their languishing (SW II/2, 605, 622, 626–37, 647).

When we turn back to the *Deities* once again, however, it is striking how strongly the views expressed there appear at an early stage of Schelling's career. His suggestive question of 1815—"Isn't it conspicuous that all higher and better faith appears right at the beginning in Greece and otherwise under the form of secret teachings?" (SW I/8, 408)—may be sufficient to indicate that he considered the privileged form of faith to be found in the mysteries themselves, at least in the ancient world. The comparative of "better faith" also indicates their anticipated completion, only indirectly named by the word *Christianity*. When Schelling writes that "only Christianity would remove all the barriers" (SW I/8, 408), the faith expressed in the mysteries is not qualitatively subordinated to Christianity; if there is a subordination, it is simply that the earlier faith lacks extension, being limited to Greece and restricted to the initiates.

A rather convoluted passage from Schelling may nevertheless help us better understand why he marginalizes the *Deities* somewhat in these final considerations and, beyond that, why he distances himself from his investigation into the Cabiri:

> In my earlier treatise on the gods of Samothrace, published as early as 1815, concerning which I have to note, by the way, that it does not completely cover the Samothracian mysteries, inasmuch as that treatise was primarily concerned only with the explanation of a passage in which the main gods of Samothrace are called by mysterious names, I fundamentally *could have said*, but to some extent I did not want to say, everything at that time—in that book, I now believe with as much probability as can be achieved in such things, that the collective name of those gods of Samothrace—the name *Cabiri*—means nothing other than the several who are indissolubly cleansed, all of whom are like one, or as we say proverbially, like one *man*. (SW II/3, 462)

Schelling's retrospect here presents a rather distorted picture of what the *Deities* originally contained. First of all, his 1815 treatise is characterized by the fact that it provides not only a comprehensive but almost a complete picture of the cult of the Samothracian gods. Even if Schelling does not include all the other places where the Cabiri were worshipped, that is to say, all the Cabirian cults elsewhere in Greece, this does not speak against the treatise and its completeness. Schelling wants to represent the deities of *Samothrace* alone. True, his later reflections gain even more importance when they include the Etruscan elements to a greater extent than his earlier reflections do. Schelling's assertion that he was interested only in the explanation of one single passage, namely, the passage of the Scholiast on Apollonius of Rhodes's *Argonauts* (verse 917), ignores not only his rich investigation into the cult of the Samothracian gods but also the obvious philosophical implications that seek to unlock the primal system of humankind and its method. Schelling's *Deities* may not have begun to analyze precisely how its individual statements are to be located historically and philologically. Rather, it implicitly presupposes such an analysis. Yet his reflections on the names of the Cabiri are philologically investigated insofar as they reveal the above-described system, which is a system constituted by hunger and longing.

Schelling now leaves these weighty thoughts aside in favor of an interpretation of the unity inherent in the Cabiri. It may not be insignificant that the Cabiri associated with unity, namely, the *complices* and *consentes*, are attributed to the Etruscans. Whereas in 1815 Schelling was able to capture the aspect of the *consentes* and *socii* primarily for the deities of Samothrace, these deities themselves are now, in the late philosophy, used only in an ancillary manner. All three aspects that for Schelling distinguish the gods of the mystery cults, namely, that they are pure potencies, that they are interlinked, and that hence they are ultimately but one God, are presented with only more or less clear reference to the Samothracian Cabiri (SW II/3, 460–464).[25] However, there is no deeper discussion of the Cabiri. The former analysis of their names, which precisely revealed the dynamic, longing moment in the unfolding of the system, is omitted. This neglect does not originate from negligence but pursues new, overriding goals that tend to minimize the motifs of hunger, languor, and languishing.

Thus when Schelling claims that he could not say everything in 1815, this is certainly true, inasmuch as he has obviously not yet developed those further considerations on mythology that subsequently reposition the mysteries as such.[26] Yet his assertion that he did not want to say everything there is surprising, inasmuch as because he does not really explain what he means by that.[27] Rather, as the indeterminacy of this statement suggests, he probably

---

25. For the marginalization of the *Deities*, see also SW II/2, 292–93 and 604–606, even if here too the Samothracian deities are conceived of as "primeval powers" (SW II/2, 605, 610).

26. See also a further reflection of Schelling on the *Deities*, which claims their supposedly systematic indeterminacy: "By the way, however, the author at that time was more occupied with the material of mythology, and still neglected the formal questions that were raised only in the present lectures" (SW II/1, 88n1).

27. What Schelling did not *want* to depict, however, could include anything that goes beyond the Phoenician background, especially the Egyptian and Indian myths. Already in a letter to Schlegel, Schelling expresses the fact that he "could not and did not want to develop the connection in this book [the *Deities*], which of course also encompasses the Indian and Egyptian context." Schelling

wanted to say something quite different at the time, namely, that the very origin of the world consists in hunger and longing. The intertwining of divine withdrawal and the positivity associated with this view, however, is regarded by the late Schelling as an illegitimate confusion. Schelling's son Karl, as we have seen, associated the *Deities* with "decisive progress in determining the first foundation of philosophy" (SW I/8, vi). One can interpret this as saying that the great importance of mysteries and mythology for the representation of Schelling's (negative) philosophy should be emphasized. Yet one can probably go a little further if one looks at the passage to which Karl Schelling is referring: "There was a time when I dared to depict this series of possibilities of a still-future being in another solely figurative series, but, as it seemed to me then and still seems to me now, a completely parallel series, and I then posited the sentence: every beginning is in a state of lack, the deepest potency to which everything is attached is nonbeing, and this nonbeing is the hunger for being" (SW II/2, 294).

This extraordinary passage is symptomatic of Schelling's handling of the mysteries in later times. The mysteries are highly appreciated but in the end are relegated to "negative philosophy." The positive elements, so to speak, which Schelling worked out in the *Deities*, are set aside. According to the logic of his late philosophy, it is only consistent to set these elements aside, because in the system as a whole, they can play only a subordinate role.

It is true to say that in 1815 the lowest deities were those whose priority did not indicate superiority; they were and they remained chthonic gods. Yet they did not merely support the whole system with their power; rather, they were also thoroughly interlaced with it. If Schelling, by contrast, calls them "formal gods" in his late philosophy (SW II/2, 333), this is not merely a neutral or even gratuitous description.[28] Already in the *Essay on Human Freedom* Schelling had discussed a "merely formal concept of freedom" (SW I/7, 352) in order to develop—in opposition to Kant and Fichte—a concept of freedom that genuinely understands it as a capacity for good and evil.

---

to Friedrich Schlegel, dated November 13, 1817, in Josef Körner, "Aus Friedrich Schlegels Brieftasche: Ungedruckte Briefe," *Deutsche Rundschau*, 175, 2 (1918): 118.

28. The whole passage of SW II/2, 333 reads as follows: "For the Cabiri were the formal gods—*Deorum Dii*, as they were also called, the gods *by whom* the others, the substantial or material ones themselves, are first posited, the causative potencies of mythology." For the definition of the formal gods, see SW II/2, 188.

The place of confession outside the northeastern wall of the Hieron.

With the notion of *formal* freedom Schelling feels he can praise Kant for having developed the highest possible notion of freedom in the modern age. Yet at the same time, he feels he can criticize Kant for having failed to depict *actual* freedom. In the same sense, the Cabiri, understood as *formal* gods, are not merely discharged; indeed, they may be considered "world regents, world rulers" (SW II/3, 514), as they are formative gods. In terms of content, however, they are supplemented by a much broader spectrum of mysteries. Specifically, they are all but superseded by the mysteries of Dionysos. Schelling is doubtless able to bring Dionysos closer to Christianity than would be possible with the primordial Cabiri. Schematically, the Cabiri can be classified as "*formal* gods," that is, gods who remain present as principles for the development of mythology in its entirety. But they are also "merely the pure reasons" (SW II/2, 663), reasons that remain subordinated, first to the material gods (SW II/2, 663–64)[29] and then to God and Christ (see, for example, SW II/4, 226). The original figures Axieros, Axiokersa, Axiokersos, and Kadmilos would thus seem to obstruct Schelling's later systematization in a way that causes him to marginalize them in his late philosophy.

It may not be too daring to claim that the genuine gods of Samothrace not only do not fit into the late philosophy but also constitute a danger to the Christian god, with whom they are incommensurable. Apart from their unifying function, they threaten to consume this god through the hunger, longing, and languishing that they undergo. The late Schelling no longer exposes God to this danger. The embers of the Samothracian deities therefore burn silently in Schelling's late philosophy. Yet it is precisely by almost disappearing and concealing themselves in the late philosophy that they may testify one last time to their uncanny power.

2. The Reception of Schelling's *Deities*

No other publication by Schelling is as far removed from the grid of philosophical research today as *The Deities of Samothrace*. Neither practical nor theoretical philosophy in our time responds to the challenge. Nor is the *Deities* understood as applying to a specific field of philosophy or the other,

---

29. On the relationship between material gods and formal gods, see also SW II/2, 609. On the mediation of formal gods and material gods by Janus as God of Gods (*Deorum Deus*), see SW II/2, 605.

for example as an exercise in aesthetics or even as belonging to the history of philosophy. The work does not fit into any of these categories. It is easy to assume that it is not a philosophical work at all, especially since it obviously deals with a subject in ancient history and develops its subject historico-philologically. But neither is it merely a historical, philological, archaeological, or religious work. The treatise is therefore "undisciplined" in the truest sense of that word: it is uninhibited philosophy.

This disorderly publication is being punished not only today, however, as philosophers generally overlook the book, which, wedged between Schelling's early and late work, cannot readily be assigned a proper place. Schelling's contemporaries too sometimes had little use for it. At first it seems as if only the King of Bavaria honored Schelling's lecture, which of course was to appreciate it superficially and ceremoniously.[30] While today we are deterred by the historico-philological framework that conceals its philosophy, Schelling's contemporaries saw it the other way around: for many of them, the philosophy distorted the mythological object and corrupted the philological work. I have already mentioned that the late Schelling criticized such misunderstanding on the part of his contemporaries (SW II/1, 196n. 1). Yet already in 1818, after the echo of these misunderstandings had come to resonate, Schelling wrote to Goethe's friend Johann Diederich Gries thanking him for affirming the book that "so few have understood."[31]

This lack of understanding is manifest in the many contemporary reviews of the *Deities*. Schelling's book was literally torn apart by the critics, at least initially; however, the main criticism was not directed against his philological abilities and his historical research. On the contrary, praise for the latter can be found in almost all the reviews and was already present in the brief advertisements of the book.[32] The testy criticism of Schelling's explanations of the mysteries of Samothrace is directed against the philosophical approach, which, beyond the philological discussion, asserts levels and

---

30. Schelling received an honorarium of 600 gulden from the king. See the copy of a decree by Maximilian I. Joseph to the Royal Academy of Arts, October 29, 1815, Main Bavarian State Archives in Munich, MF 53692, 1r.

31. Schelling to Johann Diederich Gries, December 29, 1818, M. Grunwald, "Miscellen," *Archiv für Geschichte der Philosophie* 9:2 (1896): 445–57, esp. 446–48.

32. For example, see the anonymous announcement in *Intelligenzblatt der Jenaischen Allgemeinen Literatur-Zeitung* 57 (November 1815), col. 450.

contexts of meaning not accessible to a purely historico-philological method. In some cases, praise of the scholarship ironically implies a lack of critical evaluation of the available resources. Schelling's philosophical approach, which is ultimately his main concern, is rejected or denigrated by virtually all the reviewers.[33]

I cannot offer here detailed documentation of the entire reception of the *Deities*. By focusing on the reviews, however, I will analyze symptomatically the reception of the *philosophical content* that Schelling's text offered its readers. The book received a whole range of possible treatments, from open contradiction or uninformed rejection to productive appropriation. As an example of this last, allow me to highlight only the reaction of Friedrich Schlegel, since the letter Schlegel addressed to Schelling on July 18, 1817, has not yet been published:

> For your text, *On the Deities of Samothrace*, I thank you most heartily. I have read the text with the greatest interest and share in many points your convictions. I am glad that you have trod this old Hebrew-Phoenician path of language and ancient history and have brought them back to light again. Together with the rich Indian yield of the last years and the abundance of new outcroppings and new riddles posed by extensive work on the Egyptian tradition, this path will serve as a guide to approach the goal, which is blocked only by the cherub with the flaming sword.[34]

With this last sentence, Schlegel alludes to Genesis 3:24, where the cherubim and the flaming sword block the path to the tree of life that stands in the

---

33. Among many of Schelling's contemporaries who commented on his *Deities*, Karl Otfried Müller is symptomatic of the sometimes benevolent, sometimes poisonous rejection of Schelling's work: "*Schelling's* treatise, as witty as it is scholarly, could not be taken into account here, because the principles from which everything is derived with great consistency had to be rejected." See Karl Otfried Müller, *Geschichten Hellenischer Stämme und Städte*, 2 vols., *Orchomenos und die Minyer* (Breslau [formerly belonging to Prussia; now, Poland]: Josef Max, 1820), 1:451.

34. Bayerische Staatsbibliothek, Hss Ana 608.B.II. Schlegel, Friedrich von, 2r–v. The letter is a response to Schelling's letter, January 10, 1816, with which Schelling sends Friedrich Schlegel a copy of the *Deities* and a certificate of Schlegel's new membership in the Royal Academy of Arts as a foreign corresponding member. See Plitt II, 364–65 or KSA 29, 129–30. In his letter, Schlegel adds the impatient question that we may still ask: "When may we expect your work on *The Ages of the World*?"

garden of Eden, from which Adam and Eve have been expelled. The allusion once again illustrates the ecclesiastical risk that Schelling is taking with his investigation. For not only Schlegel but also the theologians and priests will recognize in Schelling's book a challenge to the flaming sword.[35]

A. On the Background of the Reviews; the *Deities* within the Debates of Modernity

We must not underestimate how daring Schelling's venture to combine philosophy with mythology truly was. In the aftermath of Schelling's late philosophy, with the appearance of Nietzsche, Cassirer, Levi-Strauss, Blumenberg, and Calasso, it seems natural to us to work philosophically with both mythologies and mystery cults. Indeed, after Vico, Fontenelle, Herder, and Heyne, Schelling's preoccupation with mythology was no longer completely new. On the contrary, it was a part of modernity, whose understanding of society and science was expressed in opposition to the myths of earlier or even prehistoric times.[36] Schelling too stands in this tradition. Yet he lends a new dimension to the interpretation of myths by trying to understand cults and rituals, along with the ideas associated with them, as what they actually *are* and not what they merely seem to be or strive to convey. His preoccupation points ahead to his own later philosophy and its reflections on mythology, which take myth *as* myth; in other words, Schelling takes myth at its word, understanding it "tautegorically" (SW II/1, 196). If not the first to do so, Schelling nonetheless makes the decisive connection that characterizes thinkers since Nietzsche: he does not separate philosophy and myth but works precisely toward the dissolution of this separation. He endeavors to elaborate a thinking that is fundamentally mythological, a thinking that takes mythology entirely seriously.

---

35. In 1816, due to the impression made by the *Deities*, Schelling was not reappointed to the University of Jena. From the point of view of the theologians, it was only consistent that Schelling be refused a professorship since he wished to be active not only in philosophy but also explicitly in theology. For the appalled reactions to Schelling's *Deities* of those entrusted with the appointment, see CD 181–82.

36. For an excellent overview, see Burton Feldman and Robert D. Richardson, *The Rise of Modern Mythology, 1680–1860* (Bloomington: Indiana University Press, 2000).

Against the background of "the quarrel of the Ancients and the Moderns," two basic tendencies can be discerned as important for understanding the *Deities*. With regard to the debate, Schelling's supposedly surprising turn to the historical object of myth actually seems quite consistent. In an extension, but also a modification, of the debate conducted primarily in France and England, the distance of modernity from antiquity is first of all acknowledged in both tendencies. In effect, the debates concern the way in which one should deal with the distance of modernity from antiquity. Whereas for the one tendency Greek antiquity becomes the ideal that can be opened up historically and philologically but otherwise should not be touched, the other undermines this ideal by wanting to understand philosophically both what characterizes antiquity and how it was first constituted. While the latter path leads researchers to the secret mystery cults, the former at least tends to influence them in the direction of the "official" or traditionally received mythology.

Beyond the euhemeristic and historical interpretations of myths, that is, the interpretations of the gods as the mere glorification of the mortal heroes of a people, and far from the classical division into *genus philosophicum, historicum*, or *poeticum*, that is, into myths of philosophical, historical, or poetic content, Schelling stands at eye level, as it were, with the mystery cults of Samothrace. Schelling follows Christian Gottlob Heyne (1729–1812), whose importance for many interpreters of myths and cults, including Schelling, is indisputable.[37] As the teacher of four authors who wrote reviews of Schelling's *Deities*, Heyne's influence continued to be felt up to Schelling's day.[38] In an essay of 1763, published in 1785–86, on the consciousness of mythical times (*Temporum mythicorum memoria*), which unfortunately has been neglected

---

37. For the significant influence of Heyne's pupil Johann Gottfried Eichhorn on Schelling, see, for example, Christian Danz, "Hermeneutik zwischen Text und Kontext: Überlegungen zur theologiegeschichtlichen Einordnung der Bibelauslegung des jungen Schelling," *Wiener Jahrbuch für Theologie*, 8 (2010): 85–107. For the direct reference to Heyne, see Schelling's early work, *De malorum origine*, AA I/1, 108 and his *Ueber Mythen, historische Sagen und Philosopheme der ältesten Welt*, AA I/1, 204–207 and 225–229, as well as the later dissociation from Heyne in Schelling's *Historical-Critical Introduction to the Philosophy of Mythology*, trans. Mason Richey and Markus Zisselsberger (Albany: State University of New York Press, 2007), 25–28; see also 214 (SW II/1, 30–34 and 149).

38. Grotefend, Mahn, Tychsen, and Creuzer all studied in Göttingen under the guidance of Heyne. For their reviews, see subsection B, below.

almost totally by the scholarly community,[39] Heyne understands myth as the original mode of human expression in a way that extends far beyond all the abovementioned classifications. Heyne determines the nature of myth or, more precisely, the *possibility* of myths as dependent on the mental preconditions of those who originally narrate them. Any purely figurative sense of the myths is therefore initially disregarded in favor of their sheer facticity, which at the same time permits a broad spectrum of characterizations. In myths, writes Heyne, "there are some things that are characterized by simplicity, by the truth of judgment, and by a certain natural grace; some things that are excellent and sublime in form and that shake the very meaning of souls; but mixed with them are error, childishness, disgrace, and atrocity."[40]

According to Heyne, myths can be sorted into three varieties. First, he characterizes some as having the ability to tell the unadulterated truth. Second, however, others are said to have a shocking effect. In general, myths find a commendatory mention in Heyne, and this has to be emphasized, although Heyne just as often classifies them in the third category, namely, that of the absurd and underdeveloped.[41]

Schelling affirms the first description of myths, understanding them as an original form of expression, one that cannot be communicated in writing. Myth is thus not a lie or a deception but is as such an expression of its own truth. Even if Schelling radicalizes Heyne, however, his proximity to

---

39. See HT. See also Arnold Hermann and Ludwig Heeren, *Biographische und litterarische Denkschriften* (Göttingen, Germany: Johann Friedrich Röwer, 1823), 83 as well as their bibliographical overview, ibid., 416. For examples of the rather sparse research in this area, see Marianne Heidenreich, *Christian Gottlob Heyne und die Alte Geschichte* (Munich, Germany: K. G. Saur, 2006), 421–580, esp. for the classification of the present text at 424 and early Greek history at 471–96; see also Ralph Häffner, *Johann Gottfried Herders Kulturentstehungslehre: Studien zu den Quellen und zur Methode seines Geschichtsdenkens* (Hamburg, Germany: Felix Meiner, 1995), 142–43.

40. Translation of HT, 6: "in iis nonnulla simplicitate, iudicii veritate et naturali aliqua venustate se commendantia; alia specie preaclara, augusta, sensum animorum percellentia; cum iisdem alia admixta absurda, puerilia, turpia, foeda."

41. Axel E. A. Horstmann, "Mythologie und Altertumswissenschaft: Der Mythosbegriff bei Christian Gottlob Heyne," *Archiv für Begriffsgeschichte*, 16 (1972): 82 argues that Heyne regards myths overall as something backward, despite some individual words of appreciation.

Heyne is far too rarely taken into account in discussions of Schelling's *Philosophy of Mythology*. Yet whereas Heyne attributes the myths to the limited abilities of early humans,[42] Schelling emphasizes that myths in themselves announce a reality that does not need to be polished by reinterpretation. In this way he understands the statements made and the connections drawn in the mysteries as sheer truths: the Samothracian mysteries themselves are already philosophy and do not have to be reinterpreted philosophically. The seemingly obvious assumption that Schelling determines the Samothracian mysteries under the rubric of the *genus philosophicum* is true only insofar as the mysteries themselves are already philosophical. It is not necessary to add a philosophical meaning to them; rather, one must show what is already philosophical about them. Schelling takes the Samothracian myths seriously and proclaims their philosophical importance in a way that runs counter to all late Enlightenment tendencies, which generally find only superstition and falsehood in them.

Schelling runs the risk of exploring what can be called a prehistoric system on the basis of historical data, filling in the gap between history and prehistory systematically but perforce speculatively. Historical criticism, then and now, excoriates such an approach.[43] In view of the uncompromising demands of philology, researchers prefer to remain silent before making room for theoretical constructions and speculative ideas in questions of

---

42. HT, 14–15: "Multa, *quae antiquorum hominum, inprimis poetarum, ingeniis tribuuntur, ad prisci sermonis infantiam et inopiam,* . . . partim etiam *ad opiniones et notiones religiosas ab eadem inopia sermonis* nondum usu rerum et varietate locupletati *profectas, referenda esse.*" "Much of what is attributed to the powers of thought of the human beings of antiquity, especially the poets, must be attributed to the childhood and poverty of very early speech, . . . in part also to the opinions and religious ideas that had not yet been shattered in this very poverty of speech by means of the involvement with things in all their rich variety."

43. For the contemporary debate on the cultural conflict, see Andrea Polaschegg, "Athen am Nil oder Jerusalem am Ganges? Der Streit um den kulturellen Ursprung um 1800," in *Fremde Figuren: Alterisierungen in Kunst, Wissenschaft und Anthropologie um 1800*, ed. Alexandra Böhm and Monika Sproll (Würzburg, Germany: Königshausen und Neumann 2008), 41–65. For more recent research into this skeptical sense, see the discussion of the Samothracian cult by Bengt Hemberg in section 4 of Krell, "Schelling *archaeologicus*," in the present book and Jan N. Bremmer, *Initiation into the Mysteries of the Ancient World* (Berlin and Boston: Walter de Gruyter 2014), 21–54.

myth. Johann Heinrich Voss can certainly be regarded as the patron saint of all these philological studies based on Enlightenment skepticism. A letter to Cotta from 1816 indicates that Schelling had from the beginning expected criticism from Voss. Schelling had seen the caustic allusions Voss made in his preface to the *Hymn to Demeter*, which had been published earlier, as referring to himself. In this preface, Voss sharply attacks any speculations that in the end deal only with the "possible," that is, speculations that declare as "certainties" whatever only "wishful thinking" or an overactive imagination (*wünschende Einbildung*) conceives.[44] When Voss declares that historical investigations into "prehesiodic mysticism in Greece" and "prehomeric mysticism" are "ridiculous,"[45] Creuzer and Schelling are being pilloried. Schelling not only feels himself addressed, however, but also meets these barely concealed accusations with the confidence he believes can be attributed not least to his thorough knowledge of the source material: "As far as I'm concerned, he [i.e., Voss] hardly realizes how well equipped and armed I am in this matter. I have put more diligence and effort into this research than one seems to think I am capable of; all will be well, however."[46]

Voss did not write a review of Schelling's book, but his sharp criticism of Schelling in general, formulated in 1824, summarizes what is typical of many reviews criticizing Schelling's *Deities*:

"Meanwhile, *Schelling* remained true to his symbolic wisdom and the enthusiasm of the Indian primeval demon. This is demonstrated by his miraculous allusion to the Cabirian mysteries in Samothrace, which, for all the resplendent symbolic priestly ornaments of the Orient, do not possess a single unholy fibril of historical knowledge, nor (what a concession on the part of a philosopher!) of logical criticism as it was practiced in the good old days by *Lessing*. Schelling's reward is a bacchanalian welcome drink extended by—*Creuzer!*"[47]

---

44. Johann Heinrich Voss, "Eleusis. Hymne an Demeter, griechisch und deutsch, als ältestes Denkmal der Mystik," *Morgenblatt für gebildete Stände* 144 (June 15, 1816): 573–575, 574. See also Johann Heinrich Voss, *Hymne an Demeter* (Heidelberg, Germany: Christian Friedrich Winter, 1826), vii. Voss may have been referring in particular to Schelling's critical remarks on Homer in SW I/8, 363.

45. Voss, "Eleusis," 574 but also Voss, *Hymne an Demeter*, VII.

46. Schelling to Johann Friedrich Cotta, June 25, 1816, SC 125.

47. Johann Heinrich Voss, *Antisymbolik* (Stuttgart, Germany: J. B. Metzler'sche Buchhandlung, 1824), 371. Giles Whiteley also uses this passage in GW:282n5 but

Almost every adjective and noun sparkles polemically against Schelling's philosophy. However, Voss not only exaggerates Schelling's approach but also distorts it to an extent that vitiates what would otherwise be a thoroughly appropriate critical view of Schelling's procedure. Apart from the fact that Schelling repeatedly refuses to accept Indian explanations of mythology or mysteries, it is precisely in the *Deities* that we find references to manifold ancient sources and a consistently executed logic based on Schelling's philosophy and his theory of potencies. True, it is not historical knowledge and logic in the Enlightenment sense but rather knowledge in a sense that arose from the philosophies of German Iidealism and Romanticism.

Voss's central point of criticism, however, is the "symbolic priestly ornaments," which he wants to deride as the dazzling and thus deceptive accessories of the ancient priests of the *mysteries*, from which the original Greek *mythology* is distinguished by its purity and superiority. The differentiation between the mysteries and mythology, upon which Schelling had insisted early on,[48] is not considered to be valid by the Enlightenment philosopher Voss. For him, this is all paganism, which stands in sharpest contrast to Christianity, whereas Schelling was able to see in the mysteries a seamless transition to Christianity, such that Christianity "emerged ... merely by making the mystery cults public."[49] Voss, known for his translations of Homer, can view Homer alone as a pre-Christian luminary, one who narrates

---

translates Voss there as if Schelling were showing an "'unholy fuzziness' [*unheiliges Fäserchen*] of historical knowledge and of 'logical criticism.'" Voss criticizes the Romantics' "fuzziness" in principle, but here Voss is concerned with the polemical intention of showing that Schelling does not possess even the smallest fiber of historical knowledge or logical criticism; in other words, Schelling's claims would not be merely "blurred" but not knowledgeable at all, precisely because Creuzer and Schelling do not possess this knowledge and do not hold such criticism to be sacred at all, although they otherwise supposedly praise everything holy. On the significance of Voss's fundamental critique, see Hartmut Fröschle, *Der Spätaufklärer Johann Heinrich Voss als Kritiker der deutschen Romantik* (Stuttgart, Germany: Akademischer, 1985), esp. 112–139. For a description of Voss's criticism of Heyne, which can be regarded as a precursor to the later criticism of Creuzer and Schelling, see 28–33.

48. F. W. J. Schelling, *Philosophy and Religion (1804)*, translated, annotated, and with an introduction by Klaus Ottmann (Putnam, CT: Spring, 2010), 52–53; see SW I/6, 67–68.

49. F. W. J. Schelling, *Philosophy and Religion* (Ottmann, 52, and SW I/6, 66).

mythological stories but is not himself woven into mythology. Mythology itself is a means of education for humans only as proper history. To identify those symbols in the mythological realm as pointing to an infinite or an absolute within the finite, as Voss accuses Schelling of doing, runs counter to this educational mission. The forms of perception implied by Schelling's readings are held to be confusing, not only because they cannot be soberly categorized but also because they are open to endless interpretation.

Yet Voss not only disapproves of the symbolism identified in ancient Greek culture but also spurns the aim of tracing such symbolism back to the "Orient." In addition to the illicit "mythization" or even mysticism within myth, there is the spurious transplantation of myth from sources beyond and outside of Greece. The ostensible purity of Greek mythology is denigrated by its supposed seedbed in foreign lands. While Schelling recognizes in the "oriental" elements the foundation upon which a higher religion can build, Voss asserts that this higher religion is falsified and undermined by the connection with oriental alien religions. However, Schelling's approach, which assumes a "primal system," implies a fundamental applicability to all ancient and premodern mythologies, a view that Schelling explicitly expresses to Schlegel as early as 1817. For Schelling, the "different religious systems are only fragments of a large edifice raised to heaven, which covered all countries with its ruins, in which each people and each cult had some part, but never the whole, as far back as our historical knowledge reaches."[50] In fact, it is Schelling's late philosophy itself that will honor this eclectic approach and deal more comprehensively with all known mythologies.

Voss's book, highly entertaining as it is, at least in its polemics, actually illuminates the important relationship between Friedrich Creuzer and Schelling. This is also remarkable in the sense that Schelling's *Deities* is in Voss's view a mere critical sideshow to a much larger debate surrounding Creuzer's works.[51] Voss regards Schelling's *Naturphilosophie* as the basis for

---

50. Schelling to Friedrich Schlegel, November 13, 1817, in *Deutsche Rundschau*, 175:2 (1918): 104–127, 118–9. Schelling adds, "In this thought I count you as the main predecessor" (ibid.). For the many passages that show the proximity of Schlegel and Schelling, see Friedrich Schlegel, *Ueber die Sprache und Weisheit der Indier* (Heidelberg, Germany: Mohr und Zimmer, 1808), 68, 95, 98, 163 (KSA VIII, 172–73, 198–99, 200–01, 262–63).

51. See Ernst Howald, *Der Kampf um Creuzers Symbolik: Eine Auswahl von Dokumenten* (Tübingen, Germany: J. C. B. Mohr [P. Siebeck], 1926); also Éva

Creuzer's mythological research, in particular Creuzer's *Symbolism and Mythology of the Ancients*.[52] While Schelling's increased use of Creuzer in the notes to the *Deities* alone is enough to make it obvious that he received essential impulses from Creuzer's writings, the *philosophical* influence of Creuzer on Schelling is much less obvious. Even though Voss may exaggerate here, he nevertheless points out the productive interrelationship of philosophy and ancient studies. Creuzer and Schelling reciprocally provide one another the theoretical basis and much of the content of their research.[53]

Schelling himself therefore might have felt all the more addressed by the criticism that was raised extensively against Creuzer.[54] Already the *Letters on Homer and Hesiod*, published jointly by Gottfried Herrmann and Friedrich Creuzer in 1818, bear witness to a profound dissent in the study of antiquity, which not least consisted in understanding Greek mythology either purely on its own terms or in tracing it back to non-European origins, as Creuzer does.[55] Schelling is directly implicated in this dissent when he uses the Phoenician language to explain Greek mystery cults. In this respect, Hermann's criticism that there is another, namely, "a beautiful and interesting perspective . . . on how to consider this myth [of the Cabiri]"[56] might also apply

---

Koczisky, "Samothrake: Ein Streit um Creuzers Symbolik und das Wesen der Mythologie," in *Antike und Abendland*, 43 (1997): 174–189.

52. See Voss, *Antisymbolik* (1824), 371.

53. For the fruitful interaction between Schelling and Creuzer, see Alexander Bilda and Fernando Wirtz, "Unveröffentlichte Briefe von Creuzer an Schelling aus den Jahren 1813–1844," *Schelling-Studien*, 7 (2019): 217–243.

54. Arnaldo Momigliano, "Friedrich Creuzer and Greek Historiography," *Journal of the Warburg and Courtauld Institutes*, 9 (1946): 152–163; see also the excellent overview by Frank Engehausen, Arnim Schlechter, Jürgen Paul Schwindt, eds., *Friedrich Creuzer 1771–1858: Philologie und Mythologie im Zeitalter der Romantik: Begleitband zur Ausstellung in der Universitätsbibliothek Heidelberg 12. Februar-8. Mai 2008* (Heidelberg, Germany: Regionalkultur, 2008); for Creuzer and Voss, see Gerhard Schwinge, "Creuzers 'Symbolik und Mythologie' und der Antisymbolikstreit mit Voß sowie dessen Kryptokatholizismusvorwurf," ibid., 73–88.

55. Gottfried Hermann and Friedrich Creuzer, *Briefe über Homer und Hesiodus, vorzüglich über die Theogonie* (Heidelberg, Germany: August Oswald, 1818). Instructive is also Glenn W. Most, "Hermann gegen Creuzer über die Mythologie," in *Gottfried Hermann (1772–1848), Internationales Symposium Leipzig 11.-13. Okt. 2007*, ed. K. Sier and E. Wöckener-Gade (Tübingen, Germany: Narr, 2010), 165–179.

56. Hermann and Creuzer, *Briefe über Homer und Hesiodus*, 81.

to Schelling. While the conflict between Herrmann and Creuzer was still amicable, Voss's polemics in the mid-1820s were caustic. Christian August Lobeck, admired by Goethe[57] but later spurned by Nietzsche,[58] criticized Creuzer in his two-volume *Aglaophamus* in a more scholarly manner. In this comprehensive work, Lobeck interprets the Greek mystery cults as autochthonous and thus independent of influences such as those proposed by Creuzer or Schelling.[59]

Schelling's *Deities* shares the same critical fate as Creuzer's *Symbolism and Mythology*. Admiration is accompanied by acute philological criticism. Schelling's approach is taken to be at best a diversion, or rather a detour, from the main path that enlightened research on antiquity should take.[60] The way in which Schelling turns to mythology in his late philosophy may also be understood as a reaction to criticisms of Creuzer. The mysteries are led, as it were, from darkness into the light of mythology. Thus Schelling does not

---

57. Johann Leuchtbecher, *Ueber den Faust von Goethe: Eine Schrift zum Verständniß dieser Dichtung nach ihren beiden Theilen für alle Freunde und Verehrer des großen Dichters* (Nuremberg, Germany: Renner, 1838), 324.

58. Friedrich Nietzsche, *Twilight of the Idols, The Anti-Christ, Ecce Homo*, in *Twilight of the Idols, and Other Writings*, ed. Aaron Ridley and Judith Norman (Cambridge: University Press, 2005), 227: "*The famous Lobeck* in particular crawled into this world of mysterious states with all the venerable certainty of a worm that had dried up between books, and persuaded himself that it was scientific to be glib and childish to the point of nausea,—Lobeck spared no expense to scholarship in establishing that these curiosities really did not amount to anything."

59. The entire third book of Lobeck's second volume deals with the Samothracian mysteries; see Christian August Lobeck, *Aglaophamus sive de theologiae mysticae graecorim causis, idemque poetarum Orphicorum dispersas reliquias collegit* (Königsberg, [formerly belonging to Prussia, today Kaliningrad, Russia] Germany: Bornträger, 1829), 2:1104–1348; on the Cabiri of Samothrace see esp. 1202–1295. However, Lobeck does not explicitly discuss Schelling's views.

60. In recent years, Schelling's and Creuzer's approach is taken up by some classical scholars, especially Walter Burkert. See, for example, Walter Burkert, *The Orientalizing Revolution: Near Eastern Influence on Greek Culture in the Early Archaic Age* (Cambridge: Harvard University, 1992); see also B87 and B93 in the references below. For a very good overview of the ongoing debate, see Beat Schweizer: "'Frühes Griechenland': Zum 'Problem' des Orients in fundierenden Geschichten des Okzidents," *EAZ – Ethnographisch-Archäologische Zeitschrift*, 51:1/2 (2010): 191–214.

surrender the enormous importance of the mysteries for his philosophy, but their reorganization within his large-scale late philosophy makes them more manageable for his "positive" philosophy and its monotheism.

B. The German Reviews of Schelling's *Deities*

Despite widely differing views and all the possible classifications, the reviews of Schelling's *Deities* can be treated systematically. A categorization according to the positive or negative tendency of the review may exclude some individual judgments about specific matters, but it does provide an orientation within the complex history of the book's reception. All the reviews have in common the fact that they criticize isolated elements, often the etymologies of certain words. No review, therefore, offers an entirely positive assessment of Schelling's text. Of the seven German reviews, four were rather negative and three generally expressed agreement with Schelling. All the reviews except the last two are anonymous, but the authors of all the German-speaking reviews can be identified with high probability.

The negative reviews reach their apotheosis in a fundamental critique from Schelling's archenemy, Heinrich Eberhard Gottlob Paulus (1761–1851). Scholars have failed to recognize that the publication of Schelling's first Berlin lecture in 1843 was not the first time Paulus publicly railed against Schelling. The first explosion transpired more than two decades earlier, exposing their different philosophical approaches.[61] It should not come as a surprise, not least because of this history, if Schelling later rejects the publication of his lecture solely because of Paulus's proposed editorship of it.

The positive reviews culminate in Creuzer's critical appraisal, in what also turns out to be the most in-depth examination of Schelling's effort. While Paulus is diligently expanding the foundations of his enmity with Schelling, Creuzer strengthens a long-lasting friendship, a friendship that would outlast the enmity with Paulus.[62]

---

61. Although Ute Schönwitz thoroughly treats the long-lasting relationship between Paulus and Schelling in her monograph on them, she does not mention the dispute on the *Deities*. See Ute Schönwitz, *Er ist mein Gegner von jeher: Friedrich Wilhelm Joseph Schelling und Heinrich Eberhard Gottlob Paulus* (Warmbronn, Germany: Keicher, 2001).

62. See Friedrich Creuzer, *Aus dem Leben eines alten Professors* (Leipzig/Darmstadt, Germany: Carl Wilhelm Leske, 1848), 58 and 112.

Schelling and his publisher sent the *Deities* to numerous scholars, primarily in the German-speaking world.[63] All the reviews refer to the version "Ueber die Gottheiten von Samothrace: Eine Abhandlung in der zur Feyer des Allerhöchsten Namensfestes Sr. Majest. des Königes von Baiern gehaltenen öffentlichen Versammlung der Akademie der Wissenschaften, am 12. Oct. 1815, vorgelesen von Friedrich Wilhelm Joseph Schelling. Stuttgart u. Tübingen: Cotta 1815." It was sold by booksellers in another version at about the same time as the speech was delivered, a version that adds the subtitle "Supplement to *The Ages of the World*."[64]

---

63. Already on October 15 Schelling had sent the *Deities* to several scholars throughout Europe. See Plitt II, 359–364. The Schelling-Cotta correspondence reveals that three hundred copies in quarto were printed especially for the lecture to the Academy and another seven hundred in octavo for the book trade, all of which were to be available in September (J. F. Cotta to Schelling, August 31, 1815, SC 101). From early on, Schelling had planned that the copies would be available at the end of September. See Schelling to J. F. Cotta, May 23, 1815, SC 97. However, the typesetting of the text had turned out so badly that a delay occurred, which, according to Schelling's own estimation, led to a publication date shortly after October 12 in Munich. See Schelling to J. G. Cotta'sche Buchhandlung, October 4, 1815 and Schelling to J. F. Cotta, October 4, 1815, SC 107–8.

64. It is not easy to understand how this simultaneous second edition got its slightly altered title that adds "Beylage zu den Weltalter" but omits the "presented (*vorgelesen*)" phrase. None of the reviewers seem to have taken this second edition into account, which obviously deletes the *vorgelesen* because the lecture is now a book. Neither is this subtitle mentioned in the usually complete citation of the title at the head of a review nor can the remarks of the reviewers on *The Ages of the World* within the reviews be limited to the subtitle, since Schelling also refers to *The Ages of the World* in the main text. The rich correspondence between Schelling and Cotta provides information on the order of the two printings. Schelling indicated that he would give his work the subtitle *Erste Beylage zum ersten Theil der Weltalter* (Schelling to J. F. Cotta, August 8, 1815, SC 99). It is not evident how the subtitle got altered, with the designation "First Part" being dropped, and why it was skipped for the magnificent quarto edition the Academy received. Perhaps Schelling did not want to advertise his project of *The Ages of the World* to his colleagues in the Academy. It can at least also be assumed that the title of the octavo edition, which refers to *The Ages of the World*, was added and altered by Cotta for better marketing. Goethe possessed both editions. See Friedrich Theodor Kräuter, *Catalogus Bibliothecae Goethianae*, Handschriften der Herzogin Anna Amalia Bibliothek, ohne Signatur, 744. The copy without the

But now to the negative reviews. As early as December of that same year, 1815, the *Wiener Allgemeine Literaturzeitung* published a rather unspectacular but disapproving review.[65] Its content is easily summarized in the final sentence: "As little as we can agree with the results of this treatise throughout, we do not ignore the diligence which the scientific and scholarly author has put into the exploration of his very difficult subject" (RA 1573). The author of the review seems to be Friedrich Ast (1778–1841), who might have heard Schelling's lecture due to his geographical and professional proximity to the Academy in Munich, as he was a professor in neighboring Landshut.[66] In addition to a general classification of Schelling's investigation, which Ast places in the context of the as yet unpublished *Ages of the World*, Schelling's fundamental considerations are called into question. However, the review basically rejects Schelling without opposing his views by means of alternate

---

subtitle seems to have been lost, as it is missing in the new list of Goethe's library. Or it may be that only the edition that Goethe probably bought later, in November 1815, survives (Rech.: Fakz. 95, 144). This copy remained partly uncut. See GB 283–84 (No. 1978).

65. Christian Danz, however, classifies this review as benevolent. See CD 182n4.

66. See Hans Eichner, "Friedrich Ast und die Wiener Allgemeine Literaturzeitung," *Jahrbuch der Deutschen Schiller-Gesellschaft*, 4 (1960): 343–357. Ast is often regarded as Schelling's pupil because he studied with him in Jena and appropriated his philosophy eclectically. This supposed closeness can hardly be read from the review, however. Schelling was critical of Ast both before and after the review, apparently without having learned that Ast was the first reviewer of the *Deities*. See Schelling to Hegel, January 11, 1807, Plitt II, 112 and Schelling to Victor Cousin, November 27, 1828, Plitt III, 42. Although Eichner's remarks are plausible, they do not provide direct proof of Ast's authorship, especially since he refers to the Schelling review in only one footnote (Eichner 1960, 348n13). Thus under the abbreviation Φ, several anonymous authors from the editorial staff of the *Wiener Allgemeine Literaturzeitung* could also have been meant, all of whom can be assigned to the fields of philosophy and philology. Eichner has identified twenty-nine reviews in only two years, which is such a considerable number that could easily come from different authors. In the case of Schelling's *Deities*, the reviewers could therefore also be the orientalists Joseph von Hammer-Purgstall (1794–1856) or Thomas von Chabert (1766–1841), both of whom lived in Vienna. See Sibylle Obenaus, "Die deutschen allgemeinen kritischen Zeitschriften in der ersten Hälfte des 19. Jahrhunderts: Entwurf einer Gesamtdarstellung," *Archiv für Geschichte des Buchwesens*, 14 (1974): 1–122, 41.

readings or elaborating substantiated doubts. The reviewer also demands consideration of the physical, ethical, and poetic significance of myths in contrast to the cosmological significance that Schelling supposedly examines (RA 1572–73). Yet this merely reflects the traditional way of treating myth that we mentioned above in the discussion of Heyne, while the review fails to recognize Schelling's novel approach. Schelling takes note of this review and obviously sees himself challenged to react to what he sees as false criticism. Yet, in comparison to the immediately following and entirely destructive review, Ast's is still "the better one" (SC 120).

Ast's review is followed by reviews in the two major review sources for the German-speaking world, the *Hallesche Allgemeine Literatur-Zeitung* (ALZ) and its competitor, the *Jenaische Allgemeine Literatur-Zeitung* (JALZ). Halle, as the more conservative bastion, pounces on Schelling, while Jena yields more conciliatory tones. Only two months after the review from Vienna, the next review appears in the ALZ. This review also attacks Schelling's scholarly investigation at its core, but augments its predecessor both in the sharpness of its tone and its accusation of a mass of putative errors. In view of Schelling's great ambitions for his little book, this response can only have been a bitter disappointment. But Schelling also understands these reviews as a provocation to which he intends to react. Thus he writes to his faithful publisher Cotta: "I would not be averse to having this and another (albeit far better) review printed together, with very short notes."[67]

Indeed, the review in the ALZ is piquant insofar as it has a clear political dimension, signaled by the city in which it was published, Halle. It is worth noting that the ALZ was initially located in Jena, where German Idealism originated. But after the departure of Fichte, Schelling, and Hegel, among others, this journal left Jena and afterward appeared in Halle. It was at Goethe's instigation that a replacement with the same title was reestablished in Jena. As of that point, however, there were two journals that despite their identical names were symptomatic of very different approaches in the humanities during at least the first half of the nineteenth century. While the Kantian tradition of philosophy continued cum grano salis in Halle, JALZ opened itself to all the currents beyond Kant and the Enlightenment.

---

67. Schelling to J. F. Cotta, April 6, 1816, SC 120. The review mentioned here must be the one in the Vienna ALZ, unless I have overlooked some other review. For the informative remainder of Schelling's letter, see SC 119–20.

Schelling could quite rightly assume that no review from Halle would be in his favor, whereas Jena might well be kinder.

In several letters,[68] Schelling expressed his suspicion that Friedrich Köppen (1775–1858), a pupil of Schelling's opponent Jacobi,[69] was the author of the review in the ALZ of February 1816. In 1803 Köppen had published *Schelling's Doctrine, or the Whole of the Philosophy of Absolute Nothingness* (1803), whose very title clearly indicates his opposition.[70] After Schelling finally broke with Jacobi in his polemic *Memorial of the Treatise on Divine Things* (1813), corresponding counterreactions could be expected from Jacobi. Such an opportunity presented itself with the *Deities*. The first two reviews thus originate from Schelling's immediate vicinity, namely from the University of Landshut, which at that time was still a state university in competition with the two academies in Munich, where Schelling was employed.

Köppen's review is characterized by a consistently polemical and even insulting tone, which appears even more acerbic when one considers that any reader of the review would initially assume that the reviewer was neutral. The criticism begins with the title of the *Deities* and extends to many other aspects, often presenting Schelling's fundamental interpretations as simply false. Moreover, a number of anachronisms, along with all the etymologies that Schelling proposes for the names Axieros, Axiokersa, and Axiokersos are held against him and dismissed as "root illusions [*Wurzelphantasmagorien*]"

---

68. See the letter in the previous footnote and Schelling to Heinrich Karl Abraham Eichstädt, February 24, 1816, Jena, Universitäts- und Landesbibliothek; Signatur: NL Eichstädt 7, Voigtii Epistolae 1816, Bl. Shortly before this, Christian Gottlob Voigt had suspected that the historian Barthold Georg Niebuhr was the reviewer. See Christian Gottlob Voigt to Heinrich Karl Abraham Eichstädt, February 21, 1816, Universitäts- und Landesbibliothek Jena; Signature: NL Eichstädt 7, Voigtii Epistolae 1816, Bl.65.

69. Köppen was a professor of philosophy in Landshut. After the university was moved to Munich in 1826, where his place was taken by Schelling, Köppen was transferred to Erlangen. See Carl von Prantl, "Köppen, Friedrich," *Allgemeine Deutsche Biographie*, 16 (1882): 698–699. I did not find any positive proof that Köppen actually is the author of the review, so we have to trust Schelling's assumption.

70. See Friedrich Köppen, *Schellings Lehre oder das Ganze der Philosophie des absoluten Nichts: Nebst drey Briefen verwandten Inhalts von Friedr. Heinr. Jacobi* (Hamburg, Germany: Friedrich Perthes, 1803).

(RK 230). Schelling's reaction, one may easily surmise, is not at all sanguine. In his view it was only a "denigrating review... from the Jacobian workshop," which represents an "inversion [of the *Deities*] into untruth."[71]

Accordingly, Schelling condemns Köppen himself: "It is disgraceful in itself that in the ALZ all my philosophical works are left to my notorious opponent, who antagonizes me as an author and as a person; but that a thoroughly learned treatise is also surrendered to him is nevertheless too crude, particularly if on the subject in question the reviewer completely lacks any knowledge of his own. I am not mistaken in this assumption, for although the review seeks to clothe itself in a mantle of erudition, it shows no knowledge other than that drawn from the treatise itself, and merely twists it."[72]

In the end, Schelling did not release a public statement regarding this review, perhaps not least because the more balanced handling of his text produced by the JALZ might have consoled him. During the four months after Köppen's review, the JALZ responded with a pair of reviews, one negative and one positive.[73] The JALZ takes into account the two angles from which the book may be viewed, namely, in terms of the opposition between Heyne and Voss described above. Accordingly, Ernst Philipp August Mahn's (1787–1845) negative review, in language and content, follows Köppen's[74] It

---

71. Schelling to Johann Christian Pfister, June 6, 1816, Plitt II, 373.

72. Schelling to J. F. Cotta, April 6, 1816 (SC 119).

73. Schelling had sent his book by way of Cotta to the writer and "original friend" of Goethe, Karl Ludwig von Knebel (1744–1834) and the translator Johann Diederich Gries (1775–1842) in Jena. (See Schelling to J. F. Cotta, October 14, 1815, SC 112; the letter Schelling enclosed with the consignment to Gries is preserved; see Plitt II, 363–64.) It can be assumed that reviewers were selected for Schelling's book through the mediation of Knebel and Gries. See for some of the other recipients of the book SC 111–12: Eberhard Friedrich Georgii (1757–1830), Christoph Friedrich Cotta (1758–1838), Schelling's brother Karl Eberhard Schelling (1783–1854), Christian Friedrich Schnurrer (1742–1822), Karl August von Wangenheim (1773–1850), Carl August Eschenmayer (1768–1852), Barthold Georg Niebuhr (1776–1831), Friedrich August Wolf (1759–1824) and Tychsen and Paulus who actually wrote a review.

74. The review is signed with a "j." in one edition. This probably does not refer to the philologist Christian Friedrich Wilhelm Jacobs (1764–1847), who like Schelling worked in Munich from 1807–1810. Schelling sent Jacobs the book on October 14, 1815. See Horst Fuhrmans, "Schellings Briefe," *Zeitschrift für philosophische Forschung*, 8 (1954): 437–437.

is merely descriptive and largely ironic, asserting that Criticizing Schelling's method is "uncritical" (RM 430). Mahn raises points of criticism that, as in the previous reviews, cast doubt on particular etymologies. Furthermore, Schelling is also accused of plagiarizing the book *The Origin of All Cults, or Universal Religion* by the French historian Charles-François Dupuis.[75] Finally, Schelling's assumption that the mystery cults contain an esoteric doctrine compatible with exoteric doctrines is refuted. Instead, the mystery cults, which in the reviewer's opinion enter into Christian monotheism, are more valuable "than anything the jester's cap [*Schellenkappe*, that is, reduced intelligence] of the people can handle" (RM 437). For the reviewer, the mysteries must therefore be distinguished from the ordinary mythologies that the masses were able to understand.

While all the reviews after this one basically respond approvingly, the series of critical replies to Schelling's *Deities* finds its climax nearly six years after its publication in the comprehensive review by Paulus. Paulus, long a friend and patron of the youthful Schelling but later his archenemy,[76] wrote

---

Rather, according to the supposition of Karl Bulling, the review probably comes from Ernst Philipp August Mahn (1787–1845). See KB 70. Mahn, who, like the other reviewers, Grotefend and Tychsen, essentially received his academic training in Göttingen with decisive input from Heyne, did not necessarily incline to strong criticism. However, a certain distance resulting from Mahn's training is reflected insofar as he himself did not receive a proper position in Göttingen despite repeated attempts. In addition, the year after his review, 1817, he dedicated one of his books to Paulus, who cultivated an almost contradictory academic approach to methodical criticism, as his own later review of the *Deities* would show. See Johannes Tütken, *Privatdozenten im Schatten der Georgia Augusta. Zur älteren Privatdozentur (1734 bis 1831)*, Part II, *Biographische Materialien zu den Privatdozenten des Sommersemesters 1812* (Göttingen, Germany: Universitätsverlag, 2005), esp. 508–518; on the book dedicated to Paulus, see ibid., 516.

75. Charles-François Dupuis, *L'origine de tous les cultes, ou la religion universelle*, 4 vols. (Paris: H. Agasse, 1795). The work was republished in several new editions. The accusation of plagiarism, however, has never been confirmed.

76. Schelling had published one of his earliest essays in Paulus's magazine. See Schelling, "Ueber Mythen, historische Sagen und Philosopheme der ältesten Welt," in *Memorabilien: A Philosophical-Theological Journal Dedicated to the History and Philosophy of Religions, Bible Study, and Oriental Literature*, 5 (1793): 1–68 (AA I, 1, 194–246). Later it was Paulus who, against Schelling's will, published his inaugural lecture in Berlin in the winter of 1841–42, the so-called

the last known review of Schelling's treatise on the Cabiri.[77] It is at the same time a reaction to the previous reviews (in particular the two positive ones from 1817, described below) and the debate described in the previous section about the correct method of research into the secrets of the oldest human faith.

The fact that the review was written so late, almost six years after the publication of Schelling's work, can probably be explained by the opportunity that Paulus seized on when he was reviewing Friedrich Sickler's newly published work.[78] Both works intended to pursue the same method (RP 545). Paulus, who was asked by Schelling himself to express an opinion on the matter (RP 568),[79] therefore draws a comparison between these two books, Sickler's and

---

Paulus-Nachschrift. See H. E. G. Paulus, ed., *Die endlich offenbar gewordene positive Philosophie der Offenbarung. Entstehungsgeschichte, wörtlicher Text, Beurtheilung und Berichtigung der v. Schellingschen Entdeckungen über Philosophie überhaupt, Mythologie und Offenbarung des dogmatischen Christenthums im Berliner Wintercursus von 1841—1842: Der allgemeinen Prüfung vorgelegt* (Darmstadt, Germany: Carl Wilhelm Leske, 1843). In a letter to Gotthilf Heinrich Schubert of December 31, 1810, Schelling characterized Paulus in a way that could hardly have been more pejorative: "I have met many evil people and experienced much evil from others; but I never met anyone more evil than Paulus and I have never received so much evil from anyone as from him" (Plitt II, 243). Even if it be a sheer ad hominem, one has to wonder whether at least part of Paulus's animus against Schelling had to do with the fact that Paulus was fourteen years older than the wunderkind of German idealism. How difficult it must have been to be in competition with so young—and so admired—a colleague!

77. There is admittedly another, review-like evaluation of Schelling's text in a part of Sickler's book (see the following note). But since Schelling is not specifically named in the title of this review and the comments do not go significantly beyond those of Paulus, this mere mention suffices. See Wilhelm von Schütz, "Homers Hymnus an Demeter... von Dr. F. K. Sickler...," *Jahrbücher der Literatur*, 17 (1822): 37–66. However, Schütz clearly recognizes the "philosophical approach" (ibid., 54) in Schelling's project, even though he does not see himself as capable of understanding it.

78. F. K. L. Sickler, *Homers Hymnus an Demeter. Griechisch, mit metrischer Uebersetzung und ausfuhrlichen [sic] Wort- und Sacherklärungen, durch Auflösung der ältesten Mysterien- und Tempelsprache in Hellas vermittelt* (Hildburghausen, Germany: Kesselringsche Buchhandlung, 1820).

79. As of 1806, Schelling had categorically forbidden himself every correspondence with Paulus. See Schelling to H. E. G. Paulus, March 3, 1806, Plitt I, 347.

Schelling's, a comparison based on the all-decisive task of "examining their *methods*": "Everything depends on the method, which is to say everything depends on the route to the final destination; but, in addition, the forces and means to traverse that route need to be examined" (RP 545). Paulus therefore not only disputes the method but also insinuates that Schelling lacks the capacity to sustain it.

The rather late drafting of the review, however, also confirms the ongoing struggle to find the correct method and to gauge the significance of Schelling's contribution to this wide-ranging dispute. After reading Paulus's review, Creuzer also felt compelled to react. He published his reaction immediately in 1821 in the preface to the fourth part of the new edition of his *Symbolism*.[80] In a previously unpublished letter to Schelling, Creuzer conveyed the obligation he felt to join the fight between the two different methodologies.[81] Creuzer had to restrain himself to ensure that his "preface did not become a book."[82] Yet once again Creuzer takes up the whole discussion, emphasizing the methodological differences in particular and not hesitating to enlist other scholars in support of his own point of view.

Indeed, there are general considerations about the importance of method in scholarship, the matter with which Paulus begins his review. He unmistakably and repeatedly asserts that any result that "proceeds in advance from

---

However, in 1815 he had a copy of his book, along with a letter to Paulus sent by Cotta. See Schelling to J. F. Cotta, October 14, 1815, SC 112. Paulus himself seems to refer to this letter. The letter, and yet another that reacts to a criticism by Paulus, are printed in Horst Fuhrmans, "Schellings Briefe," 414–437, 434–436. The second letter refers, among other things, to Paulus's criticism of the interpretation of Axieros. Schelling counters that his Semitic interpretation of the deity is in fact ingenious.

80. For the passages concerned with Schelling in the preface, see Friedrich Creuzer, *Symbolik und Mythologie der alten Völker, besonders der Griechen*, Part Four, second, completely revised edition (Leipzig/Darmstadt, Germany: Heyer und Leske, 1821), vi–vii.

81. See Creuzer to Schelling, September 9, 1821, in Alexander Bilda and Fernando Wirtz, "Unveröffentlichte Briefe," 236: "The fact that our Dr. Paulus in the *Heidelberg Yearbooks*, which are sinking lower and lower every day, talks about your book in *his* own way will not seem strange to you, but it will also be entirely indifferent to you. Meanwhile, I thought it my duty, precisely because I live *here*, to express *my* views in the preface to the fourth volume of *Symbolism*."

82. Friedrich Creuzer, *Symbolik*, Part Four, second ed., xix.

unprovable assumptions about the most arbitrary applications of the means" (RP 546) stands on wobbly feet. Here one can already guess what sort of verdict will be delivered on the works under review. In particular, it must be understood as a dig at Creuzer's Schelling review and the tone of many other reviews when Paulus criticizes the "ordinary reviewers' remedy" that "one notes much depth and ingenuity, but cannot agree with everything" (RP 546). For Creuzer himself in particular had made sufficient use of such formulations. In addition, Paulus takes up the points of criticism of the review in the *Göttinger Gelehrten Anzeigen* in order to drive them home.

Paulus first demonstrates that Sickler assumes unprovable prerequisites for his method, which is to say that his method is fundamentally flawed; even worse, Sickler himself makes mistakes in the application of his own method (RP 546–567). Paulus then turns to Schelling, who supposedly uses the same method as Sickler, who, for his part, had allegedly plagiarized Schelling—and crudely so (RP 582). In contrast to Sickler, however, Schelling abstains from the worst kinds of arbitrariness, albeit without thereby making his method any more correct. Schelling proves to be his own "best defender" (RP 568). Yet even if this damns Schelling with faint praise, it also shows how seriously Paulus takes Schelling's approach, which he then meticulously discusses. Paulus's criticisms can be divided into two categories: one opposes Schelling's more fundamental assumptions and preconditions, while the other rejects Schelling's specific results and interpretations. If the extensive criticisms of rather minor issues can be ignored here, the fundamental points of criticism are certainly worth mentioning for they illustrate the dissent within German Iidealism in general about philosophy and science heretofore. These remarks are all the more interesting because Paulus clearly recognizes the philosophical dimension of Schelling's project.

For Paulus, the system of the Cabiri cannot be interpreted as either speculative or natural philosophy. Such a distinction is a modern and artificial abstraction that cannot be supported either psychologically or historically. On the contrary, the Cabiri can be understood only as useful rites, that is, as "externally benevolent forces" (RP 582), since otherwise they would not have been sustainable. Thus the consecrations on Samothrace have no higher purpose: they neither possess a relationship to a theory of creation nor do they promote a more spiritual form of incarnation, nor can they even be understood as an ethics. The philosophical significance of the Cabiri, and therefore the philosophical significance of the treatise itself, are thus nullified.

These reservations are followed by scholarly doubts concerning the history recounted in the *Deities*. Schelling falsely assumes that the Cabiri had been imported to Samothrace by the Phoenicians. Rather, they would have come from Phrygia (in central Turkey) as the Parisian Scholion of the *Argonauts* reports—and this in a text used by Schelling himself.[83] Although Paulus is correct on this point, and although it is worth noting that Schelling actually omits this information when relying on the Scholiast,[84] Paulus's conclusion is not very convincing. For this single item seems to be sufficient for Paulus to begin all his linguistic research with Phrygian sources rather than Phoenician ones.[85] In contrast to Schelling's method of "deciphering the origins of mythology with Semitic etymologies" (RP 580), Paulus affirms that research should concentrate on the ancient Egyptian language, which is incompatible with Semitic languages. Schelling, in Paulus's view, ultimately succumbs to "Semitism" (RP, 581). Paulus argues that one cannot explain the ancient names in terms of modern or more recent languages, because the oldest names are inaccessible "archaisms." Both philosophically and historically, it is ultimately unlikely, in Paulus's view, that the scholarship of his day would better understand the mystery cult, which was already barely understood in the ancient sources (RP 582).

Schelling's reaction to Paulus's trenchant criticism is comparatively phlegmatic. He suggests that the review as a whole is not what he would have "desired," but otherwise he all too easily passes over the force of Paulus's criticism of his fundamental approach. Schelling instead lauds the actually weak demarcation between him and Sickler, which Paulus had drawn.[86]

---

83. In his correspondence with Schelling, Creuzer also tries to move Schelling gently in the direction of the Phrygian origin with a reference to the *Etymologicum Gudianum* but without directly contradicting him. See Creuzer to Schelling, December 27, 1820, in *Schelling-Studien*, 7 (2019), 232–234.

84. Although Schelling does not explicitly reject the Phrygian origin of the Cabiri, he discredits Athenion, who asserts their Phrygian origin in the Scholion to the *Argonauts*, an origin that—unlike the account of Mnaseas—is not credible to him. See SW I/8, 41–2.

85. It has to be admitted, however, that current research tends to support a Phrygian origin for the cult. See Jan N. Bremmer, *Initiation into the Mysteries of the Ancient World* (Berlin and Boston: Walter de Gruyter, 2014), 47.

86. See the letter Schelling to Creuzer, September 3, 1822: "Paulus's review was desirable to me insofar as I could at least get away from Sickler through it. As for

Perhaps Schelling restrains himself because Paulus is Creuzer's colleague at Heidelberg University.[87] It is more likely, however, that Schelling had already adjusted himself to the opposition of Paulus and was trying to deal with it philosophically and systematically, not least in the *Erlangen Lecture Course*, an attempt that leads to the vast tapestry of Schelling's late philosophy.

Now, however, to the favorable reviews. The more benevolent statements about Schelling's *Deities* are relatively long in coming. Yet they testify to Schelling's unusual intentions. It is practically unheard of to associate the Greek mystery cults so closely with a general and, as it were, still existing consciousness and with a fundamentally *philosophical* system. The first of the two reviews in the JALZ, published in June 1816, features the first appreciation of Schelling's endeavor. The reviewer praises Schelling's scientific approach as such but also clearly identifies its deficits. Schelling is mainly accused of not relating the Indian doctrine of the gods to the Greek Cabiri, even though Schelling himself would have recognized the validity of such an approach. Whereas the two earlier dismissive reviews still remained within the limits drawn by Schelling himself, this positive anonymously published review, whose author is the philologist Georg Friedrich Grotefend (1775–1853),[88]

---

my explanations, I think I'll know how to protect them when the occasion arises. The explanations of Sickler are still far too expansive and up to now too mildly treated, for all of them (not a single one excluded) are philologically impossible and, according to the underlying concept, partly downright tasteless, partly devoid of spirit; in any case, this is not how one likes to speak, but in fact and in truth he is beneath criticism. I take the liberty of expressing the wish that in the French translation all the quotations of Sickler's explanations may be omitted;—grant farewell also to mine, dear friend" (Plitt III, 12–13).

87. This is not contradicted by the fact that Creuzer himself had immense scientific (and personal) reservations against Paulus. See as an example Creuzer to Hegel, June 8, 1823, *Letters from and to Hegel*, 3 vols. (1823–31), ed. Johannes Hoffmeister (Hamburg, Germany: Felix Meiner, 1969), 18.

88. The abbreviation "VI-VII," with which the review concludes, stands for Georg Friedrich Grotefend, who had studied from 1795 on under Heyne, whose tradition continued through Schelling; for the authorship, see KB 70. For more on Grotefend, see his grandson, Hermann Grotefend, "Grotefend, Georg Friedrich," in *Allgemeine Deutsche Biographie*, 9 (1879): 763–765. F. G. Welcker in 1824 observes a "learned Orientalist" at work in the review. See Welcker, *Die Aeschylische Trilogie Prometheus und die Kabirenweihe zu Lemnos, nebst Winken über die Triologie des Aeschylus überhaupt* (Darmstadt, Germany: C. W. Leske,

actually goes beyond Schelling's sources.[89] Schelling's text is said to be "as learned as it is beautifully written" (RG 425), and, of all the previous investigations of the etymological explanations of the names of the Cabiri, Schelling presents the most satisfying "derivations and ... procedural principles" (RG 426–27). That said, the reviewer doubts the strong connection to the Phoenician, by means of which Schelling explains the mystery cults.

From this point on, the basically positive tone of the reviews increases steadily. In the review appearing in the *Göttingische Gelehrte Anzeigen*, which was decisively influenced by Heyne and which still exists today as a review journal, the renowned orientalist Thomas Christian Tychsen (1758–1834), based in Göttingen, expresses strong approval and only benevolent criticism of the work.[90] The review, signed only with the first letter of his surname, can also be traced back to Schelling's and Cotta's initiative to send Tychsen a copy of the *Deities* along with a letter containing a request for a review of the work.[91] A "peculiarity in the point of view and the novelty of the results" (RT 289) is ascribed to Schelling's investigation. The reviewer acknowledges Schelling's "contemplation of antiquity according to an idea" (RT 296) that

---

1824), 166n. Schelling had sent the book to Welcker as well. See Horst Fuhrmans, "Schellings Briefe," 414–437.

89. Grotefend complains that Schelling has not consulted an essay from *Asiatic Researches*, namely, Francis Wilford, "Remarks on the Names of the Cabirian Deities, and in Some Words Used in the Mysteries of Eleusis," in *Asiatic Researches; or, transactions of the society instituted in Bengal, for inquiring into the history and antiquities, the arts, sciences, and literature of Asia*, 5 (1799): 297–301. Grotefend then draws from this essay—without referring to it specifically—the Indological explanations that Schelling is supposed to be supplementing. In Schelling's defense, readers may recall from endnote 113 Schelling's openness to the idea that the Indian *Cavi* or *Cabi* may well indicate a relation to the Cabiri of Samothrace. At all events, Grotefend highlights Creuzer as Schelling's starting point for Schelling's remarks on Ceres and Proserpina, figures Creuzer ostensibly deployed more prudently than Schelling.

90. For Tychsen's authorship, see Oscar Fambach, *Die Mitarbeiter der Göttinger Gelehrten Anzeigen 1769–1836: Nach dem mit den Beischriften des Jeremias David Reuß versehenen Exemplar der Universitätsbibliothek Tübingen* (Tübingen, Germany: Universitätsbibliothek, 1976), 324. For Tychsen's biography see also ibid., 551–52.

91. See Schelling to Cotta, October 14, 1815: "Instead of the copy on Swiss paper, I ask you to send one to Mr. Privy Councilor and Professor Tychsen in Göttingen (together with a letter)" (SC 112).

differs from the purely historical approach, but he praises "the meaningful combinations [and] the astute implementation of the idea" (RT 295). Admittedly, the reviewer takes issue with regard to some of Schelling's more daring etymologies. Yet Schelling's approach is here for the first time also decisively supported in its philosophical-systematic dimension.

Friedrich Creuzer himself wrote the first signed review of Schelling's investigation, discussing it in the context of a comprehensive literary report that was later printed in a separate book edition and then again included in excerpts as an addition to the new edition of his *Symbolism* in 1820.[92] Creuzer's review is concerned with the latest findings in the study of mythology and the history of ancient religions, research that according to Creuzer "has expanded in many ways over the past few years" (RC 737). Creuzer also stresses Schelling's special role in the newly developed research on mythology. His *Deities* is the first of four texts reviewed by Creuzer.[93] In particular, Creuzer's meticulous examination of Schelling's text enables us still today to better understand Schelling's remarks and assess their status and, as it were, their explosive force in the discourse of the humanities of his time.[94]

Creuzer acknowledges Schelling's treatise as an "important phenomenon" (RC 738) and highlights several positive aspects of the work. His

---

92. See Friedrich Creuzer, *Ueber einige mythologische und artistische Schriften Schellings, Ouwaroffs, Millin's und Welckers. Aus den Heidelbergischen Jahrbüchern besonders abgedruckt* (Heidelberg, Germany: Mohr und Winter, 1817). Goethe too possessed this separate print. See GB 280 [No. 1961]. For the further use of excerpts but also selective extensions in 1820, see Friedrich Creuzer, *Symbolik*, Part Two, second ed., 363–77, corresponding to the text RC 738–48.

93. The other works were written by Ouwaroff (RC 761–783), Millin (RC 783–805), and Welcker (RC 805–823). See RC 737 for more details. These works are then also compared to Schelling's text. Creuzer accuses Ouwaroff of either not having undertaken the comparison with the gods of Samothrace or not having known of Schelling's book. See RC 763, 770, and 777. The missing consideration of the Samothracian doctrine is also attributed to Welcker. See RC 811 and 820.

94. Creuzer had already made excerpts from the book immediately after he received it from Schelling. Schelling had sent it to him with a letter dated October 15, 1815 (Plitt II, 362). However, Creuzer dropped his plan to use these excerpts since the other reviews would have already substantially referenced the content. Accordingly, in Creuzer one finds an indication of the main points but neither reproduction of the content nor detailed justifications for and against Schelling's argumentation.

acknowledgment, which distinguishes Schelling's philosophical-historical method from those "who have repeatedly afflicted us with mythologies purely *a priori*," aims at the very heart of the contemporary conflicts (RC 738). In particular, Schelling's methodology, combining attention to detail with a comprehensive philosophical approach, is well received by Creuzer. On the one hand, Schelling adheres to what is "most conditional," namely the "individual expressions of popular belief" and the "most unique and most filigrane roots of the old language" (ibid.); on the other hand, Schelling's original and keen gaze is directed toward "the general nature of ancient religion," which places the reader "both historically and philosophically on an ... elevated standpoint" (ibid.).[95] After what we have already described, it is obvious that this verdict is very close to Schelling's own intentions. Creuzer extols Schelling's very precise language, which is able to represent the minute differences within the mythographical field. His productive inclination toward Plato, which is also symptomatic of Schelling's philosophy in *The Ages of the World*, is also praised. Creuzer especially affirms Schelling's approach to Plato's use of myths as a fragmentary resumption of an old doctrine, in contrast to a use that merely wants to recognize Plato as a "logical gymnast" (RC 742). This affirmation deals yet another blow to Voss and his circle.

Even more decisive than this praise of Schelling's methodical approach is Creuzer's presentation of its newly acquired content. Creuzer shares with his readers three of Schelling's basic theses, which he understands as underlying the "magnificent idea" of the investigation as such (RC 746). For Creuzer, it is a great achievement not only to locate the origin of a true understanding of God in Israel but also to understand the pagan Greek doctrine concerning the gods as developing from a "pure knowledge of God in early prehistory" (RC 747). This achievement is to be understood as nothing less than Schelling's way of thinking within a system that has developed in its historical form as a "primal system," a system that also underlies the Cabiri on Samothrace. This goes hand in hand with the historico-geographical expansion that Schelling here undertakes when he seeks the source outside of Europe, hence in opposition to any form of Eurocentrism. Although an explanation from the Greek language itself is needed in order to understand the Greek

---

95. Creuzer also approves of the fact that not only the passage of the Scholiast but also that of Sanchuniathon is consulted by Schelling. For Sanchuniathon, see also RC 747–8.

doctrine of myths and gods, ultimately "the Orient ... must be interrogated concerning the unity and higher meaning of those Hellenic legends and teachings" (ibid.). At the same time, by claiming "the Orient" as a source of knowledge, Creuzer is already announcing that the Phoenician alone, as Schelling essentially claims in the *Deities*, is an insufficient explanation. Finally, Creuzer emphasizes a third aspect that is rather strange—at least for many of his contemporary readers—namely, the fusion of magic and theurgy in religion. This fusion also occurs in language: θέλγειν, "to practice magic," and θέλειν, "to want something," belong together, if not etymologically, then nevertheless by analogy (RC 748–49). Creuzer thus unerringly points to an aspect that is decisive not only for the *Deities* but also for the early phase of Schelling's late philosophy, especially in the *Erlangen Lectures*: the radical inexplicability of the original divine will, an association that Schelling connects with the "capability" that is inherent in both willing and in magic.

The criticism of Schelling that Creuzer then submits is no less significant, even if it is gently stated. It is expressed on two levels. On the first level, Creuzer criticizes various factual elements of Schelling's investigation and supplements or corrects them. This level, which could be subdivided into six specific criticisms, may be overlooked here, even though it is quite instructive (RC 743–746). On the second level, a more fundamental criticism is made, one that challenges Schelling's investigation as a whole (RC 749–761). Creuzer claims that Schelling does not, as he should, derive the Samothracian doctrine from Egypt, which would simultaneously be Creuzer's own genuine concern.[96] Creuzer's detailed exposition of this fundamental critique urges

---

96. Indian *culture* is also neglected by Schelling, though Creuzer does not present this criticism in detail. See RC 758. Moreover, Creuzer leaves undiscussed the fact that he also has certain reservations concerning Schelling's views, which neither accept Ceres in Eleusis as the supreme being nor regard the system as an emanation. (See, for both claims, SW I/8, 395n74.) Creuzer, against whose explanation of emanation Schelling had explicitly turned, cites some forceful sentences of Schelling himself from a letter he had sent to him. They clarify why Schelling speaks out against every form of emanation: "Of course I cannot deny and do not deny *any* emanation from God; but I answer in the way that theologians do otherwise: *distingue tempora, et concordabit scriptura* [Augustine, *Sermones* XXXII: 'Distinguish times and Scripture will be consistent']. In order to renounce the Supreme (at any time or on any occasion in the future), the Other had to *be there* (*da seyn*), independent from God and beyond the Supreme. Well,

Schelling "in his further mythological as well as art-historical investigations to honor that great factor in the spiritual civilization of ancient mankind, namely the *Egyptian element*, in all its power, with new and lasting attention" (RC 761). For Creuzer, Schelling's skepticism toward Egypt, which, with regard to the Cabiri, is essentially derived from a position taken on Herodotus but is also of a general character, must be regarded as unfounded. The Egyptians are mistakenly disparaged by Schelling because of the overriding importance of the Hebrew cultural sphere of influence with respect to the ancient Greeks.[97]

In fact, Schelling will arguably take this critique of Creuzer into account, insofar as he will no longer place the Cabiri at the center of his mythological considerations. He will also compensate for Creuzer's criticism in his later *Philosophy of Mythology* by including not only the Egyptian but also other Eastern systems of myth in general. What in 1815 emerges as the "primal system," founding the whole of philosophy, expands in the late period to a philosophy of mythology that is indeed richer and more detailed in its scope but whose expansion doubtless dissipates some of the concentrated power of the 1815 system. Indeed, in the later, expanded philosophy of mythology, the drawing power of that "primal system" of Cabirian deities for the very thinking they inaugurate is, I would argue, notably diminished.

C. The Reception of Schelling's *Deities* in England and France

Beyond the German-speaking world, Schelling's book may have received even greater recognition, which is astonishing given the hurdle of national differences. While, in England, Coleridge worked intensely with the *Deities*, it was also the first work of Schelling's to be translated into the francophone context. Let us first turn to England.

I deny this first *being* outside God that can be explained by emanation, may it be by exposing oneself, or by *being* exposed (probably even by God). No such explanation reaches back to those primeval times" (RC 750).

97. Schelling had made it unmistakably clear that of all the oriental languages he considered only the Semitic ones, in particular Arabic, Hebrew, and Phoenician, as explanations for the names of the gods in Western civilization. Again, a letter quoted by Creuzer makes this very clear. Schelling was convinced "that all Greek, Roman, and Etruscan names of the gods, with few exceptions, not only originated from oriental languages in general but from Semitic languages" (RC 751).

The restored Doric columns of the Hieron, or "Holy of Holies," where the *epopteia* or "revelation" may have taken place.

In his careful study of Schelling's reception in nineteenth-century England, Giles Whiteley refers to the English-language review of the *Deities* in *The Classical Review*, published in 1816.[98] This, the only non-German review, basically consists of a pure reproduction of the most important aspects of the text (RF 59–63). However, some important aspects are omitted, such as the magic chain of the gods, for example. The review is further problematic

---

98. See GW, 17 and the reproduction of the review in GW 258–59. Whiteley's intention, however, is to work out not only Coleridge as a recipient of Schelling's philosophy but to examine Schelling's impact on English literature as a whole. See GW 2–3.

in that it does not differentiate clearly between those parts that reproduce Schelling's text and those that reflect the reviewer's opinion.[99] Only the last paragraph of the review praises Schelling's comprehensive erudition and the dedicated presentation of his topic. At all events, despite its brevity, this review bears witness to the widespread influence Schelling had in England.

There is some probability that Coleridge became aware of the *Deities*—which, to repeat, he studied quite closely—through this review.[100] His borrowing of Schelling's ideas is legendary and need not be discussed here. However, Coleridge's processing of the *Deities* also shows how shortsighted it may be to elevate the accusation against Coleridge to one of plagiarism, especially if we simply apply today's standards to the past. The fact that Schelling, who was notoriously plagued by the fear that someone might copy his ideas, welcomes Coleridge's very generous reference to his *Deities* (SW II/1, 196n1) provides a first hint, even if the relationship between the two thinkers is quite complex. It is not expedient to take Coleridge's *Biographia Literaria* as a basis here, since it blatantly copies passages from Schelling's 1800 *System of Transcendental Idealism*. This has already been commented on, thoroughly and correctly, often enough. More significantly, Coleridge's perhaps most important work on mythology, "On the Prometheus of Aeschylus," most clearly demonstrates the influence of Schelling's philosophy.[101]

---

99. Some of the critical remarks that Whiteley assigns to the reviewer are not turned against Schelling's statements but in fact are Schelling's own. For example, the supposedly critical statement of the reviewer that is "particularly concerned with Schelling's discussion of monotheism" is a pure reproduction of what Schelling himself (SW I/8, 362–363) states, namely, that "the idea of an empty monotheism, allowing God but one separate personality, or one single power, is as strange to the Old and the New Testament as it is repugnant to all antiquity and to the unanimous sense of the ages" (GW 258). See also RF 63.

100. Since Coleridge observed the German academic landscape carefully, it is also possible that he became aware of the *Deities* and acquired the book in other ways. It is known, for example, that Coleridge ordered *The Ages of the World* in 1817 after a meeting with Ludwig Tieck. See Earl Leslie Griggs, "Ludwig Tieck and Samuel Taylor Coleridge," *The Journal of English and Germanic Philology*, 54:2 (April 1955): 262.

101. The complete title is as follows: "On the Prometheus of Aeschylus; an Essay, Preparatory to a Series of Disquisitions Respecting the Egyptian in Connection with the Sacerdotal Theology, and in Contrast with the Mysteries of Ancient Greece." See CW 11/2, 1251. On the relationship of this essay by Coleridge

Probably the most important basis for the Prometheus lecture of 1825, published in 1834 in the *Transactions*, was a discussion with Schelling that had taken place several years earlier.[102] In the eleventh *Lecture on Literature*, the eleventh *Philosophical Lecture*, and his marginalia on G. S. Faber's *Dissertation on the Cabiri*, probably written between 1817 and 1819, we find Coleridge's confrontation with Schelling's *Deities*.[103] Coleridge's multifaceted response to Schelling's *Deities* indicates that he took Schelling's text very seriously. In fact, in this very dense and somewhat cumbersome text, Coleridge is able not only to shed light on Schelling's core historical and philosophical theses but also to highlight the close connection between historical facts and philosophy. A hitherto little-noticed passage from *Prometheus* is symptomatic of Coleridge's ingenious efforts. Coleridge draws on the whole of Schelling's philosophy and in particular on the distinction between existence and the ground of existence that was so important for Schelling since at least the 1809 *Essay on Human Freedom*:

"The Greeks agreed with the cosmogonies of the East in deriving all sensible forms from the *Indistinguishable*.... As an idea, it must be interpreted as a striving of the mind to distinguish *being* from *existence*, or *potential* being, the ground of being containing the possibility of existence, from being *actualised*. In the language of the Mysteries, it was the Esurience,[104] the πόθος, or

---

to Schelling's *Deities* and his *Philosophy of Mythology*, see the excellent study by Douglas Hedley, *Living Forms of the Imagination* (London: T&T Clark, 2008), 120–24. For a fine description of the essay, see JV, 139–57. For an overall excellent study, see Nigel Leask, *The Politics of Imagination in Coleridge's Critical Thought* (Houndsmill and London: Macmillan, 1988), 174–83 and 200–9.

102. See William K. Pfeiler, "Coleridge and Schelling's Treatise on the Samothracian Deities," *Modern Language Notes*, 52:3 (March 1937): 162–165.

103. I agree with the analysis in the introduction to the *Prometheus* essay in the historical-critical edition, which argues that Coleridge's essay exhibits the greatest affinity to Schelling's *Deities*. Only the historical-critical edition of Coleridge's works point to the references to the *Deities* to be considered here. Yet Coleridge's essay is not, as René Wellek says, a mere paraphrase. See CW 11/2, 1255n. 1 and also René Wellek, *A History of Modern Criticism, 1750–1950* (New Haven, CT: Yale University Press, 1955), 2, 152–53.

104. Coleridge coined the word *Esurience* himself, meaning by it a greedy and unfulfilled hunger. The word is since then a part of the English vocabulary, albeit scarcely an everyday expression. Deriving from the Latin, it combines the

desiderium, the unfueled fire, the Ceres, the ever-seeking maternal goddess, the origin and interpretation of whose name is found in the Hebrew root signifying hunger, and thence capacity" (CW 11/2, 1269–70).[105]

Even in a supposedly mythographic commentary on Greek thought, Coleridge emphasizes precisely the category of *capability* or *possibility* as the notion that not only underpins Schelling's Erlangen philosophy but fundamentally renews it. This dynamic element accompanies the development of Schelling's philosophy during its middle period, a development that Schelling struggles for years to elaborate. Coleridge is thus able to draw together what all too often Schelling himself is able to assemble only in a recondite way. Capability is not merely a philosophical category that supports and moves the whole system of Schelling's philosophy; it is also considered to be a historic moment in the development of spirit. For Coleridge, the historical localization of capability in the Greek mystery cults is thus much more than an example. What unfolds in the mystery cults as longing (*Sehnsucht*) in all its variations also pervades all philosophical thought as such.

In this context, Schelling adopts the word *tautegorisch* (SW II/1, 196) from Coleridge. If Schelling also believes at this point that Coleridge has understood the "philosophical content and concern" of the *Deities* and its "meaning" (SW II/1, 196), these are more than empty words, especially since Schelling does not try to equate the tautegorical with the philosopheme, as Coleridge does. These considerations of the "indistinguishable," characterized by capability and longing, are what make Schelling consider Coleridge to be a fellow thinker.[106] That Coleridge chooses the fire-bringing Prometheus

---

meanings of hunger and eating. This is the same combination that Schelling used in reference to the Hebrew. See endnotes 55 and 56, above.

105. Recently edited but otherwise quite commonly deleted versions from a notebook used by Coleridge a few years earlier, probably around 1820, bear witness to the fact Coleridge has the Samothracian mysteries at the back of his mind. See CW 11/2, 1289.

106. Vigus, on the other hand, assumes that it is precisely the assumption of this idea, which has only the "status of a necessary assumption" in Coleridge, that represents a contradiction between the two thinkers. See JV 147. But it is precisely this philosophical core recognized by Coleridge that makes Schelling praise him. Coleridge grasps what Schelling philosophically asserts as the "unprethinkable," *das Unvordenkliche*, only after the *Deities* had been delivered.

as the subject of his essay, employing the same metaphorical figures on the basis of which Schelling develops the yearning and consuming flame, confirms how amenable Coleridge's remarks are to Schelling.[107]

Despite all these similarities, however, a decisive difference must not be overlooked. Coleridge, in contrast to the statements Schelling makes in the *Deities*, classifies the significance of the mysteries, and especially the Phoenician mysteries, differently.[108] For Schelling, the Phoenician and the Greek coincide in the Samothracian mysteries; for Coleridge, the separation of the two is emphasized. Indeed, for Coleridge, a confusion occurs in the Phoenician but not in the Greek: "The Phoenician confounded the Indistinguishable with the Absolute, the alpha and omega, the ineffable *causa sui*" (CW 11/2, 1270). Coleridge, tracing a development from the Phoenician to the Greek and asserting the resulting hierarchy between them, pursues a path that the later Schelling was arguably to follow. In view of the further development of religions, the primal existence of mystery cults would have to be put into perspective. In Coleridge's eyes, Schelling's approach of 1815 unduly exaggerates the importance of the mysteries. While Schelling has already abandoned the approach of his identity philosophy, Coleridge apparently argues along its lines when he demands an "absolute identity above all intellect" to oppose the Phoenician "multëity" (CW 11/2, 1270). As we have seen, however, Schelling's concept of an ascending series in the *Deities* identifies the chthonic gods as elements of the absolute. These are precisely the elements that give it a vitality that would not be found in a pure absolute identity.

Thus the *Deities* avoids Coleridge's demotion of the mysteries. Schelling's text instead recounts the phenomenon of an unfolding desire in all its power, and to that extent it thereby remains within the "magic chain" of the mysteries. In this way, Coleridge certainly anticipates Schelling's later development for in 1825 Schelling was still on the way to his *Philosophy of Mythology*, although he was already working on it intensely, as his less extensive lectures on mythology in Erlangen attest. Because Schelling did not know Coleridge's

---

107. See also CW 11/2, 1268 and 1280–81 in addition to the above quotation.

108. These differences are certainly also connected with the different ways in which monotheism is explained. Coleridge employs an original monotheism and an original creation in the development of religions, which Schelling places in a larger developmental context. See also Leask, *The Politics of Imagination in Coleridge's Critical Thought*, 174–183, esp. 179.

essay until 1834 at the earliest, he was able to confirm its almost overwhelming agreement with his own current *Philosophy of Mythology*.

But now to France. No review of Schelling's *Deities* has been identified in French-speaking countries. Such restraint on the part of the French can certainly be attributed to the recent historical events in the shadow of which Schelling gave his address. After Bavaria became a kingdom through its alliance with Napoleon, it changed sides just in time not to be crushed by Napoleon's defeat. The "world spirit on horseback" had turned into a specter and a monster. The sentences with which Schelling concludes the *Deities*, and which try to interpret the names of the Cabiri once again, can also be read as a barely hidden allusion to the rejection of Napoleon, who would have destroyed the Bavarians after the manner of the monster Typhon: "For us, in this moment, the most fitting application of the name [of the Cabiri] may be permitted, inasmuch as it reminds us at the same time of that Cabirian confederation by which the tyranny was broken, so that the last spasms of a truly Typhonian empire, which threatened merely to end in a universal collapse of ethical life, could finally be quelled" (SW I/8, 369). Against the horror of a French empire, Schelling now affirms the new constitution in Bavaria, which is no longer based on the king alone. The monarch rules together with his ministers, like the Cabiri, who form a council as *consentes* and perhaps even *socii*.[109]

Schelling sent his book to the famous orientalist Antoine-Isaac Silvestre de Sacy in France.[110] The package also contained a letter in Latin in which Schelling introduces himself and his booklet (*libellus*) to de Sacy. The letter

---

109. The end of the tyranny can even be linked to Napoleon's deposition in 1814; the spasmodic convulsions are his reign of *Cent-jours*, of which Waterloo is a quasilast convulsion—the battle Napoleon lost only three months before Schelling's address. Which leaves us only to reflect on the *earlier* "Typhonian empire." Who, in Schelling's view, was the "Napoleon" the Cabirian alliance defeated? Who, indeed, but our usual understanding of the demiurge? That thought we leave for another day.

110. For the following, see Schelling to Silvestre de Sacy, October 15, 1815, Plitt II, 361–62. In the *Deities* Schelling had referred to Antoine Isaac Silvestre de Sacy, *Lettre au citoyen Chaptal, ... au sujet de l'inscription égyptienne au monument trouvé à Rosette* (Paris: Imprimerie de la République, 1802). See SW I/8, 387. For an English translation of the letter, see Robert F. Brown, *Schelling's Treatise on "The Deities of Samothrace": A Translation and an Interpretation* (Missoula, MT: Scholars Press for the American Academy of Religion 1977), 41.

is interesting because Schelling expresses his interest in oriental literature, an interest that had existed since his earliest youth. He identifies his father, Joseph Friedrich Schelling, who was known to de Sacy,[111] and his professor in Tübingen, Christian Friedrich Schnurrer, as his teachers. Schnurrer, who was well-versed in oriental languages, was a friend of de Sacy, to whom he dedicated his *Bibliotheca arabica* (1811).[112] In addition, Schelling once again explicitly distinguishes himself from his predecessors of the seventeenth century, Vossius and Bochert, who had tried to explain the names of the Cabiri. But Schelling also distances himself from Nicolas Fréret,[113] while he remains neutral toward Sainte-Croix, merely emphasizing his frequent use of Sainte-Croix for his own work.[114] In doing so, he leaves unmentioned what de Sacy could learn from the work itself, namely, that Schelling is rather critical of Sainte-Croix.[115]

Although no review of Schelling's work by de Sacy has been discovered, de Sacy mentions Schelling in the new 1817 edition of Sainte-Croix's famous work, *The Ancient Mystery Cults*. To what extent Schelling's criticism of Sainte-Croix plays a role here cannot be determined.[116] The publication of the work, however, may also be understood as a self-assertion by the French

---

111. Joseph Friedrich Schelling's *Abhandlungen von dem Gebrauch der Arabischen Sprache* (Stuttgart, Germany: 1771) was part of the library of de Sacy; see Romain Merlin, *Bibliothèque de M. le baron Silvestre de Sacy*, vol. 2 (Paris: Benjamin Duprat and Julien, 1846), 183 (no. 2717).

112. Christian Friedrich Schnurrer, *Bibliotheca arabica*, (Halle a.d. Saale: I. C. Händel, 1811).

113. Schelling mentions Fréret's essay on the Cabiri twice disapprovingly, but Fréret himself never by name. See SW I/8, 375n23 ("author") and 392n67 ("another").

114. Besides Creuzer, the historian Guillaume-Emmanuel-Joseph-Guilhem de Clermont-Lodéve de Sainte-Croix (1746–1809) was one of Schelling's main reference points. See his famous *Mémoires pour servir à l'histoire de la religion secrète des anciens peuples; ou recherches et critiques sur les Mystères du paganisme* (Paris: Nyon 1784) crowned in 1777 by the Académie royale des Inscriptions et Belles-Lettres. This book was translated into German by Carl Gotthold Lenz as *Des Freyherrn von Sainte-Croix: Versuch über die alten Mysterien* (Gotha, Germany: Karl Wilhelm Ettinger, 1790).

115. For Schelling's frequent and often critical references to Sainte-Croix, see SW I/8, 361, 372, 374–75, 382, 384, 392, 395, 400, and esp. 411–12.

116. De Sacy was commissioned to reprint the work by Sainte-Croix, who was unable to publish it himself before his death. See SS viii.

scholarship of antiquity. De Sacy was not only to reedit the work but also to correct some errors in content and editing that Sainte-Croix had made.[117] De Sacy inserts a footnote in which he both describes Schelling's criticism of Sainte-Croix and rejects Schelling's own etymologies of the Samothracian deities as "unnatural" (SS 43n). With the exception of a letter from de Sacy to Schelling, which again takes up the theme of the deities of Samothrace, this line of reception, however, came to nothing.[118]

Adolphe Pictet de Rochemont, a Swiss student at the time, received Schelling's treatise on the Cabiri in a completely different way. It was on the recommendation of Schelling's publisher Cotta that Pictet met Schelling at the end of 1821.[119] His enthusiasm for Schelling's philosophy, which can also be read in his letters to his father, Charles Pictet,[120] led him to translate Schelling's *Deities* into French.[121] This is probably Schelling's first work ever to be translated into that language and at least the first translation of the *Deities* in general. From today's point of view, it may be astonishing that of all his books, this was the one that received the honor. But as the above remarks at least indicate, Schelling's treatise was part of a larger debate that was of great interest to the European scholarly world. Such interest is reflected in the French translation. However, the relative obscurity of the translation's

---

117. However, Sainte-Croix had already corrected some mistakes himself. See SS xviii.

118. Schelling, however, knew of de Sacy's remarks about Sainte-Croix's work—the thoroughly critical, albeit benevolent, remarks. See Schelling's 1830 speech "About the Arabic Names of Dionysos," SW I/9, 335. Schelling was later to deliver a small memorial speech on the death of de Sacy. See Schelling, "Worte zum Andenken des Freiherrn von Moll und Sylvestre de Sacys," SW I/9, 297–300, 299–300. For the letter, see Silvestre de Sacy to Schelling, 1819, Archive of the Berlin-Brandenburg Academy of Sciences and Humanities, *Schelling Nachlass*, no. 611.

119. See J. F. Cotta to Schelling, December 20, 1821, SC 146. Another letter of recommendation came from Cousin. See A. Pictet de Rochemont to Victor Cousin, September 12, 1821 (XT III, 35). See also LF, 15.

120. A. Pictet to Charles Pictet de Rochemont, December 29, 1821, XT I, 272: "The only reason that determines me for Erlangen is my extreme desire to see and hear Schelling."

121. Adolphe Pictet, trans., "Des Divinités de la Samothrace . . . par F. W. J. Schelling," *Bibliothèque Universelle des Sciences, Belles-Lettres et Arts* [Series: Littérature], 20 (1822):: 319–338 and 21 (1822): 3–21.

publication in France, which was also released anonymously, may explain why it has not yet been recognized by researchers.[122] The translation appeared in two volumes of the *Bibliothèque Universelle des Sciences, Belles-Lettres et Arts*, published in Geneva by Pictet's father and his brother, Marc-August Pictet.

In 1822 Pictet waited in Erlangen for Schelling to deliver a lecture on mythology, a lecture he was to give later that summer after some postponements.[123] It may well be that Pictet undertook the translation during the wait.[124] The translation is limited to a reproduction of the main text and provides the references contained in the endnotes only in a few places. Pictet translates the text quite freely, omitting some passages of the main text and expanding or even altering the text at his own discretion. The passage quoted above, from Schelling's peroration, which can be read as a critique of France, is also replaced by Pictet with new and quite general phrases on the significance of ancient times for contemporary scholarship. One can only speculate that Pictet changed and softened this passage to please a larger French-speaking audience. Schelling, in any case, was only conditionally satisfied with this translation. In a letter to Victor Cousin of 1826, in which Schelling also announces his considerably broader reflections on mythology as a *philosophy* of mythology, he sees in the translation of the *Deities* "a rather French editorial elaboration of the original."[125] As for Pictet, he was further

---

122. For an overview of all French-language translations of Schelling's works, see LF 75, from which, however, Pictet's translation is missing. Xavier Tilliette speaks of a later translation project by Pictet but probably does not know of this translation. See Xavier Tilliette, *Schelling Biographie* (Stuttgart, Germany: Klett-Cotta, 2004), 319. Already in 1954 a Swiss researcher mentions Pictet's translation of the *Deities* in passing and only with the main title of the text. See Raymond Marcel, "L'influence de Schelling en France et en Suisse Romande," *Studia Philosophica*, 14 (1954): 91–111, esp. 99.

123. See A. Pictet to C. Pictet, May 7, 1822, XT I, 273.

124. However, it can also be assumed that Pictet completed the translation, at least of the first part, at the end of 1821, during the time he visited Schelling. For, in the brief introduction to the translation, he refers to a work by Schelling on "*mythologie greque*"; also in a letter to his father he says, "He will publish a new book on the significance of Greek mythology, and I'm awaiting it with great impatience." (A. Pictet to C. Pictet, December 29, 1821, XT I, 272).

125. See Schelling to Victor Cousin, April 16, 1826, Plitt III, 18: "ill y a déjà plusieurs années, que pour la traduction ou plutôt pour la rédaction française je m'en suis remis à Mr. *Pictet.*"

inspired by Schelling's thoughts and published a quite daring book about the Cabiri in Ireland (!) only two years after completing his translation.[126]

3. Conclusion

As we have seen, it initially appears that Schelling's reflections on the deities of Samothrace merely developed what is already sketched out in the *Essay on Human Freedom* of 1809 and intensified in *The Ages of the World* (1811–1815). Yet the motif of hunger and longing, already broached in Schelling's philosophy, is not simply confirmed by the mysterious Axieros. The motif is strengthened when Schelling makes it a vital part of the whole system of Samothracian deities. Constructed on historical grounds, this new form of philosophizing is elevated to a genuinely philosophical level in the 1821 *Erlangen Lecture Course*, where an altered combination of principle and system takes shape. These Erlangen thoughts confirm the strong principle of Axieros, which now permeates the living system of philosophy. Yet a problem arises, one that confronts Schelling with the daunting task of unifying strong *capability* with a system of *hunger* and *longing*. The underlying ground of such a capability may well undermine the system and eventually subvert its construction of God. In his late philosophy, Schelling assuages the longing and reduces the hunger by minimizing their effect on the system as a whole. Although his thoughts on mythology vastly expand in scope, the deities of Samothrace do not figure prominently in what is now a system divided into "negative" and "positive" philosophy. Axieros is now quarantined, so to speak, in a theogonic process that remains remote from philosophy itself.

The *Deities* not only revitalizes Schelling's early interest in mythology but also becomes a part of the modern debate on how to interpret the myths of antiquity. Greek antiquity may be regarded as an ideal, as Voss viewed it, or the ideal may be questioned by examining how these myths themselves are historically constituted, in the way that Heyne endeavored to show. Schelling preferred the latter approach, and he further developed this position. Like Heyne, Schelling saw in myths not mere allegories but rather true expressions of ancient consciousness and speculative reality. Therefore, a non-Greek origin of the cult could be entertained, Schelling finding a Phoenician

---

126. See A. Pictet, *Du cult des Cabires chez les anciens Irlandais* (Geneva and Paris: J. J. Paschoud, 1824), where Pictet also refers to his translation of the *Deities*, ibid., 3.

origin most plausible. Yet Schelling's philological and historical explanation of the cult, as developing from Hebrew and Phoenician roots, was immensely problematic for his colleagues. They expressed their doubts in many discriminating yet sometimes recriminating reviews, with Schelling's archenemy Paulus being the most polemical. That Schelling treated the interpretation of the Samothracian cult philosophically was often neglected, and only the benevolent reviewers saw this approach as fruitful, with Creuzer being the most sympathetic. We also have seen English and French audiences receiving the *Deities* positively: Coleridge fruitfully adapts Schelling's thought to his own projects concerning antiquity and a young Swiss scholar, Adolph Pictet, even translates the *Deities* into French, making it the first Schelling translation into that language that we know of.

What we have learned is that Schelling's *Deities* plays an important and even crucial role in his philosophy, even though the book seems to be exceptional in his oeuvre, and even if the topic itself now seems somehow antiquated. Yet Schelling's text is not merely essential to the modern discussion of mythology. For Schelling himself takes it to be a philosophical grounding of consciousness and reality. The strong reaction of Schelling's contemporaries to his effort contrasts with the neglect of his text by our own contemporary scholarly community. The recently published historical-critical edition of the text (AA I/19) may change this. In any case, the fact remains that the text represents a veritable turning point in Schelling's philosophy. The philosophy that Schelling attributes to, or ascertains within, the Samothracian cult leads to a radicalization of his entire philosophy as such. This radicalization should lead us to a deeper interrogation of our own troubled world, of nature and of the nature of our fellow creatures. Perhaps it calls for a change in our worldview—maybe even our politics. It is for these eminently philosophical reasons that readers of Schelling, as *socii* and *consentes*, express the hope of a return of the Cabiri—and a return to Samothrace.

Abbreviations of Sources Cited

AA Friedrich Wilhelm Joseph Schelling, *Historisch-kritische Ausgabe im Auftrag der Schelling-Kommission der Bayerischen Akademie der Wissenschaften*. Ed. Hans Michael Baumgartner et al. (Stuttgart-Bad Cannstatt, Germany: Frommann-Holzboog, 1976-). *Ueber die Gottheiten von Samothrace* appears as volume 19 of division I (AA I/19).

CD   Christian Danz, "'Darstellung des unauflöslichen Lebens selbst [. . .] war ihrem tiefsten Sinn nach die heilig geachtete Lehre der Kabiren.' Überlegungen zum Systembegriff in Schellings Akademievortrag *Ueber die Gottheiten von Samothrake*," *Systemkonzeptionen im Horizont des Theismusstreites (1811–1821)*. Ed. Christian Danz, Jürgen Stolzenberg and Violetta Waibel (Hamburg, Germany: Felix Meiner, 2018) (System der Vernunft: Kant und der Deutsche Idealismus 5), 181–198.

CW   Samuel Taylor Coleridge, *Collected Works* (London/Princeton: Princeton University Press, 1959).

GB   Hans Ruppert (ed.), *Goethes Bibliothek* (Weimar, Germany: Arion, 1958).

GW   Giles Whiteley, *Schelling's Reception in Nineteenth-Century British Literature* (Cham, Switzerland: Palgrave Macmillan, 2018).

HT   Christian Gottlob Heyne, "Temporum mythicorum memoria a corruptelis nonnullis vindicata [On the Consciousness of the Mythical Times, Freed from Some Mistakes]," *Commentationes societatis regiae scientarum Gottingensis antiquiorum*, 8 (1785/86): 3–19.

JV   James Vigus, "The Spark of Intuitive Reason: Coleridge's 'On the Prometheus of Aeschylus,'" *Symbol and Intuition: Comparative Studies in Kantian and Romantic-period Aesthetics*. Ed. Helmut Hühn and James Vigus (Abingdon and New York: Legenda, 2013), 139–57.

KB   Karl Bulling, *Die Rezensenten der Jenaischen Allgemeinen Literaturzeitung im zweiten Jahrzehnt ihres Bestehens 1814–1823* (Weimar, Germany: Hermann Böhlaus Nachfolger, 1963).

KSA   Friedrich Schlegel, *Kritische Ausgabe seiner Werke*. Ed. Ernst Behler et al. (Paderborn, Munich, and Vienna: Schöningh, 1958).

LF   Laurent Fedi, "Schelling en France au XIXe siècle," *Les Cahiers philosophiques de Strasbourg*, 43 (2018): 13–80.

Plitt   Gustav Leopold Plitt (ed.), *Aus Schellings Leben: In Briefen*. Volumes I–III (Leipzig: S. Hirzel, 1869–70).

RA   [Friedrich Ast], "Ueber die Gottheiten von Samothrace [. . .] von Friedrich Wilhelm Joseph Schelling," *Wiener Allgemeine Literaturzeitung*, 99 (December 12, 1815): col. 1567–1573.

RC   Friedrich Creuzer, "Ueber die Gottheiten von Samothrace [. . .] von Fr. W. Jos. Schelling," *Heidelbergische Jahrbücher der Litteratur*, 10:47–48 (1817): 737–761.

RF	F., "Notice of a German Treatise, entitled [. . .] On the Deities of Samothrace . . . by F. W. J. Schelling," *The Classical Journal*, 14:27 (September and December 1816): 59–64.
RG	[Georg Friedrich Grotefend], "Über die Gottheiten von Samothrace [. . .] von Friedrich Wilhelm Joseph Schelling," *Jenaische Allgemeine Literatur-Zeitung*, 3:113 (June 1816): col. 425–429.
RK	[Friedrich Köppen], "Ueber die Gottheiten von Samothrace [. . .] von F. W. J. Schelling," *Allgemeine Literatur-Zeitung*, 1:29 (February 1816): col. 225–232.
RM	[Ernst Philipp August Mahn], "Über die Gottheiten von Samothrace [. . .] von Friedrich Wilhelm Joseph Schelling," *Jenaische Allgemeine Literatur-Zeitung*, 3:113–114 (June 1816): col. 429–438.
RP	Heinrich Eberhard Gottlob Paulus, "Homers Hymnus an Demeter [. . .] von Dr. F. K. L. Sickler [. . .] Verglichen mit Fr. Wilh. Joseph Schellings Abhandl. Ueber die Gottheiten von Samothrake," *Heidelberger Jahrbücher der Literatur*, 14:35–38 (1821): 545–606.
RT	[Thomas Christian Tychsen], "Ueber die Gottheiten von Samothrace [. . .] von Fr. Wilh. Joseph Schelling," *Göttingische gelehrte Anzeigen*, 1:30 (February 22, 1817): 289–296.
SC	Horst Fuhrmans und Liselotte Lohrer, editors, *Schelling und Cotta. Briefwechsel 1803–1849* (Stuttgart, Germany: Ernst Klett Verlag, 1965).
SG	F. W. J. Schelling, *Weltalter-Fragmente*. 2 volumes. Ed. Klaus Grotsch (Stuttgart and Bad Cannstatt, Germany: Frommann [Schellingiana 13:1/2]), 2002.
SS	Guillaume-Emmanuel-Joseph-Guilhem de Clermont-Lodéve de Sainte-Croix, *Recherches historiques et critiques sur les Mystères du paganisme*. 2 volumes. Ed. Antoine-Isaac Silvestre de Sacy (Paris: de Bure frères, 1817).
SW	F. W. J. Schelling, *Sämmtliche Werke*. Ed. Karl Schelling (Stuttgart and Augsburg, Germany: J. G. Cotta'scher Verlag, 1856–1861).
WA	F. W. J. Schelling, *Die Weltalter: Fragmente, in den Urfassungen von 1811 und 1813*. Ed. Manfred Schröter (Munich: Biederstein und Leibniz Verlag, 1946).
XT	Xavier Tilliette, ed., *Schelling im Spiegel seiner Zeitgenossen*. Volumes 1–4 (Turin, Italy: Bottega d'Erasmo, 1974–1997).

High on Mount Georgos, above the sanctuary, the possible site of an early altar dedicated to the Mountain Mother. Note the fragment of marble cladding in the foreground, a later addition to the site.

6

The Advent of the Return of the Cabiri

JASON M. WIRTH

1. Remembering the Still to Come

> Brot ist der Erde Frucht, doch ists vom Lichte gesegnet,
> Und vom donnernden Gott kommt die Freude des Weins.
>
> "Bread is fruit of the earth, yet it is blessed by light,
> And from the thundering god comes the joy of wine."
> —Friedrich Hölderlin, *Brot und Wein* (Strophe 8)

In these beautiful lines by Hölderlin, bread and wine, the highest symbols of Christian revelation and the icons of the Last Supper and the Eucharist, are associated with more ancient and less otherworldly gods, indeed, with the earth and the sun and the flashing forth of the heavens themselves. The inference is clear: these canonical symbols were somehow already present in the ancient world. Moreover, Hölderlin links "poets in a destitute age [*Dichter in dürftiger Zeit*]" to the "holy priests of the wine god," "which roamed from land to land in holy night [*welche von Lande zu Land zogen in heiliger Nacht*]" (strophe 7). Drinking such wine and feasting on such bread against an oblivion in which the force of such things can no longer be remembered, in our "holy drunkenness" with a full wine glass, we remain "wakeful at night [*wachend... bei Nacht*]" with our "holy memory [*heilig Gedächtniß*]" (strophe 2).

Hölderlin strikingly conflates the game change that is announced with the coming of the Christ—bread and wine as the new testament and the beginning of a new world—with something that precedes incarnation, even though it originally manifested itself in the form of a mystery religion

(*Geheimlehre*). Dionysos did not manifest himself publicly, in the terms of public disclosure, but rather demanded a more radical ἀνάμνησις of the potencies of being itself.[1] Moreover, although Jesus gave rise to the many public forms of Christianity, the messianic remains no less obscure and calls for an equally radical *Andenken* and ἀνάμνησις. Feasting on the bread of the earth and drunk on joyful wine suddenly revealed from the heavens, we abide in watchful awakening during the night.

These images contest at least two of the articles of faith that are most taken for granted: that bread and wine are unique Christian historical events and that their meaning entered history with the advent of Jesus. Furthermore, linking the ontological sea change associated with Christianity with the bread of the earth and the Dionysian joy of wine renders the former less staid and historically petrified. In a sense, an inkling of something still to come can already be discovered in ancient cultures. These ancient prototypes do not merely confirm later events but rather hint at something still repressed within their historical reception. We remain "wakeful at night" with our "holy memory."

The repetition of this sacrament, which revitalizes us, the earth, and our relationship to it, recalls a distinction that Schelling made in his first address in 1807 (*On the Relationship of the Plastic Arts to Nature*) before the Bavarian King Maximilian I. Joseph on his name day. "Art that wanted to present the empty shell or limitation of the individual would be dead and unbearably severe. We clearly do not demand the individual. We demand to see more, namely, the living concept of the individual" (SW I/7, 304). Just as the dogmatically positivistic science of his day merely reiterated the forms of nature without being able to think their living ground, art follows suit and copies the forms

---

1. From *Die Weltalter*: "What we call knowledge is only the striving towards ἀνάμνησις [*Wiederbewußtwerden*, "becoming conscious once again"] and hence more of a striving toward knowledge than knowledge itself. For this reason, the name Philosophy had been bestowed on it incontrovertibly by that great man of antiquity" (SW I/8, 201). An earlier, shorter, and substantially different version of the present essay appeared as "And Hence Everything Is Dionysus: Schelling and the Cabiri in Berlin," *Rethinking German Idealism*, ed. Sean J. McGrath and Joseph Carew (Hampshire, England: Palgrave Macmillan, 2016), 271–291. An indispensable companion to serious study of the Samothrace address is *Schellings Gottheiten von Samothrake im Kontext*, ed. Christian Danz (Vienna: Vienna University Press, 2021).

of the past with no sense of their underlying vitality. "How strange it would be for those who denied all life to nature to put it forward in art for imitation! The words of the profound man [J.G. Hamann] would apply to them: Your mendacious philosophy has done away with nature, so why do you demand that we imitate it? So that you could renew your enjoyment by committing the same act of violence against the students of nature?" (SW I/7, 293).[2]

Just as in art and nature, ritual that merely recapitulates the form, bereft of its living ground, is "sterile imitation" or even "dead imitation." Just going through the motions murders what it imitates, delivering only its empty husk. "Only insofar as they grasp this in living imitation have they created something true" (SW I/7, 301).

In a sense, the Dionysian prototype of the Eucharist invigorates its repetition as the latter, releasing it from its historically sclerotic forms and hinting at a life to come from out of its repression. This is, as it were, the revelation of the Nietzschean Antichrist—"Dionysos crucified"—as the prophet of a future Christianity. It is to hearken to the Dionysian power of wine. Among the many epithets of Dionysos is Eleutherios, the liberator, and just as wine loosens and frees up what habit and decorum otherwise control, the coming of Dionysos was an event of freedom interrupting the vice grip of order and regularity. As Schelling remarked in *The Ages of the World*: "Panthers or tigers do not pull the carriage of Dionysos in vain. For this wild frenzy of inspiration in which nature found itself when it was in view of the being was celebrated in the nature worship of prescient ancient peoples by the drunken festivals of Bacchic orgies" (I/8, 337).[3] The power of wine "to enchant, to

---

2. In a new footnote in the reprinted edition that immediately precedes the first appearance of the *Essay on Human Freedom* in the 1809 *Philosophische Schriften*, Schelling clarifies this allusion that tact likely prohibited him from delivering before a royal audience. "These are the words of J. G. Hamann from the *Kleeblatt hellenistischer Briefe* [*Cloverleaf of Hellenistic Letters*], II, 189, moderated in the context of the present address. Here are the words in the man's own expression: 'Your murderously mendacious philosophy has done away with nature, and why do you demand that we should keep imitating it? So that you could renew your enjoyment by also murdering the students of nature?" Schelling incorrectly cites the source of Hamann's words. They stem from the concise and quite marvelous essay, *Aesthetica in Nuce*.

3. My translations of *Die Weltalter* (1815) originally appeared in F. W. J. Schelling, *The Ages of the World* (Albany: State University of New York Press, 2000).

inspire, and to raise up the spirit," Walter Otto tells us in his study of Dionysos, "brings even us in contact with the ancient belief that a god reveals himself in wine."[4]

This is also precisely how Schelling understood the problem of all philosophical thinking: everything comes down to who we are in relation to the bread of the earth and the wine of the heavens. How does philosophy negotiate the feast and the holy inebriation of thinking? As eager audiences in Berlin awaited the dispensation of yet another new philosophy, Schelling took positive philosophy into this bewildering realm of the gods whose coming we drunkenly but vigilantly remember. "Where there is no madness that is governed and brought under rule, there is also no powerful understanding."[5] Stupidity (*Blödsinn*), however, does not consist of a lack of intelligence—the intelligent are even more dramatically inclined to stupidity than are the dim-witted—but rather of the "absence of this originary matter," the lack of "the madness, the *potentia* that lies concealed in the depths of the human *Wesen*" (PO 186). In the *Urfassung* of the *Philosophie der Offenbarung*,[6] Schelling had already linked this to both art and philosophy in a manner that strikingly anticipated the early Nietzsche: "The mystery of true art is to be *simultaneously* mad and levelheaded [*wahnsinnig und besonnen*], not in distinctive moments, but rather *uno eodemque actu* [altogether in a single act]. This is what distinguishes the Apollonian inspiration from the Dionysian" (U 422).

This was, moreover, a distinction that Schelling had first ventured in *The Ages of the World*:

> But where there is no madness, there is also certainly no proper, active, living intellect (and consequently there is just the dead intellect, dead intellectuals). For in what does the intellect prove itself other than in the coping with and governance and regulation of madness? Hence the utter lack of madness leads to another extreme, to imbecility (idiocy), which is an absolute lack of all madness. But there are two other kinds of persons in which there really is madness.

---

4. Walter F. Otto, *Dionysos: Myth and Cult*, trans. Robert B. Palmer (Dallas: Spring, 1981), 145.

5. Schelling, *Philosophie der Offenbarung* 1841/42 [The *Paulus Nachschrift*], second, expanded edition, ed. Manfred Frank (Frankfurt am Main: Suhrkamp, 1993), 97. Henceforth PO.

6. *Urfassung Philosophie der Offenbarung*, 2 vols, ed. Walter E. Ehrhardt (Hamburg, Germany: Felix Meiner Verlag, 1992), 708. Henceforth U.

Red-figured clay shard of a dancing satyr, presumably from the fifth or fourth century BCE, found on Samothrace.

There is one kind of person that governs madness and precisely in this overwhelming shows the highest force of the intellect. The other kind of person is governed by madness and is someone who really is mad. (SW I/8, 338–339)

Thinking is an ongoing negotiation with Dionysos. In 1815, Schelling, *simultaneously* mad and levelheaded, published his last work of lasting significance, a *Beilage* to the unpublished and never completed *Ages of the World* called *Über die Gottheiten von Samothrake* or *On the Deities of Samothrace*. As Alexander Bilda demonstrates in his essay in this volume, with the exception of thinkers like Coleridge and Creuzer, the address had little positive impact. It seemingly remains a sort of outlier in Schelling's corpus. Its intense and extremely sober philological detail, which far exceeds the length of the address itself, is accompanied by a radical genealogical unpacking of the repressed potencies of religiosity as such. This was no science of mythology with its taxonomies and compilations of data but rather the excavation of a radical revolution, or conversion, of consciousness itself. Schelling endeavored, as he would claim in Berlin in 1842, to "expand" both "*philosophy* and *the philosophical consciousness itself*" (SW II/1, 252).

The Dionysian prototype of the Eucharist, or the appearance of the theurgy of the gods in Axieros-Demeter, Axiokersa-Persephone, and Axiokersos-Hades, or Dionysos, finally coming together in the embodiment of Kadmilos or Hermes, does not merely signal that the form of historical Christianity is neither unique nor original. At stake is not simply the claim that these forms have appeared before. What can be discerned at the living depths of the ruins and scattered testimonies of Samothrace is neither a form nor an assemblage of forms. What Schelling's vital philological investigation claims to have discovered is the sacred and multidimensional ontology of nature (being) itself in its genesis. "Yet the Cabiri exercised their magic not singly but only in their indissoluble sequence and linkage; by dint of such magic, they drew the transmundane into actuality. Now the gods, brought to revelation by this magic, are also caught up in a magical connection with those forces. The entire Cabirian sequence thus constitutes a chain of enchantment that binds the deepest with the highest. Not a single link in this chain can go missing or can fail to be efficacious, lest the magic vanish" (SW I/8, 356).

This "chain of enchantment" is not a spiritual supplement to nature, something supernatural and consequently wholly otherwise than the putatively "natural." It is, we learn in *The Ages of the World*, nature itself in its multidimensional life and creativity. "But such a succession of states is also found in natural life, where the preceding always becomes the past in respect to the subsequent. The health and fullness of life depends solely on the constancy of the progression, on the uninhibited succession of potencies" (SW I/8, 261). The difference between the gods and humans is not simply that they are different kinds of things. Both have their lives in the same ontological concatenation. As we see in the 1809 *Essay on Human Freedom* and again in *The Ages of the World*, this concatenation is soluble in humans, while it is insoluble in the divine. Humans can repress this living ground, elevating their own existence to the ground and sundering their extrahuman one. Only humans imagine themselves and their forms, rituals, artworks, concepts, ambitions, and deeds to be the lord of nature. This is the mad idiocy of Ahab, that he would rule the unruly sea, subjugate it to himself, and exact revenge on the white whale—although even Ahab, in chapter 132, "The Symphony," succumbing to the beauty of the natural day, drops a tear into the sea, "nor did all the Pacific contain such wealth as that one wee drop." The prevailing ecological crisis is in this respect, for Schelling, a spiritual one: the elevation of ourselves over the earth systems that make us possible. And this is the mad logic of evil: in elevating itself over the living processes that make it possible, it destroys itself. The ecological crisis cannot be wholly separated from our deafness and blindness to the ontological revelation of Samothrace. We are of this system and wholly dependent on it. It is suicide to declare war on the gods, although in our spiritual malady we imagine that it is in our self-interest to do so.

What makes thinkers like Nietzsche (or his French spiritual successor, Georges Bataille) so interesting from a religious perspective is their capacity to demonstrate how lifeless and boring our religiosity can be. As Nietzsche would protest, "Almost two thousand years and not a single new god!" All we have is the "pitiable god of Christian monotono-theism."[7] As dangerous as such a claim can be in (yet again) such a violently dogmatic time—itself a sign of decadence for Nietzsche and self-destructive evil and sickness for Schelling—Schelling and Hölderlin would likely not resist Oscar Wilde's claim in *De Profundis* that Jesus did not seek "to turn an interesting thief into a tedious honest man."

This is the thrill and welcome sense of danger and risk that still radiate from Schelling's Samothrace address. What Schelling in *The Ages of the World*

---

7. *Nietzsche Werke: Kritische Gesamtausgabe*, volume VI, 3, eds. Giorgio Colli and Mazzino Montinari (Berlin: Walter de Gruyter, 1969), 183.

called "the mother, the birthing potency, of everything posterior" (SW I/8, 260) here manifests itself as "obsession," that is, an essence that has less to do with being than with the struggle to be. "For that reason, the Egyptians held that Ceres is the queen of the dead. The dead are generally thought to be in a state of helplessness, a state of impotent striving for actuality" (SW I/8, 253). Even this manifestation as not being but rather hungering to be is itself a decision, a cutting off from itself, a displacement of its anterior absolute nothingness, much in the way that the Lurianic tradition speaks of צמצום (*tzimtzum*), "contraction," inhaling itself and wanting to exhale as something. How can absolutely nothing ever be? Yet it *is*, and that is its magic. "Persephone weaves the raiment of mortality and spins the bedazzlements of the senses. She is, moreover, the first link in the chain that connects the deepest to the highest, the beginning to the end" (SW I/8, 355). Persephone's magic, that there is something rather than nothing, is in the end a properly Dionysian thought, a thought whose genesis is inexhaustible and whose variations are "unprethinkable," *unvordenklich*.

2. Excavating Mythology

By the time Schelling ascended to a professorship in Berlin in 1841, the public conditions for receiving this kind of thinking and investigation had grown only dimmer. Although Schelling, as Alexander Bilda demonstrates, would not return to a sustained defense or further development of his Samothrace investigations, they were in part the seed that bore the fruit of the later *Philosophy of Mythology and Revelation*. Even if we grant that the latter sacrifices the drama and sweep of the Samothrace address or that the *Philosophy of Revelation* blunts the force of the mother of being, *sehnsüchtig* and languishingly endeavoring to be while in herself always contesting whatever she may be, it does not follow that Schelling in the end ceased his restless resistance and ceded everything to the status quo of religion. Schelling on both myth and revelation generally mystified his audience.

What was already true in 1815 was even truer in 1841, prompting Walter Otto to remark that "μῦθος remained in an age in which poesy was lost."[8] For

---

8. Walter F. Otto, "Der Durchbruch zum antiken Mythos im XIX. Jahrhundert," *Die Gestalt und das Sein* (Darmstadt, Germany: Wissenschaftliche Buchgesellschaft, 1955), 221.

Schelling, art emerged from the same groundless ground from which the mythic more originally issued, but now the ruin of the gods and the rise of the night of worldwide *Blödsinn* had reduced the gods to dead positivistic objects, toothless data, neutralized things stored in our historical catalogs. The λόγος had been demoted to the task of deflating the mythic into a science of mythology, a science that bore as little on the tautegory of the gods (the gods do not mean something beyond themselves; they come as themselves) as did positivistic natural science on the earth. Just as Schelling's *Naturphilosophie* tirelessly combated the humiliation of the earth, Schelling's philosophy of mythology, especially his 1842 *Historical-critical Introduction to the Philosophy of Mythology*, battled the *Blödsinn* of scientific mythology.

Dogmatic theology and its reactionary hold no doubt contributed to the deafness and disinterest that greeted Schelling's project (think of Alexander Bilda's characterization of the obsessed Dr. Paulus) but so did the unfolding death of God and the rise of the *Blödsinn* of positivism and the disenchantment of the earth and its celebration in the arts that Nietzsche would also soon diagnose. As Schelling warns: "A fable has originated in France which has also found followers in Germany: that something new should take the place of Christianity" (PO 97).

Yet Schelling, whose Berlin lectures would generally fail—Kierkegaard, for example, thought that Schelling belabored the point endlessly—was unperturbed. Schelling argued that the defense of status quo Christianity or its rejection have the same root problem, namely, the presumption that we know what it is that we are either defending or rejecting. As early as the Samothrace address and *The Ages of the World*, what he called a "genealogy of time,"[9] the genetic and sacred concatenation of nature, demanded that one now (the present) remember (the past) what was still to come (the future). This has nothing to do with the putative obviousness of Christianity. "Have you even understood Christianity? How so, if a philosophy must first unlock its depths?" (PO 97). It was not enough simply to imagine that one is religious. Religion is first and foremost a philosophical question that demands a transformative, philosophical *Andenken* and ἀνάμνησις of the free system of the gods, whether it be the triumvirate of Axieros-Demeter, Axiokersa-Persephone, and Axiokersos-Hades or Dionysos or the kenotic trinity.

---

9. Manfred Schröter, ed., *Die Weltalter. Fragmente in den Urfassungen von 1811 und 1813* (Munich: C. H. Beck'sche Verlagsbuchhandlung, 1946), 75.

Schelling was not using philosophy to offer yet another apology for institutional Christianity. The secret depths of revelation had not been revealed in the public event of revelation, depths which made it a kind of *Geheimlehre* or mystery doctrine. The key to making the esoteric exoteric was what Schelling called *philosophical religion*.[10] Religion, left to its own devices, lacked full access to itself, and the key to revealing its concealed depths, philosophical religion, depended on the event of positive philosophy.

The latter is, as Schelling says, *toto coelo verschieden*, diametrically opposed, by the whole extent of the heavens, to Christian philosophy, and it even offers for the first time ever the "true concept of religion" (PO 148). Religion has been sealed, awaiting philosophy to unleash its power. Schelling's Christianity is associated with John, who, we might surmise, was somewhat like Kadmilos. The latter "is therefore not one of the prior gods; rather, he is a ministrant {only} to a future god, a god yet to come" (SW I/8, 358). This was not a Christianity that we have had but rather a Christianity to come, a prophetic Christianity made possible by a new kind of philosophical thinking. Schelling was a kind of second John the Baptist, with a premonition (*Ahnung*) of another kind of future, a future rooted in the ongoing κένωσις[11] of a living God, "who comes out of itself through its own power and becomes other to itself in its unprethinkable being" (PO 170). Reason is beholden to the ongoing revelation of being such that being always remains unthought in its *coming* to be thought. Reason must navigate the nonreason of the ground and the unprethinkability (*Unvordenklichkeit*) of existence. Being is what is always still to be thought in whatever has been thought.

That said, Schelling did not turn to the future by looking directly toward it to imagine what otherwise might be. He looked to the future by turning to the concealed depths of the past. What is still yet to be is already intimated

---

10. For more on philosophical religion, see my *Schelling's Practice of the Wild: Time, Art, Imagination* (Albany: State University of New York Press, 2015), chapter 2. See also the important new study, Sean J. McGrath, *The Philosophical Foundations of the Late Schelling: The Turn to the Positive* (Edinburgh: Edinburgh University Press, 2021).

11. ἀλλὰ ἑαυτὸν ἐκένωσεν μορφὴν δούλου λαβών, ἐν ὁμοιώματι ἀνθρώπων γενόμενος: "Rather, he made himself nothing by taking the very nature of a servant, being made in human likeness" (Philippians 2:7, NIV). Strikingly, Schelling also cautiously links Kadmilos with the servant of the god still to come.

in what is deeply buried and repressed in the past. The rudiments of this problem were already at the heart of the *Ages of the World* project, and the initial exercise in such an excavation was already undertaken in the 1815 Samothrace address:

> What if in Greek lore concerning the gods (to say nothing of Indian and other Near-Eastern teachings) the ruins of an insight [*Trümmer einer Erkenntniß*] jut forth, indeed, the debris of a scientific system in the most ancient written documents known to us that far exceeds the scope of Revelation? What if, in general, Revelation did not so much open up a new stream of insights as constrict what earlier flowed freely to a more narrowly circumscribed but precisely for that reason more secure and sustaining riverbed? What if Revelation, after the ancient lore had been corrupted and had degenerated irremediably into idolatry, wisely restricted itself to one part of that primal system, but in so doing preserved precisely those traits that might lead us once again to the magnificently encompassing whole of the system? (SW I/8, 362–63)

Among the *Trümmer einer Erkenntniß*, the ruins of a mode of knowing and the debris of a subsequently unintelligible and degenerate mythology, lies a repressed or buried insight into the problem of revelation that allows revelation itself—which proclaimed itself as something brand new that as such ended the reign of the mythic gods—to at last more fully reveal itself. The riverbed of revelation was revealed before revelation as such publicly revealed itself, and the path to the latter goes through the ruins of the former. "For the doctrine of the Cabiri serves as the key, so to speak, to all other systems, by virtue of its antiquity as well as its clarity and simplicity of outline" (SW I/8, 423, *Nachschrift*).

Schelling's approach does for what is concealed and dissembled in the *Trümmer einer Erkenntniß* what Alasdair MacIntyre argued he was doing for ethical discourse in *After Virtue*. Likening the ruins of ethical discourse to the intellectual experiment of a future in which fragments of scientific discourse survive, but the general sense of what is at stake in science as a whole is lost, MacIntyre argued that although we use ethical utterances all the time, we have no idea what we are doing and have "no rational way of securing moral agreement in our culture."[12] We speak in inherited ethical fragments but have no general idea what ethics as such is. In the same fashion, mythology

---

12. Alasdair MacIntyre, *After Virtue*, second edition (Notre Dame, IN: University of Notre Dame Press, 1984), 6.

collapsed into unintelligibility even as the gods and rites persisted. Polytheism, for example, has something haphazard about it, as if there were just a bunch of gods roaming the earth and the heavens and that the main point was to identify who and what each god was. Merely to know *what* each god is avoids the more difficult problem: *that* there *are* gods. Schelling's philology is not reliant solely on lexicons and dictionaries and does not only seek linguistic equivalencies or approximations. "In an era when everyone quite readily feels equal to any and every challenge, it could well be that a new etymological craze jumbles everything with everything else; such a craze, in hectic, harebrained fashion, might scramble all the ancient fables of the gods. And yet investigation of the provenance and derivation of words, when pursued not blindly but artfully and in accord with the rules pertinent to that art, will always constitute the noblest portion of linguistic research" (SW I/8, 351).

Concealed within the *Trümmer einer Erkenntniß* and, as such, no longer intelligible within what remains of that ruined *Erkenntniß*, lurks a more comprehensive revelation of the original potencies of the divine (the "*that* there *are* gods" and the sacrality of the whole free and genetic system of nature). Hence, Schelling does not take any of the public accounts of the gods at face value but rather subjects them to a thoroughgoing genealogical critique as he seeks to discern what remains otherwise hidden, "the covert [*geheim*] magic of those deeper connections" that come to the fore even in ancient times within the esoteric realm "of the mystery doctrines [*Geheimlehren*]" (SW I/8, 363). To be sure, the Cabirian gods did not mean anything else other than themselves. They have no hidden meaning. They came as themselves, that is, "tautegorically." They are already a philosophical articulation of the ontology of nature as genetic and sacred.

It is rather the gods themselves who remain hidden, who demand the intellectual transformation and shifts of consciousness practiced in the mystery rites and resurrected creatively by Schelling as philosophical religion. "As a result of these rites, the initiate himself became a link in that enchanted chain, he himself a Cabir, taken up into that indestructible nexus and, as an ancient inscription puts it, welcomed into the company of the higher gods" (SW I/8, 368). Philosophical religion cannot simply report this but must also endeavor to enter the mystery as a condition of articulating it.

The Cabir experienced "inalienable life itself as it advances in a series of enhancements from the deepest to the highest levels, and that the Cabirian system presented the universal magic and the theurgy that endure forever in the cosmos, whereby the invisible—which is in effect the transcendently actual—is ceaselessly brought to revelation and actuality" (SW I/8, 368). A Cabir, Schelling confesses, would never have articulated the esoteric revelation at the heart of their mystery religion in quite this way, but nonetheless "the doctrine proper was directed toward life and toward a reflection [*Gesinnung*] on how life should be lived" (SW I/8, 368). The mystery transformed one's very disposition, or *Gesinnung*, for life.

The Cabirian initiates, even when depicted as among the gods in the cosmos, were not *Naturphilosophen*. The initiation was healing and transformative. "Those who were initiated into the rites were better prepared to live and to die, and happier in both their living and their dying" (SW I/8, 348). Even those who were down on their luck, including criminals, could go to Samothrace to receive a second chance, a new beginning, and thereby a new lease on life (SW I/8, 348).

Twenty-six years later, when Schelling came to Berlin amid all the controversies and conflicts that comprised its Hegelian legacy, he did not announce a new line of attack and a new, counter-Hegelian position. (Simply opposing Hegel is a dialectical move that as such already cedes the ground to Hegel.) Schelling came to give philosophy a new lease on life. Yes, he accuses Hegel of confusedly making the dialectic, a purely negative movement of thought, into a positive philosophy, but he did not conclude that there was no place for negative philosophy, including Schelling's own earlier *Naturphilosophie*. Negative philosophy is not wrong, but it can only formally (negatively) account for the self-presentation of being. The Samothrace address inaugurated positive philosophy—it is research into an ancient theurgic theological reality—yet in concluding with the formal system of sacred nature in general, it also risks being merely negative philosophy. Schelling did not renounce this research, and it reemerges at the heart of the *Philosophy of Mythology and Revelation*, with the latter being the fulfillment of the former. "It was a time when I dared to depict this series of possibilities of a still-future being only figuratively in another, but, as it seemed to me and still seems to me now, a completely parallel series, and I thereby posited the sentence: every beginning is in a state of lack, the deepest potency to which everything is attached is nonbeing, and this is the hunger for being" (SW II/2, 294).

Even if *On the Deities of Samothrace* analyzes a positive event in history (the gods came as themselves and mean nothing other than themselves), it is also an early figuration of what Schelling sketches in *Ages of the World* as his "formula for the world" (SW I/8, 312). To speak of either the world formula or Hegel's dialectical philosophy as negative, however, is not to dismiss or denigrate it but rather to mark its limits. Schelling claims that he did not come to Berlin to wage war. "I do not want to lash the wounds but rather heal the wounds ... I am not here to destroy, but rather to build, to found a castle in which philosophy can dwell securely from now on" (PO 95).

How secure a castle can be when built on the contraction of its ground into *Sehnsucht* and esurience is not clear. Will philosophy always find a way to govern its foundational madness? Schelling is clear he is not replacing his earlier philosophy with a newer one, or peddling a new system, but rather presenting "a new science that heretofore had been regarded as impossible" (ibid.) and somehow securing its mysterious ground. This was nothing less than the healing of German thought by way of healing the wound within, *Wissenschaft* as such. In other words, it was to excavate a healing insight from the *Trümmer einer Erkenntniß*. The prophet of the Cabiri had come to Berlin!

3. The Positivity of Revelation

What is this mysterious, recalcitrant, and heretofore concealed ground Schelling sought to secure and, so to speak, *reveal*? Had not reason endlessly spun its own wheels trying to orient itself to its own proper activity? Although Schelling was not abandoning reason, he had come to announce that the ground of reason is not itself reasonable, even if it is "the innate content of reason" (PO 100). It is rather that which continuously offered itself to reason and, so to speak, reveals itself in a manner that can never be specified in advance. "Revelation must contain something transcending reason, yet something that one cannot have without reason" (PO 98). Reason, left to its own devices, discerns *what* something *is* (*das Was, quid sit*), but as such, it cannot entertain the question of *existence* as such (*das Daß, quod sit*). "What takes shape through the movement of the concept in the purely logical concept is not the actual world, but only the world as quiddity" (PO 99)!

When reason comes to the ground of some "what" that exists, it comes to "what serves as the foundation or ὑποκείμενον" (PO 104) of that something, but, in such an account, the ground is still conceived logically as something, *ein Was*, and can be apprehended as ground by being thought in relationship to the existent that it grounds. This is even true if one thinks of it as *prima materia* or *das reine Seinkönnende* (the pure capacity to be). What we have done is to reason toward this idea, and in a sense, we can say that thinking has arrived at "the pure what [*quid*] of the Godhead" (PO 109). We have arrived at the omega but not the alpha, the final cause but not the efficient cause (PO 109). We come to the idea of God but not to the actual existence of God outside its concept. As such, in this approach "God . . . is only the end of the world, not its creator" (PO 119)! This is the "God who is only end, who has no future and who cannot say 'I will be,' who is only final cause and not principle" (PO 132). This is the force of negative philosophy (see PO 119), which cannot yet reason from *das Wesen* but merely toward it, rendering it a regulative idea, that is, something without any positive content, at best, a world formula, something that does not posit and that is not the life of that positing. This is the godhead, which exists only in our minds, not in the unfolding evolution of the universe. There is no natality, because nothing has begun outside of thinking itself (PO 110). This is the godhead whose only home is reason, indeed, as the "most immanent concept of reason" (PO 110).

Positive philosophy, "*diese zweite Wissenschaft*," therefore proceeds "from what is outside of reason" (PO 110). The first hint of this could already be detected in Schelling's *Auseinandersetzung*, or confrontation, with Fichte,[13]

---

[13]. See Michael Vater and David W. Wood's fine translation of the Fichte-Schelling letter exchange, *The Philosophical Rupture between Fichte and Schelling: Selected Texts and Correspondence (1800–1802)* and Hegel's defense of Schelling's thinking in this regard in the so-called 1801 *Differenzschrift*, rendered into English in 1988 by H. S. Harris and Walter Cerf as *The Difference Between Fichte's and Schelling's System of Philosophy*. Schelling broke decisively with Fichte along these kinds of issues. In the 1806 confrontation with Fichte, *Darlegung des wahren Verhältnisses der Naturphilosophie zu der verbesserten fichteschen Lehre*, Schelling quite severely attacked Fichte's inability to think the question of nature outside of the ground of subjectivity and its interests, accusing Fichte of *Schwärmerei*, "enthusiasm." The *Schwärmer* or enthusiast, following Luther's condemnation of those who, claiming to have seen God, fanatically and uncritically swarmed into sects and schools, claim to know what the ground is, and, in Fichte's case, posit nature outside of the subject as something that resists the subject but which should be brought under the subject's control. Schelling went on to excoriate Fichte's thinking as *Bauernstolz* (SW I/7, 47), literally the self-congratulatory pride of a peasant who profits from nature without really grasping it. This lopsided and self-serving cultivation is at the heart of a contemporary nature-annihilating *Schwärmerei*. "If an inflexible effort to force his subjectivity through his subjectivity as something universally valid and to exterminate all nature wherever possible and against it to make non-nature a principle and to make all of the severity of a lopsided education in its dazzling isolation count

although, in freeing the thought of nature from the subject, one still had not yet confronted the problem of existence. "Fichte fashioned the thought of elevating Kant's critique into a science of knowledge that would no longer borrow anything from experience but would posit everything in a self-determining manner. But right from the start he failed to secure for reason the free stance it should have, since he demanded a being at the beginning, indeed something immediately certain. That could only be the certainty: *I am*. [His] philosophy turned it into everyone's personal I [*die eines jeden Ich*]."

Schelling did not think that in lieu of a subjective absolute foundation from which everything else would follow one could substitute an objective foundation. The absolute as ground was always for Schelling something that one could not properly think, subject only to intellectual intuition, and, at best, a *nicht denkendes Denken*, "a thinking that doesn't think" (SW I/10, 151). Schelling reaches toward this insight already in the Samothrace address with the contraction of being that restlessly hungers to be. Such hunger will always elude the system, even as one endeavors to think its relationship to all the other genetic potencies of the system. It is the part of the concatenation that always already exceeds itself. If one does not take the freedom part of the system of freedom seriously, Schelling argues, "the most severe misunderstanding it could encounter was the charge that, on the analogy with other systems, it had a self-warranting principle from which the truth of other parts of the system could be derived" (PO 115). It has no such principle.

What is at stake in the problem of the positive, however, is not the transformation of a subjective idealism into an objective one but rather the limits of idealism as such. This is what led, for example, Manfred Frank[14] to separate

---

as scientific truths can be called *Schwärmen*, then who in this whole era swarms in the authentic sense more terribly and loudly than Herr Fichte?" (SW I/7, 47). Nonetheless, Fichte's *Schwärmerei*—the absolute as *die eines jeden Ich*—was close to overcoming itself; a single step was required that would have lifted it out of the reduction of the absolute to an idea. "Only one more step was required to recognize the essence [*Wesen*] that is the prior condition of all being [*Prius alles Sein*]. One had only to leave aside the limitation [of being] to self-positing [*Sichselbstsetzens*] in order to find the absolute point of evolution. Rejecting that limitation, science would have become independent of the subject" (PO 111).

14. Manfred Frank, "What Is Early German Romantic Philosophy?," *The Relevance of Romanticism: Essays on German Romantic Philosophy*, ed. Dalia Nassar (Oxford and New York: Oxford University Press, 2014). Henceforth GRP.

the romantics from the idealists. For Frank, there is a clearly discernible *Denkraum* or space of thought (GRP 16) that makes the romantics something like proto-speculative realists, eschewing dogmatic thought while denying any positive foundationalist role for the absolute. The Jena philosophers were in part responding to the Austrian philosopher Karl Leonhard Reinhold, the first chair of critical philosophy at Jena, and his *Elementarphilosophie* (elementary philosophy), which attempted to develop Kant more systematically by making the principle of consciousness a first principle and confirming Fichte's critical appropriation of this position in his subjective idealism—"an 'I' that was boosted into something absolute" (GRP 26). For the Jena philosophers, including Schelling, the subjective absolute could not serve as a clear ground because it eluded clarity and thereby could not be contained within any domain, including the human subject. "Instead, they considered subjectivity to be a derivative phenomenon that only becomes accessible to itself under a condition or presupposition (*Bedingung, Voraussetzung*), which is beyond its (subjectivity's) control" (GRP 18).

Rather than a foundationalist approach that derives everything from the absolute subject, the romantics held to the "irrepresentability of the Absolute and redefined striving after the infinite as an endless striving" (ibid.). This not only liberated thinking from its obsession with the human subject as the inevitable starting point for all that is cognized but it also cracked the negativity of the subject-object correlation and first opened up the problem of existence. In a way, this also anticipated some aspects of what contemporary speculative realists call the problem of correlationism, which Quentin Meillassoux defined as "the idea according to which we only ever have access to the correlation between thinking and being, and never to either term considered apart from the other," hence "disqualifying the claim that it is possible to consider the realms of subjectivity and objectivity independently of one another."[15]

Frank grounded a speculative realism—what he calls an "ontological realism" (GRP 27)—in the structure of self-consciousness itself, which in reflection discovers within itself "the notion of the essence of absolute identity as

---

15. Quentin Meillassoux, *After Finitude: An Essay on the Necessity of Contingency*, trans. Ray Brassier (London: Continuum, 2008), 5. Meillassoux, it should be here noted, is a thinker of the necessity of contingency. Schelling stresses the contingency of any possible necessity.

enclosing a ground that repels all consciousness" (GRP 22). This ground cannot operate as a first principle from which to derive systematically all other principles nor can it be reduced to anything in particular, not even the absolute "I." It simultaneously prohibits all dogmatic claims: "If there is no safe foundation that presents itself to our consciousness as evident, then it is possible to doubt each of our beliefs" (GRP 23). The ground in both Reinhold and Fichte's systems therefore "loses its stabilizing function" (GRP 25). What emerges is a speculative realism that (a) is not derived from the subject as a stabilizing ground and (b) renders the objects of knowledge only speculatively knowable. Beliefs, Friedrich Schlegel claimed, "are eternally valid only for the time being" (GRP 24), or, put in a more contemporary way, are *necessarily contingent*. After his rupture with Fichte, Schelling continuously thought toward this sovereign and destabilizing ground, but the task was not merely to discover this ground at the heart of reason but to learn to think *from* it.

Negative philosophy, either of a subjective or an objective kind, does not proceed from the *prius*. It thinks the prius as an idea and the omega but not as the alpha of thinking. Perhaps, in the end, Schelling conceded, the negative was only a "poetic invention ... a poem that reason itself poeticized" (PO 115). Indeed, "the whole only happened in thought" (PO 116). This science "is a merely logical science" (PO 117). This does not make it merely analytical, left only to deduce the logical relations among ideas, because, although it does not proceed from the alpha, it proceeds toward and arrives at it as the omega of this science.

That said, *Naturphilosophie* is not in the end concerned with the "now and here" of any actually existing plants but rather with the genus and species of plants. Sensuous plants that sit on my table exist outside of their thought, "as being able to be outside of thinking" (PO 118).[16] One could not even say that negative philosophy was the kind of hardcore account of idealism that Kant refuted (that nothing exists outside our experience of it) since it was not concerned with experience at all (PO 119–120).

---

16. From the Munich lectures on modern philosophy: "Everything can be in the logical Idea without anything being *explained* thereby, as, for example, everything in the sensuous world is grasped in number and measure, which does not therefore mean that geometry or arithmetic explain the sensuous world." There remains that which "strives beyond the boundaries" of reason (*Vernunft*) (SW I/10, 144).

For Schelling, Hegel's mistake, despite all his brilliance, was not that he misunderstood negative philosophy but rather that he attempted to make it into what it is not: positive philosophy. God becomes the dialectical process itself and hence "He is the God of eternal action, but he always does only what he has done" (PO 133). There are no radical surprises. The eternally avaricious ground has not already contracted even in its hunger to be. The formula always holds, even as its contents shift. Hegel's position does not own up to its "honest poverty" (PO 137), indeed to the poverty of negative thought as such.

Not only is negative philosophy not positive philosophy, but it is also not in the final analysis even the ground of positive philosophy. Negative philosophy does not end where positive philosophy begins, if by that one means that it establishes the grounding principle of the project of positive philosophy. "The end of one is not the beginning of the other" (PO 138). Negative philosophy ends in freedom. Yet that is not the principle, but rather the task of positive philosophy (PO 138), a task already inaugurated in the *Essay on Human Freedom*, as Schelling endeavored to think the problem of human freedom from the alpha of freedom as such. In this regard, negative philosophy becomes occupied with *Wegschaffen*, removal, clearing the way, making possible "the ongoing subversion of reason" (PO 152) so that thinking originates in an "absolute beginning" (PO 153). Just as the Cabirian initiates discovered, thinking and living from this secret ground was not merely an academic exercise; negative philosophy is for school and academics, but positive philosophy is for life (PO 153). The initiates did not just know something intriguing about the structure of being. Their manner of thinking was transformed, and they were "taken up into that indestructible nexus and, as an ancient inscription puts it, welcomed into the company of the higher gods" (SW I/8, 368).

Positive philosophy is a kind of *mystical empiricism*, not in the sense that its ground is derived from experience, mystical or otherwise, but rather in the sense that experience is understood to concretize and express the free movement and life of the a priori. It should in no way be confused with any form of mysticism as such, which Schelling eschews in the positive philosophy as precisely what cannot speak concretely, what cannot proceed from the mystical to the empirical. In the Munich lectures on the history of modern philosophy (1827), Schelling decries the indolent and reckless invocation of mysticism as an act of what we would now call *mystification*. Every time we do not understand something, we invoke the mystery or regard our intellectual fuzziness as mystical. Hence, Schelling regarded mysticism as "a hatred of clear insight" (SW I/10, 192). The term itself, τὸ μυστικόν, can, however, mark the accomplishment of negative philosophy insofar as it simply marks the hidden and concealed, but this would simply be an idea of the hidden and, in a way, *the hidden merely as an idea, not a life.* In this strict sense, we can say that the ground of nature (*natura naturans*) is secret and as such mystical (SW I/10, 190–192). Yet saying it is not the same as being transformed by and for it.

Positive philosophy is therefore also a kind of a priori empiricism, in which the latter plays out the former. In a sense, experience is always open; it always preserves its future and, as such, the life of experience is "ongoing proof" of God (PO 147), which relegates reason to *die gelassene Vernunft* (PO 157), to "the reason that lets be." What is this a priori? What begins any possible beginning? Schelling is clear: "I posit being before all ideas and exclude all ideas" (PO 159). In this respect, Schelling's positive philosophy resonates with Gilles Deleuze when he speaks of his own empiricism as "a mysticism and mathematicism of concepts."[17] The ground of such mystical empiricism is resolutely transcendent, but this is not to say that it is based on an *idea of transcendence,* a supreme concept that grounds all other concepts. That is mere relative transcendence. Positive philosophy's transcendence is "absolute and resolute" (PO 159). Negative philosophy's content is, therefore, the a priori *begreifliche Sein,* "being that is grasped a priori," whereas that of positive philosophy is the "a priori inconceivable being that it a posteriori makes into the conceptual" (PO 159–160). Positive philosophy begins with the genetic natality of being, the ongoing hunger to be, and becomes mindful of its ongoing life. It does not get fixated with reiterating its prior forms as if genesis were not ongoing.

Hence Schelling discloses in Berlin what was also already at the heart of his unpublished *Weltalter* project: "Das *unvordenkliche* Sein, als allem Denken vorausgehend [the *unprethinkable* being as what precedes all thinking]" (PO 161). Its task is to proceed from what has always already not yet been thought. "What is the beginning of all thinking is not yet thinking" (PO 161). There is no idea that gives rise to philosophic thought. Its inception begins with a shock or fissuring of the quotidian cogitation that we conventionally

---

17. Gilles Deleuze, *Difference and Repetition,* trans. Paul Patton (New York: Columbia University Press, 1994), xx. *Différence et répétition* (Paris: Presses universitaires de France, 1968), 3.

but stupidly consider to be thinking. Thinking is occasioned, as Plato and Aristotle had also seen, by wonder, *admiratio*, θαυμάζειν (PO 161).

Here one awakens to the erotic dimension of what is merely destitute in its negative exercise. Recall the famous *Symposium* myth (203b–d) that Schelling evokes in Samothrace address, the myth in which Ἔρως is the child of Πόρος and Πενία, plenty and destitution. At the birth of Aphrodite, the gods celebrated a great feast and Πόρος (literally, "way," "passage," "resource," which Schelling glosses as *Reichthum* and *Überfluß*, wealth and excess) became inebriated on nectar and passed out in Zeus's garden. Πενία ("poverty" or "need"), showing up to beg, seduced Πόρος and had his child. A philosophical idea is such a child, an intermediary, neither wholly true nor wholly false, settling nothing yet always discovering something. In *The Ages of the World*, Schelling writes, "Considered in itself, Nature is like Πενία showing up at Zeus' feast. From the outside, Πενία was the picture of poverty and extreme need. On the inside, she shut away divine plenitude which she could not reveal until she had wed Wealth, Excess himself, that effusively and inexhaustibly garrulous being (A^2). Even then, however, the child wrested from her womb appears under the form and, so to speak, press, of that originary negation. It was the bastard child of Need and Excess" (SW I/8, 244).

Positive philosophy gratefully desires what it can never have but always wants it in new ways. The idea is erotic in this strict, ontological sense: an intermediary between what it can never succeed in thinking and what it has just successfully thought. The penury of thinking confronts ever anew the unprethinkable Πόρος or *eternal beginning* or divine plenitude of thinking, producing the endless erotic offspring that are the inexhaustible life of thought. This is not idealism but more like what the Jena romantics (and Manfred Frank), perhaps following Heraclitus's fragment B 122, ἀγχιβασίη, called *unendliche Annäherung*, infinite approaching.[18]

---

18. See Manfred Frank, *"Unendliche Annäherung": Die Anfänge der philosophischen Frühromantik* (Frankfurt am Main: Suhrkamp, 1997) and *Auswege aus dem deutschen Idealismus* (Frankfurt am Main: Suhrkamp, 2007). "Being, the late Schelling will say, is prior to thought (*'unvordenklich'*). In other words, there is no thought—no real predicate—that can be inserted or presupposed in order to function as a ground for deducing or grasping existence" (SW II/3, 227f.; see also 262). "What Is Early German Romantic Philosophy?," *The Relevance of Romanticism: Essays on German Romantic Philosophy*, 22.

A dancing Maenad, companion of Dionysos, at the cult site.

4. Conclusion: "Everything Is Dionysos" or The Return of the Cabiri

In the Samothrace address, Schelling spoke of the A^1, not as a mere figure of thought but as the historical emergence in consciousness of Demeter's debilitating languor (*schmachtende Sehnsucht*), her penury and languishing and becoming sick, her loss of health and vitality. She is Axieros, who, according to Schelling, first means in the Phoenician dialect "hunger," "poverty," and consequently, "languishing [*Schmachten*]," "obsession [*Sucht*]" (SW I/8, 351). This is Πενία, endlessly searching for means. "For this is not to say that in the concept of *every* commencement there lies the concept of a lack. We hasten instead to recall something quite specific, to wit, Plato's figure of Penury, who, having mated with Superfluity, becomes the mother of Eros" (SW I/8, 352). This is also Ceres, who, before coming to be thought as the plenitude of the bread of the earth, was for the Egyptians the queen of the dead, "generally thought to be in a state of helplessness, of an impotent striving for actuality" (SW I/8, 353).

The A^1 comes to be with Axiokersa, Persephone, the power of magic, a word related not to *Macht*, some external power or efficient cause, but to *mögen*, which, when transitive, means to like or admire and when intransitive, used as an auxiliary, that something *may* happen, *may* come to be. Demeter becomes potent because she now has the means to express herself as her daughter. Persephone is not merely the existence of Persephone but an expression of the Demeter who cannot otherwise appear. That which in itself has no being appears now as having being. "Axiokersa and Axiokersos together construct the universe by means of a dual magic, inasmuch as the later form does not cancel or annihilate the earlier form, but merely overcomes it" (SW I/7, 386).

The A^2 reveals the Dionysian and erotic mystery at the heart of the belonging together of the two potencies. This is the person of Axiokersos, Hades, Dionysos, and the Egyptian Osiris and German Odin. "This doctrine, according to which the *amiable* god Dionysos is Hades, is indisputably the felicitous conviction that was communicated by the mystery religions." Finally, all potencies can be thought in the existence of the A^3, Kadmilos, Hermes, the "mediator between the higher and the lower gods" but not therefore the weakest of the four but rather the strongest. "Kadmilos is the last, but also the highest." As such, all potencies are "transfigured *in one supreme personality*" who speaks as if a prophet or herald (SW I/8, 359) of another manner of being altogether. This is the whole concatenation, the *Consentes* and *Complices* (SW I/8, 367). This is also the realm of the positive, the personhood of the divine, the presence of the gods as both present and gods.

Schelling returned to the mystery religions in Berlin, whose "main content" remained "the reconciliation of the consciousness wounded from severance from the real God" (PO 230). It is the reconciliation of Demeter with her daughter (PO 235), the bread of the earth with the earth itself, and toward this end we are given little bits of help along the way. Dionysos already knew what Jesus would later teach: "The wine is the gift of the already spiritualizing God" (PO 234). Philosophy, if it is to take joy in existence, drinks this wine as its happy sacrament. The three figures of Dionysos (PO 242) are nonetheless Dionysos, just as Axieros-Demeter, Axiokersa-Persephone, and Axiokersos-Hades or Dionysos are all part of the magic of nature, the magic that opens thinking to unprethinkable being in its ongoing genesis. This was personified in history by Kadmilos and it is also being personified, for Schelling, by the event of a Christianity to come.

This is indeed a revelation (PO 248), and Dionysos in "the highest potency was the meaning of the whole mystery teaching" (PO 248). This is the revelation—that thinking, like the cosmos itself, is the Dionysian mystery: "For everything is Dionysos; only in the tension do the potencies become different. That was the highest insight" (PO 237).

The public revelation of Christianity, too, under the genealogical analysis of Schelling's gesture toward philosophical religion, is revealed to contain its own *Geheimlehre*, its own nonpublic *inner* possibilities (and by *inner* we do not mean Luther's reduction of interiority to human consciousness). The Johannine Church, the church for everyone and everything—for all things human and for the mysterious creativity of the earth itself—is the "being everything in everything of God" (U 708–709), a "theism that contains within itself the entire economy of God" (U 709). This religion, what Bataille would later call "radical economy," not only excludes nothing but also includes everything as alive, where "everything has its inner process for itself" (U 710). This is religion beyond the dualism of the Petrine empire (the imposition of external forms of religion) and the Pauline revolt (the recovery of the esoteric soul of religion). It is, so to speak, to activate philosophy by thinking the problem of existence beyond mere quiddities (what there is) and beyond their groundless ground (nothing ultimately explains a priori why they are what they are) so that the problem of why there is something rather nothing is revealed to be the vital and discontinuous history of an inexplicable prius, the κένωσις at the heart of a revelatory and speculative realism.

Of course, all this discourse may well be impossible. Setting aside our associating the promise of religion even with a radical and future form of Christianity with its roots in the reality of the mythological and Semitic world, religion as a compelling and honest articulation of the great matters of living and dying continues to suffer from its historical failure to deliver on its promises. For Schelling, this belongs to the immense repression at the heart of institutional religion, a repression that demanded the extraordinary depths of his excavation of both the deities of Samothrace and Christianity. Today's world may be too late for Samothrace, Dionysos, and Jesus as the mystery doctrine (*Geheimlehre*) that will one day become a paradoxically *public secret* that reveals and preserves the joy that we take in the fecundity and inexhaustible earth of existence. Perhaps what remains, however we name it, is the secret that animates the creativity of our artworks, the patience and devotion of our scientific research, and the utopian hint that is at the impetus of our desire to philosophize. Samothrace, hidden in the ruins that David Farrell Krell details in this volume, universally befuddling archaeologists, is for the "wakeful at night," with their full wine cups and "holy memory," always still to come, regardless of the names of history, past and present.

INDEX

Abraham, 58
acolytes, 32, 62, 166, 207–8
acroamatic, 26, 108. *See also* secret teachings
actuality, 4, 19–20, 31–32, 286, 288, 293, 303
addiction, 95–96, 98, 222, 224–26. *See also* obsession (*Sucht*)
Aegean Sea, 6, 13, 91, 122, 145, 157, 220
Aeginetan sculptures, 94
Aeschylus, 21, 46, 102, 260n88, 267, 277
Agricola, Georg, 30, 71–72, 111
Ahriman, 47, 130
Alexander the Great, 14, 25, 39, 95, 106, 122–23, 162n8
Anatolia, 94, 110, 150, 164–66, 170, 174–75, 179, 189. *See also* Phrygia, Phrygian; Turkey
Angel of the Visage, 23, 59, 105, 130, 150
Aphrodite, 97, 113, 155, 157n5, 165, 169, 176, 181, 186, 191, 195, 209, 301. *See also* Venus
Apollo, 46, 56, 63, 82, 94, 103–4, 109, 134, 137, 155, 189, 200, 284

Apollonius of Rhodes, 35, 39–40, 75–76, 78, 87, 154–55, 168, 179, 214, 233
Apuleius, 85, 137
Arabic, 43, 50–51, 54, 58, 72, 74, 85, 124, 171, 187, 265n97, 273n118
archaeology, 148, 176, 183, 215
Argonauts, 14, 41, 91, 112, 154–55, 168, 233, 259
Aristophanes, 44, 49, 97, 125, 169
Aristotle, 35, 108, 117, 151, 181n16, 191, 301
Arnobius the Elder, 72, 85, 138
Artemis, 21, 103, 155, 170, 186. *See also* Diana
ascending sequence, 24, 107
Ast, Friedrich, 251, 277
Astarte, 77, 95, 97, 111, 157n5
Athena, 163, 165, 180–81. *See also* Minerva
Athenians, Athens, 19, 28, 44–45, 94, 98, 105, 151–52, 160n6, 181, 215
Attis, 69, 179–82, 185, 189, 203
Augustine, 78–79, 86, 137, 164n96
Axieros, 6, 15–17, 20, 23, 42, 44, 46, 48, 53, 57, 61, 94–96, 98, 113, 124, 127, 129–31, 146, 155, 163, 165–66,

Axieros (cont.)
170, 172, 179, 185, 222–24, 229–30, 237, 253, 257n79, 275, 279, 286, 303–4. See also Demeter
Axiokersa, 6, 15, 20–21, 40, 48, 52, 94, 101, 113, 117, 128–29, 146, 155, 168, 172, 176, 181, 185, 237, 253, 286, 289, 303–4. See also Persephone
Axiokersos, 6, 15, 20–21, 40, 52, 62, 94, 101, 113, 127–29, 146, 155, 168, 172, 176, 181, 185, 237, 253, 286, 289, 303–4. See also Dionysos; Hades

Bacchus, 22, 76, 93. See also Dionysos
Bentley, Richard, 64, 67–68
Bochart, Samuel, 27, 36, 42, 53–54, 58, 60, 62, 64, 70, 73, 95, 108–9, 134
Boeotia, Boeotian, 28, 60, 93, 105, 110, 150, 162n9, 188, 203, 207
Burkert, Walter, 149, 187n21, 194–95, 215, 248n60

Cabiri (Κάβειροι), 6–7, 14–16, 23, 29–33, 37, 39, 59–60, 64–65, 69–76, 78, 80, 82–84, 89, 92–94, 96, 103, 109–10, 112–13, 116, 123, 128, 134–37, 145–48, 150–51, 153–54, 157, 161, 166, 168, 172, 176, 182–84, 187, 190, 195–97, 200, 220, 223, 227, 230–31, 233–35, 237, 247–48, 256, 258–61, 263, 265, 268, 271–73, 275–76, 281–82, 286, 291, 294, 303
Calasso, Roberto, 99, 105, 111, 135, 174, 183, 186, 198, 200–201, 216, 240
Callimachus, 36, 46, 50
capability (Können), 228–31, 264, 269, 275
Carthage, 95, 110, 116
Castor and Pollux (Polydeukes), 77, 112. See also Dioskouroi

Ceres, 18–20, 22, 26, 37, 42, 44–46, 48, 50, 55–57, 60, 62, 75–76, 82, 100–101, 104, 123, 125, 127, 129–31, 137, 174, 176, 223–24, 261n89, 264n96, 269, 288, 303. See also Demeter
chain, 21, 24, 31–32, 115, 137, 224, 228, 230, 266, 270, 286, 288, 292. See also concatenation
Chaldean, 50, 56, 58, 68
Chaos (χάος), 19, 63
Choiseul-Gouffier, M. G. F. A. de, 36–37, 40
Christianity, 60, 73, 112, 232–33, 237, 245, 282–83, 286, 289–90, 304–5. See also Jesus; religion, religious
chthonic gods, 235, 270. See also underworld gods
Cicero, 41, 44, 65, 72
Clement of Alexandria, 56, 65–66, 131, 201
cobolds (Kobolde), 1, 72, 101, 111, 135. See also dwarfs; sprites
Coleridge, Samuel Taylor, 113, 265–70, 276–77, 286
community, 31, 160, 165, 192, 242, 276
companions, company, 7, 22, 32, 56, 58, 72, 75, 81, 116, 137–38, 181, 196, 198–99, 207, 209, 292, 299. See also consentes et complices; socii
concatenation, 26, 82, 224, 231, 287, 289, 296, 304
consciousness, 7, 107, 131, 204, 241, 260, 275–77, 286, 292, 297–98, 303–4
consentes et complices, 31, 85, 116, 304. See also companions, company; socii
cosmic egg, 18, 97
cosmology, 19
Creation, 5, 19–20, 25, 61, 107, 109, 137, 182, 198, 258, 270n108

INDEX

Crete, 95, 110–11, 122, 136, 147, 163, 175, 189
Creuzer, Friedrich, 20, 39–40, 43–44, 48–52, 56–57, 60–61, 64, 66–67, 69–70, 77, 83, 101–2, 130, 147, 183, 220–21, 228, 241n38, 244–49, 257–65, 272n114, 276–77, 286
cult, 6, 14–15, 20, 28–29, 60, 69, 75–76, 95, 99, 104, 108, 111–13, 116, 122–23, 130, 135–36, 139, 147–49, 152–53, 157–63, 165, 167, 169–70, 172, 174–76, 178, 182, 184, 186–89, 192, 194, 201, 203–4, 206–7, 211, 215–16, 221, 233–34, 240–41, 243n43, 245–48, 255, 259–61, 269–70, 272, 275–76, 284n4, 302. *See also* initiation, rites of; mystery, mysteries; religion, religious; rites, rituals; secret teachings
Cupid, 48–49. *See also* Eros

Daktyloi, 30, 75, 106, 111–13, 136, 165, 197–98
Danz, Christian, x, 106, 172n10, 220–21n2, 241n37, 251n65, 277, 282n1
death, dying, 1, 7, 14, 32, 52, 93–95, 97, 100, 112, 115, 117, 125, 138–39, 155, 173, 178, 181n15, 192, 194–95, 198–201, 203–5, 209, 227, 229–30, 272–73, 289, 293, 305
Demeter, 2, 6, 15, 20, 22, 44–45, 50, 56, 58, 80, 92, 94, 96, 98–101, 107, 109, 112–13, 123–25, 127, 129–31, 137, 146, 148–50, 155, 157, 159, 162n9, 163, 165, 170, 174, 176, 177, 180–82, 185, 192, 197, 200, 205, 208–9, 212, 214, 224, 232, 244, 256n77–78, 278, 286, 289, 303–4. *See also* Axieros; Ceres

demiurge, 2, 4, 25–26, 55, 57, 61–62, 64, 106–7, 113, 128–29, 131, 134–35, 137, 146, 148, 151, 166, 170, 176, 271n109
Derrida, Jacques, 101, 107–8, 129, 139
desire (*Himeros*), 6–7, 48–49, 98, 100–1, 127, 151, 155, 180, 183n18, 191, 225–26, 228, 270, 273n120, 305
Diana, 137. *See also* Artemis
difference, 47, 192–94, 198, 223, 230, 287, 295n13, 300n17
Diodorus of Sicily, 37, 39, 69, 75–76, 94, 153, 172, 215
Dionysos, 6, 15, 21–22, 26, 51–53, 56–57, 61–63, 68, 70, 78, 80, 92–93, 103–5, 127–29, 133–34, 136–37, 146, 163, 172, 174, 181, 188–89, 191, 193–94, 197, 200–203, 209, 210, 212, 232, 237, 273n118, 282–84, 286, 289, 302–5. *See also* Bacchus
Dioskouroi, 30–31, 82–83, 112, 113, 115, 165–66, 183, 185, 196, 208
Dodona, 28, 109, 189n23
duality, 48, 64, 78–79, 125, 132, 137–38, 178
dwarfs, 1, 29–30, 71–72, 111. *See also* cobolds (*Kobolde*); sprites
dyas, 62, 108, 125, 131, 176, 178

Earth (Gaia), 6, 8, 36, 42, 46, 48, 52, 64, 73, 75–77, 79, 87, 92, 97, 99–100, 102–3, 106, 111–12, 115, 123–25, 136–37, 148, 163, 170, 175, 189, 193–94, 196, 201, 204, 208, 210, 281–82, 284, 287, 289, 292, 303–5
ecological, ecology, 287
Egypt, Egyptian, 16, 18, 21, 23, 27–29, 46, 51, 53, 55, 60–61, 67–69, 73, 75, 77, 81, 95, 100, 103, 107, 109–10, 125, 132, 134, 150, 184, 189,

Egypt, Egyptian (*cont.*)
  234n27, 239, 259, 264–65, 267n101, 271n110, 288, 303
El, 24, 105–6, 131
Eleusinian, Eleusis, 18, 25, 39–40, 62, 69, 99, 109, 131, 148–49, 159–60, 163, 181, 185, 197, 216, 224, 244n44–45, 261n89, 264n96. *See also* Demeter; Kore (the maid)
Elohim, 86, 106, 130, 132–33, 138
emanation, 23–24, 60, 64, 130, 264–65
enchantment, 31, 115, 221n2, 228, 286
epidemic (*Seuche*), 96, 98
epopsis, epopteia (the showing), 65, 131, 160, 210, 266
Erinyes, the, 19, 100–101, 196
Eros, 17–18, 47–49, 96–97, 101, 127, 147, 169, 180, 201, 207, 209–10, 213–14, 303. *See also* Cupid; love
Erysichthon, 19, 46, 98, 100, 125
Esther, Book of, 42–43, 58
Etruscan (Tuscian), 22, 25, 29, 31–32, 55, 58–59, 85, 104–5, 116, 171, 173, 197, 233, 234, 265
etymology, 42, 53, 67–68, 110, 124, 249, 253, 255, 259, 262, 273
Euripides, 30, 41–42, 45, 56, 58, 68, 74, 111, 123, 130, 138, 198
Eusebius, 47, 52–53, 56–57, 62, 64, 69, 73, 75, 128
Exodus, 59, 68, 133

faith, 4, 14, 73, 135, 194, 232–33, 256, 282
fathers, 2, 132–33, 138
fear of death, 32, 117, 139
feminine, 7, 31, 44, 49, 75, 79, 127, 130, 137, 176, 178–79, 189n23
Festus, Sextus Pompeius, 50, 62–63
Fichte, Johann Gottlieb, 3, 221n2, 235, 252, 295–98

fire, 1, 7, 18, 22, 44, 48, 53–54, 56–57, 83–84, 97, 102, 112, 114, 118, 122–23, 127–30, 134, 147, 180–81, 225, 229, 269
Frank, Manfred, ix–x, 231n24, 284n5, 296–97, 301
Freya, 21, 103
future, 14, 23, 67, 85, 127, 192, 212n30, 214, 235, 264n96, 283, 289–91, 293, 295, 300, 305

Genesis, Book of, 36, 43, 53, 58, 64, 72, 239
German, Germanic, 2–3, 21, 26, 30, 44–45, 54, 67, 71–72, 84, 95, 98, 102–3, 111, 115, 118, 122–23, 129, 133, 140, 174, 181n15, 199, 221, 229n21, 231n24, 245, 249–50, 252, 256n76, 258, 265–67, 272, 278, 282n1, 294, 296n14, 301n18, 303
Gheber, 83–84, 171
Goethe, Johann Wolfgang von, 71, 98, 145–47, 183, 223n6, 238, 248, 250–52, 254n73, 262n92, 277
gold, 41, 56, 123, 128, 135, 148, 175, 191, 193, 209
Graves, Robert, 105, 109, 154, 216
Great Gods, xi–xii, 6, 11, 22, 29, 31, 34, 38, 58, 74, 77, 92, 96, 109, 113, 116, 135, 139, 145, 148–50, 152–53, 156–57, 159, 161, 175, 178–79, 183–84, 206–7, 210, 216
Great Mother, 4, 94, 97, 112–13, 136, 165–66, 168, 170, 179, 183, 186n22, 189n24, 196, 198, 215
Grotefend, Georg Friedrich, 241n38, 255n74, 260–61, 278
Guthrie, W. K. C., 97–99, 136, 162n8, 166, 181n16, 186–94, 201–3, 205, 216

INDEX

Hades, 6, 15, 21, 46, 52, 76, 94, 100, 103, 113, 127, 146, 155, 168, 185, 194, 209–10, 286, 289, 303–4. *See also* Pluto

Hebrew, 1, 17, 19, 28, 30–31, 42–44, 50, 53–54, 56, 58, 60, 64, 68, 73, 81–82, 85–86, 95, 109, 115, 124, 128–29, 137, 171, 184n19–20, 187, 213, 228–29, 239, 265, 269, 276

Hecate, 37

Hegel, G. W. F., 2–3, 129, 132, 140, 224n9, 227, 251n66, 252, 260n87, 293–95, 299

Heidegger, Martin, 101, 108, 129, 133, 198, 199, 213–14n32

Hemberg, Bengt, 150, 182–86, 195–97, 215, 243n43

Hephaistoi, Hephaistos, 7, 25, 28–30, 48, 52–53, 61, 64, 70, 105–6, 110, 112–13, 125, 127–28, 134, 198. *See also* Vulcan

Heraclitus, 21, 27, 56–57, 66, 103, 108, 127–28, 133, 194, 215, 227, 301

Herakles, Hercules, 14, 30, 41, 92, 115, 191

herald(s), 23–25, 58–59, 62, 64, 105, 113, 130–31, 150, 176, 304

Hermes, 15, 22–23, 25–26, 57, 59–60, 62, 68, 94, 102, 113, 121, 146, 150, 152, 155, 160–61, 165–66, 176, 181, 185, 196, 286, 303. *See also* Kadmilos (Kasmilos, Camillus); Mercury

Herodotus, 16, 28, 41, 45–46, 51–52, 60, 67, 69–70, 81, 109–10, 125, 130, 134, 151, 169, 174, 184–85, 190, 265

Hestia, 18, 44–45, 97, 199

Hesychios, 36–37, 39, 75, 174

Heyne, Christian Gottlob, 46, 76, 221, 240–43, 245n47, 252, 254–55, 260–61, 275, 277

Hindi, Hindu, 51, 85, 171

Hippolytos, 161

history, 1–2, 7–8, 14–16, 27–28, 35–37, 39, 48, 59, 69, 73, 75–76, 89, 91, 95, 98, 102, 105, 108, 122, 128, 131, 135, 140, 149, 157, 159, 166, 182, 187, 191, 124n32, 215, 227n16, 238–39, 242–43, 246, 249, 255n76, 259, 261n89, 262, 268n103, 282, 293, 299, 304–5

Hölderlin, Friedrich, 2–3, 100–11, 124, 154, 191, 193, 201, 203–4, 281, 287

Homer, 27, 36–37, 48, 56, 58, 81, 92, 98–101, 109, 124, 149, 152, 167, 185–86, 188, 190, 204, 208, 244–45, 247, 256n77–78, 278. *See also Iliad, The; Odyssey, The*

Horace, 58

hunger, 7, 17–20, 26, 43–44, 95–96, 100, 123–24, 129, 131, 134, 146, 149, 190, 193, 213, 220, 223–31, 234–35, 237, 268–69, 275, 293, 296, 299–300, 303

identity philosophy, 223, 270

Iliad, The, 37–38, 46, 56, 70, 92, 134, 152

Imbros, island of, 153–54

immortality, 138, 147, 188, 192–94, 200, 201

India, Indian, 7, 16, 27, 69, 81, 84–85, 102, 108, 123, 184n19, 234n27, 239, 244–45, 260–61, 264n96, 291

Indogermanic, 175, 187, 199

initiation, rites of, 7, 32, 40, 75, 148, 154–55, 157n4, 160, 162, 164, 168, 201, 205–7, 210, 212, 216, 243n43, 259n85, 293. *See also* cult; religion, religious

Ino Leukothea, 92–93, 105, 121, 134, 179, 204–5, 209

intramundane gods, 25, 61, 134
Isaiah, Book of, 50, 54, 56, 59, 82
Isis, 18, 21, 48, 51–52, 57, 68, 77, 96, 103

Jacobi, Friedrich Heinrich, 253–54
Jehovah, 23, 67, 74, 130, 132–33
Jeremiah, Book of, 56, 58
Jesus, 282, 287, 304–5. *See also* Christianity; religion, religious
Jewish, Jews, 59, 64, 73, 80–81, 84, 95, 129–30, 134, 138
Job, Book of, 74, 135
John the Baptist, 59, 290
Jove, Jupiter, 21–22, 25, 31, 57, 62–63, 76, 78, 80, 85–86, 116, 137–38, 163. *See also* Zeus

Kabir, 55, 74, 82, 171, 182–83, 215, 260, 277
Kadmilos (Kasmilos, Camillus), 6, 15–16, 22–26, 29, 48, 57–60, 62–63, 80, 93–94, 105, 110, 113, 131, 137, 146, 150, 155, 160, 165–66, 168, 170, 173, 237, 282n17, 286, 290, 303–4
Kadmos, 28, 60, 92–93, 105, 110, 157, 184–85, 188, 216
Kambyses, 28, 110
Kant, Immanuel, 3, 5, 221n2, 224n9, 235, 237, 252, 277, 296–98
Kerényi, Carl, 99, 104, 112–13, 150, 165, 182, 185–86, 195–98, 204, 215
kersa, 20, 50, 101
Köppen, Friedrich, 253–54, 278
Kore (the maid), 21, 104, 162, 185, 197
Korybantes, 64, 74–75, 113, 115, 136, 150, 165, 168, 183, 189–90, 198, 200, 208
Kouretes, 64, 113, 136, 150, 165, 168, 183, 189–90, 198, 200, 208
Kronos, 106, 117, 136, 172, 192n26, 200

Kybele, 4, 76, 92, 97, 111, 136, 150, 157n5, 165, 168, 170, 180, 183, 186, 189. *See also* Great Mother; Rhea

Lactantius, 55, 129
ladder, 24, 137, 148, 170
language, 1, 16–17, 31, 42, 44, 47–48, 51, 54–55, 58, 60, 64, 67–69, 74, 77, 81, 83–84, 95, 101, 105, 110, 112–13, 123, 136–38, 148, 153, 165, 170, 172–73, 175, 183, 184n20, 187–88, 192, 207, 213, 215, 219, 228, 239, 247, 254, 259, 263–66, 268, 272–74, 276
languishing (*Schmachten*), 3n1, 5–7, 17–20, 44–47, 95–96, 98–101, 123–25, 127, 130–31, 135, 146, 169, 176, 178, 185, 191, 193, 200, 114, 222–23, 228–29, 231–32, 234, 237, 288, 303
languor (*Sehnsucht*), 5–7, 18–20, 44–46, 48–50, 95–100, 115, 123–25, 127, 129–31, 146–47, 176, 190, 194, 213–14, 222, 224–25, 228, 269, 232, 234, 294, 303
Lehmann, Karl and Phyllis, 152–53, 157, 159–69, 171–73, 215
Lemnos, island of, 65, 105–6, 112–13, 150, 153–54, 168, 173, 183, 197–98, 260n88
life, living, 1, 3–7, 14, 20, 24, 32–33, 35, 39, 57, 62–63, 68, 71, 94, 97, 100, 103, 108, 114, 125, 128, 134–35, 139, 147, 155, 169–70, 173, 179–80, 190–96, 199, 201, 203–4, 210, 213–14, 219, 226–27, 230–31, 239, 268n101, 271, 275, 282–84, 286–87, 290, 292–93, 295, 299–301, 305
light, 15–16, 18, 23, 32, 45, 47–48, 60, 78, 84, 89, 112, 114, 125, 127, 130, 154, 187, 193–95, 205, 225, 239, 248, 268, 281

linguistics, 16, 35, 129, 184n20
love, 19, 47–48, 96, 103, 114–15, 125, 127, 145, 180, 201, 212–14. See also Eros
Lucretius, 38
lustrous radiance (*Lauterkeit*), 225

Macedonia, Macedonian, 14, 93, 106, 122, 170, 206
Macrobius, 58, 62, 72, 74
maenads, the, 112, 135, 201, 203
magic and magicians, 20–22, 28, 29–32, 50, 52, 55, 69, 75, 82, 84, 98, 102–3, 111, 115, 117, 123, 127–29, 135, 138, 139, 175, 178, 187, 196, 224, 228–29, 264, 266, 270, 286, 288, 292, 303–4. See also sorcery and sorceresses
magnetism, 115, 122, 138, 211–12, 229n21
Mahn, Ernst Philipp August, 241n38, 254–55, 278
Maja, 21, 51, 102, 111, 228n18
Malki-Sedek (Melchizedek), 64–65, 131
Malta, 36, 54–55, 121
Manes, the, 19, 72, 100, 173
mariners, 16, 31, 93, 112, 157n5, 178
masculine, 7, 31, 43–44, 53, 75, 79, 137, 176, 179
materialization, 178
Maximilian I. Joseph, ix, 117–18, 238n30, 282
McCredie, James R., 152, 159–60, 172
mediation, mediators, 22, 24, 157, 192n25, 216, 237, 254, 303
Melville, Herman, 112–13, 194–95, 212n30
Memphis (in Egypt), 28–29, 110, 150, 184

Mercury, 22, 52, 59, 75–76, 82, 85, 86, 137. See also Hermes
metathesis, 54, 129
Metatron, the, 59, 80–81, 130
Minerva, 80, 137, 163. See also Athena
Mnaseas of Patara, 15, 40, 63, 94, 155, 179, 184, 196, 259n84
Mohammedanism, 27
monad, 62
monotheism, 3, 26, 66, 107, 132, 135, 232, 249, 255, 267n99, 270n108
mortality, 21, 178, 191, 214, 288. See also death, dying
Moses, 59, 107, 130, 132
Münter, Friedrich, 36, 40–41, 60, 67, 69, 84, 86–87
mystery, mysteries, 5–7, 14–15, 19, 21, 24, 26, 28, 32, 36, 39–40, 44, 54, 58–63, 70, 73–75, 77, 79, 87, 92, 102, 104, 108, 112–13, 115, 130–32, 135, 139, 148–49, 151–52, 154–55, 159, 162–63, 165, 168–70, 176, 178, 181–83, 185–88, 190–91, 194–95, 197–98, 200–201, 203, 207–8, 210, 212–13, 215, 227, 231–35, 237–38, 240–41, 243–45, 247–49, 255, 259–61, 267–70, 272, 281, 284, 290, 292–93, 299, 303–5. See also initiation, rites of; secret teachings
myth, mythology, 2, 3, 5, 7, 39, 55, 60–61, 64, 66, 71, 73, 94, 96, 99, 101, 105, 107, 109, 122, 130, 132, 135–36, 171–72, 174, 176, 181, 185–88, 191–92, 200–201, 203, 205, 213, 216, 219–20, 228, 231–32, 234–35, 237, 240–48, 252, 259, 262–65, 267–68, 270–71, 274–76, 284n4, 286, 288–89, 291, 293, 301

names, 15–18, 20, 22–23, 28, 31, 40–43, 48, 50–52, 55–56, 60, 67, 69,

names (*cont.*)
72, 75–77, 85, 94, 101, 113, 121, 123, 127–28, 132–35, 155, 165, 171, 176, 179, 182–85, 187, 189, 192n25, 198, 204, 207, 213, 233–34, 252–53, 259, 261, 265n97, 271–73, 305

narrative, 6, 8, 13, 18, 29, 75, 112, 117, 139, 180, 187, 193

Napoleon, 118, 132, 271

nature, 2–4, 8, 13, 17–18, 20, 22–26, 28, 30–31, 33, 38, 44–45, 47, 49, 52, 55, 57, 59, 64–65, 70, 72–73, 75, 80, 87, 102, 115, 122, 128, 130–32, 137–38, 147, 159–61, 178n14, 181n15, 184, 186, 191, 193, 199, 201, 203, 224, 228–29, 242, 253n68, 263, 276, 282–83, 286–87, 289–90, 292–93, 295–96, 300–301, 304

Near East, 1, 17, 23, 27, 36–37, 44, 50–51, 54, 95, 97, 109, 111, 175, 248n60, 291

negative philosophy, 223, 235, 293, 295, 298–300

Nehemiah, Book of, 50, 58

Neptune, 137. *See also* Poseidon

Neptunists, 91

New Testament, 27, 66, 87, 129, 195, 267n99, 281

Nietzsche, Friedrich, 101, 214n32, 240, 248, 284, 287, 289

night, 18, 65, 97, 155, 157, 168, 195, 204–5, 207, 209–10, 212–14, 281–82, 289, 305

Nordic, 30, 72, 102

number, 19, 22, 24–25, 31, 62–63, 65, 77–80, 85, 106, 111, 128, 130–31, 146, 169, 196, 298n16

obsession (*Sucht*), 17–19, 26, 45, 57, 95–96, 98–100, 123–24, 129, 176, 191, 224, 226, 288, 297, 303. *See also* addiction

Odin, 21, 51–52, 75, 103, 303

Odysseus, 39, 92–93, 102, 134, 154, 167, 180, 186, 191, 204–5, 212. *See also* Ulysses

Odyssey, The, 92–93, 102, 134, 167, 205

Old Testament, 23, 27, 42–43, 50, 58–59, 66, 68, 72, 81–82, 95, 106–7, 109, 129, 138, 150, 171

One, the, 5, 16, 22–23, 25, 27, 44, 49, 52–54, 56, 59, 61, 64, 68, 70, 86, 89, 99, 108, 131, 133, 191, 194, 201, 208, 219, 228, 231, 241, 252n67, 263, 273

Ormuzd, 47, 84, 130

Orpheus, 14, 56, 68, 92, 112, 154

Osiris, 21, 51–52, 54–57, 67–68, 103, 125, 189, 303

Ouranos, 106

paganism, 37, 48, 66, 75, 245, 272, 278

Paracelsus, 71

past, 5–6, 48, 85, 117, 127, 139, 214, 283, 287, 289–91, 305. *See also* history; narrative

Paulus, Heinrich Eberhard Gottlob, 249, 254–60, 276, 278

Pausanias, 35, 44, 49–50, 127, 203

Pelasgians, 28, 31, 61, 67, 109, 116, 151–53

Penates, 29, 31, 70, 72, 74, 82, 85, 116

Persephone, 6, 15, 20–22, 51, 57, 62, 80, 94, 99–101, 104, 107, 113, 124–25, 127–29, 131, 134, 137, 146, 154–55, 168, 170, 176–77, 181–82, 185, 190n24, 197, 205, 209, 210, 214, 232, 286, 288–89, 303–4. *See also* Axiokersa; Proserpina

Persia, Persian, 42–44, 47, 51, 83–85, 97, 102, 106, 110, 114, 124–25, 130, 137, 171, 187, 228–29

Phaethon, 20, 48–49

Pherekydes of Syros, 75, 97, 213

philology, 85, 187, 221, 243, 251n61, 267n100, 292
Phoenicia, Phoenician, 1, 6, 16–17, 19–20, 28–29, 36, 41, 47, 50, 52–56, 60, 62, 75, 77, 87, 93–95, 97, 101–2, 105, 109–11, 116, 127, 134, 153–55, 172, 174, 183–84, 187, 213, 234n27, 239, 247, 259, 261, 264, 265n97, 270, 275–76, 303
Phrygia, Phrygian, 4, 97, 110, 112, 116, 136, 150, 155, 164–65, 170, 172, 174, 179–80, 183–84, 188–90, 203, 213, 259. See also Anatolia; Turkey
Pictet, Adolphe, 273–76
Pindar, 44, 56
Plato, 2, 17–18, 27, 48–49, 61, 66, 79, 87, 96–97, 100, 106–9, 115–16, 137–38, 155, 172, 183–84, 191, 213, 263, 301, 303; *Cratylus*, 48, 97, 100; *Ion*, 115, 193; *Laws*, 97; *Phaedo*, 87, 116, 138, 192; *Phaedrus*, 97, 109, 213–14; *Republic*, 183; *Symposium*, 48–49, 96–97, 105, 109, 301; *Timaeus*, 2–3, 106–7, 137, 155, 190n24
Pliny the Elder, 20, 35, 36–37, 39–40, 48–49, 75, 169, 185
Plutarch, 21, 37, 39–40, 45, 51–52, 57, 59, 62, 68, 122, 162n8, 201, 203
Pluto, 21, 52, 75, 82, 100. See also Hades
poetry, 2, 28
polytheism, 3, 132, 187, 232, 292
Poros and Penia ("Resource" and "Poverty"), 17–18, 96–98, 301
Poseidon, 13, 36, 69–70, 92–93, 104, 134, 150, 204. See also Neptune
positive philosophy, 223, 249, 275, 284, 290, 293, 295, 299–301
potencies, divine, 6, 61, 80, 230–31, 234–35, 245, 282, 286–87, 292, 296, 303–4

Pothos (πόθος, mourning), 20, 48–50, 100–101, 127, 169, 184–85, 209
poverty, 17, 43, 95, 97, 123–24, 149, 178, 190, 200, 229–30, 243n42, 299, 301, 303
presence, 53, 98, 108, 111, 138, 163, 165, 196, 199, 205, 304
present, 48, 56, 199, 289, 305
priests, 4, 25, 52, 63, 65, 83–84, 94, 116, 132, 137, 207, 209, 212, 240, 245, 281
Proclus, 61, 68
Prometheus, 198, 260n88, 267–69, 277
prophecy, prophets, 24, 50, 122, 135
Proserpina, 18, 20, 22, 26, 50, 60, 63, 75–76, 82, 100, 104, 125, 127, 176, 261n89. See also Axiokersa; Persephone
Proverbs, Book of, 43, 46, 59
pygmy, 28–30, 72, 111, 146, 198
Pythagorean, Pythagoras, 14, 39, 59, 62, 92, 131, 138, 167

reception of Schelling's *Deities*, 184n19, 237, 239, 249–75, 277; in England, 265–71; in France, 271–75; in Germany, 249–65
Reinhold, Karl Leonhard, 297–98
religion, religious, 1–3, 7, 21, 26, 43–44, 53, 59, 67, 76, 81, 83–84, 92, 95–96, 98, 104, 106–9, 112, 135–36, 155, 159, 164–66, 168, 170, 183, 187–91, 194–95, 203, 238, 243n42, 245–46, 255, 262–64, 270–72, 281, 287–90, 292–93, 303–5. See also cult; mystery, mysteries
return of the Cabiri, 148, 276, 281, 303
Revelation, 7, 24–25, 27, 31–32, 64, 194, 232, 266, 281, 283, 286–88, 290–94, 304
Rhea, 111–13, 118, 136, 150, 165, 168, 170, 179–82, 186, 189, 200, 210. See also Great Mother; Kybele

Rhodes, island of, 35, 37, 39, 75–76, 78, 87, 105, 136, 147, 150, 154–55, 157, 168, 179, 198, 212, 214, 233
rites, rituals, 7, 14–15, 32, 40, 63, 69, 76, 87, 92, 103, 105, 123, 134, 136, 151, 154, 162–63, 165, 167–68, 172, 175, 179–81, 184n20, 192n25, 195, 197, 204–5, 207, 210, 227, 240, 258, 287, 292–93. *See also* cult; mystery, mysteries; religion, religious; secret teachings
rivers, 35–36, 159, 142, 174, 186, 207, 218
Roman, Rome, 2, 7, 14, 20–22, 25, 33, 39–40, 58, 62, 70, 77–78, 82, 86, 92, 94–95, 100, 104–5, 109, 116, 120, 123, 133–34, 136–37, 157–59, 163, 180, 184, 194–95, 206, 224, 265n97

sacrifice, 83, 108, 163, 165, 167, 169, 200–201, 206, 209–10, 288
Sainte-Croix, Guillaume de, 26, 37, 40–41, 48, 50, 57, 60, 65–66, 75–76, 108, 272–73, 278
Samos, island of, 13–14, 35–38, 92, 121, 151–53
Samuel, Book of, 62, 74, 135
Sanchuniathon, 52, 57, 63–64, 75, 127, 263n95
sanctuary, 14, 34, 38, 44, 94, 109, 120, 148, 152–53, 156–59, 161, 163, 165, 169, 174, 179, 185, 205–7, 209, 215, 280
Santorini, 36, 91, 105, 122, 173. *See also* Thera (Santorini)
Scaliger, Josephus Justus, 73, 77, 95, 183
Schelling, F. W. J.: *Ages of the World* (1811–1815), 5–6, 13, 59, 66, 86, 89, 96–97, 117, 128–29, 132, 138–39, 192–93, 213, 219–20, 222–23, 225–28, 230–31, 239n34, 250–51, 263, 267n100, 275, 283–84, 286–87, 289, 291, 293, 301; *The Erlangen Lectures* (1821), 171, 228n17, 264; *Essay on Human Freedom* (1809), 2–3, 96–98, 114, 171, 220–21, 223–25, 235, 268, 275, 283n2, 287, 299; *First Sketch Toward a Philosophy of Nature* (1799), 115; *On the Relationship of the Philosophy of Nature to Philosophy in General* (1802), 224; *Philosophical Sketches and Journals from 1814 to 1816*, 106; *Stuttgart Private Lectures* (1810), 224–25; *System of Transcendental Idealism* (1800), 221, 230, 267; *Timaeus* (1794), 2, 106
Schelling, Karl, xi, 46, 86, 106, 125, 129, 138, 216, 222, 225, 231, 235, 278
Schlegel, Friedrich, 235n27, 239–40, 246, 277, 298
Scholiast to Apollonius, 35, 39–40, 75–76, 78, 87, 155, 168
science (*Wissenschaft*), 2, 4, 66, 89, 140, 178n14, 187, 240, 258, 282, 286, 289, 291, 294, 296, 298
sea, 36, 40, 91–93, 104, 121–23, 134, 136, 146, 174, 186, 192n26, 194, 197, 204–5, 207, 214, 287
secret teachings, 232. *See also* acroamatic
Semele, 93, 105, 122, 188–89, 204
Semitic, 105, 153, 172, 184n20, 188, 257n79, 259, 265n97, 305
sexes, 31
sky, 59, 77, 114, 190, 196, 201, 209
smiths, 71, 111, 136
socii, 7, 74, 80, 82, 137–38, 192, 198–99, 213, 227, 234, 271, 276. *See also* companions, company
solitude, 49, 123, 135, 193

Sophocles, 93, 154n2, 193n27
sorcery and sorceresses, 1, 20–21, 50–51, 102–3, 127, 129, 178
sprites, 81, 101, 111. *See also* cobolds (Kobolde); dwarfs
stars, 32, 87, 112, 166, 180, 192, 204, 213, 230
Strabo, 36, 75, 152, 190
Suetonius, 55
Suidas, 53
supplement, 13, 70, 82, 89, 139, 222, 250, 286
system, 1–4, 7, 15, 21, 23, 26–27, 30, 32, 35, 42, 47–48, 53, 61, 65–67, 80–82, 84, 89, 96, 110, 116–17, 130–31, 134–37, 139, 148–49, 175, 192, 195, 197, 221, 228, 230, 232–35, 243, 246, 258, 260, 263–65, 267, 269, 275, 277, 287, 289, 291–96

Tacitus, 40, 52, 94
tautegorical, 42, 269, 292
Telchines, 75, 113, 135–36, 147, 150, 183, 190, 198
Thassos, island of, 41
Thebes (in Greece), 6, 93, 105, 123, 150, 162n9, 174, 188–89, 198
Theodosius, 40, 123
theology, 61, 107, 115, 168, 213, 240n35, 267n101, 289. *See also* Christianity, religion, religious; system
Thera (Santorini), 36, 91, 105, 122, 168, 173
Thessaly, 50, 103, 165
theurgy, 32, 103, 111, 115, 128, 264, 286, 292
Thrace, Thracian, viii, 13–14, 36–38, 92, 105, 112, 121–22, 136, 151–55, 170, 172–74, 179, 186, 188–89, 193–94, 213

time, 14–15, 18–19, 21, 33, 46–48, 65, 78, 101, 109, 114, 125, 130, 146–47, 165, 201, 225, 189–290, 298. *See also* future; past; present
tragedy, tragic, 3n1, 98, 108, 132, 201, 223n6, 201–3
transmundane, 25–26, 30, 286
trinity, 80, 137, 196–97, 289
Trojan, Troy, 13, 31, 92, 94, 110–11, 116, 134, 151–52, 164
Turkey, 121, 259. *See also* Anatolia; Phrygia, Phyrigian
Tychsen, Thomas Christian, 47, 86, 241n38, 254–55, 261, 278
Typhon, Typhonian, 33, 117–18, 200, 271
Tyre, Tyrian, 28, 44, 55, 60, 93, 95, 105, 110, 127, 172
Tyrrhenian, 22, 104–5, 153–54, 205

Ulysses, 15, 92. *See also* Odysseus
underworld gods, 82–83, 168. *See also* chthonic gods
unity, 3, 5, 23, 26, 31, 47, 125, 132, 137–38, 220, 224, 230, 234, 264
unprethinkable (*das Unvordenkliche*), 176, 269n106, 288, 290, 300–301, 304

Varro, M. Terentius, 22, 32, 40, 48, 50, 58, 73–74, 76–80, 85–86, 105, 113, 136–37, 184, 208
Venus, 20, 43, 48–49, 63, 137, 147, 157, 170, 184. *See also* Aphrodite
Vesta, 20, 50, 97, 137, 199
Virgil, 36, 66
Voss, Johann Heinrich, 38, 221, 244–48, 254, 263, 275
Vossius, Gerhard, 27, 40, 72–73, 95, 108–9, 272
votive gifts and tablets, 41, 156, 158, 163, 179, 194, 210

Vulcan, 53, 76, 137. *See also*
 Hephaistoi, Hephaistos; smiths
Vulcanists, 91

Warburton, William, 26, 107, 187
water, 7, 13, 16, 36–37, 51, 57, 69, 93, 154, 175, 204. *See also* rivers; sea
Wescoat, Bonna, xii, 159n6
wine, 104, 168, 188, 208–9, 281–84, 304–5
"Winged Victory," 157–58, 212
wonder(s) (θαυμάζειν), 71, 94, 97, 132, 301

Xenophon of Athens, 24, 105, 135

Zend-Avesta, 47, 83
Zenobius, 46
Zeruané akherené, 46, 125, 130
Zerynthian, 37
Zeus, 15, 18, 21–22, 25–27, 61–64, 66, 78, 82, 86, 92–93, 102, 104–6, 108–9, 111–13, 117, 121–23, 131, 136–37, 146, 150, 163, 165–66, 173, 180–82, 185, 189–91, 193–94, 197, 200–201, 204, 208, 301. *See also* Jove, Jupiter
Zoëga, Georg, 16, 41, 52–53, 61, 67, 94
Zohar, Book of, 64, 81
Zoroaster, 84, 102

Alexander Bilda studied philosophy, ancient history, and historical anthropology in Freiburg and Paris. His doctoral dissertation focused on Schelling's methodology and system in the Erlangen lectures of 1821 (forthcoming from Nomos Verlag in 2024). He edited Schelling's Erlangen lectures in the historical-critical edition of Schelling's works, 2021, together with A. L. Müller Bergen and P. Schwab. Articles include studies on Kant, Fichte, Hegel, Schelling, and Merleau-Ponty. He currently works as a permanent academic staff member at the University of Freiburg.

Jason M. Wirth is Professor of Philosophy at Seattle University. He is author of *Mountains, Rivers, and the Great Earth: Reading Gary Snyder and Dōgen in an Age of Ecological Crisis*; *Commiserating with Devastated Things: Milan Kundera and the Entitlements of Thinking*; and *Schelling's Practice of the Wild: Time, Art, Imagination*. He is editor (with Bret W. Davis and Brian Schroeder) of *Japanese and Continental Philosophy: Conversations with the Kyoto School*.

David Farrell Krell is Emeritus Professor of Philosophy at DePaul University, Chicago, and Brauer Distinguished Visiting Professor of German Studies at Brown University, Providence. He also teaches at the University of Freiburg, Germany. His scholarly books include *Struck by Apollo: Hölderlin's Journeys to Bordeaux and Back and Beyond*; *Three Encounters: Heidegger, Arendt, Derrida*; *The Sea: A Philosophical Encounter*; and *The Tragic Absolute: German Idealism and the Languishing of God*. He has also published a number of translations, short stories, and novels.

For Indiana University Press
Lesley Bolton, Project Manager/Editor
Dan Crissman, Editorial Director and Acquisitions Editor
Anna Francis, Assistant Acquisitions Editor
Anna Garnai, Editorial Assistant
Samantha Heffner, Marketing and Publicity Manager
Brenna Hosman, Production Coordinator
Katie Huggins, Production Manager
Dan Pyle, Online Publishing Manager
Pamela Rude, Senior Artist and Book Designer